About the Book

1. Basic monetary, fiscal, and financial institution data are provided in chart form, which encourages additional independent analysis.
2. Includes descriptions of financial systems of the United States, Canada, England, France, East and West Germany, Brazil, Yugoslavia, China, and Russia.
3. The important decisions made by the Federal Reserve throughout its history are critically analyzed.
4. The book explains the current manner in which major domestic and foreign (public and private) institutions operate and outlines trends and likely developments.
5. Government, business, and individual debt decisions are examined to determine how they affect the soundness of an economy.
6. The materials provide a summary of the basic elements of the historical development of the American system of financial institutions and monetary practices.
7. Consideration is given to the sources of foreign exchange instability and possible solutions.
8. Personal savings opportunities and pension programs are described. Nothing in this or in other areas of financial management is accepted simply because this is the way it has been done. An effort is made to examine all ongoing practices to uncover basic weaknesses and strengths.

About the Author

1. Dr. Richard W. Lindholm, Professor of Finance and Economic Consultant, at the University of Oregon, was the founding dean of the Graduate School of Management and Business at the university.
2. Former Federal Reserve Board Economist and Economic Advisor to the governments of Vietnam, Pakistan, Korea, Turkey, and Australia.
3. Author of *Money and Finance, Principles of Money and Banking, Money and Banking, Our American Economy, Introduction to Fiscal Policy*, and *Value-Added Tax and Other Tax Reforms*.
4. Economic Consultant to the First National Bank of Oregon, the U.S. Department of Commerce, the U.S. State Department, and the Ways and Means Committee of the U.S. House of Representatives.
5. Listed in *Who's Who in America* and *Who's Who in the West*. Designated Beta Gamma Sigma Scholar for 1975–1976 and Lincoln Institute Post-Doctoral Fellow in 1977.

Money Management and Institutions

by

Richard W. Lindholm, Ph.D.
University of Oregon

ROWMAN AND LITTLEFIELD
Totowa, New Jersey

Published 1978 by Rowman and Littlefield
Copyright © 1978
LITTLEFIELD, ADAMS & CO.
81 Adams Drive, Totowa, N.J. 07512

Library of Congress Cataloging in Publication Data

Lindholm, Richard Wadsworth, 1914–
   Money management and institutions.

   Bibliography: p.
   Includes index.
   1. Financial institutions. 2. Finance. 3. Money.
I. Title.
HG153.L53   1978b   332   77–28953
ISBN 0–8476–6044–3

Printed in the United States of America

Sources

Tables and charts have been reproduced from these U.S. government publications:

Credit Union National Association
    CHART XXIV
Federal Financing Bank, *Annual Report, 1976*
    TABLE 28
Federal Reserve Bank
    MAP of Federal Reserve System
Federal Reserve Bank of Kansas City Monthly Review, (June, 1976)
    CHART XXV   TABLE 17
Federal Reserve Bulletins
    TABLES—1, 2, 3, 4, 5, 13, 14, 18, 19, 20, 22
Historical Chart Book, Board of Governors of the Federal Reserve System
    CHARTS—I, II, III, IV, V, VI, VII, VIII, IX, X, XI, XII, XIII, XIV, XV, XVI, XVIII, XIX, XX, XXI, XXII, XXIII, XXVI, XXVII, XXIX, XXX
Housing and Urban Development, *Annual Report, 1975*
    TABLE 27
International Letter: Federal Reserve Bank of Chicago, (No. 298, October 29, 1976)
    CHART XXVIII
Introduction to Flow of Funds, Board of Governors of the Federal Reserve System (February, 1975)
    CHART XVII   TABLES—11, 12
National Association of Mutual Savings Banks, *Annual Report 1975*
    TABLES—15, 16

SEC ANNUAL REPORT (for fiscal year ended June 30, 1975)
  TABLE 24
SEC MONTHLY BULLETIN (July 1976)
  TABLE 23
U. S. Department of Commerce, Bureau of the Census
  TABLE 25
U. S. Department of Commerce, Bureau of the Census, and Tax
Foundations Computations
  TABLE 26
World Bank Annual Report, 1975
  TABLE 29

Some text material has been adapted from MONEY AND BANK-ING by Richard W. Lindholm © 1969 Littlefield, Adams & Co.

Table of Contents

Tables

Charts

Diagrams

Part I

Money

INTRODUCTION

Ours is an exchange economy. It runs on the ball bearings of money. The speed and quantity of today's economic exchanges require a monetary system much more highly developed than that needed by the smaller, simpler, and more primitive societies of yesterday. Nevertheless the functions of money still are very much the same as they were in the Ch'in dynasty of ancient China (200 B.C.) when bank notes, i.e., paper money, first were used.

It is reported by Marco Polo that the paper money issued by Kublai Khan, the great Mongol ruler, became authentic when the vermilion seal was pressed on it. Marco Polo wrote that "with these pieces of paper he causes all payments on his account to be made; and he makes them to pass current universally over all his kingdom and provinces and territories and whithersoever his power and sovereignty extends."

The term *fiat* is used to describe paper money of this sort. Paper money that is basically a warehouse receipt for gold and silver held in the Treasury is called *representative* money. A certificate or coin is money, because the government decrees it to be money. The ability of a government to create money by decreeing that something is money is called the power of *legal tender*. The idea that it is the power of the government making something legal tender that gives that something value is called the *state theory* of money.

A modern government does not decree how many potatoes, for example, five units of its money will purchase. Neither did Kublai Khan. When this step is taken, a government has established price controls and the possibility of rationing.

1

COMPETITION AMONG CURRENCIES

Recently a backlash has developed from the unhealthy use of the power of legal tender and of the money production monopoly of government. The concept of *choice of currency* has been gaining converts as a usable procedure to stop continuous inflation and to return to money some of its former virtues as a store of value and a provider of economic security.

Briefly, the idea treats money as it does other commodities —as was largely the situation before the growth of central banks. Under these conditions, suppliers of money would be obliged to compete for adoption by contract writers and receivers and payers of funds. The supplier of money with the most stable value surely would capture a large portion of the market.

The suppliers of competing currencies, upon seeing the use of their money declining, would establish procedures to win back the market. To do this, they would have to produce money with a more stable value.

For the whole procedure to work, foreign money must possess the same legal tender rights as domestic money. Section 102 of Public Law 89-81 of July 23, 1965, would have to be amended to read, "All coins and currencies, regardless of when coined or issued, that are designated in the contract, shall be legal tender for those debts, public and private, public charges, taxes, duties, and dues."

This would be a giant step away from a national policy built on a domestic monopoly of money. Although this is not a likely step in the near future, its mere contemplation by such serious conservative economists as F. A. von Hayek points to the desperation of the inflation problem. And after all, ten years ago, who would have thought that perpetuation of the current rate of inflation could be accepted as a likely prospect? So perhaps denationalization of money is a necessary first step in a return to money that can act as a store of value and a source of economic security.

Chapter 1

Types and Uses of Money

Definition of Money. Money in our society perhaps is defined best as something that ordinarily is spent directly and does not require a transfer into something else to permit its being spent.

To the sixteenth-century citizen *money* meant metal coins. Later the term came to include paper money issued by governments or banks. Finally, it also has come to extend to cover deposits of all financial institutions that may be spent by writing a check or draft.

The use of a draft or check (which is the use of a deposit to complete a transaction) is more limited than that of currency; however, it must be considered money, for it is in general use as a medium of exchange. And the deposit itself generally is considered the equivalent of currency.

TABLE 1

QUANTITIES AND TYPES OF MONEY OF THE UNITED STATES
(In billions of dollars, not seasonally adjusted.)

	January 1968	January 1976	July 1977
Currency outside banks	39.0	73.7	85.1
Demand deposits (adjusted)	142.0	227.6	241.6
Time deposits (all banks)	241.1	451.3	519.5
Deposits of savings and loan associations and mutual savings banks and credit union shares	—	428.6	533.4

During the past ten years, the amount of currency outstanding has grown somewhat more rapidly than have demand

3

deposits, which are deposits that do not earn interest and that can be transferred by writing a check. This is surprising, for it also has been the period of rapid growth for the credit card. The expansion has been largely in $50 and $100 bills, but the average denomination has not kept up with the rate of inflation.

In addition, government securities and evidences of short-term business and agricultural debt in modern nations have developed to the point where they possess almost all the characteristics of money. Usually, however, such credit instruments are considered near money rather than actual money.

GROWTH OF DEPOSITS AND CURRENCY.   Chart I summarizes the growth of the quantity of money (with the exception of member bank reserves) from 1910 through 1976. The three periods of largest growth were during World War I, World War II, and the Vietnamese war. In 1915 the total of deposits and currency was only a little more than $20 billion; and within five years, or by 1920, this total had expanded to $40 billion. World War II had a similar effect, and the M_2 (i.e., currency outside banks, demand deposits, plus time deposits of commercial banks) increased from $60 billion in 1939 to $178 billion in 1945. The Vietnam increase was less, but still substantial. This time, however, much of the "money" expansion showed up as time deposit growth. Between 1963 and 1968 time deposits grew by about $85 billion; demand deposit expansion was but $15 billion. The increase in the quantity of deposits and currency during the boom of 1929 was just a ripple compared to these great swells that arose during war periods.

Since 1973, M_1 (i.e., currency outside banks plus demand deposits) increased by $25 billion, whereas M_2 increased by $104 billion and M_3 by $183 billion. (Remember, M_3 includes M_2 plus deposits of mutual savings banks, savings and loan associations, and credit unions.) This was a period only somewhat influenced by military requirements; nevertheless, it was characterized by large federal budgetary deficits. In fiscal year 1976 the federal deficit was more than $70 billion. There is also an M_4, which is M_2 plus large negotiable CDs, and an M_5, which is M_3 plus large negotiable CDs.

Functions of Money.   The basic and normally the most important function of money is to make it easy to exchange goods and services. This is called the *medium of exchange function*. Objects perform this function efficiently if they possess the characteristics of *portability, indestructibility, homogeneity,*

CHART I

MONETARY AGGREGATES

ANNUALLY, 1910–46; SEASONALLY ADJUSTED, QUARTERLY, 1947–1975.

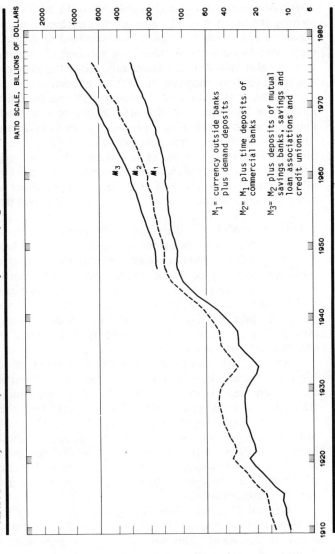

RATIO SCALE, BILLIONS OF DOLLARS

M₃

M₂

M₁

M_1 = currency outside banks plus demand deposits

M_2 = M_1 plus time deposits of commercial banks

M_3 = M_2 plus deposits of mutual savings banks, savings and loan associations and credit unions

divisibility and reunion, and *cognizability.* In addition to performing the function of (1) a medium of exchange, money also serves as (2) a unit of value, (3) a standard of deferred payment, and (4) a store of value. The medium of exchange and unit of value functions are frequently called the primary functions, and the remaining two the derivative functions.

MEDIUM OF EXCHANGE. Money performs the function of medium of exchange and also sets the major conditions of a market economy by making it possible for an individual to pursue an intelligent economic policy of selling his goods to the one offering the largest number of monetary units and buying his goods from the one who will sell for the fewest. The only feasible alternative to this type of exchange is barter, which is much more tedious and complicated if the variety of goods traded is great.

UNIT OF VALUE. The function of a unit of value is being performed when all articles and services are commonly valued by stating them in terms of a certain number of units of one particular type of good. For example, when in the United States a person asks the price or the value of an article or a service and is told that it is ten dollars, the dollar is serving as a unit of value. The practice of measuring the value of all items in monetary units greatly simplifies the problem of exchange and the determination of relative worth.

STANDARD OF DEFERRED PAYMENT AND STORE OF VALUE. Money performs the function of a standard of deferred payment when credit is extended in terms of the repayment of a stated number of monetary units. Money is performing the function of a store of value when a quantity of it is held for a period of time. Today this generally is done by making a deposit in a bank. Money obviously is not the only store of value and in fact is not the most important; its great advantage is that it can be used readily at any time to gain control over any of the large variety of goods for sale.

General Economic Function of Money. Money has had an important effect upon the direction, speed, and type of economic development. The periods of great expansion in the quantity of money have also been periods of vigorous economic activity. The revival of economic activity in Europe during the sixteenth century frequently is attributed to the expansion of the quantity of money through the Spanish conquest and exploitation of Mexico and Peru. The economic expansion of the

United States often has been related closely to its supplies of standard money, i.e. gold and silver stocks.

It is dangerous, however, to relate economic expansion solely to the abundance of money. This is illustrated vividly by the complete economic demoralization and stagnation in Germany after World War I and in China after World War II, when their money supplies were very great. In fact, part of the cause of the economic difficulties being experienced today has been too much, rather than too little, money.

In 1790 a dollar was worth $3.80, and in 1900 it was worth $6.85. Since then, it has been downhill except for the period from 1920 to 1940. The shrinkage in the value of the dollar, i.e., inflation, is a very serious problem that is understood only partially. Chart II is a summary of wholesale prices from 1800 to 1976. The increase in prices from 1973 to 1976 was one of the most severe, even though a major war was not in progress.

MONETARY POLICY. A wise monetary policy therefore is one that supplies the correct amount of money to bring national income and resulting price levels to the point producing the most efficient use of the nation's resources. This is the ideal. Its achievement may require a decrease or an increase in the amount of money; success also will be affected by the distribution of money resources and money income. The nation's resources usually are used most efficiently if the price level is rising slowly and if aggregate production is expanding. Under these conditions, more goods and services are being exchanged continually through the use of an ever-growing money supply. A money supply expanding at the same rate as the Gross National Product (GNP), or currently at about 4 percent annually, would seem to be appropriate policy during normal times.

The paper standard has a bad record of inflation, partially because it usually has been utilized during periods of war when the economy was badly disorganized. Also previous experience was prior to the development of modern methods of gathering economic data and economic analysis procedures. The provision of a good monetary system today depends upon the establishment of procedures that will make the paper standard operate efficiently. This goal has been more nearly reached by some countries than by others. However, basically the paper money standards of the world are working poorly.

The Currency, Banking, and Government Principles. The

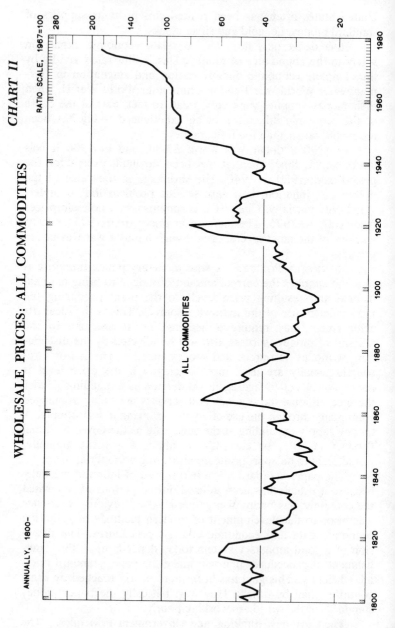

ANNUALLY, 1800—

WHOLESALE PRICES: ALL COMMODITIES

CHART II

RATIO SCALE, 1967=100

ALL COMMODITIES

currency principle requires that money be issued only in the form of gold or silver equal in value as a commodity to the value stamped on it, or that paper money be issued only as a type of warehouse receipt. A monetary authority operating under the currency principle would not permit the amount of money to exceed the value of gold and/or silver held.

The banking principle is almost the exact opposite of the currency principle. It teaches that bankers should increase the amount of notes and deposits when loans are granted and cause a decrease when loans are repaid. If this principle is followed, the amount of money increases when the business need expands and decreases when the need contracts. This principle is sound, except that it does not provide a safeguard against imprudent and reckless banking. The system of also requiring reserves to back bank credit combines features of both the currency and banking principles.

The issuance of money directly or indirectly to cover national government budget deficits has become common in peace and no longer is limited to war finance as was largely true prior to 1965. Large armament and social expenditures have not been met with equally large tax collection. The result is what might be called the government deficit theory of money issuance.

Chapter 2

Monetary Standards

General Categories of Monetary Standards. The monetary systems of most of the nations of the world are combinations of commodity money and paper money. *Commodity money* is money that possesses as great a value when in the form of goods or commodities as when stamped and is given the power of *legal tender*. Money also is called commodity money if it can be converted into standard money or a standard commodity at a fixed rate. *Paper money* is money that cannot be converted into a fixed quantity of a standard commodity.

COMMODITY STANDARDS. Commodity standards are of several types. *Monometallism*, based on one metal, usually gold, has been the most common commodity standard during the twentieth century. *Bimetallism* is based on two metals that are standard money at a fixed value in terms of one another. The legally established ratio between the two metals is known as the *mint ratio*. It has been popular in central Europe and the United States. *Symmetallism*, based on a single metallic unit in the form of a mixture of different metals in legally established proportions, has not been used. A *composite* commodity or commodity reserve standard is based on an assorted list of staple commodities that make up the standard unit. Composite commodity money is a theoretical ideal that is not out of the discussion stage.

PAPER STANDARDS. Paper standards are of two general types: *free* and *controlled*. Under the free paper standards, no restrictions are placed on the use of money to complete international transactions, and its value in relation to other currencies is permitted to be determined freely in the money markets of the world (where the value of the money of one country is determined in relation to the values of the money of other countries). Under a controlled paper standard, exchange rates and international transactions are strictly regulated.

The money standards of all the major countries are paper. The money of countries exercising least control over use is called *hard* money. This money is considered much better. That is, it can be used to purchase goods, services, and securities with greater freedom than can the money of the countries that closely control the manner of its use. The U. S. dollar is not restricted in use and therefore is favored by international businesses. The important factor determining the desirability of a nation's money is the quantity of production available for consumption in relation to the quantity and use of money; money supply can be affected by governments and the use of this power usually results in a money supply too large for price stability.

The Gold Standard. No nation of the world has been on the gold standard since the 1930s. Actually today Swiss francs, German marks, and American dollars perform many of the international functions formerly allocated to gold. In addition, the International Monetary Fund (IMF) has developed Special Drawing Rights (SDR) as usable in the international settlement of balances (*see* Index).

REQUIREMENTS OF A GOLD STANDARD. The basic requirements for a nation to be on the gold standard are: (1) laws must define the standard money unit as a particular weight of gold of a specific fineness, (2) the gold unit must be given the power of full legal tender, (3) free and unlimited coinage of gold must be permitted, (4) gold must be permitted to move freely out of the treasury into private hands and out of the country into the possession of foreigners, and (5) all types of money of the nation must be freely convertible into gold.

ADVANTAGES AND DISADVANTAGES CLAIMED FOR THE GOLD STANDARD. The principal advantages usually attributed to the gold standard are that it provides a monetary unit (1) in which the public has confidence, (2) that has a great stability of value, (3) that requires little government interference, and (4) that is international yet does not require international agreements.

The principal disadvantages of the gold standard that have caused it to be abandoned by the nations of the world are: (1) the flow of gold in a world of central banks does not determine the quantity of money, (2) great inflations and deflations can arise under the gold standard, (3) governments are not willing to permit their domestic price levels to remain at the mercy of the international movements of gold, (4) large gold movements arise even though the relative price levels of nations are in adjustment, and (5) it imposes restrictions on the independence of domestic economic activity.

TYPES OF GOLD STANDARDS. The *gold coin standard* that was in effect in most of the leading nations prior to 1914 provided for circulation of gold coins and conversion of all types of money into gold. It was abandoned because of the higher prices after World War I and the shortage of gold that made it necessary to increase the efficiency of gold use. The United States remained on the gold coin standard until 1933.

The *gold bullion standard*, which has been called the rich man's standard, provides for redemption of all types of money into gold bullion. This means that a rather large amount of funds must be possessed before gold can be obtained. It economizes the use of gold and has the effect of largely limiting it to settling international balances. The gold bullion standard was as effective as the gold coin standard in keeping the value of all types of money at par and in preventing a change in the value of a nation's money in terms of gold.

The *gold exchange standard* sometimes has been called the "limping" gold standard, because it provides for the convertibility of a nation's money into another nation's money, which is convertible into gold. Today the convertibility of one nation's money into another nation's money is as far as convertibility goes. The indirect convertibility into gold under the gold exchange standard also served to keep the monetary units of a nation at a constant value in terms of gold. It was another device introduced after World War I to economize the use of gold. The gold standard is unlikely to be reintroduced because:

1. The nations of the world are dedicated to using all monetary and fiscal powers available to maintain full employment and expand production. This necessitates conscious control over domestic prices, and thus government cannot permit prices to be dominated by international gold movements.

2. The gold standard is based on the quantity of money theory of prices. This simple explanation of price movements is partially inapplicable to the conditions existing in a modern nation.

3. The use of trade barriers and other restrictions to international trade is incompatible with the gold standard.

4. The use of the gold standard requires that the expansion of the quantity of liquid assets (money and near moneys) be determined by the expansion of the production of gold.

The Bimetallic Standard. The bimetallic standard in modern times has meant the use of gold and silver as standard monetary metals. The two outstanding examples of the use of the bimetallic standard are the United States and the Latin Monetary Union established in 1865 under the leadership of France.

The basic requirements of a bimetallic standard are (1) free and unlimited coinage of gold and silver, (2) a fixed ratio between the value of the metals for monetary purposes, (3) both metals must be given the power of legal tender, and (4) both metals must be permitted to move freely out of the treasury into private hands and out of the country into the possession of foreigners.

The principal advantages usually attributed to bimetallism are: (1) that it provides for more stable prices because the operation of Gresham's law causes the cheaper metal to drive out the more expensive, thus reducing price fluctuations due to changes in the supply of one metal; (2) that it economizes the use of gold; and (3) that it increases the base of the monetary standard.

The principal disadvantages of the bimetallic standard are: (1) the monetary demand for the two metals is inadequate to keep their prices at a constant ratio; (2) international cooperation beyond that existing is necessary to make it work; and (3) the weaknesses of the gold standard are applicable also to the bimetallic standard.

Composite Commodity Standard. The composite commodity standard would be the basis of what is called *commodity reserve currency*. The best known plan is the "Graham plan," named after Benjamin and Frank Graham, American economists who developed the scheme. The basic idea is to tie the value of the dollar or some international monetary unit to that of a "commodity composite" in exactly the same way that the gold standard tied the value of the dollar to that of gold.

The basic requirements for a composite commodity standard are: (1) legislation must provide a standing offer to buy and sell several commodities; (2) the price would be set for the bundle of commodities rather than for an individual commodity; (3) the reserves of commodities possessed by the monetary authority must be sufficient so that their sale would prevent a general price rise of the bundle of commodities used in the reserve; and (4) commodities must flow freely between nations.

The principal advantages usually attributed to the composite commodity standard are that it would (1) provide a stable price level, (2) increase the base of the monetary system, and (3) provide a reserve of goods to be used during periods of shortages. The principal disadvantages are that (1) it requires international acceptance to be effective; (2) reserves might either become too large or run out; (3) the administrative problems related to the plan are very great; and (4) it may create a very strong political bloc by combining all major raw-material producers.

The Paper Standard. The paper standard is the basic standard utilized by all principal nations. The quantity of financial claims usable as money and the manner in which they can be used are established by the banking and monetary authorities of the nation through application of certain principles established by legislation and custom. These principles, if followed, are supposed to provide a money system which will contribute to maintenance of economic stability and efficient utilization of resources.

Chapter 3

Banking and Making Money

It was the last decade of the seventeenth century before England developed a money market or a substantial bank. The banking methods utilized in this early British period can be traced back to the paleolithic age or to 10,000 B.C. However, it was not until the neolithic age or 5000 B.C. that capital and credit became important. The first professional bankers in the western world arose in the Neo-Babylonian period around 2000 B.C. Their banks were lending and depository institutions that developed out of practices evolved by religious leaders and their management of the resources of the temples.

Although evidence of rather sophisticated financial institution arrangements existed in Babylon between 1800 and 600 B.C., very little evidence exists of similar development in Egypt. The difference in the development of finance in these two great ancient empires appears to have been due to the relative strength of the central government in Egypt and to the relative importance of trade between areas under different governments and the use of money in carrying out domestic transactions in Babylon. In Egypt very little use was made of money in internal allocation of goods and services, and trading outside the Egyptian empire was much more limited than was true of the Babylonian empire.

It is said that the evolution of financial management practices around the eastern Mediterranean between 1800 B.C. and 600 B.C. was as great as that which has taken place since 600 B.C. By 600 B.C. the business of granting exchange bills and the use of documentary order on a debtor were being practiced. Also, bills were payable on demand or on a fixed rate and were payable to the bearer as well as to the original creditor. Merchants and money exchange dealers accepted deposits and paid interest on these amounts. Transfers were made from one account to another without the use of cash. In Babylon, security passed to the creditor when the loan fell in default. This was a considerable development from the older practice of having to transfer a substantial pawn when the loan was granted. The pawnbroker, of course, is still with us, but the Babylonian practice dominates lending through grant of a secured loan.

BRITISH BANKING DEVELOPMENT

English financial development in the eighteenth century was based on the previous experience of Italian money managers and later of the Dutch bankers. This English development was basic in the establishment of financial management practices in the United States.

Checks were being used occasionally in England at the end of the seventeenth century, and British merchants were lending and borrowing from each other on the basis of an "inland bill of exchange." That England did not have laws prohibiting the payment of interest, as was true in Italy and Spain, stimulated this practice.[1]

The Bank of England was established in 1694 as a joint stock bank to lend money to the government. The loan was to be repaid from a new tonnage tax. The bank could engage in trading bullion and paper arising from the sale of goods. In addition, it could issue bank notes equal to its total capital and carry out a general banking business. This general banking business, in addition to accepting government deposits and lending to the government, included acceptance of general deposits and the honoring of drafts against deposits. In carrying out these activities, the Bank of England was anticipating the modern passbook and check.

At the same time the Bank of England was developing as the sole joint stock bank, private banks owned by individuals and partnerships grew up in London and the countryside. The rural banks sent some of their deposits to private banks in London to be invested in the urban areas where returns were higher. These private banks carried out just about the same

[1] Payment of interest by Italian, Dutch, and Spanish bankers was hidden in foreign exchange contracts.

activities as the Bank of England, except that they did not accept government deposits—nor did they lend to the government.

Finally in 1775 the Bank of England was chosen as the organization that would facilitate transfer of deposits from one bank to another through acceptance of a draft on the deposit balance each bank kept at the Bank of England. The Bank of England performed the function of the London Clearinghouse. As the British Empire grew and prospered, the Bank of England became the world clearinghouse.

The rapid rise of England as a money and banking capital was due to two principal developments. First, the revolution of 1688 brought the Dutch Prince William III to the throne. The country became a constitutional monarchy, and arbitrary action by the king became impossible. Second, speculation in securities of companies engaged in international trade and debt issues of the government to finance wars (including the rebellion in North America) provided securities in which funds could be kept liquid while invested at a return.

During the eighteenth century and the formative period of the British monetary and banking system, the gold and silver standard was maintained. No deliberate debasement of the coinage of the realm took place during this hundred-year period. From this environment came the writers of the American Constitution and the managers of the first American financial institutions. The founding fathers were aware of attempts of the colonies to found banks based on the mistaken notion that the basic worth of reserves (e.g., land) would guarantee soundness and acceptance of credits extended as deposits or paper money. These land banks did not accumulate savings and extend loans from these savings. They issued notes backed by real estate. They were all failures with the possible exception of the Pennsylvania loan office established in 1722.

The first bank established in the colonies along the lines of the British experience was the Bank of North America at Philadelphia. It opened its doors for business in 1781. The charter was granted by the Continental Congress to Robert Morris. The bank was a success and an example of how government capital could be used to assist a financial institution that was managed on sound business principles. Although the federal government withdrew from the venture in 1785, the experience had been favorable and provided a portion of the environment that prompted Congress to approve Alexander Hamilton's proposal for the First Bank of the United States in 1791.

AMERICAN MONEY AND BANKING TRADITIONS

The First Bank of the United States was a creature of the members of Congress from the northern states. It was financed substantially through use of stock notes; i.e., the federal government purchased $2 million of stock and was extended a $2 million loan by the bank. The remaining $8 million of capital was three-quarters U.S. government securities and one-quarter gold.

The bank was very good to the government and the Federalist Party in power. For example, it charged the federal government 6 percent on the $2 million loan and paid 8 percent as dividends on stock held by the U.S. Treasury. Most of the lending of the bank was to the federal government, and many business interests felt deprived of needed funds. These businesses turned to state banks being established to meet their needs. The state banks felt they were prevented from operating effectively because of the liquidity forced on them by the bank note redemption policy of the branches of the First Bank.

These credit allocation problems, combined with the fact that the stock of the First Bank was largely owned by foreigners and with the basic political hostility of the South, resulted in Congress failing to renew the bank charter when it expired in 1811.

In 1816, a second Bank of the United States was established by a Congress united in the belief that a nation-wide bank providing public and private banking services was needed. The War of 1812 plus the excesses of the state-chartered banks had resulted in a disorganized national currency; only another nation-wide bank closely tied to the federal government could reverse the debilitating effects of the suspension of payments in specie, or payments in gold or silver rather than paper money. This practical approach to the money management problems of the country gained legal support in the *McCulloch* v. *Maryland* decision of the U.S. Supreme Court.

Chief Justice John Marshall's 1819 Maryland decision declared unconstitutional a state stamp tax on notes issued by the

Second Bank. The decision also acted to support the constitutionality of federal government action establishing a nationwide banking system that performed both commercial and government functions. Nevertheless, Andrew Jackson, whose first term as president (1829–1833) coincided with the fourth term of the Second Bank, continued to state his belief in its unconstitutionality. When Jackson was re-elected in 1832, he took this to be public support for his position and vetoed 1832 rechartering legislation; he removed federal government deposits in 1833. The Second Bank continued to exist until its charter expired in 1836.

The concept of federalism and the right of states to charter banks was too strong in the United States to permit the federal government to control the banking system. Also, the economic sophistication and power of the Northeast was so much greater than that of the West and South that any national banking system was destined to be managed in the interest of the Northeast. Finally, the grant of monetary power to Congress by the Constitution talks of the right to "coin money" but does not consider issuance of paper money.

The Constitution did not give the federal or state governments the right to issue paper money because of the bad experience in the United States during the colonial period and the Revolution. In addition, the writers of the Constitution were influenced by the British system. Paper money was the credit issued by commercial banks in carrying out their traditional activities, not the money issued by governments. Some involvement by government in the basically banking process of providing paper money (bank notes) was acceptable, but just barely, and then only as limited participation through provision of capital.

It was not until the Legal Tender Cases of 1871 and 1884 that the Supreme Court finally decided that the money sections of the Constitution provided monopoly power to Congress to issue paper money as well as coins. Nevertheless, when legislation was prepared in 1913 to establish another nation-wide banking system tied to the federal government, i.e., the Federal Reserve System, the issuance of paper money and deposit creation was limited to the backing that could be provided from commercial paper and gold. Bank reserves and legal tender funds could not be issued on the backing of government debt.

The people's distrust of a federal government issuing money to meet its own needs still existed.

The U.S. Treasury still does not issue paper money directly. There remains a veil between the creation of money and its placement in the hands of the people. The charade of issuing securities and offering them to the public is continued. These securities can be purchased by the Federal Reserve System (FRS) in unlimited quantities; when they are purchased, additional bank reserves are created (i.e., commercial bank deposits in the Federal Reserve) that can support a multiple expansion of commercial bank deposits, and less directly, of savings and loan and mutual savings bank deposits to be used to purchase more federal debt, and so on, and so on. Unlike paper money and deposits of the past, no provision for conversion (specie payment) exists.

Chapter 4

Establishing an American
Money System

Colonial Experience. The Indians of North America used wampum as a standard of value and medium of exchange. It served the need for money so well that the colonists used it also, and in Massachusetts in 1649 it actually was made legal tender for small amounts.

The colonists used the British pound, the Spanish dollar, and also paper money issued by the different colonial governments. (The North American Colonies pioneered in the use of paper money.) The Spanish dollar was used widely in commerce, but accounts generally were kept in pounds.

"Bills of Credit" and "Continentals." The Continental Congress in 1775 provided for printing "bills of credit" in dollar denominations. It also issued large amounts of notes, called "Continentals." By 1780 the "Continentals" had practically no value.

State Banking, 1836–1863. During this period of twenty-seven years (1836–1863) the banking activity of the nation was carried on entirely by banking institutions chartered by the states. The number of state banks expanded from about 500 to approximately 1,500. This threefold increase was due to (1) elimination of federal banking activity, (2) expansion of the population and financial activity of the nation, and (3) permission of loose banking practices.

Weaknesses. The loose banking procedures permitted led to malpractices in (1) bank capital structure, (2) bank note issues, and (3) bank assets. Frequently as little as 5 percent of the capital stock of a bank was paid for with cash; the remainder was purchased with promissory notes and the like. The effect was a strong temptation to practice reckless banking procedures, for the actual losses to the owners from bankruptcy were very small.

NOTE ISSUES. The note issues of state banks were generally unlimited and unregulated. This encouraged overissue of bank notes (the paper money of the period) and the consequent depreciation of the value of the notes issued by many banks. The effect of the issuance of bank notes possessing a theoretical, nation-wide circulation by hundreds of small, state banks was a confused and disorganized paper money system. The paper money system of the nation did not regain the confidence of the business community until national bank notes became available and gradually replaced state bank notes.

The weakness of the state banking system is discussed in terms of bank notes rather than deposits, because at that time the practice of using checks as a method of payment had not gained wide usage in the United States.

SUFFOLK, NEW YORK, AND LOUISIANA BANKING SYSTEMS AS REMEDIES. To improve the nation's currency system a number of schemes to provide ready redemption were established. The Suffolk system, which was established in Boston, offered to hold deposits for country banks for the purpose of redeeming any of their notes presented to it. Country banks failing to maintain such deposits risked having the Suffolk Bank accumulate their notes and present large amounts for redemption at one time.

In New York, the Free Banking Act passed in 1838 provided for deposit of acceptable collateral with the comptroller of the state; the comptroller printed under the bank's name notes equivalent to the value of the acceptable collateral deposited. The system worked fairly well but did not prevent failure of New York banks and the redemption of their notes at a discount. In 1853 the banks of New York City provided for redemption of their notes at a daily clearing.

Louisiana state legislation prohibited a bank from paying out the notes of another bank, and required each bank to settle weekly for its balances due other banks of the system. This, in addition to the rather large amount of specie available as a result of the trade of the port of New Orleans, provided Louisiana with one of the few acceptable currency systems of the period.

Greenbacks or United States Notes, 1862–1866. The first paper money was issued by the federal government in 1862 when notes were printed to replace the demand notes issued by the Treasury in 1861. The new notes or greenbacks were irredeemable, noninterest-bearing, demand notes and legal tender for payment of all private debts. These notes depreciated in terms of specie but did not become worthless. The $325 million total issued by 1866 provided nearly half the currency of the nation for more than ten years.

National Bank Notes, 1863–1935. The system of national bank notes was introduced originally to provide a market for government bonds, but in its long history of more than seventy years (1863–1935) it became known chiefly for its national uniformity. The plan was based upon the New York Free Banking Act and provided for issuance of notes by banks chartered by the federal government.

These notes were secured by United States bonds issued for that purpose, and no bank could issue notes of greater value than its paid-in capital stock. The state bank notes were eliminated through assessment of a federal tax of 10 percent on all state bank notes on July 1, 1866. In 1935 the U.S. Treasury used a portion of the profits from the devaluation of gold to retire bonds that could be used as collateral for national bank notes. Issuance ceased as of August 1, 1935.

Silver Certificates, 1878–1967. The first United States silver certificates were issued in 1878. Legislation of 1878 and 1890 that provided for issuance of silver certificates was repealed in 1893, but the money was not withdrawn at that time. In 1934 legislation was again passed providing for issuance of silver certificates.

The 1934 act provided that silver certificates be issued in an amount not less than the total cost of the silver purchased by the federal government under provisions of the act. Silver certificates in circulation totaled $2,257 million on May 31, 1949. The additional silver certificates issued since 1934 did not cause an expansion of the total quantity of paper money; rather they acted as substitutes for additional quantities of Federal Reserve notes.

REASON FOR USE OF SILVER. Silver was used during the nineteenth century, because the United States had had very unfortunate experiences with paper money unbacked by a commodity customarily used for monetary purposes. Examples of this unfortunate experience were the Continental currency during the American Revolution, which became worthless, the state bank notes of the middle 1800s that in many cases became partially valueless, and finally the greenbacks of the Civil War period, which fell below par. With this background it was politically impossible to obtain substantial backing for issuance of more money not backed by either gold or silver. An additional factor that must not be neglected was the desire of the mining interests of the West for a more profitable market for their silver.

Prior to the development of the Federal Reserve central-banking techniques and the utilization of deficit financing possibilities, free coinage of silver was very nearly the only usable tool available to the government for expanding the quantity of money. The use of silver in the 1930s to expand the quantity of money is an example of the slow change of established monetary practices.

HISTORY OF SILVER LEGISLATION.

1. Although federal legislation providing for free coinage of silver was passed in 1792, coinage was suspended until 1834 by an executive order of President Jefferson. The order was issued because the money was being used in the West Indies and not the United States.

2. The Coinage Act of 1834 provided for free coinage of silver and gold; however, the mint price set undervalued silver, and silver dollars were soon driven out of circulation.

3. In 1873 legislation eliminated the silver dollar. This caused little concern at the time because the mint price for silver was below the market price. The price of silver soon began to decline and the legislation became the "Crime of '73." For the first time the market price of silver fell below the $1.29 that the mint had been offering since 1834.

4. In 1878 the Silver Purchase Act, often called the Bland-Allison Act, was passed. This act required the Treasury to buy each month at least $2 million and not more than $4 million of silver to be coined into dollars of the old weight and fineness. The Treasury purchased the minimum amount provided in the act.

5. In 1890 the Sherman Silver Purchase Act was passed. This act provided for purchase of 4½ million ounces of silver monthly at the prevailing market price. The silver was paid for with new full-legal-tender Treasury notes. Despite these rather considerable Treasury purchases of silver, the price of silver continued downward. This downward trend in the value of sil-

ver was partly due to the reduced use of silver for currency by the major countries of the world.

6. In 1918 the Pittman Silver Purchase Act was passed. This act provided for sale of the silver accumulated under the Bland-Allison and the Sherman Acts to Great Britain, who needed it to pay for purchases made from India during World War I. It also provided that this silver, which was sold for $1 an ounce, be replaced with domestically produced silver that would be purchased at the same price. This was a definite subsidy to domestic silver producers, whose output was selling for about 70 cents an ounce.

7. In 1933 the so-called "Thomas inflation amendment" to the Agricultural Adjustment Act gave the President power to establish free coinage of gold or silver at a fixed ratio and to accept foreign obligations in silver at a price of 50 cents an ounce. Foreign obligations (allied war debts) to the amount of $200 million only could be repaid by this method.

8. In 1934 a new Silver Purchase Act was passed. It provided for purchase of silver by the Treasury in amounts at times and at prices (but not to exceed $1.25 per fine ounce) that it "deems reasonable and advantageous to the public interest." The law further stated that silver be purchased until its monetary value was equal to 25 percent of the monetary stocks of gold and silver held by the government. This goal was never reached. Under this legislation silver has been bought at net prices varying from 64.5 to 90.5 cents an ounce. The higher price was established in 1946. These silver purchase legislative acts resulted at one point in an accumulation by the Treasury of the fantastic amount of over 100,000 tons of silver.

9. In 1967 the demand for silver became so great that the $1.29 per fine ounce selling price was limited to buyers in the silver business. Also after June 30, 1968, silver certificates were no longer redeemable for silver. The new clad dimes and quarters have replaced the silver coins, and the fifty-cent piece is now only 40 percent silver. The Treasury sells a limited quantity of silver monthly at the existing market price. The demonetization of silver was completed over a three-year period. Now silver is one of the more useful and valuable metals—and that is all.

Federal Reserve Notes, 1913–19—. The Federal Reserve note was provided for by the Federal Reserve Act of 1913 to supply the nation with an elastic money system. The apparent need was for a currency that would increase in quantity when the public demanded greater quantities. Need for a currency to decrease with the reduction of the public's demand for currency has never existed, for the public always returns unwanted currency to the banks. By 1920 Federal Reserve notes were of greater aggregate value than all other types of currency combined, and today with the withdrawal of the silver certificate there is no other important type of U. S. currency.

AN ELASTIC CURRENCY. The Federal Reserve note was originally established as a type of paper money the quantity of which was determined by the amount of discounted commercial paper. It was believed that the amount of this collateral would vary to provide the desired elasticity. In practice, however, it soon was learned that no dependable close relationship existed between the Federal Reserve holdings of discounted commercial paper and the need for currency.

ACTUAL PROVISION OF ELASTICITY. The Federal Reserve note did not become a type of money that varied automatically to meet the needs of business. Instead the needed elasticity was provided by establishing procedures that enabled Federal Reserve officials and commercial banks to expand the amount of currency when needed. For example, in 1917 provision was made for issuing Federal Reserve notes against gold reserves held by the Federal Reserve System. Also, member banks were able to expand the currency supply by borrowing from the Federal Reserve banks on the security of federal government bonds or by depositing funds that arose from Federal Reserve purchases of securities.

Federal Reserve Bank Notes, 1913–1945. The history of the Federal Reserve bank note, which was provided for in the original Federal Reserve Act of 1913, has been varied but not very important. On June 12, 1945, Congress repealed the power of the Federal Reserve banks to issue this type of paper money. The intent of the original 1913 legislation was to use Federal Reserve bank notes to replace national bank notes. Thus the federal government bonds that could be used to back national bank notes were also eligible to back Federal Reserve bank notes. This intent did not materialize, and Federal Reserve bank notes were actually issued only during three separate currency emergencies.

USE OF FEDERAL RESERVE BANK NOTES. The first

emergency was the reduction of silver certificates during World War I that arose through sale of silver to Great Britain for export to India. These silver certificates were replaced by a special issue of Federal Reserve bank notes. The second emergency arose during the banking holiday of March 1933, when it appeared desirable, because of the shortage of gold reserves, to provide for issuance of currency not backed by gold. Each of these issues amounted to about $270 million, and each was discontinued after a few years. The third emergency started in December 1942 and arose from the need for additional currency to meet the expanded economic activity of the war. The principal justification for the issuance of $660 million at this time was that the notes were already printed and would therefore conserve labor and material during the war. The power for the World War II issue arose from the provisions of the Bank Emergency Act of 1933, which had not been repealed.

Additional Paper Money Experience. The Thomas Amendment of May 12, 1933, provided that the Secretary of the Treasury may issue $3 billion of unsecured greenbacks to be used to retire the federal debt. This legislation was not used as a basis of action and was finally repealed in June 1945.

CONFEDERATE CURRENCY. During the War between the States, the Confederacy financed a considerable part of its war expenses by issuing paper money. In addition, banks and cities throughout the South issued paper money. A large portion of this local paper money, including all Confederate currency, became worthless after the Confederate defeat.

METALLIC MONEY

The Silver Dollar. In 1785 Congress, under the Articles of Confederation, adopted the dollar as the monetary unit. The Monetary Act of 1792 under the new Constitution continued the dollar as the standard unit and provided for its coinage in gold and silver. The weight of gold and silver assigned to the standard unit was believed by Alexander Hamilton, Secretary of the Treasury, to approximate their relative values. The standard dollar in both gold and silver was declared legal tender and was the only money to possess this power until the Civil War. The establishment of independent gold dollars and silver dollars as standard units placed the United States on a bimetallic standard.

PERIOD OF SILVER DOMINANCE. Although the United States had a bimetallic standard, nearly all circulating standard currency from 1792 until 1834 was silver. This arose because the official United States mint ratio gave a higher relative value to silver than did the mint ratios of other countries or the world markets. This overvaluation of silver made it advantageous for all foreigners to pay their foreign bills in gold. The standard gold coins that did circulate commanded a premium.

The Gold Dollar. The Act of June 28, 1834, reduced the fine content of the gold dollar so that the gold dollar was undervalued. Consequently, silver flowed out of the country and gold flowed into it. Gold thereafter virtually replaced silver. The replacement was so complete that although officially a bimetallic standard existed, the actual standard money of the country was gold. The gold dollar was the circulating standard and legal tender currency from 1834 until 1861.

During the Civil War most of the gold and silver coin of the country was exported. Throughout the period of the 1870s very little gold and silver currency circulated within the country.

RESUMPTION OF SPECIE PAYMENT. The resumption of specie payment in 1879 placed the United States on a de facto gold standard with the gold content of the dollar unchanged from that established in 1834. This was the case despite the provision of legislation permitting the Treasury to redeem greenbacks, at its option, in either gold or silver. Actually the Treasury always redeemed it in gold. The Act of 1900 legally established the gold standard. This was done by requiring the Secretary of the Treasury to keep all forms of money issued at par one with another, and one type of money issued was gold. The effect was to keep all forms of money at par with gold.

ELIMINATION OF GOLD CURRENCY. Gold continued to circulate until March 9, 1933, when legislation was passed making it unlawful for the general public and the banks to hold gold and gold certificates. The legislation of 1933 and 1934 eliminated the gold dollar, which had had an important place in the circulating currency of the nation for exactly 100 years. The legislation also prohibited domestic holding of gold other than in works of art or as utilized in industrial processes. On August 14, 1974, legal restrictions on domestic ownership of gold by Americans were repealed. President Ford signed the freedom-to-own-gold bill. The legislation did not restore the freedom to enter into contracts that require payment in gold or in dollars measured in gold; that freedom had been repealed in the joint resolution of June 5, 1933.

On August 15, 1971, the United States ceased conversion of dollars held abroad into gold. On December 18, 1971, the Smithsonian Agreement established a new set of relative values in gold of the major currencies of the world. Actually the dollar's value was related to gold only as it is related to the price of any other commodity. In 1978 gold was selling for about $180 an ounce. But the U.S. government gold holdings are valued at $42.22 an ounce.

SUBSIDIARY COINAGE. The nations of the world experienced great difficulty in maintaining a satisfactory system of subsidiary coinage until the principles of token money were developed and utilized. When the metal value of subsidiary coins was equal to the coined value, the variations in the relative worth of the metals used constantly were causing an overabundance of one coin and a shortage of another. If this problem were avoided by making the seigniorage (the difference between the coined value and the metal value) great, the tendency existed to produce too many subsidiary coins and too few coins upon which the seigniorage was small. Paper money of small denominations has always been difficult to handle and expensive because of the speed of replacement necessary. Also, small-denomination paper money is not as suitable as coins for use in vending machines. Despite these disadvantages, small-denomination paper money has been issued in the United States, particularly during the period of the Civil War. This money acquired the nickname "shinplasters."

Principles of Token Money. The principles of token money considered most basic are:

1. The coins should be issued in unlimited amounts but only in exchange for standard money.

2. The market value of the metal in the coins should be well below the face value.

3. The coins should be redeemable in standard money without charge and in any amount.

4. The coins should be convenient in size, attractive in appearance, durable, and individual in feature.

The increase in the value of silver in the fall of 1965 was so great that the silver content of U.S. token coins reached the value of the coins. A shortage of coins developed as hoarders withheld some $2.2 billion of silver coins received. The difficulty was solved by making U.S. coins from a baser metal. Principle 2 (above) of token money could not be violated, even by the strongest nation in the world.

The impact of collectors of coins and paper money has been substantial. The mint has stopped putting mint marks on coins and has dated coins as though issued in previous years. The two-dollar note issued until 1966 and reissued in 1976 has been particularly attractive to collectors, and only 5 percent of the quantity issued between 1926 and 1966 was ever redeemed.

RESULTS OF THE BIG SQUEEZE
OF THE 1930s

By the fall of 1931 the Federal Reserve System, under the leadership of Benjamin Strong, president of the Federal Reserve Bank of New York, was taking seriously its role as defender of the legislative provisions restricting the expansion of deposits and currency. After all, the Fed (Federal Reserve) had been in existence for nearly twenty years; it had taken the nation safely through World War I and had engineered the great prosperity of the 1920s. Now that troubled days had descended on the people, the Fed thought it had not only a responsibility but also an ability to correct the existing unfortunate circumstances.

More than likely, from that day right up to the present, the Fed has always been involved in trying to keep the economy prosperous and on an even keel. It is difficult to believe this has been the case when the record has been so miserable. The Fed began to develop its wrong-headed record when it raised the discount rate from $1\frac{1}{2}$ percent to $3\frac{1}{2}$ percent in 1931, when the unemployment level was about 20 percent and banks were closing their doors by the hundred every month.

The troubles of 1931 had their roots in what happened in the 1920s. What did the Fed do then? Speculation in common stocks with borrowed money was rampant, and the Fed sharply raised the discount rate and therefore the cost of short-term funds to everyone. This action cut off funds to the business borrower first, but not to the speculator—not until the boom was over. The result was undercapitalized businesses forced to face a rapidly deteriorating economic climate as the boom blew itself out.

Under the conditions in the business and consumer communities in 1931 one would expect a generous acceptance of private sector loans for discount by the Fed. The law had established that Federal Reserve credit could be extended if a portion (35 and 40 percent) of the backing consisted of gold and the remainder of commercial paper. A little easing of maturity and collateral requirements would permit businesses and consumers to meet their money-denominated obligations. This approach also would have helped the banks to stay open, and the Fed would have been doing what it was supposed to do—"meet business's need for credit on reasonable terms."

Federal Money Machine. Instead, provision for federal government debt-backing to match gold required to issue Federal Reserve credit was established by the Glass–Steagall Act (February 27, 1932). This action opened the floodgates to the monetization of federal government borrowing. The whole concept of the Fed was changed by this legislation. Instead of an institution to meet the monetary needs of business and consumers, it became a governmental, money-printing press. Today the "assets" of the Fed consist largely of federal government securities, i.e., federal debt turned into high-powered bank reserves.

The purchase of federal government debt to be held more than temporarily to aid in the financing of a new federal bond issue or to increase briefly the liquidity of the economy is all that was contemplated when the Fed was founded. It was not needed to carry out a government program of finance through expansion of the money supply. Congress has this power, and all it need do to cover checks presented for collection is to order the mint to print a billion dollars to be deposited in the banks of the country.

When, instead, federal government deficits expand the money supply through use of federal bonds to back Federal Reserve credit, the Fed is being used to do indirectly what the Constitution contemplated would be done directly by the elected representatives of the citizens. The Glass–Steagall Act opened the door to irresponsible federal financing and largely eliminated the very close relationship contemplated between the liquidity needs of business and consumers and the quantity of Fed credit.

The Federal Reserve, of course, was not the only element of U.S. society in 1931 that considered backing money with federal debt a desirable development. It was, however, the institution that made use of the right, and it was the institution that fueled the crisis by failing to reduce sharply the requirements of private debt for qualification as collateral for loans from the Fed. During the 1932 presidential campaign, for example, President Herbert Hoover said that the Glass–Steagall Act "saved us by a narrow margin from going off the gold standard" and from having "grass growing in our streets!"

In 1920 and 1923, as in 1931, the Fed had experienced a shortage of free gold to back its credit. But it didn't talk about going off the gold standard then. Instead it acted to increase discounting by member banks. Obviously the crisis in 1931 was more serious. In 1931 action to ease acceptability requirements for discount would have been the appropriate procedure to ease the situation while keeping the rate of interest (discount rate) low to encourage investment.

It is ironic that the leadership of the Republican Party and the conservative wing of the Democratic Party pressed for a solution to a temporary gold shortage at the Fed that was destined to lay the basis for practically unlimited federal deficits and unlimited expansion of the supply of money. The Glass–Steagall Act contained two other amendments to the Federal Reserve Act that made it easier for member banks to borrow from the Fed. Neither of these turned out to be important, although at the time they were considered comparable in impact to the provision permitting use of federal government securities to back Federal Reserve credit. The advocates of sound money and continuation of the gold standard destroyed a major bulwark of this approach to monetary policy in their effort to preserve it.

Since 1932, the quantity of federal government debt provided by government deficits has never proven to be in short supply. However, the gold needed to make that portion of the backing of Federal Reserve credit did run into supply shortages, and legislation was passed to eliminate this requirement. So the Glass–Steagall Act, the sponsors of which were advocates of a *sound* money system, provided a basic step to a money backed only by a batch of government debt. And much of the relation of the money supply to operations of the private sector was eroded. At the same time, the growth of rigidities in labor costs and corporate pricing reduced the ability of flexible prices to carry out needed supply-and-demand adjustments between different industries and products.

In 1932 the wholesale price index of all commodities with 1926 = 100 had declined to 64.8. This was the level that had existed in 1907 and only 8 index points above the 1890 level. Farm prices in 1932 were lower than in 1891, and the interest rate on commercial paper in 1936 had fallen to 0.75 percent, the lowest in the nation's history. Prices of basic products were remarkably stable, i.e., the value of money did not change much during the fifty-year period ending in 1940. Prices went up, but they went back down again. Prices went down, but they came back up again. And this had been true of interest rates prior to the sharp drop in the mid 1930s.

Money prior to 1932 was closely associated with demand-and-supply movements of goods and services. Its quantity could not move violently for any period of time, because basic production and consumption levels had a built-in stability. The technology and labor at hand could produce a certain level of a variety of goods and services. Pressures were constantly pushing toward full utilization at this level. The money available was tied to economic basics and not to government budget deficits arising from politically motivated, administrative decisions having little relation to needed goods and services and production potentials. This was all changed with the passage of the Glass–Steagall Act—as we were to learn.

PART I: SELECTED REFERENCES AND SOURCES

Jane Anderson and Thomas M. Humphrey, "Determinants of Change in the Money Stock, 1960–70" (Federal Reserve Bank).

William Burke and Yvonne Levy, *Silver: End of an Era* (San Francisco: Federal Reserve Bank of San Francisco, 1969).

William Fellner, "The Dollar's Place in the International System," *Journal of Economic Literature*, September 1972, *10*, 735–756.

Irving Fisher, *100% Money* (New York: Adelphi, 1935).

M. Friedman and A. J. Schwartz, *Monetary History of the United States, 1867–1960* (Princeton, N.J.: Princeton University Press, 1963).

John Kenneth Galbraith, *The Great Crash* (Boston: Houghton Mifflin Co., 1955).

Alexander Gerschenkron, "History of Economic Doctrines and Economic History," *American Economic Review*, May 1969, *59*, 1–17.

Yustave Glotz, *The Agean Civilization* (New York: Alfred A. Knopf, 1926).

R. G. Hawtrey, *Currency and Credit* (London: Longmans, Green, 1950).

———, *The Gold Standard in Theory and Practice* (New York: Longmans, Green, 1927).

George G. Kaufman, "More on an Empirical Definition of Money," *American Economic Review*, March 1969, *59*, 78–87.

William C. Niblock, "Development of Electronic Funds Transfer Systems," *St. Louis Federal Reserve Bank of Review*, September 1976, 10–18.

Chester A. Phillips, *Bank Credit* (New York: Macmillan, 1920).

E. S. Shaw, *Money, Income, and Monetary Policy* (Homewood, Ill.: Irwin, 1950).

R. H. Timberlake, Jr., and J. Forston, "Time Deposits in the Definition of Money," *American Economic Review*, March 1967, *57*, 190–193.

J. Tobin, "Monetary Interpretation of History," *American Economic Review*, June 1965, *55*, 464–485.

Part II

The Federal Reserve System

INTRODUCTION

The Federal Reserve is the central bank of the United States. It was established in 1913; however, its purpose *then* was not to stabilize the economy—*that* goal was acquired in 1942 when Congress adopted the Employment Act. Actually, ten years earlier, in 1932, Congress basically changed the way the Fed was to function through the Glass–Steagall Act. But in 1913 the Fed was set up to tie together the economy of the country through provision of a uniform check-clearing system. Another important goal in 1913 was to avoid money panics. The Fed was able to accomplish this through lending money or granting deposits on the basis of loan contracts (commercial paper) brought to it as collateral for loans (discount) by commercial banks in need of funds.

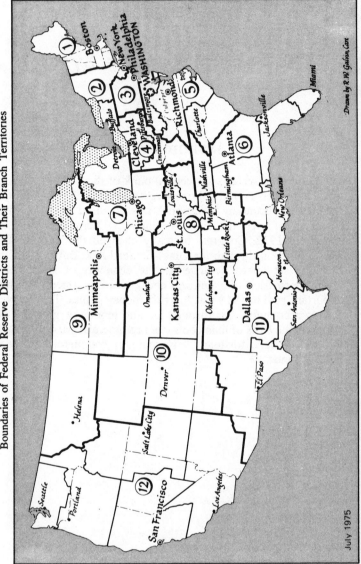

The Federal Reserve System

Boundaries of Federal Reserve Districts and Their Branch Territories

Drawn by R. W. Galvin, Cox

July 1975

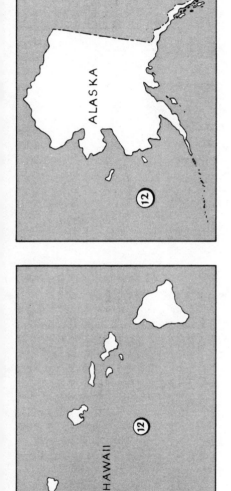

ALASKA

⑫

HAWAII

⑫

LEGEND

▬ Boundaries of Federal Reserve Districts

▮ Boundaries of Federal Reserve Branch
Territories

✪ Board of Governors of the Federal
Reserve System

⊙ Federal Reserve Bank Cities

• Federal Reserve Branch Cities

· Federal Reserve Bank Facility

Chapter 5

Organization and Jobs

Organization. The Federal Reserve System was established in 1913 to provide the services of a central bank. At this time these services were considered largely to be protection of the nation's gold stock and meeting the liquidity needs of business (a flexible money system). Instead of establishing one central bank as had the countries of Europe, it was decided to establish twelve regional banks. A Board of Governors selected by the President with the approval of the Senate was provided to coordinate the activities of the twelve district banks and to make most basic policy decisions.

FEDERAL RESERVE BANKS. Federal Reserve banks are in the following cities (the number indicates the number of the district): (1) Boston, (2) New York, (3) Philadelphia, (4) Cleveland, (5) Richmond, (6) Atlanta, (7) Chicago, (8) St. Louis, (9) Minneapolis, (10) Kansas City, (11) Dallas, and (12) San Francisco. In addition to the twelve banks, the system includes twenty-five branch banks.

More than 50 percent of the assets of the twelve banks are possessed by the New York, Chicago, and San Francisco banks. The New York bank is by far the largest of the twelve, and it largely dominated the Federal Reserve System until 1930. The Minneapolis bank is the smallest and possesses assets only about one-twelfth as great as that of the New York bank. The banking legislation of 1935 expanded the powers of the Board of Governors so that the board is able to dominate the activities of the twelve district banks. This reduced the independence of each Federal Reserve bank and substantially diminished the power of the New York bank.

MEMBER BANKS. The member banks of the Federal Reserve System are the commercial banks of each district that have met minimum requirements, requested admission, and been admitted. All commercial banks that are also national banks must be member banks. The member banks include about 39 percent of the nation's commercial banks; these banks hold about 74 percent of all commercial bank deposits.

Recently, state banks have hesitated to join the system because: (1) the reserve ratios required by the Federal Reserve Board have been higher than those of most state banking commissions; (2) the requirement of par clearing reduces earnings; (3) the restrictions on interlocking directorates; (4) the high capital requirements if a member bank is to establish out-of-town branches; (5) the restrictions on loans to executive officers, reports required, and the like; and (6) the advantages of membership have been reduced through the pressure of non-member banks upon Congress to force the Federal Reserve System to be very liberal in making its services available to all banks, members and nonmembers. With certain limitations, nonmenber banks may use the Federal Reserve clearing system, borrow from Federal Reserve banks, and use other facilities. On the other hand, the most important material advantage of membership is direct access to the discount and loan facilities of the Federal Reserve System.

The funds for the establishment of the Federal Reserve were obtained through a required stock subscription by all member banks. Each member bank is required to pay into its Federal Reserve bank an amount equal to 3 percent of its own paid-up capital and surplus. Federal Reserve banks are owned wholly by their member banks but are not controlled by these member banks. The stock held by member banks is similar to nonvoting stock of a corporation. In effect, all voting stock of the Federal Reserve banks is held by the federal government through its control over the Board of Governors.

Administration and Control.

BOARD OF GOVERNORS. The federal government controls the actions of the Federal Reserve System through the Board of Governors. The board is composed of seven members, each appointed by the President with the approval of the Senate for a term of fourteen years. They are ineligible for reappointment if a full term has been served. The President designates one of the board members as chairman. The chairman in 1978 is G. William Miller, a business executive.

OPEN-MARKET COMMITTEE. The most powerful instrument in setting the quantity of deposits of the Federal Reserve System is the purchase and sale of government obligations, acceptances, and credit instruments in the open market. This activity directly controls the reserves and hence the lending activity of member banks.

The group name for these activities is open-market operations. This activity formerly was conducted individually by each district bank, with the New York bank dominating the policy. Since 1935, open-market activities have been conducted by the Federal Open-Market Committee (FOMC), which is composed of the seven members of the Board of Governors and five members selected by the twelve Reserve banks. The Reserve bank representation is determined by relative size. Only the New York bank has a representative of its own on the committee. The open-market policy now is officially definitely in the hands of the board and may soon be more so, for many now believe it is unconstitutional to have nonpresidential appointees such as presidents of Federal Reserve banks serve on a policy committee as important as the FOMC.

FEDERAL ADVISORY COUNCIL. The final central governing body of the Federal Reserve System is the Federal Advisory Council. One member of the council is selected by the board of directors of each bank. It acts as an advisory group, and its power depends upon the prestige of the individual members.

Bank Boards of Directors and Executive Officers. Each of the twelve Federal Reserve banks has a board of directors of nine, composed of three classes of three each. Each class is differently appointed and has varying responsibilities. Class A directors are appointed by the member banks to represent them. Each of three size groupings of member banks appoints one director. Class B directors are appointed in the same manner, but they represent important industries of the district rather than banking interests. Class C directors are appointed by the Board of Governors. The chairman also acts as Federal Reserve Agent and in this capacity is the official representative of the Board of Governors in carrying out its functions. Another director acts as deputy chairman.

The chief executive officer of each bank is the president.

He is appointed by the directors of the bank and must be approved by the Board of Governors. The first vice-president is appointed in the same way. Other executive officers are appointed by the directors, and the board has only the power of removal.

The Federal Reserve banks possess little independent power today. For purposes of understanding the manner in which the system functions, each bank should be considered as a branch of the central bank, which is the Board of Governors, with some independence of action.

Routine Work. The principal routine jobs or chores of the Federal Reserve System are: (1) banking supervision, (2) clearing and collection of checks, and (3) fiscal-agency functions.

Bank supervision of the traditional type has become relatively less important and perhaps should be relinquished entirely to the Federal Deposit Insurance Corporation (FDIC). However, the new powers given to the Fed in the Bank Holding Company Act has substantially increased its supervision responsibilities. Clearing and collection of checks by Federal Reserve banks has provided collections at par and has speeded up the process from frequently over two weeks to approximately three days. Electronic clearing is technically feasible, but it has not been adopted.

The fiscal functions of the Federal Reserve System have expanded with the growth of the federal government's economic activity. The Fed holds the principal checking accounts of the U.S. Treasury and holds, sells, pays interest due, and redeems federal government obligations. In addition, the Fed along with the Treasury is responsible for maintaining the value of federal debt obligations and generally for preserving an orderly market for government securities.[1]

Credit control powers of the Fed are the traditional powers possessed by the world's central banks. Congress gave these powers with the intent to permit the Fed to control business credit and, in that manner, prices. In addition it was believed that economic booms and depressions could be avoided if price fluctuations were largely eliminated. From 1921 through 1929, the Fed appeared to be successful in maintaining price levels by

[1] See Appendix I for an official summary of Fed activities in providing payment mechanisms.

utilizing these central-bank powers. The powers proved inadequate in preventing price rises during World War I and II and inadequate for preventing price declines during the 1930s. In the late 1960s, price increases expanded and continued at an ever more rapid rate until 1975. The Fed's tools were largely powerless.

Chapter 6

Discount Rate

The discount rate is the rate of interest or schedule of interest rates charged by a Federal Reserve bank if it extends a loan or an advance to a member bank. The Federal Reserve bank is a banker's bank, and the discount rate is the rate of interest it charges when member banks exchange their credit for Federal Reserve credit. At the time the Fed was established, it was believed that an increase of this rate would decrease the expansion of credit and therefore the expansion of money, and that a decrease of the rate would increase expansion of credit and therefore the expansion of money. An increase in the rate of discount was supposed to tighten the money market and decrease credit expansion; a decrease was thought to have the opposite effect. When the power to change the discount rate was given to the Fed it was considered very important. However, it never proved as valuable a weapon of credit control in the United States as it apparently had been in Great Britain when utilized by the Bank of England.

Causes of Ineffectiveness. The inability of the discount rate to control the level of economic activity and price levels should have been expected. Despite this, its ineffectiveness surprised the leaders in American money and banking circles. The more important reasons for the inadequacy of the discount rate as a tool to control the economy are:

1. The use of fractional reserves necessitates a very great increase in the rate of discount to bring about a rather modest increase in the cost of borrowed funds.

2. A rise in the cost of borrowed funds is likely to reduce loans for legitimate commercial activities rather than speculative borrowing. The increase in cost occasioned by a rise in

FEDERAL RESERVE BANK INTEREST RATES

TABLE 2

Federal Reserve Bank	Loans to member banks—									Loans to all others under Sec. 13, last par.		
	Under Secs. 13 and 13a			Under Sec. 10(b)								
				Regular rate			Special rate					
	Rate on 8/31/77	Effective date	Previous rate	Rate on 8/31/77	Effective date	Previous rate	Rate on 8/31/77	Effective date	Previous rate	Rate on 8/31/77	Effective date	Previous rate
Boston	5¼	11/22/76	5½	5¾	11/22/76	6	6¼	11/22/76	6½	8¼	11/22/76	8½
New York	5¾	8/31/77	5¼	6¼	8/31/77	5¾	6¾	8/31/77	6¼	8¾	8/31/77	8¼
Philadelphia	5¾	8/30/77	5¼	6¼	8/30/77	5¾	6¾	8/30/77	6¼	8¾	8/30/77	8¼
Cleveland	5¾	8/30/77	5¼	6¼	8/30/77	5¾	6¾	8/30/77	6¼	8¾	8/30/77	8¼
Richmond	5¾	8/30/77	5¼	6¼	8/30/77	5¾	6¾	8/30/77	6¼	8¾	8/30/77	8¼
Atlanta	5¾	8/30/77	5¼	6¼	8/30/77	5¾	6¾	8/30/77	6¼	8¾	8/30/77	8¼
Chicago	5¾	8/30/77	5¼	6¼	8/30/77	5¾	6¾	8/30/77	6¼	8¾	8/30/77	8¼
St. Louis	5¾	8/30/77	5¼	6¼	8/30/77	5¾	6¾	8/30/77	6¼	8¾	8/30/77	8¼
Minneapolis	5¾	8/30/77	5¼	6¼	8/30/77	5¾	6¾	8/30/77	6¼	8¾	8/30/77	8¼
Kansas City	5¼	11/22/76	5½	5¾	11/22/76	6	6¼	11/22/76	6½	8¼	11/22/76	8½
Dallas	5¼	11/22/76	5½	5¾	11/22/76	6	6¼	11/22/76	6½	8¼	11/22/76	8½
San Francisco	5¼	11/22/76	5½	5¾	11/22/76	6	6¼	11/22/76	6½	8¼	11/22/76	8½

Range of rates in recent years

Effective date	Range (or level)—All F.R. Banks	F.R. Bank of N.Y.
In effect Dec. 31, 1970	5½	5½
1971—Jan. 8	5¼–5½	5¼
15	5¼	5¼
19	5 –5¼	5¼
22	5 –5¼	5
29	5	5
Feb. 13	4¾–5	5
19	4¾	4¾
July 16	4¾–5	5
23	5	5
Nov. 11	4¾–5	5
19	4¾	4¾
Dec. 13	4½–4¾	4¾
17	4½–4¾	4½
24	4½	4½

Effective date	Range (or level)—All F.R. Banks	F.R. Bank of N.Y.
1973—Jan. 15	5	5
Feb. 26	5–5½	5½
Mar. 2	5½	5½
Apr. 23	5½–5¾	5½
May 4	5¾	5¾
11	5¾–6	6
18	6	6
June 11	6–6½	6½
15	6½	6½
July 2	7	7
Aug. 14	7–7½	7½
23	7½	7½
1974—Apr. 25	7½–8	8
30	8	8
Dec. 9	7¾–8	7¾
16	7¾	7¾

Effective date	Range (or level)—All F.R. Banks	F.R. Bank of N.Y.
1975—Jan. 6	7¼–7¾	7¾
10	7¼–7¾	7¼
24	7¼	7¼
Feb. 5	6¾–7¼	6¾
7	6¾	6¾
Mar. 10	6¼–6¾	6¼
14	6¼	6¼
May 16	6–6¼	6
23	6	6
1976—Jan. 19	5½–6	5½
23	5½	5½
Nov. 22	5¼–5½	5¼
26	5¼	5¼
1977—Aug. 30	5¼–5¾	5¼
31	5¼–5¾	5¾
In effect Aug. 31, 1977	5¼–5¾	5¾

interest rates is likely to mean little to the speculator, but may cause postponement of legitimate construction.

3. The rate of discount has little effect unless the banks are forced to borrow to acquire sufficient reserves to support an expanding quantity of deposits. Under these conditions the cost cannot continue for long because of the Federal Reserve rule against continued borrowing.

4. A reduction of the rate of discount is effective only if the supply-and-demand conditions in the money market permit a reduction of interest rates.

Discount Rate Policy.   Table 2 gives the details of the Federal Reserve bank discount rate since 1970. The next several paragraphs provide a summary of discount rate changes and policy considerations since the establishment of the Federal Reserve.

RATE CHANGES (1919–1922).   The discount rate of 7 percent was established late in the spring of 1920 and was continued until the spring of 1921. This increase from the 4¾ percent rate, which had existed in 1919 when World War I federal government financing was completed, was made to reduce the great postwar inflation the country was experiencing. The increase was not made until the inflationary bubble was approaching the breaking point. The sharp increase of 2¼ percent within a few months during the winter and spring of 1920 appeared to make the break more violent than necessary and certainly was greater than needed to stop the inflationary spiral. The rate was also maintained at this high level after the threat of inflation had obviously disappeared.

Reductions of the discount rate were begun in the early summer of 1921 and continued in ½ percent steps until June 1922, when the rate was down to the 4 percent level.

RATE CHANGES (1922–1928).   From June 1922 until the spring of 1928 the discount rate fluctuated between 3 and 4½ percent. Changes in the rate of discount were not great during this six-year period, but they were frequent. In the spring of 1928 the discount rate was started on a course toward higher levels and reached a peak of 6 percent in the late summer of 1929.

The rate of discount was not the only economic indicator that remained relatively constant during this period. Generally, the period of 1922 through 1928 was one of economic stability on a high level. Very nearly every index of economic activity of the period shows a high level of activity with only minor fluctuations. For example, the wholesale price index of the Bureau of Labor Statistics was extremely steady; this was also true of the Federal Reserve index of physical volume of manufacturing production, the Bureau of Labor Statistics reports of factory employment and payrolls, and the Federal Reserve index of dollar volume of department store sales. These and a number of other indexes indicated that economic activity was steady at what was considered a desirable level. Three exceptions were the indexes of residential construction, food prices, and stock prices. The F. W. Dodge Corporation index of residential construction fell steadily from the early months of 1928, the wholesale prices of foods showed weaknesses in the early portion of the period, and stock prices indicated boom conditions.

In the 1920s the nation experienced two periods, in 1921 and 1924, of rather sharp recession and a minor drop in 1927. In all three periods the discount rate was reduced. Also, a quick return of prosperity was enjoyed, but it is doubtful if the return of prosperity was due to the reduction of the discount rate; however, at the time this appeared to be the case. In addition, the Federal Reserve System expanded its outstanding credit by increasing its open-market purchases, that is, its holdings of federal government bonds. The banking authorities can be pardoned, after these successful experiences, for believing that the tools of monetary policy they possessed (the discount rate and later open-market operations) were adequate to prevent a severe depression.

DISCOUNT RATE (1928–1931). In October 1929, a few months after the discount rate had been increased to the high of 6 percent, the stock market crashed and with it the prosperity of the economy. The discount rate had been increased gradually to this rate from the low of 3½ percent established during the slight recession of 1927. The higher discount rates did not stop the investment boom, and it appears to have run itself out when the index of 420 stocks prepared by the Standard Statistics Company reached a new high of about 220 with the base year 1926 equaling 100. Immediately after the stock market crash and the development of depression conditions, the Federal Reserve System lowered the discount rate 1 percent, shortly later by another ½ percent, and continued to lower it until a new low of 1½ percent was reached in the summer of 1931. This time, however, prosperous conditions failed to return. The public gradually learned that prosperity was *not* just around the corner and that the Federal Reserve monetary tools were inadequate to restore prosperous economic conditions.

DISCOUNT RATE (1931–1933). The low discount rate and the generally easy money policy of the Federal Reserve System were abandoned in the autumn of 1931; however, prosperity had not returned to the nation. The discount rate was increased to meet the requirements of the *international gold standard*. The use of the discount rate for this purpose was unique in the history of the Federal Reserve System but had been the principal purpose of the device in Great Britain during the nineteenth century. (It was in Great Britain that this tool of monetary policy first was developed and where its use reached the highest degree of perfection.)

In 1931 Great Britain went off the gold standard. This caused an uncertainty of the ability of the United States to remain on the gold standard. Also, the low discount policy of the Federal Reserve Board had reduced interest rates in the United States below those prevailing in other money centers. Both of these had the effect of draining gold out of the United States.

The uncertainty made people with dollar credits desirous of converting these into gold while it still was possible, and the low rate of interest induced foreign depositors to shift their accounts to higher interest areas. The gold shortage was intensified by an expansion of the need for gold to be used as reserves for Federal Reserve notes and by deposits and gold hoarding by United States citizens. The additional gold reserves were needed because the depression had seriously reduced the quantity of commercial paper available to back Federal Reserve notes. Under these circumstances the Federal Reserve Board acted in the traditional central-bank manner to prevent loss of gold and serious credit complications; it raised the rate of discount.

By the autumn of 1931 the discount rate was back up to 3½ percent. The effect of this action is doubtful, but it did prevent the withdrawal of several large accounts to the credit of foreign central banks. It might have been better if the Federal Reserve Board had not attempted to keep the United States on the gold standard, for in less than two years the United States was to leave the gold standard under conditions that were perhaps less favorable than those existing in 1931. Also, in 1932 the Glass–Steagall Act was passed to permit the Federal Reserve System to use federal government bonds as a backing for its notes as a substitute for commercial paper. If this had been done earlier, it probably would have made unnecessary the high discount rate in the midst of a depression.

DISCOUNT RATE (1933–1970). The discount rate was gradually reduced in 1933, and early in 1934 it was back to 1½ percent. From 1934 until the 1957–1958 period, the discount rate was permitted to remain constant for long periods of time, and when it was changed the change was very small. The discount rate from 1934 through most of 1937 remained at 1½ percent. Late in the summer of 1937 it was reduced to 1 percent as a halfhearted aid to the economy during this period of sharp decline in economic activity. Nobody considered the change particularly important, and this general opinion undoubtedly was right.

The discount rate of 1 percent was continued until late in 1942, when it was reduced to ½ percent. (Technically the 1 percent rate was maintained, and the lower rate was applicable only to discounted federal government securities.) The rate was continued throughout the War. In the spring of 1946 the discount rate was increased to 1 percent where it remained until January 1948. Then it was increased by ¼ percent, and later the same year it was increased by another ¼ percent. The discount rate of the New York Federal Reserve Bank in the summer of 1957 was 3½ percent, which was higher than it had been at any time since the summer of 1931; it was an increase of more than 100 percent since 1954. The discount rate was down to 1¾ percent in April 1958, but by November it had been brought back up to 2½ percent.

The discount rate was used more actively to control the credit expansion of 1955–1957 than at any time since the 1920s. The increased rate was made feasible by the abandonment of the program to support federal government bonds in 1951 and the increased political support given monetary policy since 1954.

DISCOUNT RATE (1959–1976). From March 1959 to the spring of 1974, the discount rate trend was upward. The rate in 1968 was up to 4¼ percent from the 1959 level of 3 percent. This rate was first established in August of 1968. In

1969 the discount rate was raised to 6 percent as interest rates increased; the Fed was attempting to decrease speculation and the deficit in our balance of international payments.

The discount rate from mid-November 1970 to May 1973 fluctuated within the range of 4½ percent to 5¾ percent. It started a climb in the spring of 1973 that resulted in an 8-percent high—a new, all-time peak—in April 1974. Historically high rates continued for two years. In August of 1976 the discount rate of Federal Reserve banks was back down to 5¾ percent and in April, 1978 up to 6½ percent again.

Member banks borrow from the Fed without being out of line when it is done to meet seasonal needs, requirements of a short-term adjustment of their credit program, or a local emergency. Security for the borrowing is usually short-term federal government securities. The minimum rate can also be enjoyed on collateral of municipal securities of not over six months to maturity that are tax anticipatory. Commercial paper, the original federal loan collateral, is still used. The maturity maximum is 90 days. Congress has also provided that housing mortgages may be discounted at the lowest rate.

Chapter 7

Open-Market Operations

The Federal Reserve can create deposits for member banks (reserves) by purchasing securities in the open market. The securities purchased are largely federal government obligations. It can contract deposits of member banks (reserves) by selling securities in the open market. Federal Reserve deposit contraction activities through the open market are limited by the number of securities the Fed owns. Purchases are no longer limited by a gold certificate backing requirement on Federal Reserve credit. Policy alone dictates purchase limits. The gold certificate backing requirement of deposits was removed in 1965. Open-market operations were not contemplated as a method of credit control when the Federal Reserve System first was established; this tool developed through trial and error. From 1923 until 1942 it was considered the most important power the Federal Reserve Board had to control the quantity of credit. Its usefulness during a boom, however, was greatly reduced when the Fed and the Treasury assumed the obligation of preventing long-term, federal government obligations from falling below par between 1942 and 1951. Since 1951 open-market purchases and sales along with reserve requirement changes have been used to set appropriate money-market conditions as seen by the Fed.

Historically, the Fed has entered into open-market operations for five purposes: (1) to obtain earning assets, (2) to control the quantity of commercial bank reserves, (3) to stabilize the general values of securities, (4) to maintain a pattern of interest rates on federal government obligations, and (5) to set growth rate goals for both M_1 and M_2—a requirement placed on the Federal Reserve chairman in March 1975. The first and third goals are now of secondary importance.

PURCHASES AND SALES (1920–1923). The Federal Reserve use of open-market sales and purchases to control the economy did not develop as a well-understood policy until the middle of the 1920s. In 1920 and 1921, open-market sales were not made despite the inflationary pressure. The obvious reason for the lack of action, other than the failure to understand the effect, was the relatively small quantity of Federal Reserve holdings of federal government bonds; the total was about $0.75 billion. In 1922 the Fed entered into open-market purchases that helped to ease credit conditions, but this effect was not the reason for the action.

In 1922 Federal Reserve purchases of about $0.5 billion of federal government bonds were made to expand the earnings of the Fed. The reduction of member bank borrowing from $2.75 billion toward the close of 1920 to $0.4 billion had caused Federal Reserve earnings to fall below levels needed to meet expenses. In this unintentional fashion, large-scale, open-market operations were initiated. It soon was recognized that open-market operations could be performed much more effectively, in relation to general credit conditions, if the activities of all Federal Reserve banks were coordinated. This was done through the establishment of a committee of Federal Reserve bank presidents. Later, in 1933, legislation provided for the Federal Open-Market Committee (FOMC).

PURCHASES AND SALES (1923–1933). Federal Reserve holdings of federal government bonds were decreased to about $0.25 billion in the autumn of 1923. In 1924, business conditions deteriorated in the United States, and the Fed expanded its holdings of federal government bonds to a peak of $1.25 billion in the autumn of 1924. But by the spring of 1925 they had been reduced again to $0.75 billion. This approximate level was maintained until the autumn of 1927.

The open-market operations of the Fed during this period were counteracting the fluctuations in outstanding Federal Reserve credit arising from changes in the quantity of commercial bills discounted with Federal Reserve banks. In 1922, 1924, and 1927 the quantity of commercial bills discounted decreased due to the reduction of business activity, but the full impact on the quantity of Federal Reserve deposits was modified through open-market purchases. The fact that government deficits did not expand caused interest rates to decline.

In 1923, 1925, 1926, 1928, and 1929, the holdings of federal government securities were reduced. This lessened the impact on the quantity of Federal Reserve deposits of the expanded business conditions of the period and the resulting greater quantity of commercial bills. These actions of the Fed show an abandonment of a major principle of its establishment; that is, that the quantity of Federal Reserve credit was to fluctuate with the needs of business as indicated by the quantity of commercial paper (elastic credit). *Instead, by as early as 1924 the policy had become one of preventing the quantity of commercial paper from affecting the amount of Federal Reserve credit.*

The great test of effectiveness of open-market operations as a tool to stablize the economy was made in 1932. It will be remembered that the rate of discount was sharply dropped immediately after the crash of the stock market in the autumn of 1929. This failed to bring back prosperity; it actually appeared to have little effect on the level of economic activity.

The discount rate was raised in 1931 to save the United States' gold supply. This was contradictory to the general policy of credit relaxation. A little later the Fed inaugurated the largest open-market operations up to that date. Within a span of a few months in the spring and summer of 1932 (an election year), over $1 billion of federal government bonds were purchased; in the summer and autumn of 1933, another $0.5 billion were purchased; this brought the holdings to about $2.5 billion. *They were maintained at approximately this level until World War II.*

Twofold Purpose of Open-Market Activity. The use of open-market operations to maintain a constant level of Federal Reserve earnings, which was their original purpose, is not inconsistent with the additional use of those operations to maintain the proper level of Federal Reserve credit. They both point to simultaneous expansion or contraction of holdings, that is, expansion during a business depression and contraction during a business prosperity.

Beginning with the 1930s, Federal Reserve commercial paper activity became unimportant. The quantity discounted and bought by the Fed, after a brief surge during the period of the bank holidays in 1933, became insignificant. Since 1933 the Federal Reserve deposits extended to purchase federal government bonds have been the total credit extended, not merely credit extended to compensate for fluctuations of discount or purchase of commerical bills.

The increase of discounts and advances at the end of 1952 and the first part of 1953 was a brief exception to this generalization. Again during the period of a shortage of commercial bank deposits in the Fed in 1969 and 1973 the Fed extended loans to commercial banks of somewhat over $1 billion. Commercial banks adjust their individual deposit balances in the Fed through the federal funds market; i.e., those with a surplus of deposits needed to meet reserve requirements lend to those with a shortage.

PURCHASES AND SALES (1942–1949).   The holdings of federal government bonds reached a new peak in 1942 when they went above $6 billion, and they climbed steadily until the end of 1945 when they totaled $24 billion. The increase was largely determined by the credit needs of the federal government as they were seen by the Treasury and the Federal Reserve Board. During the period of large-scale federal borrowing, open-market purchases were made to permit expansion of federal debt without placing an undue strain on the money markets of the nation. The principal aim was to give commercial banks sufficient reserves to enable them to expand their deposits by the amount needed to buy the government debt that savers were unwilling to purchase at the prevailing interest rates. The postwar activities until the summer of 1949 were largely directed at keeping long-term federal government bonds up to par. On occasion this required large open-market purchases during a rather short period; for example, the large purchases during the fall of 1948.

There was a fantastic expansion in commercial bank excess reserves during the World War II period. These arose because commercial bank lending was sharply restricted while the Federal Reserve supported U.S. Treasury borrowing through massive open-market purchases that resulted in expanded commercial bank deposits in the Fed.

REVERSAL OF POLICY IN 1949.   In the spring and summer of 1949, interest rates began to fall. The continuation of the policy of keeping uppermost a fixed interest rate on long-term federal government bonds necessitated substantial open-market sales. From April 27 to June 29 (when the policy was changed) the Federal Reserve System sold $1.7 billion of federal government bonds. This tended to raise interest rates and reduce member bank reserves by reducing deposits of member banks at the Fed. This took place during a period of business recession when the opposite would have been the more desirable monetary policy.

Open-market activities to supply suitable credit conditions would *contract* the quantity of Federal Reserve deposits during a *boom* through open-market sales and *expand* Federal Reserve deposits during a *depression* through open-market purchases. Open-market activities to maintain long-term, federal government bonds at par would *increase* the quantity of Federal Reserve deposits during a *boom* when interest rates tend to be rising and would *decrease* the quantity of Federal Reserve deposits during a *depression* when interest rates tend to be falling. The effect of these two goals that required almost opposite types of action made open-market activities from the end of World War II until March 1951 very indecisive.

POLICY DEVELOPMENT BETWEEN 1949 AND 1958. From June 29, 1949, until March 4, 1951, there were varying degrees of official disagreement between the Treasury and the Federal Reserve as to what should be the interest rate policy on government securities. It was the general position of the Federal Reserve that it could not continue to be responsible for controlling the quantity of deposits in the best interests of the country restricted by a pattern of interest rates on federal government securities established at the outset of World War II. It was the general position of the Treasury that if the existing pattern of interest rates were not maintained and particularly if long-term marketable securities were permitted to fall below par, the federal government would find it very difficult to carry out refunding and new borrowing operations. Therefore the Treasury maintained that the best interests of the country were served by maintaining the interest rate pattern.

Finally, on March 4, 1951, these differences were settled in the announcement of a policy "accord" that relieved the Federal Reserve of the responsibility of maintaining any given pattern of market interest rates on federal government securities. The effect of the "accord" was to restore to the Federal Reserve the power to control the quantity of central bank deposits in a way that the board, acting under its basic mandate from Congress, believes best meets the needs of the economy.

During the 1954 recession the board interpreted this mandate to require a massive expansion of Federal Reserve deposits. During the boom of 1957 the board refused to expand bank reserves, and the effect was a shortage of loanable funds. During the recession of late 1957 and 1958 the board failed to act as forthrightly as it had in 1954.

POLICY DEVELOPMENT BETWEEN 1959 AND 1968.   Early in 1959 member bank indebtedness to the Federal Reserve was permitted to average more than $500 million. Despite rather large open-market purchases, member bank borrowing rose to a billion-dollar average by midyear. This was largely due to a decline of $780 million in the gold stock and a sharp outflow of currency. Tight money and higher discount rates were the order of the day until mid-1960. During the remainder of 1960 through to late 1962, monetary ease prevailed. By mid-1963 a tighter monetary policy had been initiated. This was the period of "the twist" when the Federal Reserve attempted to keep short-term interest rates relatively high by making a large portion of open-market purchases in the over-one-year maturity portion of the market. The aim of the policy was to keep long-term interest rates down while avoiding a lowering of short-term interest rates. Later in 1970 and 1973, long-term interest rates moved up to approximate the high, short-term rates. (See Charts III and IV.)

Higher short-term interest rates would avoid an outflow of U.S. funds and a worsening of an already serious balance-of-payments problem. Relatively low long-term rates would permit a continuation of investment commitments in housing.

In late 1964 interest rate ceilings under Regulation Q (which sets bank interest payments on deposits) were raised as was the discount rate. Higher interest rates were established in the market, and these rates continued to increase until the end of 1966. In the fall of 1966 the Federal Reserve credit outstanding actually was permitted to decline while the economy was in the midst of a war boom. Interest rates reached thirty-year highs only to be bested again in late 1967. In early 1968 the liquidity of the economy was very high, and interest rate trends were downward. However, the availability of Federal Reserve deposits was not expanding as rapidly as it had during most of 1967. To care for this shortage of Fed deposits to supply reserves to back member bank deposits the banks have been permitted to count currency as reserves since 1960.

SHORT-TERM MONEY MARKET
SALES AND PURCHASES

Most FOMC decisions to buy and sell federal government securities are not aimed at affecting the money supply. An example of this more common type of open-market operation is the net open-market purchases made in December of every year. At this time commercial bank loans are high, and the cash held by the public is much larger than usual. Both of these increase the need for central bank reserves, and it is largely through open-market purchases that the reserves are provided as needed. After Christmas central bank reserve requirements are reduced, and at this time open-market sales are made to decrease the amount of central bank credit.

Other times when money market-type, open-market action is likely are on quarterly income tax payment dates and when the Treasury is engaged in a new borrowing or refunding operation. In the latter case, what was originally intended to be a temporary increase in central bank credit is more likely to become permanent than are increases related to seasonal needs or tax payment requirements.

Short-Term and Long-Term Interest Rates. Shortly before the United States entered World War II the interest rate on three-month bills was $\frac{3}{8}$ percent and that on long-term bonds was $2\frac{1}{2}$ percent. When the nation entered actively into the conflict it was determined to maintain these rates despite the quite conclusive evidence that the spread between the long-term and short-term interest rates was too great. The success of this effort is illustrated in Charts III and IV. Gradually after 1946 short-term interest rates and longer-term rates increased. In 1969 and 1975, long-term rates of Baa-rated corporate bonds (high-level, investment-type bonds) reached the peaks of the 1930s and 1920s.

The monetary powers of the federal government during a popular war are sufficiently great to obtain any quantity of funds at any rate of interest. But maintenance of an artificial spread between interest rates of different types of obligations is another story. The results of the attempt during World War II were mostly undesirable. It resulted in (1) long-term bonds selling above par, (2) speculation in government securities aris-

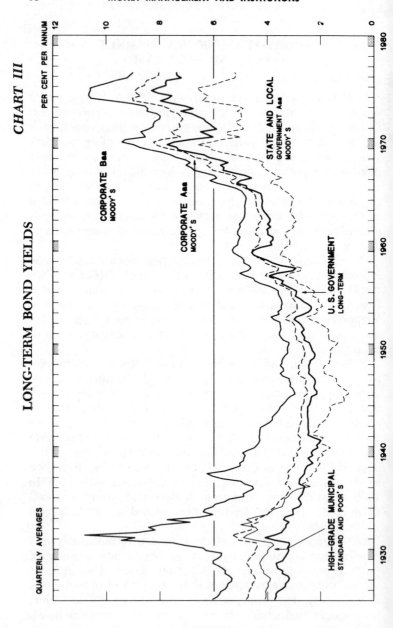

CHART III

LONG-TERM BOND YIELDS

QUARTERLY AVERAGES

PER CENT PER ANNUM

CORPORATE Baa
MOODY'S

CORPORATE Aaa
MOODY'S

STATE AND LOCAL
GOVERNMENT Aaa
MOODY'S

U. S. GOVERNMENT
LONG-TERM

HIGH-GRADE MUNICIPAL
STANDARD AND POOR'S

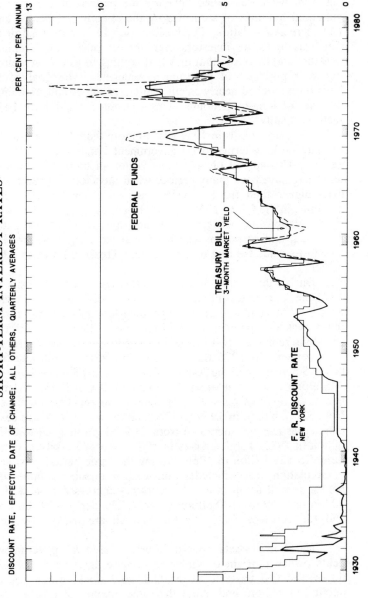

CHART IV

SHORT-TERM INTEREST RATES

DISCOUNT RATE, EFFECTIVE DATE OF CHANGE; ALL OTHERS, QUARTERLY AVERAGES

PER CENT PER ANNUM

FEDERAL FUNDS

TREASURY BILLS
3-MONTH MARKET YIELD

F. R. DISCOUNT RATE
NEW YORK

ing from what was called "playing the pattern of rates," (3) increased holdings of securities by the commercial banks, and (4) increased inflation. The basic reason for the original decision was to assure investors that interest rates would remain constant and therefore that they had nothing to gain from delaying their purchase of government securities. The goal could have been reached nearly as efficiently through establishing only the rate of long-term bonds. This guarantee could have been realized readily.

The rate on bills in 1957 rose to more than 3 percent while the rate on long-term federal government bonds was about 3.4 percent. This spread of .4 percent is not an unusual situation, and there have been many periods when the short-term rate was even higher than the long-term rate. This was the case, for example, in the fall of 1966. But in the spring of 1968, the more usual relationship between short- and long-term interest rates prevailed, and corporate Aaa bonds carried a 6.10 percent interest rate while the rate on three-month Treasury bills was 5.01 percent.

During the period of a severe shortage of Fed deposits in 1974 the four- to six-month, prime commercial paper rate averaged 9.87 percent, and the average, long-term rate on Aaa-rated bonds was 8.47 percent. In 1975 the rate on three-month Treasury bills remained well below the long-term rate and averaged 6.26 percent. In 1976 the three-month Treasury bill rate fell below 5 percent, and the Aaa-rated bonds below 8 percent.

POLICY DEVELOPMENT BETWEEN 1969 AND 1978.   Member bank reserves consisting of deposits in the Fed increased from $23.1 billion in 1969 to $26.5 billion in 1977. Vault cash counted as reserves increased from $4.9 billion in 1969 to $8.7 billion in 1977. Total reserves in 1977 were $35.2 billion compared to $28 billion in 1969. During the same period currency in circulation, which includes vault cash of member commercial banks, as well as all other U.S. currency increased from $53.6 billion in 1969 to $100 billion in 1977. The deposits of the Fed and the currency issued by the Fed all are backed by Fed assets.

The Fed's assets consist largely of federal government debts owned outright or under repurchase agreements. In addition, the Fed has title to the U.S. gold stock, which equals about $11 billion, and about the same amount of outstanding Treasury currency. The Fed is practically out of the business of discounting commercial paper or lending to business. However, in 1977 loans to commercial banks totaled about $1.6 billion.

The business the Fed is in basically is the business of turning federal government debt into money—and a lot more money than the debt amount, because commercial banks need keep reserves only of about 12 percent of demand deposits. In mid-1977 when federal debt held by the Federal Reserve was approximately $100 billion, the quantity of M_1 was about $327 billion, M_2 about $783 billion, and M_3 about $1,317 billion. The whole business of how our money supply is backed is very confusing, but one more point should be mentioned now. The FOMC's net purchases of federal government securities between 1969 and 1975 totaled $30,780 million. These additional holdings of federal government debt make up nearly all the additional assets the Fed acquired. On the other hand, the Fed is the source of reserves supporting a total commercial bank deposit increase during the same period of about $367 billion.

The FOMC goal during the 1969–1977 period shifted from an emphasis on interest rates to one on the rate of increase of the money supply. In most cases, the emphasis has been on M_1; however, M_2 is a concept that enjoys more intellectual support. The first year of experience with money-rate expansion goals rather than interest-rate goals worked out rather well. Interest rates fell during the 1975 period and more modestly during 1976. Therefore the FOMC, in reporting its policy decisions, talks about increasing M_1 at annual rate of 4 to 8 percent and M_2 at rates of between 7 and 11 percent. Emphasis on interest rates is not completely gone, however; and reference is made to an expected federal funds rate.

The average federal funds rate reached a new high in 1974 of 10.51 percent for the year, and the prime rate reached 12 percent on July 5, 1974. These high interest rates lived side-by-side with unemployment of 5.6 percent, a wholesale price index increase from 134.7 to 160.1, and a decrease in private housing starts of about 700,000 to 1,338,000 with no change in the level of industrial production. The experience was unsettling, and the descriptive economic phrase "stagflation" was coined and came into wide use. It was, perhaps, the death knell of monetary economics as developed during the past forty years.

Chapter 8

Reserve Requirements

The Federal Reserve Board requested the power to set member bank reserve requirements as early as 1916. In 1917 Congress eliminated the old correspondent-bank deposit pyramid system and amended the Federal Reserve Act to require all member banks to keep their reserves with the Fed. The power to vary reserve requirements was not granted until 1935. Reserve requirement changes as they existed in 1975 and 1976 are summarized in Table 3. Chart V summarizes reserve excess and borrowings from 1930 to 1976. The borrowings in the 1970s were by far the largest.

It was thought that an increase in member bank reserve requirements would reduce the quantity of credit and that a decrease in reserve requirements would increase the amount of credit. An increase in reserve requirements was supposed to have a great effect, because the theory assumed that banks were utilizing all their reserves and that reserves required were only a fraction of deposits. Therefore, an increase in reserve requirements would force a reduction of deposits and, as a result, would force a reduction of credit extended by commercial banks. A change of reserve requirements also changes commercial bank profit possibilities and interest charged on loans.

Reserve Requirements 1936–1978. The federal banking legislation of 1935 gave the Federal Reserve Board the power to double member bank reserve requirements from the level that had existed since June 21, 1917. The 1917 demand deposit requirement was 13 percent for central reserve city banks, 10 percent for reserve city banks, and 7 percent for country banks. The time deposit requirement for all member banks was 3 percent. The special session of Congress in the summer of 1948 passed legislation giving the Federal Reserve Board power until

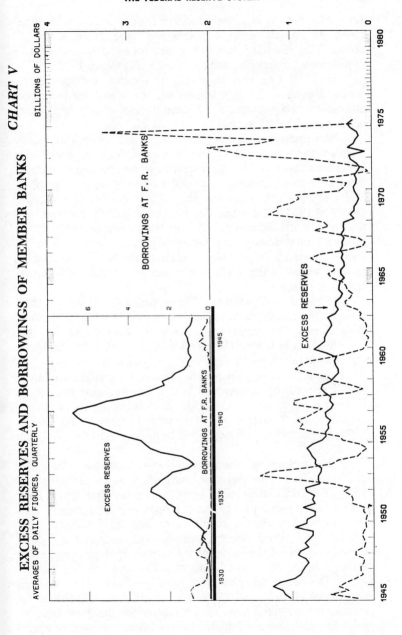

EXCESS RESERVES AND BORROWINGS OF MEMBER BANKS *CHART V*

AVERAGES OF DAILY FIGURES, QUARTERLY

BILLIONS OF DOLLARS

June 30, 1949 to increase all demand deposit reserve requirements by an additional 4 points and time deposits by 1½ points. The 1948 legislation was not renewed, so the reserve requirement powers reverted to those in effect since 1935.

In 1959 Congress legislated to modify reserve requirements. Acting under this legislation, the board made reserve minimums and maximums of central reserve city banks and reserve city banks identical.

The reserve requirements of December 1949 were nearly identical to those in effect from 1938 up to the war period. This is perhaps about as high as reserves can be maintained without member banks beginning to consider Federal Reserve membership onerous rather than beneficial. The higher reserve requirements of 1951 on demand deposits were quickly reduced, and the trend continued downward until 1968 when demand deposit reserve requirements were increased by ½ percent. The increase was made to partially counteract the additional reserves made available when vault cash became a portion of commercial bank reserves.

1936–1938 CHANGES. The undesirable banking conditions of the country reached a climax in 1933 when all banks were closed. The banks gradually were reopened as they put their finances in order. The election of a Democratic President, the change in the psychology of depositors and borrowers, and the large imports of gold resulted in the accumulation of huge excess reserves by commercial banks. The situation caused the Federal Reserve Board to decide in 1936 to use its newly acquired power to raise deposit reserve requirements. By May 1, 1937, all reserve requirements had been doubled (the maximum possible).

This decision to raise reserve requirements had a generally desirable effect. However, the sharp increase in the spring of 1937 resulted in unnecessary credit stringency that should have been relieved more quickly through open-market puchases. This large increase in reserve requirements and the hesitancy in reducing the pressure through open-market purchases are often considered two of the causes of the very sharp drop in economic activity during the second half of 1937 and the first half of 1938. The action and the effect were quite similar to previous experience in 1920 and 1929. The reaction on these three instances is very likely part of the reason for the great caution, prior to 1957, that the Federal Reserve Board showed in applying deflationary measures during the post-World War II boom.

1941–1942 CHANGES. The member bank reserve requirements were reduced in the spring of 1938 and remained at that level until late in the fall of 1941, when they again were set at the maximum permissible. The reserve requirements, with the exception of those of central reserve city banks, remained at this level through the World War II period. The reserve rates of commercial banks in New York and Chicago (central reserve cities) were reduced from the 26 percent requirement established in the fall of 1941 to 20 percent set in the fall of 1942.

The reserve requirements of the commercial banks of New York and Chicago were reduced to facilitate the huge federal borrowings of the period. Loans obtained by the federal government in these financial centers were spent in all the production and training centers of the nation; this caused a heavy drain on the reserves of the central reserve city banks, and reduction of reserve requirements of these banks prevented this drain from increasing Treasury borrowing difficulties.

1948–1949 CHANGES. The post-World War II inflation gained momentum through 1946 and 1947, and by the summer of 1948 consumer prices had reached a new all-time high—some 52 percent above 1945 levels. The special session of Congress called in the summer of 1948 to decrease the inflation and expand housing facilities passed inflationary housing legislation and deflationary banking legislation. Congressional action expanded the Fed's ability to increase reserves, and the board utilized this new power in the early fall of 1948 to set reserve requirements at the highest point in history.

The danger of inflation subsided during the first months of 1949, and by the early summer of 1949, fear of deflation had replaced that of inflation. The Fed took cognizance of the changed situation and began gradually to reduce reserve requirements in the spring of 1949. By September, member bank reserve requirements were at the approximate level established in the spring of 1938.

1950–1958 CHANGES. The inflationary impact of the Korean War caused Federal Reserve banks in cooperation with the board to increase commercial bank reserve requirements sharply; and by February 1951, they had been set at a new, relatively high plateau that was held until July 1953. In 1951 wholesale prices were 10 percent above the 1948 record levels. In 1952 prices declined by 2.1 percent and continued stable for

TABLE 3

RESERVE REQUIREMENTS ON DEPOSITS OF MEMBER BANKS

PER CENT OF DEPOSITS

Type of deposit, and deposit interval in millions of dollars	Requirements in effect August 31, 1977		Previous requirements	
	Per cent	Effective date	Per cent	Effective date
Net demand:				
0–2	7	12/30/76	7½	2/13/75
2–10	9½	12/30/76	10	2/13/75
10–100	11¾	12/30/76	12	2/13/75
100–400	12¾	12/30/76	13	2/13/75
Over 400	16¼	12/30/76	16½	2/13/75
Time:				
Savings	3	3/16/67	3½	3/2/67
Other time:				
0–5, maturing in—				
30–179 days	3	3/16/67	3½	3/2/67
180 days to 4 years	2½	1/8/76	3	3/16/67
4 years or more	1	10/30/75	3	3/16/67
Over 5, maturing in—				
30–179 days	6	12/12/74	5	10/1/70
180 days to 4 years	2½	1/8/76	3	12/12/74
4 years or more	1	10/30/75	3	12/12/74

	Legal limits, August 31, 1977	
	Minimum	Maximum
Net demand:		
Reserve city banks	10	22
Other banks	7	14
Time	3	10

four years. An increase of 6.6 percent in wholesale prices between 1955 and 1957 was followed by relative price stability until 1965. During the slight recession of 1953 and 1954 the reserve requirements were reduced by approximately 20 percent to 20, 18, 12, and 5 percent of deposits for central reserve city banks, rseerve city banks, country banks, and all member bank time deposits, respectively. This level of reserve requirements was continued through 1957. In early 1958 reserve requirements were reduced again.

1959–1968 CHANGES.   Since 1959 vault cash has been counted in meeting reserve requirements. In 1960 reserve requirements were decreased on demand deposits of central reserve city banks to the level of reserve city banks. On July 14, 1966, the category *central reserve city banks* was eliminated. The rapid expansion of time deposits (especially large CDs, or certificates of deposit) brought forth a gradual increase of the reserve requirements on these deposits from 4 percent in 1962 to 6 percent in 1968. In 1978 this still was the time deposit reserve requirement of 30- to 179-day CDs of banks with more than $5 million of deposits.

1969–1977 CHANGES.   The legal limits of reserve requirements provided in Table 3 are the same as those established in 1935. However, the gradations within the general limitation have become more complex. A major change in 1972 eliminated the reserve city concept and made the top reserve requirement applicable to all commercial banks with more than $400 million of net demand deposits. Since 1974 the maximum applied has been 16½ percent, some 3½ percentage points below the legal maximum the Fed could establish. Time deposit reserve requirements have been declining; and the rate of 6 percent for large banks is not really applicable, because the rate on long-term time deposits is below the minimum and banks are only required to provide reserves equal to a 3 percent average.

During the immediate post-World War II period, the expansion of member bank reserve requirements largely resulted in a reduction of the holdings of federal government securities by member banks and an expansion of holdings by the Federal Reserve banks. This decreased the earnings of member banks and increased those of the Federal Reserve banks. This reversal of ownership also reduced the economic burden of the federal debt, because nearly the entire expansion of Federal Reserve earnings is paid into the federal government as a self-imposed tax. Another effect of increased reserve requirements is that Federal Reserve membership becomes less desirable, which tends to decrease the number of state bank members.

More recently the change of reserve requirements has been aimed at changing the quantity of commercial bank credit available to private borrowers. For example, a decrease of reserve requirements would be effective in expanding lending if money needs of unsatisfied, willing borrowers could be met by banks after a reduction of reserve requirements had caused a drop of interest rates through increased offerings of lendable funds. Reserve requirements are a blunted tool so long as they apply only to member commercial banks. The Fed has recommended for a number of years that it be given the power to establish uniform reserve requirements for all deposits that serve as part of the public's money balances, regardless of the type of institution holding these balances. These institutions, however, would not be required to join the Fed. Congress has not been willing to grant this power. All the savings and loan associations and state banks whose competitive position would be worsened by such action have lobbied against the change.

Marginal Reserve Idea. Starting in 1969 the concept of marginal reserve requirements was introduced by the Fed as a method of influencing the sources of bank funds or to minimize the pressures arising from market interest rates that were higher than the maximum that banks could pay. A special 10 percent reserve was set on additional borrowings of Eurodollars; a Eurodollar is a dollar deposit in a bank or branch located in Europe. In 1971 the Eurodollar reserve requirement was set at 20 percent and gradually reduced to 4 percent by 1975. In 1973 a marginal reserve requirement of 11 percent was placed on increases in large denomination CDs issued by banks above a base figure. In 1977 only the 4 percent rate of foreign borrowings remained.

State Nonmember Reserve Requirements. The percentage of banking business done by nonmember banks has been increasing. This trend has effectively placed a ceiling on Fed reserve requirements.

The ideas behind bank reserves include their use to limit or encourage monetary expansion, to meet losses on loans and investments, and to fulfill deposit withdrawal demands. State reserve requirements follow the safety and precautionary reserve idea. The Fed has control of monetary quantities through reserve levels required to support deposits. The two reasons for reserve requirements do not exactly operate at cross-purposes, but neither do they compliment each other.

Nonmember bank reserve requirements vary from state to state. Enforcement of state reserve requirements, to the extent they exist, is spotty. Also, reserves of nonmember state banks held as deposits in other banks or as liquid securities (either directly through interest receipts or indirectly through the provision of services) provide earnings not available on reserves kept as deposits in the Fed.

Although the direct higher reserve costs of Fed membership over state-chartered commercial bank reserve requirements is obvious, studies do not seem to demonstrate that the difference is sufficient to affect profit levels. It is clear, however, that the approximately 26 percent of bank deposits held by nonmember banks reduces the effectiveness of the Fed to control monetary quantities. This impact arises from two sources: first, from the fact that state nonmember banks are not directly affected by reserve requirement changes of the Fed; and second, because the currently reported banking data do not reflect current changes in about one-fourth of the deposit total of the nation. The data inadequacy was very troublesome during the 1973–1975 period. At this time monetary control was seen to be important; but agriculture was the dynamic portion of the economy and a substantial percentage of the banks in rural areas were nonmember banks. As a result, policy makers had to operate largely in the dark where information was needed badly to make accurate judgments.

Chapter 9

Central-Bank Policy Evolution

The central-bank policy that was developed in Great Britain during the nineteenth century and then incorporated into the Federal Reserve System and further refined and expanded was based on squeezing the financial structure at its most sensitive and critical points. These points were found by experimentation and observation of results. Since the 1930s the most sensitive and critical points of the financial structure of the United States and other nations have changed. It is a prime duty of the Federal Reserve Board and other central-bank authorities to determine and understand the exact types of national financial structure changes. The next job is to determine the new sensitive and critical points and devise policy to effect changes at these points.

Aim of Central-Bank Policy. The use of what is called "the bank rate technique"—its use in the United States has been described above—resulted from the development of effective procedures to hit the sensitive and critical points in the nineteenth- and early twentieth-century financial structure. The changed financial structure of the 1970s and 1980s requires new techniques, which more than likely will require much more refined and direct action than is provided by changes in the rate of interest.

The development of such direct actions as control of margin requirements and consumer credit are likely to set the pattern for the new tools of central-bank policy. Again, the tools utilized will be aimed directly at the sensitive and critical areas of the existing financial structure, that is, at fluctuations in consumer expenditures and in capitalization of business earnings.

Reduction in the importance of the older tools and procedures of central-bank policy and the development of new, direct control techniques does not mean an abandonment of traditional central-bank policy. Rather, it signals a return of the traditional approach. It returns central-bank techniques to the old principle that monetary tools must operate on the most sensitive and critical points of the financial structure to be effective. For example, on September 1, 1966, the presidents of the Federal Reserve banks sent a letter to all member banks asking their cooperation in cutting back their expansion of business lending. When the need for this approach disappeared in late December 1966, the letter was rescinded. Business borrowing was out-of-line; it was hit, and a serious situation was avoided.

Additional Tools.

TREASURY BILL TECHNIQUE. The *Treasury bill technique* utilized during World War II permitted commercial banks to use all their reserves by eliminating the need to maintain reserves to meet contingencies. The banks could always sell Treasury bills without loss when they needed additional reserves. Also, the sale included a repurchase agreement if the bank in the near future should again desire to hold Treasury bills. It was better than Federal Reserve loans or advances, because it avoided the popular prejudice related to being in debt to the Federal Reserve System; yet the effect was the same. Also, the device was better than open-market operations, because the additional reserves were made available only to the banks needing them and only in the amounts required.

QUALITATIVE CREDIT CONTROL. Qualitative credit control was formerly an important power of the Federal Reserve Board that could be used to encourage extending credit for what were considered legitimate commercial purposes. When the Federal Reserve System was established, only limited types of debt obligations (largely commercial paper) were eligible for a grant of Federal Reserve credit (security for an advance from Federal Reserve banks); gradually the list has been expanded. Now under certain circumstances, almost any type of obligation may be used to obtain Federal Reserve credit. However, it is still true that the interest rate is ½ percent higher if advances are extended on the basis of collateral other than banker's acceptances or federal government obligations. The Fed frequently has requested modification of Section 10(b), the portion of the Federal Reserve Act requiring the penalty. Some progress has been made, and reserve banks now may make advances on one- and four-family homes at the regular discount rate. Nevertheless, many perfectly sound bank loans cannot qualify for Federal Reserve advances except at a penalty rate of ½ percent above the discount rate.

INTEREST RATE MAXIMUMS.   The wisdom of controlling interest rates was intermittently debated in the United States for nearly a century before federal legislation was passed. The original legislative action that finally was taken in 1933 arose because it was believed that the introduction of deposit insurance made interest maximums necessary to guarantee sound banking.

No interest may be paid on demand deposits. The maximum payable on time deposits of commercial banks is set by the Federal Reserve Board under Regulation Q. These rates remained constant from 1936 to 1957. Between 1962 and 1966 the maximums were changed each year. In 1966, for the first time, the maximum rate was related to deposit size. The rate permitted on CDs over $100,000 was removed entirely to permit domestic banks to meet foreign as well as domestic competition. Although savings and loan associations and mutual savings banks now offer deposits very similar to demand deposits, they continue under Regulation Q to pay interest on these deposits above the level commercial banks can offer on passbook savings accounts. See Table 4 for a summary of the situation in 1967. Regulation Q does not apply to credit unions although their shares are also insured by the federal government.

MARGIN REQUIREMENTS.   The Federal Reserve Board continues to possess another direct instrument of credit control. Since 1934, it has had the power to change margin requirements from 40 percent to 100 percent. The control applies to all margin transactions in stocks on registered security exchanges and since 1967 on convertible debentures (securities that can be changed into stock under certain conditions). Margin requirements apply to all bank loans for the purpose of carrying on transactions in the above types of securities traded on exchanges. Those requirements were as high as 90 percent between 1958 and 1960. Table 5 includes a summary of changes since 1968.

This power was considerably expanded by the 1968 action that placed convertible bonds and securities traded over-the-counter (OTC stocks) under margin requirements.

CONSUMER CREDIT CONTROL.   Another direct credit control was provided under Regulation W. Under Regulation W, the Federal Reserve Board was able to *regulate the conditions under which installment and consumer credit could be extended.* The power was first granted shortly before World War II and was removed on November 1, 1947, only to be restored on September 20, 1948, and permitted to expire on June 30, 1949. Then after the outbreak of the Korean War the board was again given power to regulate consumer credit, and Regulation W was reimposed September 8, 1950, and suspended May 7, 1952. Regulation W permitted the Federal Reserve Board to set the period of time over which consumer credit could be extended and the size of the down payment. Data gathered indicate that Regulation W was much more effective in reducing the quantity of consumer credit during World War II than during the Korean War.

REAL ESTATE CREDIT CONTROL. On October 10, 1950, under Regulation X the board introduced procedures to limit the quantity of credit extended to purchase new and old homes. The regulation was suspended on September 16, 1952.

Future Possibilities. The 1966 letter asking commercial banks to cut back their lending to business could have been a first, major new step toward direct Federal Reserve control over the extension of loans and quantity of deposits. This has not turned out to be the case. The Fed continues to operate with the aggregate and direct control tools that were brought into existence prior to 1950. During the past twenty-five years it is only in the areas of monopoly and holding company activities that the Fed has initiated new approaches.

For many years it has been pointed out that a reserve requirement based on deposits and the size of an institution fails to accomplish many worthwhile bank management influences that are within the grasp of such a tool. If the reserve requirement varied with asset rather than deposit, then the rate could be varied to stimulate banks to use their credit to best meet economic needs of the period. Also the reserve requirement could be related to the risk the bank was undertaking in how it was lending and investing its funds.

Progress in this direction did not even develop during the exposure of the misallocation of commercial bank resources during 1973 and 1974. Instead, Congress and the Fed seemed to be mesmerized by efforts to set quantity of money goals, without any clear idea of the boundary between money and other guaranteed claims to spending power. The problem of defining either money or the relationship between money and

TABLE 4

MAXIMUM INTEREST RATES PAYABLE ON TIME AND SAVINGS DEPOSITS

PER CENT PER ANNUM

Type and maturity of deposit	Commercial banks				Savings and loan associations and mutual savings banks			
	In effect August 31, 1977		Previous maximum		In effect August 31, 1977		Previous maximum	
	Per cent	Effective date	Per cent	Effective date	Per cent	Effective date	Per cent	Effective date
1 Savings..........	5	7/1/73	4½	1/21/70	5¼	(6)	5	(7)
2 Negotiable order of withdrawal (NOW) accounts[1]........	5	1/1/74			5	1/1/74		
Time (multiple- and single-maturity unless otherwise indicated):[2]								
30–89 days:								
3 Multiple-maturity.......	5	7/1/73	4½	1/21/70	(8)		(8)	
4 Single-maturity........			5	9/26/66				
90 days to 1 year:								
5 Multiple-maturity.......	5½	7/1/73	5	7/20/66	[3] 5¾	(6)	5¼	1/21/70
6 Single-maturity........				9/26/66				
7 1 to 2 years[3]...........	6	7/1/73	5½	1/21/70	6½	(6)	5¾	1/21/70
8 2 to 2½ years[3]........	6½	7/1/73	5¾	1/21/70	6¾	(6)	6	1/21/70
9 2½ to 4 years[3]........			5¾	1/21/70		(6)	6	1/21/70
10 4 to 6 years[4]........	7¼	11/1/73	(9)7¼	11/1/73	7½	11/1/73	(9)7½	11/1/73
11 6 years or more[4].....	7½	12/23/74			7¾	12/23/74		
12 Governmental units (all maturities)....	7¾	12/23/74	7½	11/27/74	7¾	12/23/74	7½	11/27/74
13 Individual retirement accounts and Keogh (H.R. 10) plans[5]	7¾	7/6/77	(8)		7¾	7/6/77	(8)	

[1] For authorized States only. Federally insured commercial banks, savings and loan associations, cooperative banks, and mutual savings banks were first permitted to offer NOW accounts on Jan. 1, 1974. Authorization to issue NOW accounts was extended to similar institutions throughout New England on Feb. 27, 1976.

[2] For exceptions with respect to certain foreign time deposits see the Federal Reserve BULLETIN for October 1962 (p. 1279), August 1965 (p. 1094), and February 1968 (p. 167).

[3] A minimum of $1,000 is required for savings and loan associations, except in areas where mutual savings banks permit lower minimum denominations. This restriction was removed for deposits maturing in less than Nov. 1, 1973.

[9] Between July 1, 1973, and Oct. 31, 1973, there was no ceiling for certificates maturing in 4 years or more with minimum denominations of $1,000; however, the amount of such certificates that an institution could issue was limited to 5 per cent of its total time and savings deposits. Sales in excess of that amount, as well as certificates of less than $1,000, were limited to the 6½ per cent ceiling on time deposits maturing in 2½ years or more.

Effective Nov. 1, 1973, the present ceilings were imposed on certificates maturing in 4 years or more with minimum denominations of $1,000. There is no limitation on the amount of these certificates that banks can issue.

[4] $1,000 minimum except for deposits representing funds contributed to an Individual Retirement Account (IRA) or a Keogh (H.R. 10) Plan established pursuant to the Internal Revenue Code. The $1,000 minimum requirement was removed for such accounts in December 1975 and November 1976, respectively.

[5] 3-year minimum maturity.

[6] July 1, 1973, for mutual savings banks; July 6, 1973, for savings and loan associations.

[7] Oct. 1, 1966, for mutual savings banks; Jan. 21, 1970, for savings and loan associations.

[8] No separate account category.

NOTE.—Maximum rates that can be paid by Federally insured commercial banks, mutual savings banks, and savings and loan associations are established by the Board of Governors of the Federal Reserve System, the Board of Directors of the Federal Deposit Insurance Corporation, and the Federal Home Loan Bank Board under the provisions of 12 CFR 217, 329, and 526, respectively. The maximum rates on time deposits in denominations of $100,000 or more were suspended in mid-1973. For information regarding previous interest rate ceilings on all types of accounts, see earlier issues of the Federal Reserve BULLETIN, the Federal Home Loan Bank Board *Journal*, and the *Annual Report* of the Federal Deposit Insurance Corporation.

TABLE 5

MARGIN REQUIREMENTS

PER CENT OF MARKET VALUE; EFFECTIVE DATE SHOWN.

Type of security on sale	Mar. 11, 1968	June 8, 1968	May 6, 1970	Dec. 6, 1971	Nov. 24, 1972	Jan. 3, 1974
1 Margin stocks..........	70	80	65	55	65	50
2 Convertible bonds.......	50	60	50	50	50	50
3 Short sales.............	70	80	65	55	65	50

NOTE.—Regulations G, T, and U of the Federal Reserve Board of Governors, prescribed in accordance with the Securities Exchange Act of 1934, limit the amount of credit to purchase and carry margin stocks that may be extended on securities as collateral by prescribing a maximum loan value, which is a specified percentage of the market value of the collateral at the time the credit is extended. Margin requirements are the difference between the market value (100 per cent) and the maximum loan value. The term "margin stocks" is defined in the corresponding regulation.

Regulation G and special margin requirements for bonds convertible into stocks were adopted by the Board of Governors effective Mar. 11, 1968.

the reserve base (basically Fed deposits) has worsened as the uncertain impacts of floating exchange rates have been realized, and close substitutes for demand deposits have mushroomed. Finally, the effect of the expanding use of electronic money and credit cards is having an uncertain effect on the reliability of relationships between the quantity of money and the level of the Gross National Product (GNP).

In the past when the Fed attempted to moderate interest rate shifts, it had to work with the problem of changes in the interest rate of securities with different maturity dates. Need for concern over interest rate levels did not disappear with the Fed's new emphasis on money supply. Long-term interest rates and their relation to capitalization of corporate earnings and investment in construction continue to be important in any Fed policy aimed at affecting the economy.

With the money supply replacing interest rate goals as the aggregate monetary policy emphasis, the need for more direct controls to affect the direction of the flow of funds has become more important. The establishment of bank reserves based on asset holdings rather than on deposits, the activation of investment and consumer credit controls of the World War II period, plus the use of Fed letters such as that of 1966 become likely policy directions if the world remains politically and economically unstable, which is very likely, too.

In February 1977 the general level of consumer prices was 77 percent higher than ten years earlier, and wholesale prices were 90 percent higher. Adjustment through inflation rather than through shifts of prices both up and down continues to be basic policy in the United States and in industrial countries other than Germany and Switzerland. One result of this approach has been a substantial increase in the vulnerability of the economy to a prolonged and severe economic disturbance. This is true because the ability of the federal government to stabilize economic conditions has been largely destroyed by the previous inflationary policy.

Chapter 10

Treasury Influence

In 1913 when the Federal Reserve Act originally was written, it was assumed that the decisions of businessmen to produce or not to produce would be nearly the only factor determining the quantity of employment, the amount of production, and the level of prices. Business decisions have remained important, but in addition today there is a very vital area of government economic decision. With the growth of economic activity of the federal government, economic policies of the Treasury and credit agencies of the federal government have become very important (*see* Index). As a result, efforts to coordinate government monetary activity are necessary to prevent operation at cross-purposes.

DURING WORLD WAR I AND THE 1920s. It was not until the United States became an active participant in World War I that Treasury policy had a vital effect upon Fed activities. The Treasury's desire and need to borrow on convenient terms during World War I forced the Fed to adopt a very lenient credit policy.

Again during the 1920s the Fed was forced to some extent to follow a policy against its better judgment as a result of the Treasury's activity in reducing the World War I federal debt. The reduction of federal credit throughout the 1920s made it necessary that additional credit be extended; otherwise the quantity of credit (money) would have been reduced. If this had been permitted, prices might have fallen during the 1920s. The Fed thought that this would be depressive and would cause undesirable economic developments; therefore it extended credit on rather easy terms during this period. This resulted in the use of credit inflation to maintain stable prices and prosperity. It also provided the groundwork for the stock market boom, consequent crash, and the following serious depression.

DURING THE 1930s. Policy designed to increase prosperity after the crash of 1929 was seen to be a failure by the mid-1930s. It was then that the Treasury program began to dominate the drive toward prosperity. The Treasury began to expand the quantity of credit through direct government borrowing from commercial banks. Also, during the latter part of the 1930s, the Treasury began war finance borrowing. Corporate profits were not restored, however, until World War II. Since then, undistributed corporate profits and later, capital consumption allowances, have provided a large portion of the capital used by U.S. industry to expand and introduce new techniques (see Chart VI). Inflation has reduced the real value of these internally generated funds.

DURING WORLD WAR II AND THE POSTWAR PERIOD. During World War II, the Federal Reserve considered it expedient to follow a liberal credit policy, despite the rapidly expanding inflationary pressures. Here again, Fed policy was dominated by Treasury needs and desires. The Federal Reserve Board did not find it practical to thwart or even seriously criticize Treasury war finance procedures.

The postwar Federal Reserve credit policy supplied banks with liberal quantities of reserves and set low discount rates while inflationary price rises were occurring. This procedure is directly contrary to the objectives of Federal Reserve credit-control policy. However, it was the program followed by the Federal Reserve banks during the first year of the postwar inflation.

The goals of postwar Fed policy have been varied. Some of the more obvious and important were: (1) to enable the Treasury to continue to refund federal debt at low interest rates, (2) to prevent a fall in the market value of long-term government bonds, and (3) to encourage investment, particularly investment in home construction.

During the period between 1946—the end of World War II—and 1951, the Treasury blocked all efforts of the Fed to decrease the availability of credit. Finally, on March 4, 1951, the Treasury accepted the Federal Reserve position that the availability of Fed credit would be limited. The "accord" worked out at this time continues to be the basis of the working relationship between the Treasury and the Fed.

The Board of Governors as originally constituted com-

CORPORATE PROFITS, DIVIDENDS, AND TAXES *CHART VI*

SEASONALLY ADJUSTED ANNUAL RATES, QUARTERLY

BILLIONS OF DOLLARS

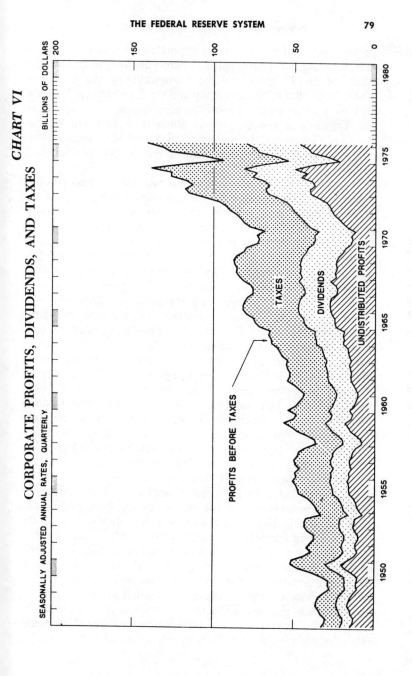

PROFITS BEFORE TAXES

TAXES

DIVIDENDS

UNDISTRIBUTED PROFITS

prised twelve members to be appointed especially as board members and two additional members who were to be the Secretary of the Treasury and the Comptroller of the Currency. The Comptroller of the Currency and the Secretary of the Treasury were removed from board membership in 1935. Although the Treasury is not at present officially represented on the Board of Governors, the actions of the board have such a direct effect on Treasury debt management responsibilities that close collaboration is necessary.

In 1913 the Fed was considered essentially "a cooperative enterprise among bankers for the purpose of increasing the security of banks and providing them with a reservoir of emergency resources." This continues to be true. But it also has become one of the most potent institutions involved in national economic policy. Since the Glass–Steagall Act of 1932 the Fed has been busy accepting U.S. securities in exchange for its deposits (reserve base); in this way it has permitted the U.S. Treasury to finance its huge war and peacetime deficits.

Since the banking and monetary legislation of 1935, the money activities of the Fed definitely have been under the control of its Board of Governors, which functionally is similar to any other independent agency of the federal government; however, its budget is not voted by Congress. The Fed is financed basically from the interest it receives as the owner of about $100 billion in U.S. securities. Also, since the Great Depression, the federal government has been interested in promoting a desirable level of economic activity. This aim has been advanced through requiring coordination of Federal Reserve actions with those of other economic agencies, particularly the Treasury and the Council of Economic Advisors.

Interest Rate: An Economic Gauge or an Economic Controller? The transmission belt of the impact of the Fed on the economy is still largely dependent on the effectiveness of the interest rate in regulating economic activity. The rate of interest has been considered important in economic activities, because of its close relationship to the quantity of savings and investment and therefore to the size of the national income. Also, a fall in the rate of interest causes the market value of previous investments to rise, and an increase in the rate of interest causes a fall in the market value of previous investments. If the real rate of interest is causal and not merely a measurement, and if it can be moved up and down by Fed action, then the Fed can very largely determine economic conditions.

SUPPLY OF LOANABLE FUNDS. The total savings of individuals are equal to income received that is not spent for consumption. The portion of additional income received that is spent for consumption is called the *marginal consumption function* or the *marginal propensity to consume*. If the marginal propensity to consume is large, savings arising from the additional income are small. The marginal propensity to consume tends to be greater if the income level of the income recipient is low.

The other principal determinant of the supply of loanable funds is *liquidity preference*. Liquidity preference refers to the unwillingness of people to tie up their money in such a way that it will not be immediately available to meet current or emergency needs or for use in taking advantage of special opportunities for profitable speculation. Extra interest is paid to induce people *not* to make short-term investments from unconsumed income but to make long-term investment commitments.

DEMAND FOR LOANABLE FUNDS. From the aspect of demand for loanable funds, the rate of interest is related primarily to earnings from new investments. This is called the *marginal efficiency* of capital. Actually at any given time, anticipation concerning the future marginal efficiency of capital rather than the efficiency ratio currently prevailing is more likely to control the actions of business people. Thus the Fed tends to encourage investment through any activity that reduces the real rate of interest without reducing the real level of profitability. Reducing the real rate of interest increases the quantity of loanable funds that can be used profitably but it also tends to reduce the supply of savings. The market rate of interest is set through an expansion or contraction of the disposable income, which of course is affected by investment and savings decisions.

The demand for funds for new, productive investment is determined by the cost of funds in relation to the marginal efficiency of capital. If the marginal efficiency of capital is constant, the Fed (by causing an increase in credit [cash]) would tend to cause a decrease in the real rate of interest and expand the quantity of real investment if the economy were not inflation sensitive. This method of expanding the quantity of investment may be quite important in such investment areas as housing and public utilities, where interest payments are a large portion of the total cost. The goal would be liquid assets in excess of the amounts that members of the economy are willing to hold and interest rates that are sufficiently low to stimulate additional investment. Along with the high interest rates of 1974 came a reduction in the portion of disposable income spent on durables. Despite an increase in disposable personal income of $83 billion over the 1973 level, durable consumer goods purchased decreased by $1 billion. However, in 1974 this did not cause a large increase in personal saving, because expenditures for services and nondurable consumer goods increased by $70 billion. It was the year of the sharp increase in fuel and food prices.

RELATED TO FEDERAL RESERVE POLICY. The rate' of interest can be affected by Fed policies related to the economy's liquidity. The expansion of liquid assets will reduce interest rates. The effectiveness of this program is limited by the willingness of people to substantially increase their holdings of deposits and cash when interest rates fall. Thus, very great increases in liquidity seem to be required before investment expands, and then the inducement is accompanied by price rises that reduce consumer real purchasing power and the ability to purchase the products produced by the new investment. The effectiveness of Federal Reserve policy to cut off a boom through a program aimed at raising interest rates is considerably greater.

The experiences of 1973 and 1975 demonstrated that rising and high interest rates and rising and high unemployment go together. Because rising prices are associated with increasing quantities of money, the belief that monetary ease decreases interest rates relative to the marginal efficiency of capital and expands investment and employment is being critically examined.

MONETARY POLICY AND TIME LAGS. Studies indicate it may take one and a half to two years for monetary policy actions to cause the effect that ultimately will flow from the action. Because of this long period—called the *outside lag*—some analysts favor monetary policy by formula. The most popular one is to have money supply change with the average change of GNP in the past. This type of program would mean an annual 3 percent or 4 percent increase of the money supply, (defined perhaps as M_2 or M_3), because real GNP has tended to increase at this rate. This type of policy fits in with quantity of money goals for the Fed rather than interest rate goals.

Debt Carrying Cost. The debt of the federal government (total gross public debt) is now more than $700 billion. The U.S. Treasury must pay interest on this debt. The Fed therefore is being constantly urged to do what it can to decrease debt carrying costs, i.e., to keep interest rates low.

The ability of the Fed to control interest rates is apparently something like the ability of dikes to keep a river in its channel; i.e., a pretty good job can be done if the pressures are moderate. Therefore, when huge federal government deficits combined with high unemployment and rapidly rising prices became the order of the day, the Fed became largely powerless to control the torrent. Short-term interest rates moved up to 12 percent, and long-term funds were not far behind. The result was stagflation in a developed nation that was very similar to what the LDCs (less developed countries) had been experiencing through the years, i.e., inflation, low investment levels, and high unemployment.

PART II: SELECTED REFERENCES AND SOURCES

American Bankers Association, *The Cost of Federal Reserve Membership* (New York, 1967).

O. K. Burrell, *Gold in the Woodpile* (Eugene, Oregon: University of Oregon Press, 1967).

Commission on Money and Credit, *Money and Credit.* (Englewood Cliffs, N.J.: Prentice-Hall, 1961).

Federal Reserve Bank of Kansas City, "Is the Federal Reserve Hitting Its Money Supply Targets?" *Monthly Review*, February 1976, 4–10.

Federal Reserve System, *The Federal Reserve System, 50th Anniversary* (Washington, D.C., 1963).

George G. Kaufman, *Money, the Financial System, and the Economy* (New York: Rand McNally, 1963).

Willis H. Parker, *The Federal Reserve System* (New York: Ronald, 1923).

Walter B. Smith, *Economic Aspects of the Second Bank of the United States* (Cambridge: Harvard University Press, 1953).

Beryl W. Sprinkel, *Money and Markets* (Homewood, Ill.: Irwin, 1971).

Charles N. Stabler, "Marketing Fed Funds," *Wall Street Journal*, May 17, 1976, 30.

Peter Temin, *Did Monetary Forces Cause the Great Depression?* (New York: W. W. Norton, 1976).

U.S. Treasury, "A Treasury History," *Treasury Papers*, January 1976, 23–24.

Part III

Commercial Banking

INTRODUCTION

A revolution of major proportions has occurred in how banks operate and how they influence individual and government decisions. The revolution, started in the 1960s, first was seen to be largely an electronic revolution leading to push-button paying and depositing. Later it became apparent that this technical development was not where the real action lay. The real change was when the Fed no longer required banks to sell off a portion of their investment portfolio to make new loans and when money substitutes were developed for a strange array of bank customers—from the most affluent corporation of the private sector to the poorest LDC of the public sector. They all, or nearly all, had one thing in common; they were deeply in debt, and unless they were kept afloat huge losses would have to be realized by the lenders, i.e., the banks.

As pointed out in Part I, banking has been a troublesome institutional arrangement because of its close relationship to a basic power of government—control over money used by its citizens—and its possession of power to influence the direction of business and individual spending and investing. Much of the activity and many of the powers of the Fed only make sense when thought of as a method for the people to keep enough control over money and the decisions made through use of money (defined very broadly) to guarantee a relatively orderly and sensibly functioning economy.

Several times in our national history, it has been thought that the complex relationships included under the term *banking* finally had been brought-to-heel, only for it to be learned that such belief was not warranted. Bank failures and wastage of bank equity in 1974–1975 demonstrated again that banks still have the power, combined with a built-in intemperance, to bring the American and world economies to the brink of disaster.

Chapter 11

Small Banking Units

A fundamental feature of the commercial banking system of the United States is its decentralization. There are about 14,500 different commercial banks in the United States; Canada has ten, and Great Britain and France each have four dominant banks. Canada, Great Britain, and France have extensive nation-wide branch bank systems that permit a few banks to serve the whole nation. The number of branches in the United States has more than doubled in the last ten years, while the number of individual banks has remained about the same. There are now about 29,000 branches. Chart VII summarizes the commercial bank office trend in the United States from 1920 to 1972 and also the trend toward state nonmember banks.

Modest Financial Resources. Because the United States has many independent banks, many of them are small. In fact, about 50 percent of the commercial banks have deposits of less than $5 million. At the other end of the scale, about eighty-five commercial banks have deposits of more than $1 billion each. The trend through mergers and consolidation is definitely in the direction of larger commercial banks. However, this trend has been its strongest in the large cities where the banks that are brought together are already large. Chart VII provides a summary of the trend in the number of commercial banks from 1915 to 1976. The very sharp decrease in the number of banks in the 1930s arose from, and also caused, the great deflation of the period. The term "state member" in the chart refers to state banks that are members of the Federal Reserve System, and "nonmember" refers to state banks that are not members of the Fed.

Setting Monetary Policy. One problem that has arisen from this large number of banks is how to develop a monetary

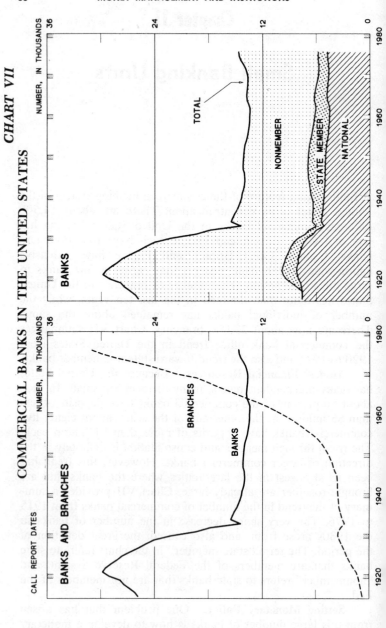

CHART VII

COMMERCIAL BANKS IN THE UNITED STATES

BANKS AND BRANCHES

CALL REPORT DATES

NUMBER, IN THOUSANDS

BRANCHES

BANKS

BANKS

NUMBER, IN THOUSANDS

TOTAL

NONMEMBER

STATE MEMBER

NATIONAL

policy. The presidents of all the banks could not be consulted as it is possible to call in the heads of the four commercial banks of Great Britain. Also, it would not be proper to consult only the heads of the largest big city banks, for the other banks, and rightly so, would feel that they were being made objects of discrimination.

The establishment of the Fed with its twelve district banks and branches, which was given the responsibility of establishing monetary policy, was the answer that was finally taken in 1913. In the mid-1930s some Federal Reserve powers were transferred to the Treasury. However, even after the grants of additional powers through the years, those that Congress saw fit to bestow upon the Fed frequently prove inadequate to control monetary policy as it actually is developed by the commercial banks. This proved to be the situation in the mid-1960s, and the Federal Reserve requested and was granted still more powers. And now in 1978 the Fed wants the power to set reserve requirements of all banks.

Providing Deposit Safety. Another very important problem related to the large number of independent banks and their small size has been how to assure the safety of the repayment of the monetary units deposited in these banks. Because these independent banks were relatively weak financially, and because they were only able to keep a fraction of their deposits in specie or readily salable assets, a bit of imprudence on the part of one banker would be very likely to lead not only to losses to his depositors but to those of many sound banks. This impact was likely, because the losses of one group of depositors would destroy the faith of depositors in other banks; they then would request specie payment, which would force the commercial bank into bankruptcy.

The first efforts to solve this problem established minimum reserve requirements to assure that all commercial banks could at least meet for a time demands of depositors for specie (or paper money). This was helpful, but many banks continued to fail. Later this was supplemented by establishing supervisory agencies that carefully examined bank records to prevent commercial banks from following a policy that would lead to later insolvency. Also, commercial bank chartering legislation has established ratios of capital to deposits. This was another effort to provide greater assurance that depositors in commercial banks would not lose through bank failures. The final de-

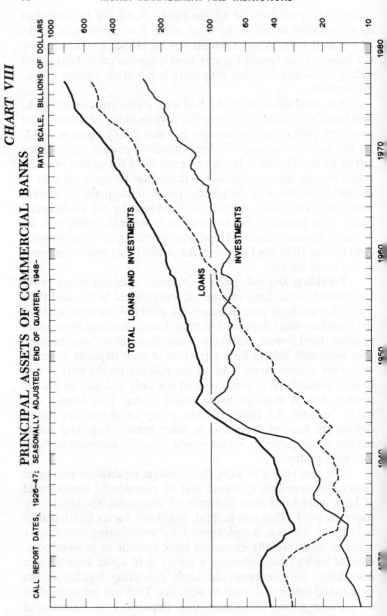

CHART VIII

PRINCIPAL ASSETS OF COMMERCIAL BANKS

CALL REPORT DATES, 1926–47; SEASONALLY ADJUSTED, END OF QUARTER, 1948–

RATIO SCALE, BILLIONS OF DOLLARS

TOTAL LOANS AND INVESTMENTS

LOANS

INVESTMENTS

velopment to protect the depositors of the relatively weak commercial banking units of the United States was the establishment by Congress of a system of deposit insurance. Several states had experimented, largely unsuccessfully, with the procedure before, but it was done on a national level in 1934, when the Federal Deposit Insurance Corporation (FDIC) was established.

Dual Banking System. The United States is a federal republic; and a second fundamental feature of our commercial banking system is the "dual banking system," which has arisen from both state and federal government chartering of commercial banks. In the past this power of chartering and regulating commercial banks has been the focus of many sharp political battles, and the issue is still very much alive. The net effects of the chartering of commercial banks by state governments and by the federal government, side by side, have been an increase in the number of banks and a reduction in the strictness of commercial bank regulation by government agencies.

Chart VII shows that during the past ten years the number of state banks included in the Federal Reserve System has been declining. This has arisen at least partially from the higher reserve requirements set by the Federal Reserve. The increasing number of state banks has resulted in an increase in the portion of commercial bank business carried out by banks not directly reporting to the Federal Reserve System.

Long-Term Liabilities with Short-Term Assets. A third feature of the American commercial banking system that has caused much trouble, but has also probably been a very important factor in the rapid development of the country, has been the extension of long-term loans. The basic liability of commercial banks in the United States are demand deposits and individual business time deposits, both of which are fundamentally short-term liabilities. Conventional commercial bank development provides for the backing of these deposits with short-term loans so that in case of need the management of the bank could meet depositor withdrawal demands by calling in loans extended.

Nevertheless, throughout history U.S. commercial banks have become engaged in making loans for real estate development and for the expansion of productive facilities. These loans have always been relatively long-term and could not be called in quickly to meet a sudden demand of depositors for their money.

This method of operating a commercial bank is obviously likely to cause trouble. The banking system expands loans and deposits when times are good and every project seems to have profit possibilities. A few over-optimistic commitments and a liquidity crisis develops. Under the old banking rules loans would be called and security holdings reduced. Under the new banking operation procedures, new loans are made to those in trouble, and security holdings are increased as the Fed supports deficits of the U.S. Treasury. (See Chart VIII.)

Recently commercial banks have become an operating unit of a holding company (see Index) that owns mortgage companies, leasing companies, and other finance-related businesses. A popular type of operation in 1973 was the Real Estate Investment Trust (REIT). Although under the holding company arrangement the commercial bank was not supposed to be affected by financial troubles of other operating companies owned by the holding company, this turned out not to be the case during the troubled times of 1975 and 1976. The bank of the holding company, being the dominant member, has found it necessary to bail out troubled operating units of the holding company.

Chapter 12

Ownership, Control, and
Management

Fractional Reserves. The earliest type of English bank was an institution for the safekeeping of gold and silver owned by private individuals. These banks provided a warehouse function, charged for the service, and issued warehouse receipts to persons owning the *specie* on deposit. It was convenient for the owners of gold to transfer their warehouse receipts when an expenditure was made rather than actually carrying the gold to the place of business of the creditor. This became important when added to the fact that the operators of these warehouses and goldsmiths, private bankers, and some chartered institutions learned that only a small portion of the gold left for safekeeping was removed. It made possible the extension of rights to withdraw gold of a greater aggregate value than gold in storage—the expansion of the quantity of money.

BANK NOTES. The second stage was reached when these institutions paid their depositors to store their gold rather than charging them for the service. Also, the deposit became the property of the bank, and the understanding between banker and depositor was that equivalent rather than the same funds would be returned to the depositor by the banker when the depositor desired them. This arrangement made it possible for the banker to lend money, that is, issue *bank notes* backed by *fractional reserves* of gold and silver. The banker obtained interest from the borrowers to whom the bank notes were issued, which made it profitable for the banker to expand the amount of gold and silver on deposit to permit expansion of loans. The banker encouraged deposits by paying interest on amounts deposited in his bank.

DEMAND DEPOSITS. The final development was when loans were extended in the form of bank *demand deposits* rather than bank notes. Demand deposits were promises to pay issued by the bank in the form of a bank account. The amounts in these accounts could be transferred by written orders, that is, *checks*. The importance of gold and silver left in banks decreased, and deposits were increased and decreased through the presentation of credit instruments. The modern commercial bank continues to perform the first function in its safe deposit department. The second function is performed when *bullion* or coins are accepted by a bank as deposits and these coins or bullion provide a reserve for expanded deposits. However, the third phase of the development of deposit banking dominates current commercial banking.

Deposits by Origin. Basically the deposits of a modern commercial bank originate in two ways: (1) the *primary deposit*, which arises when a depositor deposits a check upon another bank or when he presents currency for deposit (for the entire banking system, primary deposits arise only when currency is deposited); (2) the *derivative deposit*, which arises when a bank extends its credit. The portion of the total deposits of a single commercial bank that may be classified as primary are much greater than the derivative, because the typical individual, firm, or institution obtaining bank credit through the sale of an investment or a grant of a loan quickly withdraws the resulting deposit. He does this to make the payments for which the grant of credit was needed and obtained or to enjoy earnings from idle funds.

Deposits by Withdrawal Right. The two principal types of deposits by withdrawal right are (1) *demand* and (2) *time*. Total demand deposits of commercial banks in 1978 were about 60 percent of total time deposits. In 1958 the demand deposit total was twice as great as that of time deposits.

Only demand deposits of commercial banks can be drawn upon through use of a check. Demand deposits, as the name indicates, can always be drawn upon demand, but the right to withdraw time deposits may be withheld for a period of thirty days or more, if so stipulated in the bankbook or signed agreement. The conditions of withdrawal determine whether a deposit is classified as a demand or time deposit. A third type that is sometimes introduced and called an *interbank* deposit actually is a type of ownership rather than a type of deposit. It is largely in the form of demand deposits.

In 1977 movement toward the reduction of the distinction

between demand and time deposits has become apparent. Time deposits are readily made available in checking accounts, and legislation to permit payment of interest on demand deposits is being actively advocated.

Bank Certificates of Deposit. One reason for the rapid growth of time deposits was the invention in 1961 by the New York commercial banks of a new money market asset. They are the interest-bearing, negotiable certificates of deposit (CDs). They are largely issued to business corporations, and they are a portion of the time deposit total. The period to maturity is three months or a year. In addition all deposit institutions have some form of check system to offer their customers.

Deposit by Ownership. The deposits of commercial banks are owned by all the individuals, groups, and institutions that make up the society. Data are not available, nor would they be particularly valuable, that show the quantity of deposits owned by the many different segments of the economy. The deposits of commercial banks by ownership are divided into just a few classifications: (1) interbank deposits; (2) federal government deposits; (3) state and political subdivision deposits; and (4) the demand deposits of individuals, partnerships, corporations, foreign governments, and foreign commercial banks. In 1977 the demand deposits possessed by individuals, partnerships, and corporations were $242 billion, and the deposit total of banks was $823 billion.

Control of Increasing Bank Power. Both commercial and savings banks are chartered by the states. The federal government charters only commercial banks. The regulations governing the operation of state commercial and savings banks vary from state to state, but a large degree of uniformity is provided through membership in the Federal Deposit Insurance Corporation (FDIC). All national banks possess charters from the federal government. All such banks are primarily commercial, but since 1903 they have been permitted to accept savings deposits as well. All national banks must meet the requirements of the National Banking Act, which are administered by the Comptroller of the Currency. In addition, all national banks must be members of the Federal Reserve Systems and subscribers to Federal Deposit Insurance Corporation insurance. State banks are only voluntary members of these agencies.

In 1975 state commercial banks were 9,747 of the 14,457 commercial bank total. About 1,072 of these banks are Federal

Reserve members. The branches of all commercial banks total 28,237 (see Chart VII). The foreign branches of member commercial banks total 762 and are found in 83 countries and overseas areas of the United States.

STOCKHOLDERS AND DIRECTORS. Except for the very few private banks, all commercial banks are operated as corporations, and the source of all authority and control is the shareholders. These shareholders elect a board of directors who delegate authority to the number of officers considered necessary. The courts hold the directors personally liable for violations of bank regulatory laws committed by officers or employees of the bank.

EXECUTIVE OFFICERS. Each common stockholder may cast one vote for each share of stock for each director. Or, he may accumulate his votes and cast all for one director. The directors are elected annually and must possess certain qualifications related to stock ownership, residence, and the like. It has always been held that extension of loans is a power that the directors cannot delegate. However, that power can be delegated in part by authorizing the officers to extend a *"line of credit."* Regulations prevent directors from receiving from the bank favors that are not also available to other borrowers or depositors.

Prior to 1933 all national bank stock was common stock, but since 1933 national banks have been permitted to issue preferred stock as well. Also the banking legislation of 1933 and 1935 abolished double liability, and by 1937, all national banks were operating under the provisions of this legislation.

The *president* is the principal executive officer of the bank, and his authority is frequently very great due to expressed or tacit delegation of powers by the directors. Frequently the president is also the chairman of the board of directors; this is less likely if the bank is a large institution. The *cashier* conducts all money operations of the bank. The cashier's duties are gradually becoming more routine, and the president is assuming active direction of functions formerly controlled by the cashier. Another officer often provided is the *comptroller* who handles personnel, auditing, planning, and the like. Despite changes arising from a more active president and the introduction of the comptroller, the cashier remains the focal officer of the medium-sized commercial bank.

DEPARTMENTS OF A COMMERCIAL BANK. The activities of a bank are frequently divided into departments, the number of which varies with the size of the bank. All department heads and clerks are subordinates of the cashier. Two departments, or clerks, possessed by all banks are the paying teller and the receiving teller. The paying teller pays bank funds out over the counter and cares for the funds in the vault. The *receiving teller* accepts deposits over the counter and by mail. The *check desk* is the department responsible for the general bookkeeping activity of the bank. The *note teller* is responsible for collecting amounts due on notes and often for a large portion of the bank's correspondence.

The *discount department* is responsible for the work involved in making loans and discounts. If the bank is small, all assets are acquired by this department; as the bank becomes larger, this department frequently is subdivided into a discount department, loan department, credit department, bond department, and customers' securities department. It is this department that prepares the paper for discount with the Federal Reserve bank.

The typical large and medium-sized commercial bank has a *mortgage department* and an *installment credit department*. Installment credit is a new development in commercial banking. It was introduced in the 1930s and has grown rapidly. In the 1970s installment credit classified as bank credit cards has grown most rapidly. In addition, most commercial banks have a *savings and time deposit department* and a *safe deposit department*. The modern commercial bank is truly a department store of credit and safety provision.

The services offered by commercial banks are considerably greater today than they were twenty years ago. Nevertheless, as Chart IX illustrates, earnings continue to arise largely from interest on loans. The higher interest rates during the past ten years have resulted in a rapid rise in income from this source. The second half of Chart IX shows that interest has also risen rapidly as an expense.

The increase in earnings from securities shown in Chart IX arose from increased holdings of state and local government securities (municipals) until 1974 and 1975 when holdings of federal securities increased rapidly. The net result of rising costs and rising incomes has been rising commercial bank net income during the past ten years. This is shown in Chart IX. The year 1975 was an exception. Earnings were weak in 1975, as many large banks wrote off substantial loan losses.

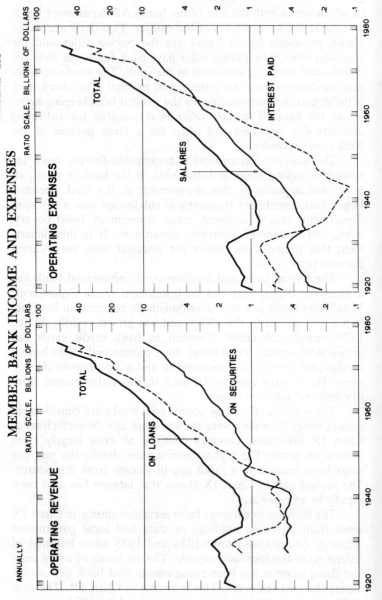

CHART IX

MEMBER BANK INCOME AND EXPENSES

OPERATING EXPENSES

RATIO SCALE, BILLIONS OF DOLLARS

TOTAL

SALARIES

INTEREST PAID

OPERATING REVENUE

RATIO SCALE, BILLIONS OF DOLLARS

ANNUALLY

TOTAL

ON LOANS

ON SECURITIES

Commercial Bank Operations in the United States.

DEVELOPMENT PRIOR TO 1930s. From 1791 to the 1930s, American commercial banking legislation had been built on the real-bills doctrine—that is, that credit should be extended as short-term loans for commercial purposes; it also is called self-liquidating short-term credit. This was the ideal of commercial banking policy. It was believed it would prevent the money supply from increasing more than trade, provide it with the elasticity required, and in addition largely prevent bank failures. However, the goal was more honored in its breach than in its accomplishment.

From the establishment of the nation to the 1930s (with the possible exception of the brief period of the First and Second Banks of the United States) commercial banking is correctly characterized as a large number of small, independent, and frequently inefficient banking establishments. (This characterization is still partly true.) Prior to 1933 hundreds to thousands of banks were forced into bankruptcy during each period of economic crisis. Although these banks were theoretically operated as commercial banks, which at this time meant that they extended only self-liquidating, short-term credit, actually they frequently extended credit that possessed only the outward appearance of being short-term; that is, the length of time was short but renewal of the credit was assumed. Also, the credit definitely was not self-liquidating.

STATE BANKS. Prior to the Civil War, a large number of banks possessed the right to issue notes as well as to create secondary deposits. These banks (again with the exception of the First and Second Banks of the United States) were state banks. They possessed many privileges including the right of note issue and deposit creation. In nearly all instances, the activities of these banks were inadequately regulated. Provision for the control of banks by the federal government was not made until 1863 with the establishment of national banks.

NATIONAL BANKS. The federal national banking legislation did not substitute national banks for state banks. Actually, the national bank legislation merely added an additional group of individual banking units and a new type of regulation to the already confused and overexpanded banking industry. The national banks were, however, larger than most state banks, and the inspections to enforce regulations were more rigidly conducted. The end result was an improvement in the banking conditions of the nation. The greatest immediate benefit developed from the Congressional provision establishing national bank notes and taxing out of existence state bank notes. This eliminated the paper money confusion and provided paper money that was readily recognized and that circulated at par throughout the nation. The notes were backed with federal debt but proved unattractive and did not replace state bank notes until the federal government in 1864 placed a 10 percent tax on state bank notes.

Federal Reserve System.   The establishment of the Federal Reserve System in 1913 provided an additional nationwide regulatory agency. The Federal Reserve System was given the power to inspect all member banks, that is, all national banks and most of the larger state banks. Duplication of inspection resulted from this arrangement, with national banks being inspected by the Comptroller of the Currency as well as by Federal Reserve examiners and later by the Federal Deposit Insurance Corporation. This gradually has been eliminated. However, waste continues and quality appears to be spotty. Nevertheless, efforts to reform the procedure in 1976 failed to gain sufficient Congressional support.

The three great contributions of the Fed to the improvement of the money, credit, and banking system of the nation have been: (1) it gave checks on nearly all banks *par value* in all parts of the country and (2) it removed the danger of a credit crisis arising from reserve shortages. Later (3) its policies also largely eliminated the danger of banks losing their liquidity.

Federal Reserve coverage, powers, and inspections proved inadequate to establish a banking system free from either numerous bank failures or depositor losses. Bank failures continued to be so frequent that when they decreased slightly in 1932, it brought forth the quip from Will Rogers "that the country was running out of banks."

In the 1920s and 1930s: (1) the portion of the paper money consisting of national bank notes decreased; (2) the number of commercial banks decreased; (3) the average size of commercial banks expanded; and (4) the portion of the total commercial banking business conducted under federal regulations increased.

The development of the commercial banking system up to the 1930s included an expanding amount of supervision that proved to be surprisingly ineffective. The assets held by the commercial banks of this period were largely loans extended to private economic units interested in producing, transporting, processing, storing, and selling goods and/or services. These loans were extended to individuals and firms by the commercial banks' responsible officers, after these officers had become convinced, through examining the proposed economic venture and becoming acquainted with the entrepreneur, that the loan would expand the profit of the bank. All too frequently the value of the asset became inadequate to support the loan.

During the period between the Civil War and the 1930s the right of note issue was strictly controlled, but demand deposit creation remained relatively free. The degree of federal control exercised over demand deposits was obtained through the establishment of the Federal Reserve System and its acquisition of central banking powers in the 1920s. More than likely, the federal government's power to control both note issue and demand deposit creation was weakened by the war finance measures of World War II.

Bank Legislation of 1933 and 1935.

FEDERAL BANKING ACT OF 1933. The provisions of the 1933 legislation were sweeping, the main purpose being provision of conditions that would restore public confidence in the nation's banking system. The act provided for the Federal Deposit Insurance Corporation, which was later expanded in 1935. Mutual savings and industrial banks became eligible for Federal Reserve membership. The Board of Governors was given power to restrict member bank credit for speculative purposes. A Federal Reserve Open-Market Committee was set up to determine open-market policy. New national banks in towns of less than 3,000 population were to have a capitalization of at least $50,000; also, the branch banking powers of national banks were extended. Interest payments on member bank demand deposits were prohibited, and the Board of Governors was given the power to fix the interest rates on time deposits. Member banks were prohibited from lending to their own executive officers, and investment affiliates were ordered divorced from commercial banks.

FEDERAL BANKING ACT OF 1935. The 1933 legislation was partly concerned with the Fed, but the major concern was with the safety of the nation's banking system. The 1935 legislation was nearly entirely related to extending and redefining the scope and powers of the Fed. The board was given the power of doubling the basic reserve requirements, which were established as the minimum reserve requirements. It also was given power to review and determine rediscount rates more often than every two weeks and to determine the types of paper ineligible for advances to member banks. The board was given a majority in the Federal Open-Market Committee. The title of the head of each Federal Reserve bank was changed from governor to president. National bank real-estate loan powers were expanded.

After 1935. The 1930s were a period of great economic turmoil, which was reflected in banking and monetary legislation of the period. The monetary legislation was based on old and disproved assumptions, but the banking legislation was generally enlightened.

REGULATORY AGENCIES. Bank regulation was largely carried on by the individual states until a series of events concentrated regulation and public banking policy in the federal government. The formal acts leading to this change were the National Banking Act of 1863, the Federal Reserve Act of 1913, and the Federal Deposit Insurance Act of 1933. In addition, legislation of 1933 and 1935 strengthened the power over commercial banks of the Board of Governors.

Effect of Safety Legislation. Up to the time of this writing, the legislative development aimed at increasing the safety of bank deposits has been successful, but the changes aimed at increasing the power of the Federal Reserve System have been neutralized somewhat by special legislation and pressure groups tending always to keep abundant and cheap credit available to meet housing, agriculture, and government needs.

These have combined to reduce substantially the Federal Reserve restrictions on the creation of deposits through the discount rate and control over quantity of reserves through reserve requirements and open-market operations. It was not until 1966 that the liquidity of the economy had become sufficiently reduced so that a failure of the Federal Reserve to continue to increase reserves developed a very stringent credit situation.

The rapid growth of the money supply is illustrated by the monetary aggregates of Chart X. Time deposits of various types grew particularly rapidly during the 1960s.

The new, aggressive management of commercial banking has been taking full advantage of federal government guarantees initiated in the 1930s to revive the nation's credit system. These thirty-five-year-old laws combined with a technology and population explosion in the United States and around the world are causing traditional ideas embedded in legislation to be examined for their appropriateness.

New Banking. The 1970 amendments to the Bank Holding Company Act had a landmark effect. They have permitted a single bank to branch out and gain control over any business the Fed deems to be "closely related" to banking. This has brought banks into fifteen different businesses, from mortgage companies to leasing industrial equipment.

The new banking results in giant conglomerates that fret because they haven't yet been given the power to gain control over savings and loan associations and cannot openly engage in nation-wide banking. Despite these restrictions, fifty commercial banks of the United States control directly about 50 percent of all banking activity and perhaps another 25 percent indirectly.

A large portion of the new banking is concerned with Eurodollars and the transfer of American savings to deposits of branches of large U.S. banks in London. The other basic and related element is the transfer of banks into one unit of a one-bank holding company. In both instances the action is taken in carrying out "liability management," i.e., maximizing earnings from the money purchased from businesses and individuals through interest payments and sale of debt securities.

Foreign lending by banks in the United States has been growing steadily since the federal government's "voluntary" restraint program administered by the Fed was removed in 1973. In 1975 the loans were up $29 billion from the restraint level and totaled $59.4 billion. This lending was dwarfed by the lending activity of foreign branches of these and other American banks, which reached $135.9 billion, or a total of $195.3 billion. This foreign total is about 35 percent, or one-third, as large as all domestic loans of commercial banks. Indeed this aspect of "new banking" is very impressive and also poses serious and largely unsolved problems of supervision by U.S. regulatory agencies. In September 1976 assets of foreign branches of U.S. banks totaled $158.5 billion—very big business, indeed.

Bubbling below the one-bank holding company development and Eurodollar operations is an aggressive attitude of going out after deposits and debt capital and not waiting for money to be brought in by savers. New devices to attract funds have been developed. For example, the certificate of deposit

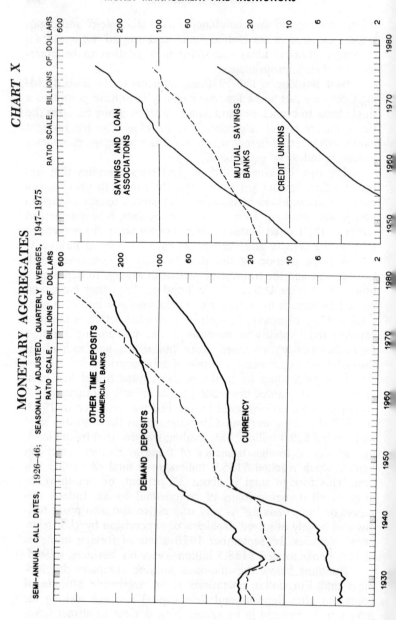

CHART X

MONETARY AGGREGATES

SEMI-ANNUAL CALL DATES, 1926–46; SEASONALLY ADJUSTED, QUARTERLY AVERAGES, 1947–1975

RATIO SCALE, BILLIONS OF DOLLARS

RATIO SCALE, BILLIONS OF DOLLARS

OTHER TIME DEPOSITS
COMMERCIAL BANKS

DEMAND DEPOSITS

CURRENCY

SAVINGS AND LOAN
ASSOCIATIONS

MUTUAL SAVINGS
BANKS

CREDIT UNIONS

(CD) was introduced by the nation's leading commercial bank in 1961.

Automation and Bank Supervision. The expansion in the number of bank branches and the growth of business activities controlled by single-bank holding companies has increased the problems of bank supervisory agencies. The growth of automation and computer systems during the same period has permitted the development of procedures adequate to maintain supervision.

The cooperative procedures required to get a handle on the overall impact of diverse domestic activities of a one-bank holding company and the international operations of branches and finance companies controlled by the same group are just in the process of implementation. For example, in 1971 a pilot program called Standardized Examination Automated Reports (SEAR) was the result of a joint effort of the Florida Bankers Association, the Banking Department of the State of Florida, and regional representatives of the comptroller of the Currency, the Federal Deposit Insurance Corporation, and the Atlanta Federal Reserve Bank.

The tools of SEAR are computer programs that produce standard bank examination reports. An example of the information provided is demonstrated by the items reported on commercial loans, which includes collateral descriptions, loan review reports, unposted items, and director and officer indebtedness. Loans purchased and sold also are given.

In a short time supervisory authorities themselves can be expected to develop data bases. By showing trends of loans and deposits by bank size and location these data can become important bank management inputs. Usefulness of the growth of banking data bases can only become a reality if the data become a portion of public information and available to bank managers, bank supervisors, and bank analysts generally.

Through the years borrowers from banks have benefited less from government aid and supervision than have depositors. Federal legislation does exist limiting interest rates that can be charged; also, government lending agencies, particularly in agriculture, have been established, but the popular appeal of this type of legislation has been considerably less.

The creation of the FDIC in 1933 was the last government legislation to protect depositors. The establishment of the FDIC is an admission that the regulation of banking cannot protect the monetary value of deposits. The FDIC, of course, does not protect the depositor from loss arising from reduced purchasing power of the dollar.

MAINTAINING ECONOMIC STABILITY. The public interest today is largely focused on (1) changes of the purchasing power of money and (2) the efficiency of the operation of the economic system, rather than the guaranteed liquidity of deposits. This need to maintain satisfactory business conditions has been recognized by the Board of Governors, who have stated this to be the chief problem of government banking policy. Actually, banking policy alone is not sufficiently potent to provide satisfactory business conditions. This fact was recognized by the Board of Governors as long ago as 1938. The aim of satisfactory business conditions is only a practical government goal as a joint project of the Fed and Congress. It now is well recognized that the most desirable level of economic activity cannot be maintained by simply changing discount rates and entering into open-market operations.

PURPOSE OF REGULATION. Bank examination is to prevent and expose abuses and to provide information of use to government and business policy makers. The examination of a bank not only involves gathering the facts but also appraising the information obtained. Appraising economic activity is very difficult. Appraisals during periods of boom and prosperity are likely to be too optimistic, and appraisals during depressed conditions too pessimistic. During prosperous times bank examiners tend to overrate bank assets, while during a depressed period they tend to underrate them. See Chart XI for balance sheet ratio trends.

The 1938 ruling established four categories to be used to evaluate bank loans and investments for examination purposes. Loans are given the highest rating if payment seems assured, and the lowest if they are to be counted as losses and charged off. The intermediate classifications represent intermediate degrees of risk, and call for corresponding action on the part of the bank officers. Securities are placed in the four classifications largely on the basis of the ratings given in *Poor's* and *Moody's* security rating manuals. Those given the highest investment rating are placed in category I and the others from II through IV depending upon the degree of risk and speculation. Securities in category I are given book value with the proviso that any premium paid be properly amortized. Until the summer of

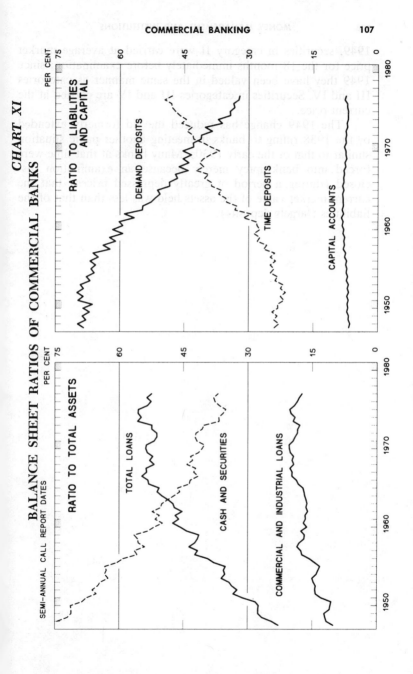

CHART XI

BALANCE SHEET RATIOS OF COMMERCIAL BANKS

SEMI-ANNUAL CALL REPORT DATES

1949, securities in category II were carried at average market price for the 18 months immediately before examination; since 1949 they have been valued in the same manner as categories III and IV. Securities in categories III and IV are carried at the current price.

The 1949 change has reduced the aid formerly extended by the 1938 ruling to banks in meeting another panic stiuation similar to that of the early 1930s. Many banks at that time were forced into bankruptcy merely because an examination disclosed (during a period of greatly depressed prices) that the current market value of the assets held was less than that of the liabilities (largely deposits).

Chapter 13

Credit Extension Evolution

The expansion of federal and also state and local government debt has reduced sharply the portion of commercial bank assets that are "commercial." For example, during the economic revival of early 1976 most of the increase in commercial bank assets was accounted for by an increase in acquisitions of federal government securities. The assets held by commercial banks underwent a great change during the 1930s. The shift proceeded with accelerated speed during the World War II period. Basically the change then was from business loans and discounts to government bonds and private consumer and real estate loans.

During the 1930s, the federal government rapidly expanded its credit activities aimed at expanding economic activity. It was considered desirable policy that a large portion of the securities arising from spending and lending activities be purchased by commercial banks. This had not been the case with federal government borrowing during World War I, when a great effort was made to have the bonds held by individuals. By 1934, the value of securities owned by commercial banks (largely federal government debt) exceeded the value of loans, and by 1943 the income from investments held by commercial banks went ahead of income from loans. During the World War II period, federal government debt expanded at a very rapid rate, and again a large portion of the securities arising from this debt became assets of commercial banks. In 1948 earnings from loans went ahead of investments, but the quantity of investments remained the greater. By 1957 both the earnings and the quantity of loans of all commercial banks were considerably greater than investments. This trend continued until 1974 when loans in relation to bank deposits became so great that the liquidity of the commercial banking system was threatened—a far cry from the situation in 1943.

Economic Power of Commercial Banks.   In 1978 the commercial banks have over $1 trillion in assets and are much more important in the determination of the manner and direction of national economic life than they were in the 1950s and 1960s. There is a strong trend currently toward a monopoly role for commercial banks that shows signs of returning banks to the dominant position they held from 1791 to 1930. Commercial banks in their purchase of investments do not actively determine use of credit but merely purchase the best instruments (after consideration of earnings and security) that are available. The over two-thirds of commercial bank credit extended as loans is also to an important extent determined by the activities of individuals other than the managers of commercial banks. This is particularly the case with real estate loans and loans for purchasing and carrying securities, which together amount to nearly one-third of total commercial bank loans. The quantity and type of real estate loans is affected greatly by federal government programs that set conditions for the guarantee of this type of loan. The loans to carry securities are affected by the margin requirements established by the Federal Reserve Board. Even the extension of loans to consumers has on occasion been partially determined by government action as, for example, under Regulation W of the Federal Reserve Board during World War II and the Korean War.

Chart XII provides a summary of short-term borrowing to meet business and consumer credit needs. Between 1950 and 1970 the level of borrowing remained relatively constant with rather regular modest expansions and contractions. In the 1970s the data show an entirely new situation. Business and consumer short-term borrowing expanded very rapidly and business bank loans fell to new low levels in 1974. There was a large-scale boom and bust in the extension of short-term credit.

Prime Rate.   The interest rate charged by large banks on loans to their best customers tends to be uniform after a few days of adjustment. This rate is called the *prime rate* and to a large extent is the minimum rate at which funds are available; it acts as the base interest rate. All other interest rates adjust themselves to this prime rate base.

In August of 1974 the prime rate went to 12 percent, a record high. The rate gradually declined, and a year later it was

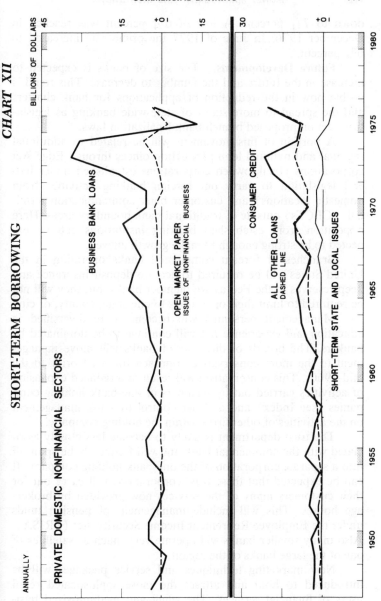

CHART XII

SHORT-TERM BORROWING

ANNUALLY

BILLIONS OF DOLLARS

PRIVATE DOMESTIC NONFINANCIAL SECTORS

BUSINESS BANK LOANS

OPEN MARKET PAPER
ISSUES OF NONFINANCIAL BUSINESS

CONSUMER CREDIT

ALL OTHER LOANS
DASHED LINE

SHORT-TERM STATE AND LOCAL ISSUES

down to 7¾ percent. A low of 6¼ percent was reached in December 1976. In June of 1977 the prime rate increased to 6¾ percent.

Future Developments.   The size of banks is expected to increase in the future and the number to decrease. This trend is visible now in the reduction of applications for bank charters and the spread to more states of state-wide banking as legislatures act on proposed branch bank legalization laws.

A portion of this movement will be related to additional regional and national loan production offices through Edge Act corporations (bank-owned corporations established under federal legislation to carry out foreign banking activities from domestic locations) and customer bank communication terminals (CBCTs) outside of traditional bank boundary areas. Here opposition from established banking institutions can be expected to be strong enough to make growth uneven.

Branches of foreign commercial banks operating in the United States will be required to acquire deposit insurance and keep reserves in the Fed as are member banks, but they will not be required to limit their operations to one state, county, or city.

Management personnel will become more diversified in education and experience but will continue to be dominated by bankers. The boards of directors of banks will move management to the more conservative approach followed prior to the mid-1960s. This conservatism will result in a reduced expansion of activities carried out by members of one-bank holding companies (see Index) and a closer control by bank management on the activities of other firms within the holding company.

The trust department is likely to become less closely associated with the commercial bank and will frequently be spun off into a separate corporation of the one-bank holding company. It can be expected that these trust corporations will carry out for their customers many of the services now provided by brokerage houses. This will include management of pension funds under the Employee Retirement Income Security Act (ERISA). Also many smaller banks will operate very much as satellites of one of the large banks of the region.

New marketing techniques and service packages will be introduced to hold and attract the more sophisticated retail users of financial services. The small and medium-sized businesses will return to commercial banks to find good financial advice and short- and long-term loans. One can expect limited

TABLE 6
CLASSIFICATION OF CREDIT INSTRUMENTS

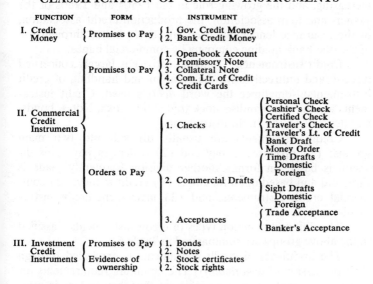

FUNCTION	FORM	INSTRUMENT	
I. Credit Money	Promises to Pay	1. Gov. Credit Money 2. Bank Credit Money	
II. Commercial Credit Instruments	Promises to Pay	1. Open-book Account 2. Promissory Note 3. Collateral Note 4. Com. Ltr. of Credit 5. Credit Cards	
	Orders to Pay	1. Checks	Personal Check Cashier's Check Certified Check Traveler's Check Traveler's Lt. of Credit Bank Draft Money Order
		2. Commercial Drafts	Time Drafts Domestic Foreign Sight Drafts Domestic Foreign
		3. Acceptances	Trade Acceptance Banker's Acceptance
III. Investment Credit Instruments	Promises to Pay	1. Bonds 2. Notes	
	Evidences of ownership	1. Stock certificates 2. Stock rights	

insurance of business credit extensions as a new service of commercial banks to their customers.

The basic retail banking development will be toward a single customer account divided into portions bearing different degrees of liquidity and therefore varying interest rates. Along with this all-purpose, general account there will develop procedures for personal overdrafts and for the extension of long-term credits with interest rates that change with market shifts. The variable rate mortgage (VRM) will become more competitive and acceptable as interest rates fall as well as increase.

These new opportunities in commercial banking will require personnel with new skills acquired in mid-career as well as from precareer programs. To go along with the personnel with new skills will come new computer hardware and software and systems capable of reporting accurate customer and product profitability including adequate consideration of risk differentials of income sources. Although electronic funds transfer (EFT) networks and operational management systems will reduce the relative role of clerical personnel, large numbers will continue to be required by commercial banks.

The partial monopoly of commercial banks over financial resources in the small and medium-sized community is currently increasing, and the growing role in the 1950s and 1960s of the savings and loan association, the production credit association, or the insurance lender has been effectively halted through use of the one-bank holding company by commercial banks.

Credit Instruments. Banking activity is largely concerned directly and indirectly with the creation and handling of credit instruments; sometimes the word *debt* is used. Credit instruments are the merchandise stock traded by banks. Notes, bonds, and deposits are all credit instruments.

Credit instruments are usually divided into two main groups: (1) promises to pay and (2) orders to pay. This division is based on form. Another division frequently made is threefold and based upon function: (1) credit money, (2) commercial credit instruments, and (3) investment credit instruments.

The different common types of credit instruments classified in the above groups are summarized in Table 6.

The usefulness of credit instruments is expanded through their possession of *negotiability*. The minimum requirements for credit instruments to be negotiable are that they (1) be in writing and signed by the maker or drawer; (2) contain an unconditional promise or order to pay a certain sum of money; (3) be payable on demand or at a fixed or determinable future time; (4) be payable to order or bearer; and (5) when addressed to a drawee, name him with reasonable certainty.

Clearing and Collection of Checks. The clearing of checks is the procedure worked out to get this type of credit instrument back to the banks upon whom they are drawn so that the amount may be deducted from the writer's (drawer's) account. In performing this function clearing also determines the amounts different banks owe other banks. If the total value of the checks written on Bank A is greater than the total value of checks Bank A accepted from other banks to cash or as deposits, then Bank A will lose reserves.

LOCAL CLEARING. Checks drawn on local banks and used in the same trading area are usually cleared through an institution called a *clearinghouse*. The clearinghouse gathers together all the checks drawn on members of the clearinghouse that have been accepted by these banks. The total value of all checks and credit card claims written on one bank that were accepted by the other banks is deducted from the total of the checks accepted by the first bank. If the result is a negative number the bank has experienced an adverse clearing and must make funds available to meet the deficit. If the figure is positive the bank has experienced a favorable clearing and will receive funds. A bank loses reserves in an adverse clearing and gains them in a favorable clearing.

INTRADISTRICT CLEARING. Clearings that involve checks that are not drawn on and accepted for deposit by banks belonging to the same local clearinghouse are cleared through the Federal Reserve banks. The same functions are performed by these clearings as are performed by local clearings. See Appendix I for additional detail.

Table 7(a) indicates the procedure of clearing a check drawn on a bank and accepted for deposit by another bank belonging to the same Federal Reserve district.

INTERDISTRICT CLEARING. The process of clearing a check that is used in two Federal Reserve districts is fundamentally the same. The difference is that the clearing includes a second Federal Reserve bank as well as the interdistrict Settlement Fund in Washington. The steps involved are briefly outlined in Table 7(b).

Loans and Discounts. A loan is a credit grant on which interest is paid at the maturity of the loan or at stated intervals.

A discount is a credit grant on which the interest is paid at the time of original negotiation. A discount is usually granted for a shorter time than a loan.

COMMERCIAL LOANS. There are three principal types of loans extended by commercial banks to business firms: (1) working-capital loans, which provide funds to buy raw materials and to pay wages; (2) term loans, which provide funds to purchase or construct additional facilities or to acquire other enterprises; (3) capital loans, which are used for the same purposes as term loans, but provision is made for collateral, and the loan is repaid in installments.

REAL ESTATE LOANS. These are long-term loans to finance the purchase of real property usually utilized as housing.

LOANS TO BROKERS AND DEALERS IN SECURITIES. These are short-term loans made to investment banking houses, brokerage firms, and individuals obtaining investment credit. These loans are always made with the securities purchased providing the collateral.

TABLE 7A

CLEARING OF CHECKS USED OUTSIDE OF A TRADING
AREA BUT WITHIN ONE FEDERAL RESERVE DISTRICT

1. X gives Y a check drawn on the First National Bank of Mankato. Y deposits the check in the Commerce Bank of Fargo. Y receives a credit to his bank account of the amount of the check. (+)

4. The First National Bank of Mankato charges the account of X by the amount of the check. (−)

2. The Commerce Bank sends the check to the Federal Reserve bank of Minneapolis. The Commerce Bank (within 3 days) receives a credit to its Federal Reserve account of the amount of the check. (+)

3. The Minneapolis Federal Reserve bank sends check to the First National Bank of Mankato, and charges the account of the Mankato bank by the amount of the check. (−)

TABLE 7B

CLEARING OF CHECKS USED OUTSIDE OF A TRADING AREA AND
INVOLVING DIFFERENT FEDERAL RESERVE DISTRICTS

1. X gives Y a check drawn on the First National Bank of Mankato. Y deposits the check in the Michigan National Bank of Lansing. Y receives a credit to his bank account of the amount of the check. (+)

2. Michigan National sends the check to the Federal Reserve bank of Chicago and receives (within 3 days) a credit to its Federal Reserve account of the amount of the check. (+)

6. The First National Bank charges the account of X by the amount of the check. (−)

3. Chicago Federal Reserve bank sends check to Minneapolis Federal Reserve bank and makes totals available to Interdistrict Settlement Fund.

5. The Minneapolis Federal Reserve bank charges the account of the First National Bank and sends in X's check. (−)

(+)   (−)

4. Interdistrict Settlement Fund credits the account of the Chicago Federal Reserve bank and charges the account of the Minneapolis Federal Reserve bank. (−)

CONSUMPTION LOANS, AGRICULTURAL LOANS, OVER-
DRAFTS, AND OTHER LOANS. Consumption loans are for less
than two years, and the funds obtained are used to finance
purchase of durable consumer goods. Agricultural loans are
short-term and usually extended to finance purchase of feeder
stock, purchase of equipment, or expenditures related to plant-
ing and harvesting of crops. In this area commercial banks must
meet stiff competition from federal-sponsored cooperative lending institutions. Overdrafts arise when customers overdraw their
accounts. This results in short-term loans. They are much less
important today than during the 1920s. Other loans represent a
miscellaneous group of loans. Loans to other banks are the
most important element. See Chart XIII for loans trends since
1848.

Legal Limitations on Bank Lending Power.

1. A national bank is not permitted to lend more than 10
percent of its capital to any one borrower. However, the exceptions to the rule that have been gradually adopted are so
numerous that the 10 percent limitation is largely meaningless.
Its effect today is limited to the provision of a point beyond
which prudent bankers realize they should not go.

2. National bank lending on real estate loans is somewhat
limited by regulations of the Comptroller's office. If the loan is
fully amortized, it can amount to 90 percent of the appraisal
value and be for 30 years. This rule is modified if insured by the
Federal Housing Administration (FHA) or the Veterans' Administration (VA). An FHA insured loan can be granted with
only a 3 percent down payment on the first $15,000 and the
maturity can be up to 35 years. FHA insurance of the loan costs
0.5 percent of the loan and is paid by the morgagor (borrower).
A VA loan can be for 100 percent if the appraised value of the
property is up to $12,500. Again the mortgage can run for 35
years.

If no provision is made for amortization or for government
insurance, the loan can only be for 50 percent of the appraised
value and cannot be for longer than 5 years.

3. All banks must obey the margin requirements established by the Federal Reserve Board under the conditions of the
Securities Exchange Act. These requirements are applicable to
loans to finance brokers, dealers, and their customers, who purchase securities on margin. (See Table 5.)

4. A number of minor limitations on bank lending are also

TABLE 8

A SIMPLIFIED COMMERCIAL BANK STATEMENT

Description	Assets	
Cash on hand to carry on day to day business. If a large cash drain developed the deposits in other banks would be reduced and short term securities sold or used as collateral for an advance. Non-earning asset.	Cash in vault	$ 120,000
Deposits in other banks. Non-earning asset.	Due from other banks	250,000
A non-earning asset also. Required by law of commercial banks members of the Federal Reserve system. Requirement is less on country banks and time deposits.	Reserve Deposit at Federal Reserve Bank	900,000
Principal earning asset. Discounts on present loans on which interest is prepaid.	Loan and discounts	2,000,000
These are obligations issued by the United States government or fully guaranteed obligations of its agencies. Book value stands at par at maturity or first call date.	United States Government obligations	815,000
These are mostly state and local government securities. The interest income from these securities is exempt from the Federal income tax.	Other securities	450,000
Equal to 3 per cent of capital and surplus. Stock purchased prior to 1942 is exempt from the Federal income tax.	Federal Reserve Bank Stocks	15,000
Space occupied by bank and value of equipment. Part of this may be income producing property because the bank does not occupy the entire building.	Building, furniture, and fixtures	500,000
Mainly property taken over in foreclosure of mortgages or chattel loans.	Other real estate	600,000
		$5,650,000

TABLE 8 (Continued)

Liabilities		
Demand deposits	$4,000,000	Non-interest bearing since 1933.
Time deposits	450,000	Federal legislation sets maximum rates, currently 6¼ per cent.
Reserve for taxes	100,000	Income taxes not yet due but for which the bank is liable.
Reserve for losses	120,000	This is the amount the management is permitted by law to set aside for this risk.
Liability on acceptances	80,000	The bank's liability on payments it has guaranteed.
Reserve for contingencies	240,000	This item is really a part of capital and reserves.
Undivided profits	160,000	Profits that have been set aside to be paid out to stockholders as dividends.
Capital	200,000	The par value of shares issued by the bank's board of directors.
Surplus	300,000	Capital funds beyond par value of stock.
	$5,650,000	

in effect. For example, with permission of the board of directors, a member bank can loan up to $30,000 to an officer for any purpose. Permission is not required for a loan up to $10,000 for education of an officer's children and $30,000 on real estate occupied by an officer as a residence.

There has been a very rapid rise of commercial, real estate, and consumer loans during the postwar period. The current expansion of direct real estate lending by commercial banks is not the dangerous type of lending it was in the 1920s. The change in the desirability of real estate loans has arisen from the federal government guarantee activity through the FHA and the VA. However, this cannot be said of much of the real estate lending made through REITs that were usually a unit of the

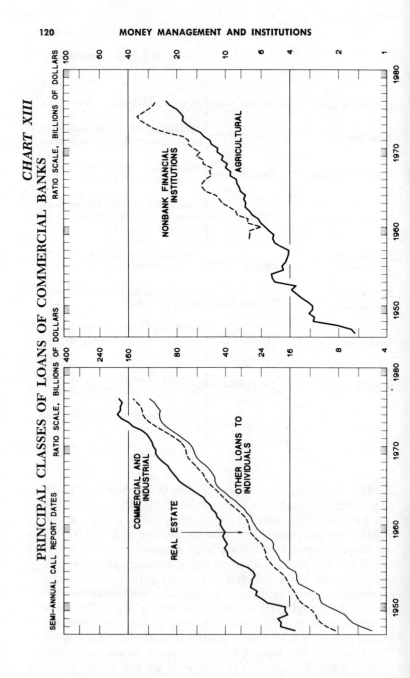

CHART XIII

PRINCIPAL CLASSES OF LOANS OF COMMERCIAL BANKS

SEMI-ANNUAL CALL REPORT DATES

RATIO SCALE, BILLIONS OF DOLLARS

RATIO SCALE, BILLIONS OF DOLLARS

NONBANK FINANCIAL INSTITUTIONS

AGRICULTURAL

COMMERCIAL AND INDUSTRIAL

REAL ESTATE

OTHER LOANS TO INDIVIDUALS

PRINCIPAL LIABILITIES OF COMMERCIAL BANKS *CHART XIV*

CALL REPORT DATES, 1926–42;
QUARTERLY AVERAGES, 1943–46; SEASONALLY ADJUSTED, QUARTERLY AVERAGES, 1947–   RATIO SCALE, BILLIONS OF DOLLARS

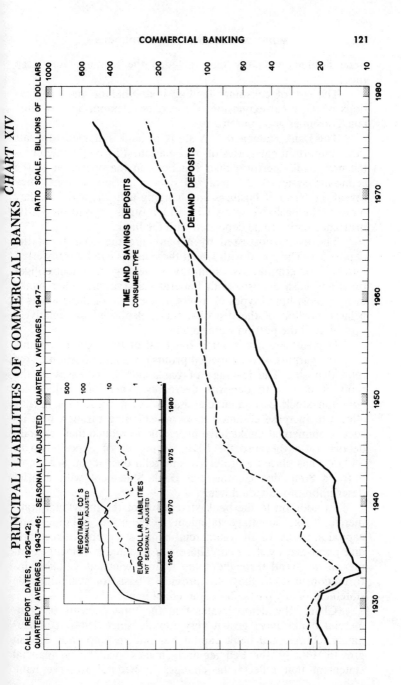

same holding company that included the lending bank (see Index).

The rise of consumer lending is another of many indications of the great expansion of the relative importance of durable consumer good purchases.

The Bank Statement. A study of bank statements reveals three important categories of information: (1) bank statements tell how banks perform their functions in the operation of the economic system; (2) analyzed over a period of time, they reveal the trend of business and banking activity; and (3) they indicate the probable safety with which funds beyond the FDIC insurance limit can be deposited with the bank.

The assets possessed by a bank are the security of the depositors. The speed with which these assets can be transferred into cash determines asset liquidity. Federal government obligations and cash deposits with Federal Reserve and other banks are the most liquid types of assets. If the total of these assets is a large portion of the deposits, funds deposited are relatively safer than if the portion were smaller.

Deposits are also safer if the total of the capital accounts (capital, surplus, and undivided profits) is a large portion of the total deposits. The leverage of bank capital increases as the ratio of capital to deposits decreases. Therefore holders of common stock of commercial banks resist regulatory agency efforts to increase common stock outstanding through new issues. Commercial banks have been able to reduce their capital–deposit ratios because the FDIC insurance of deposits up to $40,000 has placed a protective umbrella over them. See Table 8 for a Simplified Commercial Bank Statement with a brief description of individual items.

In addition to the bank statements of the individual commercial banks, summary statements of the assets, liabilities, and capital accounts of all commercial banks are prepared regularly and published by the Fed. These consolidated statements summarize the trend throughout the nation, which is valuable information in itself; they also provide a basis for evaluating the statement of any particular commercial bank.

Chart XIV demonstrates that the total deposits of commercial banks have grown very rapidly since 1960. Unfortunately, commercial bank capital has not kept up with deposit growth. Finally, the Fed regularly makes available a financial statement that reflects the changes in Federal Reserve bank assets, liabilities, and capital accounts. These statements recently have revealed a great preponderance of federal government obligations and a relatively small quantity of business and commercial obligations in Federal Reserve portfolios. Nearly all the earnings of the Federal Reserve System arise from receipt of interest on federal government obligations.

Careful examination of the Federal Reserve System statement shows, among other things, the quantity of (1) *member bank reserves*, the quantity of (2) *Federal Reserve notes*, and the quantity of (3) *gold certificates*, and (4) Special Drawing Rights (SDRs). Changes in these items always should be considered important guideposts in estimating existing and possible credit expansion.

Chapter 14

Liquidity Attitude Shifts

The movements in prices and business activity that are registered through changes in commercial bank assets and deposits are based on fundamental changes in the desires of businesses and individuals to be in debt, or to have a cash balance, or to purchase new businesses and expand, or to reduce operations and contract. These psychological changes are called "changes in liquidity desires." Three areas of increased liquidity have developed in the United States.

LIBERALIZED CENTRAL BANK POLICY. The first area arose from money and banking legislation that liberalized the restrictions placed on the transfer of various debt obligations into deposits and currency. The original legislation establishing the Fed permitted only the transfer of commercial paper into Federal Reserve Deposits, which act as reserves to support additional bank deposits arising from new loans. In addition, sound banking practice frowned on the indebtedness of member banks to the Federal Reserve banks that arose from rediscounting. Today the Federal Reserve banks stand ready to purchase or accept as collateral for loans (turn into Federal Reserve deposits or notes) nearly all types of assets held by a commercial bank. The liberalization has been terrific, and the danger of the commercial banking system being short of funds to meet the demands of depositors has been replaced with the danger of flooding the economy with an excess of liquidity.

EXPANSION OF FEDERAL GOVERNMENT DEBT. The second area has been the great expansion of federal government debt. The debt of a government possessing the power to issue money must always possess a high degree of liquidity. Also over nearly all conditions the debt of a government with these powers is more liquid than other types of debt. Therefore, the relative expansion of government debt causes an expansion of the liquidity—i.e., the moneyness—of the total debt structure.

FEDERAL GOVERNMENT CREDIT GUARANTEE ACTIVITY. Finally, the government, through establishing credit institutions to guarantee debt arising from such sources as agriculture and home finance, has expanded the liquidity of debt instruments arising from these borrowings. The liquidity has been expanded in the case of agriculture by substitution of the well-known and very sound credit of the agricultural credit institutions of the federal government for the credit of the individual farmer. In the case of home finance, the credit liquidity was expanded through extension of government credit guarantees on approved loans and the development of bonds backed by insured mortgages.

Effects of Liquidity Changes on Economic Analyses. This tremendous expansion of liquidity should have changed the emphasis of monetary theory and policy discussions, but it did not. Current analyses of the late 1960s and early 1970s continued to emphasize the quantity of money narrowly defined as M_1 or M_2 and failed to consider the different ways that existing liquid assets may be used. Finally, in 1976, it was realized by many that the examination of the quantity of money had lost much of its usefulness because such a huge portion of the assets of the economy possesses a liquidity that makes it money for purposes of analysis.

The really important monetary questions are related, therefore, to the manner of use of the existing huge quantity of liquid assets. Some of these questions are:

1. Will the holders of assets with a high degree of moneyness wish to exchange them for goods or equity investments; that is, for example, exchange demand and time deposits for corporate bonds and/or shares of stock?

2. What is the effect of changing currency and demand deposits into time deposits and federal government bonds?

3. Will bank and savings and loan interest rates paid and charged be sufficiently flexible to attract and hold deposits while meeting the credit needs of individuals and businesses?

As institutions, however, the commercial banks have been becoming less liquid year by year since 1946. Between 1961 and 1968 loans of all commercial banks increased by some $104 billion while federal government securities held decreased by about $5 billion. During this same period the liquidity of the business corporation was also declining. The result of the trend has been more active bidding for available funds and higher interest rates, with the large federal deficits crowding out uninsured borrowing or being financed with an expansion of Federal Reserve deposits and fiat currency.

In 1977 the equity capital of all commercial banks totaled $73.6 billion, and the total of deposit liabilities was $823.1 billion. A decline of 10 percent in the value of loans and securities held would use up all the equity capital of the commercial banking industry.

Public Attitudes.   In the depression period of the 1930s, everyone considered it very wise to keep as large a portion of his assets in cash or in claims on a definite number of monetary units (deposits in banks and bonds, for example) as possible. Their reasoning was based on past experience that had shown that cash assets were the best, because all others lost value with the price decline of the period. During the World War II period such thinking continued. This time it was partly due to the 1930 experience, but it was also due to the unusually high prices and the scarcities of goods, which were considered to be temporary war phenomena. The net effect of these factors was a great willingness to hold liquid assets.

Availability of Goods.   In the postwar period more goods did become available, but prices did not fall; instead, they rose higher. This raised some doubts regarding the desirability of liquidity, which was expressed in the phrase, "hedge against inflation." Private debt of all types expanded, and the purchase of a government security began to look like an investment inferior to the purchase of common stock or investment in a new home. The desire for liquidity began to decline. The severe losses suffered by holders of common stocks and those in debt in the 1930s became more distant, and the business leaders who had gone through this period were replaced by younger men who knew of the crash of 1929 only as a historical episode.

Rate of Capitalization.   The effect of these relationships was to increase the rate of capitalization of the earnings of corporations. Common stocks that were selling at eight times earnings per share in 1949 were selling at twenty times earnings in 1968, and growth stocks at forty times earnings became common in 1973. The effect has also been to use savings to purchase a new car, to expand a factory, or to modernize a house rather than to increase a bank account or holdings of government securities. Rising prices reduce the desirability of liquidity.

Despite these influences liquidity as measured by savings in commercial banks, savings and loan shares, and mutual savings banks has continued to grow. The growth is shown in Chart XV. On the other hand, as is also shown in the chart, the quantity of life insurance and pension fund reserves has remained relatively constant; and money balances—i.e. demand deposits—that totaled more than time and savings deposits in commercial banks in 1960 are now much less. The higher interest earnings have reduced the attractiveness of money as no-interest demand deposits.

Holding of Government Debt. The very great liquidity preference that the depression and deflation of the 1930s instilled in the American people made it possible for the federal government to sell large quantities of its debt obligations to savers during World War II. Ordinary wage earners and corporation treasurers purchased government securities with their surplus funds, because they thought government securities a good investment. When they did this they were saying in part that they believed prices would fall after the war; that is, they feared another depression. They also were saying that after the war there would be lots of things that they would want to buy and that it would be well for them to have cash on hand at that time. In other words, a considerable portion of the desire for liquidity was a temporary state of mind arising from the unusual conditions of the war and immediate prewar and postwar periods.

As the unusual conditions of all-out war were dissipated and the fears of another depression faded, the liquidity preference of individuals and corporation treasurers became less. However, while it lasted, it was very useful to the federal government. The federal government was able to sell securities at a much lower interest rate than it would have been able to do under conditions of a more normal liquidity preference. It was also able to borrow large sums of money through an expansion of bank credit and to do so with only minor inflationary pressures.

By 1966, because of a belief in further price increases that would be reflected in common stock prices and also because of high income taxes and the attractiveness of undistributed profits, investors were willing to purchase a common stock paying dividends of 3 percent while high-grade corporate bonds earned 6 percent. The pendulum had swung a long way from the situa-

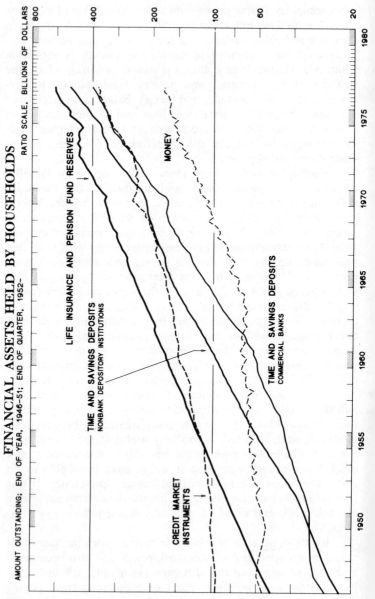

CHART XV

FINANCIAL ASSETS HELD BY HOUSEHOLDS

AMOUNT OUTSTANDING; END OF YEAR, 1946–51; END OF QUARTER, 1952–

RATIO SCALE, BILLIONS OF DOLLARS

LIFE INSURANCE AND PENSION FUND RESERVES

TIME AND SAVINGS DEPOSITS
NONBANK DEPOSITORY INSTITUTIONS

MONEY

TIME AND SAVINGS DEPOSITS
COMMERCIAL BANKS

CREDIT MARKET
INSTRUMENTS

tion in the 1940s when dividends were 10 percent of the market price of common stock and interest rates on corporate securities were less than half as high.

The earnings–price ratio of the 500 stocks of Standard and Poor's corporate series was higher in 1974 than previously in 1970, but the New York Stock Exchange index reached a high in 1972 and then fell sharply reaching its low in 1974. In 1977 the New York Stock Exchange index was still below the 1972 level.

The willingness to capitalize corporate earnings at differing rates and rather wide shifts in profit levels have caused the stock market to fluctuate widely during the 1970s. This has acted to increase the attractiveness of investment in bonds and savings accounts and the desire for liquidity. On the other hand, the high inflation rate of the 1970s has acted to make nonliquid investments in natural resources, land, and structures even more attractive. A result was the land boom of 1976 and 1978.

Chapter 15

Fractional Reserve Credit Systems

A very basic feature of the banking and monetary system of the United States is that the commercial banking system, because of the fractional reserve requirement, is able through its day-to-day operations to change the money supply. The commercial banking system does this daily through the decisions made by loan and security portfolio officers of individual banks. However, the decisions of these officers must operate within the general credit atmosphere that is created by the availability of bank reserves and the profitability of borrowing as seen by the business community.

Forgetting for the moment these interrelationships and a multitude of other factors affecting the operations of our fractional reserve commercial banking system, let us concentrate on just the mechanics of commercial bank deposit creation and destruction.

As you have seen, a commercial bank is primarily in the business of holding debt. The debt owed to the bank is of two general types: (1) loans and (2) securities and investments. The amount of all these debts owed to the bank is approximately balanced by the debt of the bank to its depositors. It is through the expansion of the debt owed to it that the commercial banking system increases the debt it owes—deposits—which is a part of the money supply. However, originally because depositors may ask for some type of debt instrument (money) other than the bank's IOU's and currently largely as a method of regulation, banks are required by law to keep a certain portion of their deposits in legal reserves. In the United States, as we have seen, these legal reserves for all the bank members of the Fed are deposits with the Federal Reserve Bank of the Federal Reserve District in which the commercial bank is located.

CHART XVI

RESERVES AND RELATED ITEMS OF MEMBER BANKS

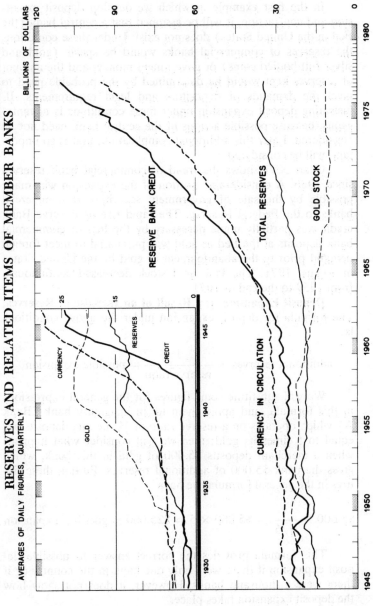

AVERAGES OF DAILY FIGURES, QUARTERLY

BILLIONS OF DOLLARS

RESERVE BANK CREDIT

TOTAL RESERVES

GOLD STOCK

CURRENCY IN CIRCULATION

GOLD

CURRENCY

RESERVES

CREDIT

In the first example in which we develop deposit expansion and contraction, it will be assumed that a central bank (the Fed in the United States) does not exist. Under these conditions the reserves of commercial banks would be specie (gold and silver full-bodied coins) or government money, and the amount of reserves kept would be determined by the probable need to meet the demands of depositors and legal requirements. Illustrating deposit expansion under these conditions is advantageous, because possible actions of the central bank need not be considered. Later this additional complication, that is so important, will be considered.

Chart XVI shows the trend of commercial bank reserves since 1930. A considerable portion of the expansion was made possible by the sale of government securities of commercial banks to the Federal Reserve. The rapid rise of Reserve Bank credit was partially made necessary by the loss of commercial bank deposits at the Fed as gold was purchased to meet foreign demand prior to the abandonment of gold by the United States in August 1971. The U.S. gold stock decreased continuously from 1957 to the end of 1971.

Deposit Expansion as a Result of an Increase of Reserves. The formula for deposit expansion under the above conditions is:

$$\text{additional reserves} \times \frac{1}{\text{reserve ratio}} = \text{possible expansion}$$

We will substitute some figures for the general expressions in this formula, and apply them to an imaginary bank (Bank A) which operates on a reserve ratio of $\frac{1}{5}$, i.e., its deposits are equal to 5 times its gold; then we will consider what happens when a merchant deposits $5,000 of gold in this bank, which gives the bank $5,000 of additional reserves. Putting these figures in the general formula, we have

$$\$5,000 \times \frac{1}{1/5} = \$5,000 \times 5 = \$25,000 = \text{possible expansion}$$

This formula provides the correct answer to possible deposit expansion if there were only one bank in the country or if there were a thousand banks. However, it does not show how the deposit expansion takes place.

To make our example more illustrative but still simple, we

will assume there are a number of commercial banks and not just one in the country. The expansion of deposits will be shown by the use of a very abbreviated commercial bank balance sheet. As a starting point, let us assume that the balance sheet of our bank has just changed by the deposit of $5,000 of gold.

Bank A

Assets		*Liabilities*	
Gold holdings increased	$5,000	Demand deposits increased	$5,000

Because, as was shown in the formula, Bank A need keep only 20 percent of its demand deposits as reserves, and as gold is considered to be reserves, Bank A has $4,000 of excess reserves. It has $4,000 of excess reserves because only $1,000 of the additional gold is needed to give the increase of demand deposits a 20 percent reserve coverage.

Our next assumption will be that Bank A lends to a customer $4,000. When this transaction has been completed, Bank A's balance sheet looks like this:

Bank A

Assets		*Liabilities*	
Gold holdings	$5,000	Demand deposits	$9,000
Commercial loans increased	4,000		

The loan was granted to the customer by increasing his checking account (demand deposits) by $4,000. When the customer wishes to use his loan he will write checks or withdraw gold on his expanded account. Notice also that the note which the customer signed indicating that he owed the bank $4,000 is an asset of the bank; it represents the amount owed to the bank, which is just equal to the increase in the amount the bank owes—its demand deposits.

In order to continue this illustration of the expansion of demand deposits in a system of a number of commercial banks, we will assume that the customer spends his deposit by withdrawing gold. The effect of this is very like the situation of a modern commercial bank in the United States because a person receiving a loan is not very likely to spend it in such a way that the expenditure only results in the transfer of deposits from one account to another within the commercial bank.

Therefore we will have our borrower spend his deposit in gold, which causes the balance sheet of Bank A to change so that it looks like this:

Bank A

Assets		Liabilities	
Gold holdings	$1,000	Demand deposits	$5,000
Commercial loans	4,000		

Our next step is to include another bank. This shall be called Bank B, and it is the bank in which the gold is deposited after the borrower from Bank A has spent his $4,000 loan. Bank B's balance sheet as a result of this new deposit of gold changes as follows:

Bank B

Assets		Liabilities	
Gold holdings		Demand deposits	
increased	$4,000	increased	$4,000

If Bank B also utilizes its excess reserves to expand its lending, the commercial loans of Bank B will expand by $3,200 and so will its demand deposits. This will cause the balance sheet to change again so it would look like this:

Bank B

Assets		Liabilities	
Gold holdings	$4,000	Demand deposits	$7,200
Commercial loans			
increased	3,200		

Again the loan was granted by increasing the customer's checking account. Also, let us again assume the borrower spends his new deposit by withdrawing gold that is deposited in yet another commercial bank. This causes the balance sheet of Bank B to look like this:

Bank B

Assets		Liabilities	
Gold holdings	$ 800	Demand deposits	$4,000
Commercial loans	3,200		

Table 9 provides a summary of the transactions that have been explained in some detail. It also provides space for continuing the expansion of demand deposits from bank to bank.

Actually the data of Table 9 are an infinite geometric series that never quite reaches but comes very close to the answer provided by the formula of the expansion of deposits.

TABLE 9

DEPOSIT EXPANSION AS RESERVES BECOME DISTRIBUTED
AMONG THE DIFFERENT BANKS OF THE BANKING SYSTEM

	Reserves Received	*Deposit Increase*	*Reserve Increase*	*Loan Increase*
Bank A	$5,000	$5,000	$1,000	$4,000
Bank B	4,000	4,000	800	3,200
Bank C	3,200	—	—	—
Bank D	—	—	—	—
Bank E	—	—	—	—
Bank F	—	—	—	—
Total	—	—	—	—

Deposit Contraction as a Result of a Reduction of Reserves. The process of deposit and loan contraction through the reduction of reserves is the reverse of expansion of loans and deposits as a result of an expansion of reserves, and the same formula may be used. For example, if the reduction of reserves is $5,000 and the reserve requirement is 20 percent, the reduction of deposits (liabilities) and loans and investments (assets) is shown by putting these data into the formula (it is assumed throughout that the commercial bank does not possess excess reserves).

$$-\$5,000 \times \frac{1}{1/5} = -\$5,000 \times 5 = -\$25,000$$
necessary contraction.

The way in which this reduction of commercial bank loans or investments and deposits takes place can be shown in a system of a number of commercial banks by going from bank to bank in the same way as we went from bank to bank in the case of the expansion of commercial bank reserves. In this case, let us call the first commercial bank, Bank Z. A customer of Bank Z decides to withdraw $5,000 of gold to use in paying for goods purchased abroad. This reduces the gold reserves of Bank Z, and it is now short of reserves, and it must act to replenish its depleted reserves. This can be shown in its balance sheet as follows:

Bank Z

Assets		*Liabilities*	
Reduction of gold holdings	$5,000	Reduction of deposits	$5,000

The deposits of Bank Z are down by $5,000 but so are its gold holdings. The reduction of deposits by $5,000 relieved Bank Z of the need for 20 percent of $5,000 or $1,000 of reserves, but Bank Z has lost $5,000 of reserves and is therefore short $4,000 of reserves. We will assume it recovers its reserve ratio by selling $4,000 of its assets to a depositor of Bank Y who pays for the securities by reducing his deposit in Bank Y by $4,000. As this makes Bank Y's obligations to Bank Z $4,000 greater than those of Bank Z to Bank Y, it is necessary for Bank Y to make the payment of the $4,000 check written by its customer by remitting $4,000 in gold to Bank Z. This causes Bank Z's balance sheet to change as follows:

Bank Z

Assets		*Liabilities*
Gold holdings increased	$4,000	No change
Securities decreased	4,000	

Bank Z is now in balance again because its decrease of deposits of $5,000 resulting in a loss of gold of $5,000 and therefore a $4,000 shortage of reserves has been rectified. But Bank Y is now short of reserves. Bank Y lost $4,000 of deposits and also $4,000 of gold, and therefore it is short $3,200 of reserves. The changes in Bank Y's balance sheet as a result of the first transaction would be as follows:

Bank Y

Assets		*Liabilities*	
Gold holdings decreased	$4,000	Demand deposits decreased	$4,000

To rectify the reserve shortage, Bank Y would make the following additional changes in its balance sheet:

Bank Y

Assets		*Liabilities*
Gold holdings increased	$3,200	No change
Securities decreased	3,200	

After this action, Bank Y's reserve position is again satisfactory, but the purchaser of the securities has made the reserve position of his bank unsatisfactory. Again we have the impact of a change in reserves flowing from bank to bank and finally bringing about the reduction in deposits indicated in the formula.

Table 10 provides a summary of the transactions that have already been explained and in addition provides space for continuing the contraction of demand deposits from bank to bank. Also, again it is an infinite geometric series that never quite reaches but comes very close to the answer provided by the formula of the contraction of deposits.

TABLE 10

DEPOSIT CONTRACTION AS OTHER COMMERCIAL BANKS
SHARE IN THE ORIGINAL LOSS OF BANK RESERVES

	Reserves Lost	*Deposit Decrease*	*Final Reserve Reduction*	*Decrease of Securities Held*
Bank Z	$5,000	$5,000	$1,000	$4,000
Bank Y	4,000	4,000	800	3,200
Bank X	3,200	—	—	—
Bank W	—	—	—	—
Bank V	—	—	—	—
Bank U	—	—	—	—
Total	—	—	—	—

Introduction of a Central Bank. The basic procedure of the way the increase or the reduction of reserves available to a commercial bank may cause demand deposits, i.e., the quantity of money, to decrease or increase is not changed by the introduction of a central bank, such as our Federal Reserve System. The change caused by the central bank is that it can through its actions determine the quantity of reserves that will be available to commercial banks. A central bank if it had desired could have prevented (open-market purchases) the loss of $5,000 of gold by Bank Z from having any effect on the total reserves available to commercial banks. Also a central bank could have prevented (open-market sales) the increase in the reserves of Bank A from having any effect on the total reserves available to commercial banks. Another change resulting from the original introduction of a central bank was a conservation of the basic reserve, which usually has been gold.

Since 1965 the Federal Reserve has not been required to provide a gold certificate backing of its deposits. And since 1968 a gold certificate backing has not been required of Federal Reserve notes. Prior to 1945 the gold certificate backing ratio of notes was 40 percent and deposits 35 percent. For the next twenty years the ratio required to back both notes and deposits was 25 percent. Now no gold or SDR reserve is required.

KEY CURRENCY. The U.S. dollar is still the "key currency" of the world. This means that the dollar: (1) serves as unit of account in international matters, (2) acts as a widely accepted means of making international payments, and (3) is used as monetary reserves for the currency and deposit liabilities of other countries.

The effect of having your money a "key currency" is to make you the international banker for the rest of the world. Recently the nations of Western Europe have been unhappy with this situation and in cooperation with the United States have initiated plans to make the International Monetary Fund a type of international central bank and to make its credit (SDRs) function as a "key currency."

Prior to the American abandonment of gold in 1971 and the initiation of the floating international exchange rate in 1972 the United States had initiated devices and procedures for stabilizing the international monetary situation. One procedure that continues is *swap lines*. A swap line arises when a central bank agrees to exchange on request its own currency for the currency of the other party up to a maximum amount and over a limited period of time. In 1977 the United States through reciprocal exchange arrangements actively supported the international value of the dollar.

Another procedure used until 1968 was called the *central bank's gold pool*. It was managed by the Bank of England and was set up in 1961. The cooperating countries included Western Europe, with the exception of France who withdrew in 1967. They added gold to the pool to meet speculation against the set price of $35 an ounce, which had not been changed since it was established by the United States in 1933. This price for gold was reaffirmed when the International Monetary Fund was established in 1944. In 1968 a two-price gold system was established. The price of gold not traded between central banks was permitted to fluctuate freely.

Also the elimination of the gold certificate backing of Federal Reserve deposits and notes freed the $12 billion of U. S. gold for use to stabilize the price of gold.

In 1963 the United States entered into standby arrangements with the IMF to withdraw other currencies from the fund in exchange for dollars. This right was exercised during the period of dollar abundance in the international money markets. The need for this and most of the other devices was eliminated when the United States abandoned gold and floating exchange rates were initiated.

The Rio Agreement of 1967 provided for adding a new reserve to supplement gold—Special Drawing Rights or SDRs. They are distributed to IMF members in proportion to their fund quotas as a result of a deliberate decision of IMF members. The claims represented by the SDRs are backed by the obligation of member countries to accept them in exchange for convertible currencies up to certain limits. As SDRs replaced gold as the IMF reserve currency the need for gold by the IMF declined. As a result in 1976 the IMF began to sell gold to provide funds to assist low-income LDCs.

Conclusion. This is the bare skeleton of the Western world's money machine. The machine in real life is made to operate through the effect of a myriad of private and governmental decisions to borrow or repay their loans, to hold more cash or to hold less cash, to invest abroad or to invest at home. The details of the uses and sources of credit available in the money and credit markets of the United States are provided partially by the flow of funds accounts. The flow of funds matrix possesses many data shortcomings, particularly in demonstrating how the supply of credit is reduced and increased (see Index). The explanation of the relationship between commercial bank credit and bank reserves and the central bank described in this chapter is only a bare-bones picture that is limited largely to the domestic portion of the credit creation and contraction process in the United States.

Banking and general business activity have become more international, and about 25 percent of the business of U.S. banks is offshore. In this large area the expansion and contraction of credit takes place through the Eurodollar market located in London. The activities of the market are unregulated and largely unreported. The governors of the central banks of the world could place reporting and reserve requirements on the banks operating in the market, but they have decided not to do so. Therefore an expanding portion of the money manufacturing system of the world operates outside of government-set reserve requirements and quantitative limits.

PART III: SELECTED REFERENCES AND SOURCES

David A. Alhadeff, *Monopoly and Competition in Banking* (Berkeley: University of California Press, 1954).

David R. Allardice, "State-Owned Banks: New Wine in Old Bottles," *Federal Reserve Bank of Chicago, Business Conditions*, July 1976, 3–10.

Richard I. Bloch, "The Bank Secrecy Act and Personal Privacy," *Michigan Business Review*, November 1973, 1–9.

Howard D. Cross, *Management Policies for Commercial Banks* (Englewood Cliffs, N.J.: Prentice-Hall, 1962).

Donald R. Hodgman, *Commercial Bank Loan and Investment Policy* (Champaign, Ill.: University of Illinois, 1963).

Paul F. Jessup (ed.), *Innovations in Bank Management* (New York: Holt, Rinehart, 1969).

Robert E. Knight, "Account Analysis in Correspondent Banking," Federal Reserve Bank of Kansas City, *Monthly Review*, March 1976, 11–20.

Lewis Mandell, *Credit Card Use in the United States* (Ann Arbor: University of Michigan, 1972).

Robert P. Mayo, "The Challenges for Small Banks," *Federal Reserve Bank of Chicago, Business Conditions*, March 1971, 10–20.

Stephen L. McDonald, "The Internal Drain and Bank Credit Expansion, *Journal of Finance*, December 1953, 407–21.

Sanford Rose, "They're Still Pioneering at Wells Fargo Bank," *Fortune*, July 1976, 120–128, 130.

P. F. Smith, *Economics of Financial Institutions and Markets* (Homewood, Ill.: Irwin, 1971).

Dana L. Thomas, "Going Checkless," *Barrons*, September 20, 1976, 5, 13.

U.S. Treasury, "Commercial Banks and the Securities Markets." *Treasury Papers*, January 1976, 6–7.

Part IV

Credit Uses, Sources, and Creation

INTRODUCTION

The monetary and financial portion of the operation of our economy is connected to the production and purchase of products and services by the net flow of money claims and the ownership and location of the accumulation of these claims. This process is affected by the considerable powers and a willingness to exercise them possessed by Congress, the Fed, and the commercial banks. It is a process that goes considerably beyond these three institutional inputs, however.

The economy is continually busy meeting and creating needs. The production and exchange of goods and services to meet these needs requires financing procedures at all stages, i.e., from planning to final disposal. The credit needs include liquidity of various types, i.e., from a million-dollar line of credit from a large commercial bank to a large manufacturer, to enough paper money to meet someone's spending needs over a weekend. Because of the great variety of credit uses and sources and the inability to consider all the interrelationships of each credit use, a combination of an overall look and an examination of specialized activities is the basis of the approach generally taken in this book.

The chapters of this part are concerned largely with an overall look at credit uses, sources, and creation. The manner in which the system functions is affected, of course, by the decisions of Congress and the Fed and by the type of commercial banking and financial institution system that exists.

Chapter 16

Flow of Funds: General Concept

The flow of funds matrix is a statement of the capital account for the economy as a whole. The whole matrix in a simplified form with hypothetical data is given in Table 11.

Investment in assets is in the "uses" columns, and means of financing that investment is in the "sources" columns.

The matrix operates under two basic restraints. First, each sector makes real investments or financial investments that are by definition equal to saving. In the example "saving" is shown in row one for the sector.

Second, the sum of the uses of funds across the columns is equal to the sum of the sources of funds in that row. This means there is a vertical balance between saving and investment and a horizontal balance between payments and receipts. Each row and each column constitutes one full account of the structure. The relationships among columns and rows demonstrate the interlocking provided for in the accounting system used.

For example, if savings of the private domestic nonfinancial sector decrease, then some particular uses of funds must also decrease. It might cause a decrease in deposits of financial intermediaries by an equal amount. If this takes place financial intermediaries as a source of funds will decrease and the users of loans or funds from the sale of securities to financial intermediaries will have fewer resources to spend. The result of the development would be less investment and reduced employment and profits in the capital goods sector, resulting in less taxes and a larger government use of funds. When the analysis gets to this point the flow of funds approach gives way to central bank policy and whether or not it will "manufacture" the funds needed by the government through purchase of securities held by financial intermediaries so that these intermediaries can become a source of funds for use by the government.

TABLE 11

MODEL FLOW OF FUNDS MATRIX

(HYPOTHETICAL DATA; BILLIONS OF DOLLARS)

Transaction category	Private domestic nonfinancial sector		Government sector		Financial intermediaries sector		Rest of world sector		Totals		Memo: domestic totals	
	Use	Source	Use	Source	Use	Source	Use	Source	Use	Source	Use	Source
Nonfinancial:												
1. Saving		179		−10		5		−4		170		174
2. Capital outlays	170		--		--		--		170		170	
Financial:												
3. Net financial investment	9		−10		5		−4		0		4	
4. Total financial uses and sources (5+6)	69	60	5	15	70	65	3	7	147	147	144	140
5. Deposits at financial intermediaries	50		3			55	2		55	55	53	55
6. Loans and securities	19	60	2	15	70	10	1	7	92	92	91	85

NOTE.— This table compresses about 20 sectors in the full system into four columns for sector types that are to be distinguished in the present discussion, and the rows are a similar grouping of transaction categories. In addition, the matrix is simplified by omitting the row and the column for discrepancies and a number of items peripheral to the main stream of financial transactions. These omitted items are treated in the model as nonexistent in the simple economy shown. Specifically, the relation of transactions in this table to the full matrix is conceptually as follows:

Full matrix	Model
Gross saving	Saving
Gross investment	Omitted
Private capital expenditures, net	Capital outlays
Net financial investment	Net financial investment
Financial uses, net and financial sources	Total financial uses and sources
Gold, foreign exchange, Treasury currency	Omitted
Demand deposits, currency, and time and savings accounts	Deposits at financial intermediaries
Insurance and pension reserves, and interbank items	Omitted
Credit market instruments	Loans and securities
Security credit, trade credit, taxes payable, noncorporate equities, miscellaneous, and sector discrepancies	Omitted

The Government sector should be interpreted as central Government only, with State and local governments omitted as another simplification. Of the omissions, the most important for the discussion that follows is insurance and pension reserves, which are a major form of intermediation. This item is left out because part of such reserves are liabilities of governments and complicate the relation between intermediation on the one hand and financial institutions on the other. The present section is focused only on the broad outlines of structural relationships, and a more detailed description requires many qualifications and additions to the broad form in order to incorporate these governmental reserves and the other omitted items.

CHART XVII

FLOW OF FUNDS: CURRENT PAYMENTS

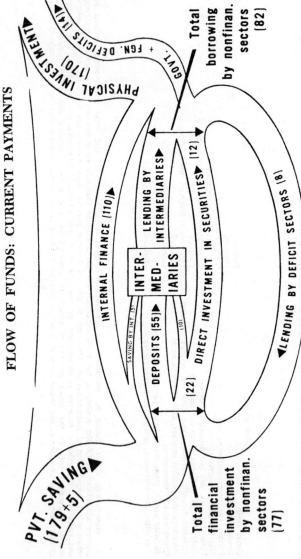

PVT. SAVING ▶ (179+5)

PHYSICAL INVESTMENT (170)

GOV'T. + FGN. DEFICITS (14)

INTERNAL FINANCE (110) ▶

LENDING BY INTERMEDIARIES ▶

SAVING BY INT. (5)

INTER-MED-IARIES

DEPOSITS (55) ▶

(10)

(22)

DIRECT INVESTMENT IN SECURITIES ▶

(12)

◀ LENDING BY DEFICIT SECTORS (8)

Total borrowing by nonfinan. sectors (82)

Total financial investment by nonfinan. sectors (77)

In Table 11, nonfinancial transactions are placed in the first two rows. These uses and sources of funds include sale and purchases of goods and services, taxes of all kinds, and transfer payments and receipts. The following rows are financial transactions. Here the net changes in the capital amounts of claims owed as liabilities or assets are recorded. This means all financial transactions of a sector are combined into a net borrowed or net investment position.

The model of Table 11 shows only a two-way breakdown of the financial portion of the accounts. In the full matrix, as shown in Table 12, the financial category is given in considerable detail.

Chart XVII is a diagram of Table 11. The numbers given in the flow accounts are taken from Table 11. It is, of course, an abstract of the full complexity of the system.

Saving in Chart XVII is the total of private sectors, including intermediaries. Therefore, intermediary saving is an internal source of funds for lending in Chart XVII.

Also, all private sector saving is kept on the left of the chart, even though the total is a net sum of savers and dissavers. These savings are pictured as entering the capital account as a diversion from the current payments stream. As investments are made by various institutions and individuals the funds are injected back into the spending stream.

Internal finance is the amount of capital goods purchased without borrowing funds, and it amounts to the excess of capital outlays (170) over private borrowing (60).

The saving going into financial assets goes partially directly to nonfinancial borrowers (12). Most of these savings become deposits (55) with security claims on intermediaries. These savings are used by these institutions to extend credit as mortgages and bank loans (70). This (70) combined with the (12) of internal finance make up the total (82) borrowing by the nonfinancial portion of the money market. The funds borrowed are used to finance investment not coming from internal sources and the deficits of consumers and others.

The bottom portion of Chart XVII shows the reverse flow of funds from the borrowing to the lending side of the structure. This flow is equal to the investments in financial assets coming from the government sector and the rest of the world sector, i.e., the two deficit sectors. In carrying out their activities these deficit sectors have added to their asset position (8) to carry

TABLE 12

FINANCIAL TRANSACTION CATEGORIES

Gold and Special Drawing Rights
Official foreign exchange position
   IMF gold tranche position
   Convertible foreign exchange
Treasury currency
	Monetary reserves

Demand deposits and currency
   Private domestic
   U.S. Government
   Foreign
Time deposits at commercial banks
Savings accounts at savings institutions
	Deposit claims on
	financial institutions

Life insurance reserves Pension fund reserves	Insurance and pension reserves
Interbank claims Corporate equities	

U.S. Government securities
   Treasury issues
      Short-term
      Other marketable
      Savings bonds
   Nonguaranteed agency issues
   Loan participation certificates
State and local obligations
Corporate and foreign bonds
Home (1- to 4-family) mortgages
Other mortgages
   Multifamily residential
   Commercial
   Farm
Consumer credit
   Instalment
   Noninstalment
Bank loans n.e.c.
Other loans
   Open market paper
   Finance co. loans to business
   U.S. Government loans
   Sponsored credit agency loans
   Loans on insurance policies
	Credit market instruments

Security credit
   Owed by brokers and dealers
   Owed by others
Taxes payable
Trade credit
Equity in noncorporate business
Miscellaneous
   Deposit claims
   Equities
   Insurance claims
   Unallocated claims and bank floats
	Other claims

Sector discrepancies	

out lending programs in the case of government plus some increase in the liquidity of others.

A point to keep in mind relative to the reverse flow of funds shown at the bottom of Chart XVII is that nonfinancial institutions perform considerable quasi-financial intermediary activities. All of this activity creates reverse flows that add another dimension to the flow of funds concept.

The savers provided (179), which was greater than capital outlays of (170). However, some (69) went into financial investments, and some (60) were borrowed again on the other side of the market in different forms. The result is an increase of both assets and liabilities but no change in the net position.

The Fed, which has done a considerable portion of the work in developing the flow of funds data, reports that, "It is this detailing of credit transactions in the capital account that brings the financial statistics of the economy into coherent relation to one another and into direct relation to the nonfinancial statistics in income and product accounts," i.e., national income data.

The total of net financial investment of the flow of funds is the quantity that provides the accounting link to national income amounts. However, in the economic analysis sense, it is the specific credit flows and their relation to specific income generating or income reduction actions that is of interest.

The flow of funds data organized into a matrix permits examination of the ways the economy can be affected by this activity. The transactions of each sector, no matter how little or great the detail, are divided into uses and sources. This approach recognizes that each individual, within the limits of his net worth and income, can decide to save or spend, to invest in securities or physical assets, to pay off debt or go into debt. When the data are analyzed in terms of the impact of these decisions, much is learned of how the economy operates; and therefore one gains some idea as to what future economic levels will be if certain actions are taken.

Financial Structure. Chart XVII provides a visual summary of the nation's capital account. The basic relationships, i.e., government and foreign deficits, of Table 11 are continued in Chart XVII. One way to look at the approach is to view each sector as a single person in an economy made up of only four persons, each different from the other.

Savings are shown as flowing out of the general expenditure stream. These savings then pass through a number of channels as they move toward the financing of capital, consumer borrowing, and government deficits. The portion of capital goods financed out of depreciation and retained profits is financed internally and appears as the excess of capital outlays (170) and private borrowing (60).

Finally, there is a savings flow that goes into cash, deposits for liquidity, and marketable securities for capital gains. This is financial investment and some goes immediately to nonfinancial borrowers (12); however, a much larger portion (55) is put into deposits and security claims on intermediaries (10). The intermediaries through mortgages and bank loans relend this money. The total (82) of borrowing is financial with direct investment of savings (12) and lending (70) of intermediaries.

At the bottom of Chart XVII the government and international deficits are shown to consist in part of investment in financial assets. This extra borrowing (8) for investment in financial assets is done largely by government to carry out public goals. In a fashion the government sector in borrowing and relending is acting a good deal like a financial intermediary, i.e., a savings and loan association.

Chart XVII illustrates in a general and aggregate fashion the relationship between savings and investment and the decisions to borrow directly or through intermediaries. However, it must be realized that these quantities are not directly determinants of the total of either saving or investment. This is true because of opportunities for internal finance and of borrowing to carry financial assets.

When this lack of a relationship between savings and investment is realized it also becomes understandable why a restrictive or expansive credit policy does not immediately influence these aggregates. Rather, credit policy actions of the Fed and commercial banks tend to be diffused throughout the economy. One difficult aspect of analyzing financial markets arises from the problem of defining supply and demand separately. Many would agree that useful solutions to the problem of separate analysis of supply and demand, i.e., use and source, still need to be worked out.

Chapter 17

Flow of Funds: Definition of Sectors and Financial Transaction Levels

The sector structure of the flow of funds matrix was given in Table 11. In the most detailed approach there are about twenty sectors. The broadest useful sector division is fourfold and consists of: private domestic nonfinancial, U.S. government, financial, and foreign. The data included in the foreign area are much less reliable those that of the three domestic sectors. The unreliability of foreign financial data plus the reduced interest in balance of payments trends since the introduction of floating international exchange rates has caused the U.S. Department of Commerce to discontinue its publication of these data.

The private domestic nonfinancial sector is made up of four divisions. These are: *households, farm business, nonfarm noncorporate business*, and *corporate nonfinancial business*. The detail of the composition of each of these four groupings is highlighted below. An understanding of developments in the components of the aggregate makes possible a forecast of changes in the level of the uses and sources of funds of financial transaction categories as used in the flow of funds accounts.

The *households* sector includes persons of households, personal trusts, nonprofit organizations serving individuals such as foundations, private schools and hospitals, labor unions, churches, and charitable organizations. The sector excludes farm and noncorporate business activity of individuals. The data on personal trusts and nonprofit organizations are very sparse and perhaps constitute 10 percent of the total for the sector.

Farm business covers all farming activities in the United States including both cooperative and corporation farms. In addition, credit cooperatives are combined with farmers who own and manage them as are housing activities. Owner investments are a portion of the equity in the noncorporate business transaction account. Farm business is really a combination of the household sector and the proprietors' equity transaction account.

Nonfarm noncorporate business includes nonfinancial proprietorships and partnerships plus individual rental activities and the professions. Like farming all income and savings are transferred to the household account. Net saving becomes zero, and gross saving is equal to capital consumption allowances; all changes in equity capital appear as net inflows in "proprietors' net investment."

Corporate nonfinancial business covers the same area as in the national income accounts except that farm corporations are not included. It includes holding companies, closed-end investment companies on a consolidated basis, real estate firms, and all private corporations not specifically covered in financial sectors.

State and local governments—general funds does not include employee retirement funds, which are shown separately as a financial sector. This category does include all political subdivisions plus corporations, enterprises and debt-issuing authorities, and trust funds other than pension funds.

Rest of the world is based on U.S. Commerce Department data on balance of payments for financial transactions and national income quantities for nonfinancial transactions. The "errors and omissions" in the balance of payments data is the sector discrepancy reported by the U.S. Commerce Department.

U.S. government covers all the items developed in the federal budget in 1969 with one exception—the District of Columbia, which is included in the state and local government sector. Also the Fed and certain monetary accounts are not included but are instead included in the monetary sector. It does include federal employee retirement and life insurance funds and all corporations that are wholly or partially owned by the federal government.

Federally sponsored credit agencies consists of five types of specialized lending institutions that were originally federal government owned to a greater or less degree but are now excluded from the federal budget. The agencies are federal home loan banks, federal national mortgage associations, federal land banks, federal intermediate credit banks, and banks for co-operatives. Pass-through securities of GNMA (Government National Mortgage Association), with the securities as liabilities and pools of mortgages as assets, are also included.

Monetary authorities data come from the "Member Bank Reserves, Federal Reserve Bank, Credit and Related Items" table in the *Bulletin* of the Fed. The principal liabilities are bank reserves and currency in circulation. The assets consist largely of U.S. government securities, Treasury currency, Fed float, bank borrowings from the Fed, and gold.

Commercial banks is a category that can be broken down into four categories. First there are all banks of the fifty states as defined by the coverage of all bank statistics of the comptroller of the Currency; second, the holding company parents of banks and nonbank subsidiaries; third, the Edge Act corporations and agencies of foreign banks operating in the United States and some chartered investment companies in New York; fourth, banks of the United States and foreign banks in U.S. territories and possessions.

Private nonbank finance combines the source and use of funds of some twenty different groupings of institutions. They are as follows: savings and loan associations, mutual savings banks, credit unions, life insurance companies, other insurance companies, private pension funds, state and local government employee retirement funds, finance companies, real estate investment trusts (REITs), open-end investment companies, and security brokers and dealers.

Discrepancy has the sign of net use of funds and source, or liabilities. In the case of the financial asset account it is not used. It is the balancing account of the matrix. The household account is the final resting place for most of the data inconsistencies throughout the system, for all of the household account items arise from the books of other sectors, including wages and personal taxes.

Table 13 is a summary of the flow of funds accounts (FFA). There are many relationships that warrant your study. For example, FFA treats the purchase of consumer durables as an investment and not as consumption as do the national income accounts. Also, notice how households dominate as a source of savings and that business savings are dominated by the allowance for capital consumption, i.e., depreciation.

SUMMARY OF FUNDS RAISED IN U.S. CREDIT MARKETS   TABLE 13

(SEASONALLY ADJUSTED ANNUAL RATES; IN BILLIONS OF/DOLLARS)

Transaction category, or sector	1967	1968	1969	1970	1971	1972	1973	1974	1975	1975 H1	1975 H2	1976 H1	
Credit market funds raised by nonfinancial sectors													
Total funds raised by nonfinancial sectors	83.9	98.3	93.5	100.7	151.0	176.9	197.6	188.8	210.4	184.2	236.5	242.0	1
Excluding equities	81.5	98.3	89.6	94.9	139.6	166.4	190.0	185.0	200.3	173.8	226.9	228.3	2
U.S. Government	13.0	13.6	-3.7	11.9	24.4	15.2	8.3	12.0	85.2	80.8	89.6	73.8	3
Public debt securities	8.9	10.5	-1.3	12.0	26.0	14.0	7.9	12.0	85.6	82.0	89.7	73.9	4
Agency issues and mortgages	4.1	3.1	-2.4	-.1	-1.6	1.1	.4	.0*	-.6	-1.2	-.1	-.1	5
All other nonfinancial sectors	70.9	84.8*	97.1	88.8	126.3	161.7	189.4	176.8	125.2	103.4	146.9	168.2	6
Corporate equities	2.4	.0*	3.9	5.8	11.5	10.5	7.7	3.8	10.1	10.5	9.6	13.7	7
Debt instruments	68.5	84.8	93.3	83.0	114.8	157.2	181.7	173.0	115.1	93.0	137.3	154.5	8
Private domestic nonfinancial sectors	66.9	81.9	93.5	86.1	121.1	157.7	183.1	161.6	112.2	94.9	129.4	152.5	9
Corporate equities	2.4	-.2	3.4	5.7	11.4	11.0	7.9	4.1	9.9	10.3	9.5	13.3	10
Debt instruments	64.5	82.1	90.1	80.4	109.7	146.8	175.3	157.5	102.3	84.6	119.9	139.2	11
Debt capital instruments	46.1	51.8	52.5	60.2	86.8	102.8	106.7	101.2	101.3	97.5	105.1	111.8	12
State and local obligations	7.8	9.5	9.9	11.2	17.5	15.4	16.3	19.6	17.3	16.2	18.4	18.4	13
Corporate bonds	14.7	12.9	9.0	19.8	18.8	12.2	9.2	19.7	27.2	33.4	21.0	20.7	14
Home mortgages	13.4	17.3	18.1	14.4	28.6	42.6	46.4	34.6	40.8	33.4	48.1	54.4	15
Multifamily residential mortgages	3.6	3.4	4.9	6.9	9.7	9.7	10.4	7.0	-.1	-.1	-.1	11.5	16
Commercial mortgages	4.7	6.2	5.7	5.7	9.4	10.4	18.5	15.1	10.9	8.7	13.1	5.9	17
Farm mortgages	2.0	2.2	1.8	1.6	2.9	3.6	3.6	5.1	5.1	5.6	4.8	4.8	18
Other debt instruments	18.4	30.2	37.6	20.1	22.8	44.0	68.6	56.3	1.0	-12.8	14.8	27.4	19
Consumer credit	4.5	10.0	10.4	5.1	11.6	19.1	21.7	9.8	9.8	1.1	16.0	19.4	20
Bank loans n.e.c.	9.6	13.5	15.8	6.6	6.5	18.1	34.8	26.2	-14.5	-23.5	-5.5	-12.7	21
Open market paper	1.7	1.5	1.8	1.8	1.1	6.8	2.5	6.8	-2.2	-2.2	-4.2	12.6	22
Other	2.6	5.0	9.5	8.6	6.5	6.5	9.6	13.5	9.1	9.7	8.5	8.1	23
By borrowing sector	66.9	81.9	93.5	86.1	121.1	157.7	183.1	161.6	112.2	94.9	129.4	152.5	24
State and local governments	7.9	9.8	10.7	11.3	17.8	15.2	14.8	18.6	14.7	13.9	15.9	16.8	25
Households	22.4	32.1	33.8	25.3	42.1	64.8	73.5	45.2	49.7	39.0	60.4	72.8	26
Farm	3.3	2.8	3.1	2.7	4.5	5.8	9.7	9.7	4.9	4.0	9.2	11.0	27
Nonfarm noncorporate	4.4	5.3	7.4	5.3	10.3	13.1	12.3	6.3	5.9	3.5	8.4	9.2	28
Corporate	28.9	31.9	38.4	41.5	46.4	58.8	72.9	83.1	37.1	33.5	40.6	46.8	29
Foreign	4.0	2.8	3.7	2.7	5.2	4.0	6.2	15.3	13.0	8.5	17.4	15.7	30
Corporate equities	.1	.2	1.0	.0	.0*	.*	-.2	-.2	-.1	-.1	.1	.3	31
Debt instruments	3.9	2.7	2.7	2.7	5.2	4.4	6.4	15.5	12.8	8.4	17.3	15.3	32
Bonds	1.2	1.1	1.0	2.9	5.9	4.4	1.0	6.4	6.2	5.7	6.7	15.5	33
Bank loans n.e.c.	-.3	-.5	1.3	-.8	2.1	1.0	2.8	4.7	4.0	-.6	7.4	3.7	34
Open market paper	-.5	.2	-.3	-.3	-.8	-1.0	.9	7.1	-.1	-1.2	1.0	.8	35
U.S. Government loans	2.6	2.2	2.1	1.3	1.8	-.3	1.7	1.6	2.8	3.3	2.2	3.2	36
Memo: U.S. Govt. cash balance	1.2	-1.2	-.5	2.5	3.2	-.3	-1.7	-4.6	2.9	2.9	5.2	10.8	37
Totals net of changes in U.S. Govt. cash balances:													38

Credit market funds raised by financial sectors

1	Total funds raised by financial sectors	2.0	17.2	35.2	15.8	17.0	29.1	56.7	43.0	14.8	15.1	14.6	29.7
2	U.S. Govt. related	.1	4.0	9.5	9.8	5.9	8.4	19.9	23.1	13.5	14.0	14.6	18.0
3	Sponsored credit agencies	-.6	3.2	9.1	8.2	1.1	3.5	16.3	16.6	12.3	11.4	3.3	3.9
4	Mortgage pool securities	.7	.5	.7	1.6	4.8	4.9	3.6	5.8	10.3	11.5	9.2	14.2
5	Loans from U.S. Government	-.1	.5									.6	*
6	Private financial sectors	2.0	13.2	25.8	6.0	11.1	20.7	36.8	19.0	13.5	15.1	1.4	11.7
7	Corporate equities	3.1	6.5	4.8	4.8	3.5	3.1	1.5	1.0	1.3	1.1	1.2	1.1
8	*Debt instruments*	-1.7	6.7	19.5	1.2	7.6	18.0	35.3	18.9	12.1	*		*11.0*
9	Corporate bonds		.4	.8	2.7	3.8	5.1	3.5	2.1	.9	3.2	.5	6.1
10	Mortgages	-1.0	.1	.8	.7	2.1	1.7	-1.2	-1.3	2.9	1.0	2.6	1.8
11	Bank loans n.e.c.	-2.0	1.5	1.5	.1	3.5	6.8	14.0	-7.5	-3.9	-4.7	-3.2	-2.8
12	Open market paper and RP's	-1.8	3.4	12.9	-3.5	-.9	4.4	11.8	3.9	-2.8	-7.3	-1.9	8.7
13	Loans from FHLB's	-.5	4.0	4.0	1.8	-2.7	-1.1	6.7	3.9	-4.0	-7.3		-2.3
14	Total funds raised, by sector	2.0	17.2	35.2	15.8	17.0	29.1	56.7	43.0	14.8	15.1	14.6	29.7
15	Sponsored credit agencies	.6	3.5	8.8	8.1	-1.1	3.5	17.3	17.3	3.2	15.1	4.0	14.2
16	Mortgage pools	.7	.5	.7	1.6	4.8	4.9	3.6	5.8	10.3	11.5	9.2	14.2
17	Private financial sectors	2.0	13.2	25.8	6.0	11.1	20.7	36.8	19.9	10.3	1.1	1.4	11.3
18	Commercial banks	*	.8	2.4	-2.0	2.4	4.8	8.1	-1.1	1.7	6.4	-3.0	-1.1
19	Bank affiliates		.4	4.2	-1.9	-.9	.8	2.2	-3.5	-.3	-.9	.2	-1.5
20	Foreign banking agencies		.1		.1	1.6	.8	5.1	2.9	-.3	-.9	.2	-.7
21	Savings and loans associations	-1.7	1.1	4.1	1.8	2.0	2.0	5.0	6.3	-2.1	-7.8	3.6	1.0
22	Other insurance companies		.3	-.5	1.4	.6		6.5		.9		1.0	.7
23	Finance companies	.6	3.9	7.8	2.6	2.7	6.3	9.4	4.5	.7	-1.8	-1.1	6.7
24	REIT's		1.2	1.5	2.2	2.9	6.3	6.5	1.1	-1.9	-1.6	-2.2	-1.9
25	Open end investment companies	3.0	5.9	4.9	2.8	1.3	-.5	-1.2	-1.5	.8	1.5	*	-1.1
26	Money market funds								2.4	1.3	2.6	*	-.7

Total credit market funds raised, all sectors, by type

1	Total funds raised	85.9	115.5	128.7	116.4	168.1	206.0	254.3	231.8	225.2	199.4	251.1	271.7
2	Investment company shares	3.0	5.9	4.9	2.8	1.3	-.5	-1.2	-.5	.8	1.5	.7	-1.1
3	Other corporate equities	2.5	.6	5.2	7.7	13.7	13.8	10.4	5.4	10.4	10.2	10.7	15.4
4	*Debt instruments*	80.4	109.0	118.6	105.9	153.1	192.8	245.2	227.0	214.0	187.7	240.3	257.4
5	U.S. Government securities	13.7	17.4	21.7	11.2	23.7	28.3	34.5	98.0	34.5	93.6	102.4	91.8
6	State and local obligations	7.8	9.5	9.9	11.2	17.5	15.4	16.3	19.6	17.3	16.2	18.4	18.4
7	Corporate and foreign bonds	16.6	14.4	13.8	5.9	23.5	13.6	23.9	19.6	36.3	42.3	30.3	34.4
8	Mortgages	24.6	29.8	30.7	29.9	52.5	76.8	79.9	60.5	59.0	49.1	69.0	74.1
9	Consumer credit	4.5	10.0	8.5	5.9	18.6	21.7	9.8	8.5	-14.4	-27.6	16.0	19.4
10	Bank loans n.e.c.	7.3	14.8	16.1	6.3	12.1	27.8	51.6	38.4	-14.4	-27.6	-1.2	-11.8
11	Open market paper and RP's	3.9	4.8	15.1	-1.1	1.8	4.1	5.2	17.8	6.2	6.2	-5.1	11.8
12	Other loans	2.5	8.3	15.8	7.7	4.2	8.0	18.5	22.5	8.7	6.8	10.7	13.5

NOTE.—Full statements for sectors and transaction types quarterly, and annually for flows and for amounts outstanding, may be obtained from Flow of Funds Section, Division of Research and Statistics, Board of Governors of the Federal Reserve System, Washington, D.C. 20551.

TABLE 14

DIRECT AND INDIRECT SOURCES OF FUNDS TO CREDIT MARKETS

(Seasonally adjusted annual rates; in billions of dollars)

Transaction category, or sector	1967	1968	1969	1970	1971	1972	1973	1974	1975	1975 H1	1975 H2	1976 H1	
Total funds advanced in credit markets to non-financial sectors	81.5	98.3	89.6	94.9	139.6	166.4	190.0	185.0	200.3	173.8	226.9	228.3	1
By public agencies and foreign													
Total net advances	12.0	13.0	16.5	29.2	43.4	19.8	34.2	52.7	44.2	51.9	36.6	52.6	2
U.S. Government securities	6.9	3.3	.5	15.1	34.4	7.6	9.6	11.9	22.5	32.6	12.4	26.9	3
Residential mortgages	-2.6	3.3	5.1	6.5	7.0	7.0	8.2	14.7	16.2	15.9	16.5	11.1	4
FHLB advances to S&L's	.5	.9	4.0	1.3	-2.7	*	6.7	6.7	-4.0	-7.3	-.6	-2.3	5
Other loans and securities	5.2	5.5	6.9	6.2	4.6	5.1	9.2	19.5	9.5	10.6	8.3	16.9	6
Totals advanced, by sector													
U.S. Government	4.7	5.2	3.1	2.8	2.8	1.8	2.8	9.8	15.1	14.9	15.2	5.9	7
Sponsored credit agencies	.6	3.8	.4	11.1	8.9	9.2	21.4	25.6	8.5	15.9	13.2	20.0	8
Monetary authorities	4.8	3.7	4.2	5.3	8.4	9.3	9.2	6.2	8.5	7.0	10.1	13.7	9
Foreign	2.0	-.1	-.3	10.3	26.4	8.4	9.7	11.2	11.1	14.0	-2.0	13.0	10
Agency borrowing not included in line 1	.1	4.0	9.5	9.8	5.9	8.4	19.9	23.1	13.5	14.0	13.1	18.0	11
Private domestic funds advanced													
Total net advances	69.5	89.3	82.5	75.5	102.1	155.0	175.7	155.3	169.6	135.9	203.4	193.8	12
U.S. Government securities	6.3	14.1	5.6	6.6	-3.7	16.1	18.7	22.6	75.5	61.0	90.0	64.9	13
State and local obligations	7.8	9.5	9.9	20.0	19.5	13.1	16.0	19.6	17.3	16.2	18.4	18.4	14
Corporate and foreign bonds	16.0	13.8	12.5	20.0	19.5	13.1	10.0	20.5	32.8	38.9	26.7	27.3	15
Residential mortgages	14.4	17.3	17.9	14.3	31.2	48.1	48.5	26.9	24.7	17.7	31.1	44.3	16
Other mortgages and loans	22.4	35.9	40.7	24.3	35.0	71.9	89.3	71.9	15.7	-5.2	36.5	36.6	17
Less: FHLB advances	-2.5	4.0	4.0	1.3	-2.7	*	7.2	6.7	-4.0	-7.3	-.6	-2.3	18
Private financial intermediation													
Credit market funds advanced by private financial institutions	63.4	75.5	57.4	77.0	109.7	149.4	163.8	126.2	116.0	97.7	134.3	139.2	19
Commercial banks	35.8	38.7	18.6	35.0	50.6	70.5	86.5	64.6	27.6	13.5	41.7	22.1	20
Savings institutions	15.0	15.4	14.6	17.4	39.1	47.2	36.0	27.0	51.0	49.8	52.2	68.0	21
Insurance and pension funds	12.9	13.6	13.3	17.1	14.2	17.8	23.8	30.1	39.3	36.4	42.3	43.9	22
Other finance	-.3	7.6	10.8	7.5	5.9	13.8	17.4	4.5	-1.8	-1.9	-1.8	5.1	23
Sources of funds	63.4	75.5	57.4	77.0	109.7	149.4	163.8	126.2	116.0	97.7	134.3	139.2	24
Private domestic deposits	49.8	45.9	2.3	60.7	89.4	100.9	86.4	69.4	90.5	90.3	90.3	90.9	25
Credit market borrowing	-1.1	6.7	19.5	1.2	7.6	18.0	35.3	18.9	.5	.*	.3	11.0	26
Other sources	14.7	22.9	35.6	15.1	12.6	30.5	42.1	37.8	25.4	7.4	43.4	37.3	27
Foreign funds	2.3	2.6	9.6	-2.9	-3.2	5.3	6.9	14.5	-.4	-5.5	5.0	-.1	28
Treasury balances	.2	2.2	.*	-2.9	3.2	3.7	-1.0	-1.5	-1.7	-5.7	3.5	3.5	29
Insurance and pension reserves	11.4	11.4	10.8	13.3	8.6	11.6	18.4	26.0	29.9	27.4	32.5	32.7	30
Other, net	.8	9.1	15.1	7.1	5.7	12.8	17.8	2.4	-2.4	-10.8	5.9	1.2	31

Line	Private domestic nonfinancial investors													Line
	Direct lending in credit markets													
32	U.S. Government securities	4.9	20.5	44.6	−.3	*	23.6	47.2	48.0	53.2	38.1	69.4	65.6	32
33	State and local obligations	−1.1	8.6	17.5	−7.1	−10.8	4.2	19.4	17.9	23.9	5.0	41.6	29.5	33
34	Corporate and foreign bonds	−2.6	8.2	8.5	−1.3		3.1	7.5	7.5	9.9	10.3	9.6	7.7	34
35	Commercial paper	4.0	4.2	5.4	9.5	8.3	4.2	2.9	5.3	10.4	13.6	7.2	6.0	35
36	(Commercial paper cont.)	1.8	1.8	10.0	−5.1	−8.1	3.0	12.5	4.6	3.1	3.5	2.7	10.2	36
37	Other	2.8	3.6	3.6	3.7	3.2	9.1	6.9	8.1	7.3	5.6	8.9	12.2	37
	Deposits and currency													
38	Time and saving accounts	51.8	48.5	5.1	64.2	92.8	105.3	90.3	75.4	96.7	95.7	97.7	95.1	38
39	Large negotiable CD's	38.4	33.7	−2.2	55.3	79.1	83.7	76.2	76.2	84.8	75.0	94.7	82.3	39
40	Other at commercial banks	4.3	3.5	−13.7	15.0	7.7	8.7	18.4	23.6	−9.7	−22.3	2.9	−23.5	40
41	At savings institutions	17.9	13.7	13.7	22.6	31.8	29.7	29.4	29.4	35.4	34.4	36.4	39.9	41
42		16.6	13.0	8.4	16.6	39.6	45.4	28.4	22.4	59.2	63.0	55.4	66.0	42
43	Money	13.0	14.8	7.3	8.9	13.7	21.6	14.1	8.3	11.9	20.7	3.0	12.7	43
44	Demand deposits	11.0	12.3	4.5	5.5	10.4	17.2	10.2	2.0	5.7	15.3	−4.0	8.5	44
45	Currency	2.0	2.5	2.8	3.5	3.4	4.4	3.9	6.3	6.2	5.4	7.1	4.2	45
46	Total of credit market instr., deposits, and currency	56.8	69.0	49.8	63.9	92.9	129.0	137.5	123.7	150.4	133.8	167.1	160.7	46
47	Private support rate (in per cent)	14.8	13.2	18.4	30.7	31.1	11.9	18.0	28.5	22.1	29.9	16.1	23.0	47
48	Private financial intermediation (in per cent)	91.2	84.6	69.5	102.0	107.4	96.4	93.2	81.2	68.4	71.9	66.0	71.8	48
49	Total foreign funds	4.3	2.9	9.4	2.2	22.5	13.7	7.6	25.7	5.7	8.5	3.0	13.0	49

Corporate equities not included above

Line														Line
1	Total net issues	5.6	6.5	10.1	10.5	15.0	13.3	9.2	4.9	11.2	11.7	10.8	14.3	1
2	Mutual fund shares	3.0	5.9	4.9	2.8	1.3	−.5	−1.2	−.5	.8	1.5	.1	−1.1	2
3	Other equities	2.5	.6	5.2	7.7	13.7	13.8	10.4	5.4	10.4	10.2	10.7	15.4	3
4	Acquisitions by financial institutions	9.1	10.9	13.0	10.6	17.8	15.3	13.3	5.5	8.3	9.2	7.4	11.7	4
5	Other net purchases	−3.5	−4.4	−2.9	−.1	−2.9	−2.1	−4.1	−.7	2.9	2.4	3.4	2.6	5

Notes
Line

1. Line 2 of p. A-56.
2. Sum of lines 3-6 or 7-10.
6. Includes farm and commercial mortgages.
11. Credit market funds raised by Federally sponsored credit agencies. Includes all GNMA-guaranteed security issues backed by mortgage pools.
12. Line 1 less line 2 plus line 11. Also line 19 less line 26 plus line 32.
17. Includes farm and commercial mortgages.
25. Lines 39 plus 44.
26. Excludes equity issues and investment company shares. Includes line 18.
28. Foreign deposits at commercial banks, bank borrowings from foreign branches, and liabilities of foreign banking agencies to foreign affiliates.

29. Demand deposits at commercial banks.
30. Excludes net investment of these reserves in corporate equities.
31. Mainly retained earnings and net miscellaneous liabilities.
32. Line 12 less line 19 plus line 26.
33-37. Lines 13-17 less amounts acquired by private finance. Line 37 includes mortgages.
45. Mainly an offset to line 9.
46. Lines 32 plus 38 or line 12 less line 27 plus line 45.
47. Line 2/line 1.
48. Line 19/line 12.
49. Lines 10 plus 28.

Corporate equities
Lines 1 and 3. Includes issues by financial institutions.

FINANCIAL TRANSACTION LEVELS

Tables 13 and 14 are the data on flow of funds provided in the *Bulletin* of the Fed. The data cover a ten-year period in which our financial system underwent some very serious adjustments. The attitude toward the desirability of holding assets quoted in monetary units fell sharply because of both domestic and foreign developments.

The summary of funds raised, or uses of funds (Table 13) demonstrate an increase in 1975 of $73.2 billion over the 1974 level of $12 billion in funds borrowed by the federal government. This huge quantity of borrowing by the federal government was made possible partially because of a sharp drop of $46.4 billion in credit used by private domestic nonfinancial sectors.

The sources of funds shows where the funds came from to finance the huge increase in the federal government's credit needs. The important role played by an expanding money supply in carrying the heavy need for borrowed funds by the federal government in 1975 is made clear by the increase of $21.0 billion in the total of deposits and currency (line 38 of Table 14).

The impact of monetary policy is reflected most clearly in commercial banks as a source of funds to the credit markets. In 1966 for the first time since 1937, the Fed failed to make reserves available to meet market demands, and interest rates rose above the pattern for the previous thirty years; commercial banks provided only $17.5 billion of funds (source) to credit markets. Conditions were reversed in 1967, and the commercial banks as a source of credit approximately doubled to $35.9 billion. Again in 1969 the Fed failed to meet the demand for funds, and funds provided to credit markets by commercial banks fell to $18.2 billion only to jump back up to $35.1 billion in 1970. From then until 1973 the annual provision of credit by commercial banks increased year by year and reached $86.6 billion in 1973. The Fed began to reduce the growth of reserves in 1974, and the prime rate on July 5, 1974, reached the record high of 12 percent. In 1975 commercial banks as a source of credit declined sharply to a $27.3 billion level.

Each of the rows of sources and users of funds can be analyzed to some extent from the data of Tables 13 and 14.

Full statements for sectors and transaction types quarterly and annually for flows and for amounts outstanding may be obtained from Flow of Funds Section, Division of Research and Statistics, Board of Governors of the Federal Reserve System, Washington, D. C. 20551.

PART IV: SELECTED REFERENCES AND SOURCES

L. Anderson and K. Carlson, "A Monetarist Model for Economic Stabilization," *St. Louis Federal Reserve Bank Review, 52*, April 1970, 7–25.

Board of Governors of the Federal Reserve System, *Introduction to Flow of Funds* (Washington, D.C., 1975).

———, *Flow of Funds in the United States*, 1945–62 and 1939–53 (1963 and 1955) (Washington, D.C.).

Phillip Cagan and Arthur Gandolfi, "The Lag in Monetary Policy as Implied by the Time Pattern of Monetary Effects on Interest Rates," *American Economic Review, 59*, May 1969, 277–284.

Morris A. Copeland, *A Study of Money Flows in the United States* (New York: National Bureau of Economic Research, 1952).

William C. Freund and Edward D. Zinbarg, "Application of Flow of Funds to Interest Rate Forecasting," *Journal of Finance, 18*, May 1963, 231.

Milton Friedman, "The Role of Monetary Policy," *American Economic Review, 58*, March 1968, 1–17.

Richard T. Froyen, "An Alternative Neutralized Monetary Policy Variable and the Implications for the Reverse Causation Controversy," *Journal of Economics and Business, 29*, Fall 1976, 16–21.

A. P. Lerner and F. D. Graham (eds.), *Planning and Paying for Full Employment* (Princeton, N.J.: Princeton University Press, 1946).

W. L. Smith, "On Some Neglected Issues in Monetary Economics: An Interpretation," *Journal of Economic Literature, 8*, September 1970, 767–782.

Part V

Money, Prices, GNP, and Employment

INTRODUCTION

The value of money conventionally is measured only in terms of raw materials, partially finished goods, or finished goods used up in current consumption or in carrying out the production process. The value of financial assets or of existing physical assets is not included in estimating changes in the value of the dollar. This practice has led to serious misinterpretations of what is happening in the economy.

The most famous example was the belief that because wholesale and consumer prices were relatively stable in the late 1920s the economy was sound, and that the new highs in the prices of securities quoted in the stock market were not a measure of inflation. Another misinterpretation was between prices and the quantity of money. Between the mid-1950s and the mid-1960s, wholesale prices of both farm products and industrial commodities were very stable, and M_1 was moving along at a steady upward pace of a few percentage points annually. Conditions did not appear to be developing that would support a major inflation. The analysts were wrong, however, because insufficient attention had been paid to the increasing income velocity of M_1 and the huge annual increase in M_3.

To be a useful approach to economic analysis the position of monetarists, i.e., those believing money supply is the determiner of economic activity and prices and not largely the result, must be helpful in making predictions. If money supply does determine economic activity and if money supply can be controlled by central bank actions, commercial bank control, and the regulation of other financial institutions, then the economy can also be set at the level considered best by those administering these monetary powers of government. In this part the economic theories and the quantities measuring money, prices, GNP, and employment will be examined to gain an understanding of the problems being encountered in efforts to make the economy obey the monetarists and of why the predictions of these economists have not always been useful.

Chapter 18

Measuring the Value of Money

The value of money is most frequently indicated by a concept labeled *general price level*. This is supposed to represent the average of prices of all commodities, services, and property rights currently being bought and sold.

The relationship between the value of money and this general price level is inverse and proportional; for example, a rise of 25 percent in the general price level is equivalent to a decline of 20 percent in the value or purchasing power of money. A price level of 100 increases to 125. This is an increase of 25 percent; 25 is 25 percent of 100. Divide old price level (100) by new price level (125), and you have the purchasing power of the monetary unit. In this case it is 80 percent of its former value, a drop of 20 percent.

Variation in Price Movements. This concept of general price level as a measure of the value of money would be satisfactory if all prices moved in the same direction at the same speed, but this is not the situation. For example, between 1970 and 1976 the value of the dollar in terms of hides, skins, leather, and products decreased by over 54 percent, in terms of lumber and wood products it decreased by about 89 percent, and in terms of energy and oil it decreased by about 160 percent.

Although money is a standard of value, it is difficult to determine its own value. Obviously nothing is said when it is stated that a dollar is worth a dollar, and very little more has been said when it is stated that a dollar is worth 2.36 Swiss francs. The first statement says nothing of the value of a dollar; and the second gives only the value in relation to the Swiss franc, which is only one currency of many, albeit a very strong one.

COMPLEXITY OF DETERMINING VALUE OF MONEY. Even

though the value of money is not known, the generalization can be made that its value changes. The value of money changed in relation to gold when the United States devalued the dollar in 1934. The value of money in relation to wheat changed when the price of wheat rose very rapidly during World War II and in 1973 when large wheat purchases were made by Russia. In both cases the value of money was decreased in relation to a single commodity. It is logical to measure the value of wheat in terms of money because almost all wheat grown is exchanged for money; the same is true of gold production. But it is not logical to measure the value of moeny exclusively in terms of either wheat or gold because money is exchanged for innumerable commodities, services, and property rights other than wheat and gold.

The forces that affect the supply and demand for a particular commodity do not necessarily affect the supply or the demand for all other goods. For example, in 1976 the demand for automobiles was strong and the demand for new homes was relatively weak.

Chart XVIII shows the trend of farm product and industrial commodity prices in the United States since 1910. The failure of prices to fall after World War II, as they did after World War I, is the great new price phenomenon of current economic history. It has been made possible by continued large arms expenditures, social welfare outlays, and a sharp reduction in monetary reserve restrictions plus an increasing money velocity and labor unions strong enough to keep wages rising.

The Unweighted Index Number. It is obvious from this brief discussion that the value of money cannot be stated in terms of one commodity and also that the value of money can be stated only as the purchasing power over all types of commodities. This latter concept of value is very difficult to measure. The best that can be done is to dermine an average of the prices of all goods, services, and property rights. If the average at one time were greater than at a previous time, the conclusion would be that the value of money had declined in inverse proportion. (The method of calculating this decline was indicated above.) However, all commodities cannot be included in arriving at this average; there are just too many different types of commodities.

METHOD OF CALCULATION AND USEFULNESS. It is necessary to select a certain group of commodities and calculate

CHART XVIII

WHOLESALE PRICES

FARM PRODUCTS AND INDUSTRIAL COMMODITIES   QUARTERLY

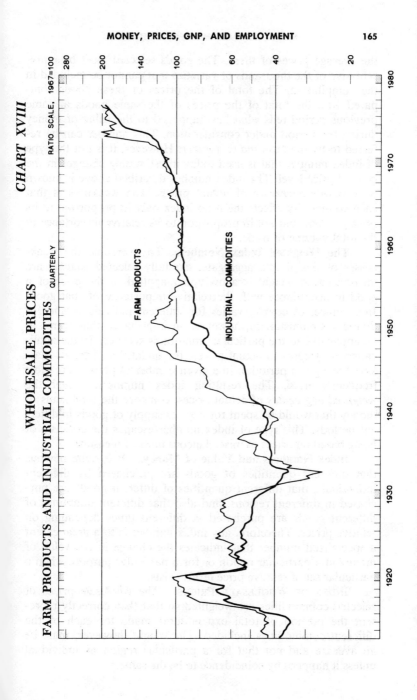

the average prices of these. The goods selected must be representative of the thousands of varieties that cannot be included in the compilation. The total of the prices of these goods compared with the total of the prices of the same goods at some previous period tells what has happened to the value of money during the period under consideration. This number can be referred to by the term *index number*. However, it is not the type of index number that is used today in estimating changes in the general price level. The index number described above is known as a *simple aggregate* of actual prices. The weakness is that each commodity affects the total index only in proportion to its *price per unit*, but not in proportion to its relative importance in the total volume of trade.

The Weighted Index Number. To overcome the weaknesses of this simple aggregate, carefully selected *weights* are introduced. A weight is a multiplier applied to the price of a good in accordance with the relative importance of that good. Importance, of course, varies for different individuals and for different circumstances; however, an importance that seems to be applicable to the particular situation is selected. In the application of weights to actual prices, the quantities of goods marketed in a given period or in a given number of periods are most frequently used. The resulting index numbers, called the *weighted aggregates* of actual prices, compare the total sums of money that would be spent for a given supply of goods in different periods. This type of index number escapes the criticism of being based on prices of miscellaneous units of measure.

Index Numbers and Value of Money. It is quite obvious that different quantities of goods are purchased by different individuals, that different quantities of different goods are purchased in different regions, and also that different quantities of different goods are purchased at different times depending on relative prices. Therefore, any index number is to a great extent a specialized number that indicates the change in the value of money in a particular region or for a particular purpose when a particular set of relative price levels exists.

INDEX OF WHOLESALE PRICES. The wholesale prices of selected commodities are weighted so that they correctly represent the portion of total expenditures made for each of the different commodities included. The weight, however, must be an average and not that for a particular region or individual unless it happens by coincidence to be the same.

INDEX OF COST OF LIVING. This index number does not represent the changes in cost to a manufacturer who buys raw materials; it indicates the changes in the cost of providing the common goods consumed by individuals. It is used extensively to indicate changes in the purchasing power or the value of money received by labor as wages.

Usefulness. A realization of the shortcomings of price indexes does not destroy their usefulness. Although a tool of analysis may be imperfect, this is not justification for casting it aside. Until better methods for measuring the value of money are developed, therefore, it is necessary to employ these currently available indexes. However, they should be employed with caution, always making allowances for their inadequacy.

Inflation Effects. Since 1968 the United States and the nations of the world generally have been experiencing inflation at rates that have seriously injured the health of their economies by distorting the way prices direct investment. The situation ten years later remains serious, although the price indexes of most countries are increasing at about one-half the rate being experienced four or five years ago.

It is easy to consider a 5 or 6 percent inflation rate as normal and not destructive. It is easy also to take for granted that wage increases that keep up with the inflation rate will protect the income earner from a reduction of his economic well-being. Both of these beliefs are not well founded.

The federal progressive personal income tax kept at its present level and an economy growing at a 3.5 percent annual rate and experiencing a 5 percent inflation rate can be destructive of the private sector. The Federal Reserve Bank of St. Louis (May 1977) reports that a person earning $3 an hour in 1976 wouldn't be liable for income taxes, but in forty-five years under the above economic growth and inflation conditions, federal income taxes would be absorbing 46 percent of a current dollar income of $117.89 an hour.

The results of what is normal are downright scary.

Spending Money. The economic concepts of real dollars and constant dollars are useful in evaluating and comparing what has happened to prices in different areas and during different periods of time, but one must not confuse this world of intellectual examination with the real world. No one has ever spent or been paid a real dollar. The only kind of dollar that is spent and received is the current dollar. It is only current dollars that are exchanged for the money of other countries, and it is only current dollars that are saved and invested. Interest and dividends also are only paid in current dollars.

The value of money is what it can buy. A few years ago dollars that the price indexes show to have been very valuable dollars could not buy a colored TV set or a pacemaker for the heart. Less dramatic production and technical development permit the average family in the Southeast to purchase a room air conditioner today for 50 hours of work, whereas thirty years ago it would have required the wages earned from 377 hours of work.

One aspect of the problem of working with money as either a store of value or a measure of value is whether business accounts should be kept on the basis of what is called current value accounting or on historical value, i.e., price paid basis. Undoubtedly machine replacement costs increase with inflation, and depreciation costs included in prices set on sales made through the years are not sufficient to purchase a new machine at current high prices. However, it is also true that depreciation allowances are not typically held as balances quoted in money units but instead are spent month-by-month to meet current needs for funds. Therefore depreciation dollars arising early have the original high value of those used in the purchase of the depreciating asset. Also it must be kept in mind that firms with equipment purchased when dollars were worth more compete with firms that must cover current higher costs. Under these conditions the firm with low-cost equipment will be earning above-average profits. This cost advantage results in a higher return on capital, permitting allocation of profits to cover replacement capital costs that are above the amount in the depreciation account, without reducing current dollar earnings below the average for the industry.

Chapter 19

Savings and Investment Shortages

A major problem of the American economy is maintenance of prices that encourage efficient production at capacity levels. The solution is most frequently discussed in relation to savings and investment and their effect on money flows to the markets where goods and services are offered for sale.

Money Flows. The major problem related to current money flows is keeping the flow correct to remove from the market the goods produced at prices that will encourage additional efficient production. This problem would solve itself if we started at a balanced situation and everyone spent his income as he received it. Say's Law of Markets (production creates its own effective demand) assumed this to be the situation. It is now realized that this assumption is incorrect.

The major cause of the irregular flow of money is that every income-receiver has several choices: (1) he may spend all of his income; (2) he may save a part of his income; (3) he may spend not only his current income, but his past savings, plus what he can borrow.

If the receivers of income should decide to save more funds than can be readily invested in housing and capital goods, for a period of time these savings will seek investment in outstanding securities, causing their price to increase and interest rates to decline. This will lay a base for additional investment, because the cost of commanding savings has been reduced.

On the other hand, the flow of expenditures may have been toward the purchase of investment goods in unusually large quantities. The quantity of investment may be so great that former levels of consumption cannot be maintained. The immediate effect of this condition will be inflationary pressures that will be relieved as the additional investment begins to provide consumer goods.

Finally, the portion of the money income allocated for consumption may be so large that the funds available for investment are not adequate to maintain plants or expand production. The result is that the quantities of consumer goods fail to increase and actually decrease. The effect is stagfation and reduced production efficiency.

LEVELS OF PERSONAL INCOME. Chart XIX shows the trends of income available for individual disposal. Notice the regular increase of disposable income during the period. The disposable income levels of Chart XIX were partly both the cause and the result of the investment expenditures. The increase in disposable income since 1968 has been absorbed largely in higher prices.

LEVELS OF SAVINGS. Savings levels during the first half of the 1940s, the period of World War II, were huge. Between 1951 and 1953 personal savings remained approximately constant, while disposable personal income grew from $226.6 billion to $404 billion.

However, in 1964 personal savings increased by over $6 billion and again in 1967 increased by another $9 billion. This was nearly a 75 percent increase in personal savings while disposable personal income was increasing by about 35 percent. In the 1970s savings as a percent of disposable income continued to fluctuate rather widely. In 1975 personal savings as a percent of personal income reached a new post-World War II high. In 1977 the level was $12 billion below that of 1975.

The data seem to demonstrate that the relationship between personal saving and disposable personal income is very uncertain.

In the National Income Accounts savings equal investment. The concept of savings used is that of gross savings, which in addition to net personal saving includes undistributed profits of corporations, corporation depreciation, and capital outlays charged to current expense, plus other less important aggregates.

With this concept of saving it is obvious that the value of machines in production and the quantity of profits withheld by the corporation are important determinants of the quantity of saving. In fact, as was pointed out above, business depreciation charges have become the most important component of saving in the United States. Gross savings in 1977 at $292 billion were $12 billion above the 1975 level.

The actual sources of savings in a modern industrial nation seem to make the traditional determinants of savings unrealistic and not very useful. The traditional determinants are: (1) the size of income (the propensity to consume is such that as incomes rise, consumption rises less rapidly than income) and (2) the rate of interest offered for savings (a higher rate of interest makes it more worthwhile to save). However, this does not weaken the basic fact that savings cannot be made without income. The necessary conclusion is that the principal cause of savings in the United States during the recent past has been the ability of the business corporation to earn huge incomes and to utilize an important portion of this income to fiance investment. The corporation is able to make savings above depreciation levels because stockholders are willing to leave earnings in the corporation rather than demanding them as dividend payments. And finally, businesses operate efficiently enough to pay good wages to workers who save a portion of their earnings.

In some nations that are rapidly increasing their industrial production, savings arise largely from the ability of the government to collect more in taxes than it spends on goods and services used up during the period. This budgetary surplus on current account permits the government to finance additional investment—which means savings have been made. Another investment speedup procedure in common use in underdeveloped countries is for the government to engage in investment activities with newly created or printed money. With this money they bid goods and services away from consumers by offering higher prices. The effect is inflation, and the type of savings caused is frequently (and rather correctly) given the label "forced savings."

In the United States most savings are made and used by businesses; however, a rising portion of savings (business and personal) are absorbed by the net borrowing of governments. Governments invest, in the American national income account sense, only when they borrow more than they repay. The construction of a road or a new building by government is not treated as an investment. All government expenditures are on current account.

Individuals invest in the American national income account sense when they build a house or purchase a new house,

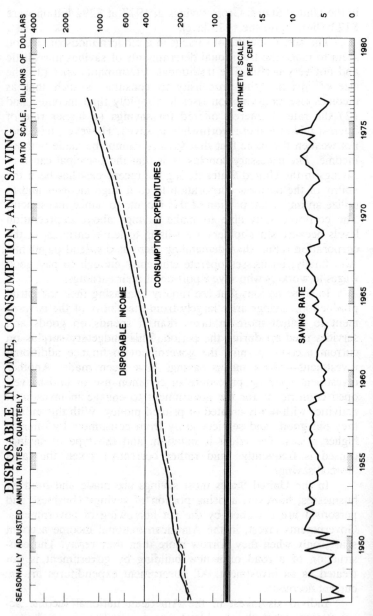

CHART XIX

DISPOSABLE INCOME, CONSUMPTION, AND SAVING

SEASONALLY ADJUSTED ANNUAL RATES, QUARTERLY

RATIO SCALE, BILLIONS OF DOLLARS

DISPOSABLE INCOME

CONSUMPTION EXPENDITURES

ARITHMETIC SCALE
PER CENT

SAVING RATE

but not when they purchase a new automobile or new furniture. However, as we saw, the money flows accounts consider durable consumer goods purchases to be investments.

SOURCE OF INVESTMENT. The most vital aspect of investment is generally considered to be that made by businesses. The most important determinants of this investment are: (1) the profits expected from the investment in relation to the interest rate charged (if profit expectations are much greater than interest cost, businesses will be very anxious to invest) and (2) the movement of interest rates (because, for example, when interest rates are falling the capitalized value, i.e., selling price, of an earning asset increases even though earnings remain the same).

Notice that the direct impact of interest rates is on investment rather than savings. Very likely this effect of the interest rate on investment carries over to savings, but it is very difficult to trace. For example, corporations seem to save less when interest rates are high, because under these circumstances the pressure for higher dividend payments is greater.

LEVELS OF INVESTMENT. Chart XX summarizes investment and source of funds in the private business sector since 1945. The level of gross internal funds and the level of business investment followed each other closely until 1965. The relationship since then has not been close. Much higher and widely fluctuating undistributed profits and bond marketing levels provide the explanations for the shift. The charts also demonstrate the degree to which capital funds and investment were a portion of the 1974 business downturn.

In the past, net foreign U.S. investment often has been below zero. This is because foreigners have found investment in American securities and business very attractive. Thus, though America is much richer than most nations, there was a tendency for foreigners to invest more in the United States than Americans invested abroad. The data for 1956 and 1957 of Chart XXI began to indicate the development of a very large net level of U.S. foreign investments. The U.S. investment in Europe was stimulated by the development of the European Economic Community (EEC), and the slowdown in the growth of the U.S. economy while the level of economic activity in Europe was growing rapidly.

Chart XV compared with Chart XXI demonstrates very clearly that when credit to support domestic investment was

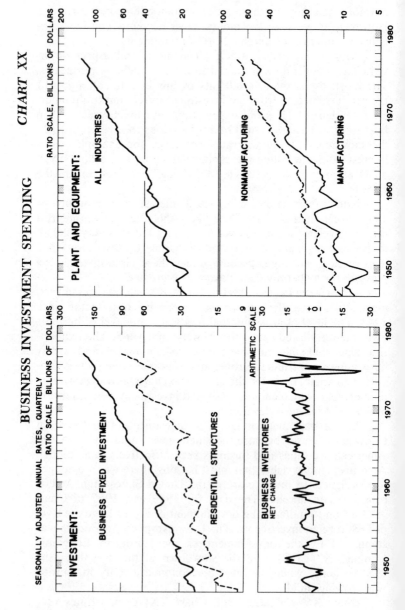

BUSINESS INVESTMENT SPENDING   CHART XX

SEASONALLY ADJUSTED ANNUAL RATES, QUARTERLY
RATIO SCALE, BILLIONS OF DOLLARS

RATIO SCALE, BILLIONS OF DOLLARS

PLANT AND EQUIPMENT:

ALL INDUSTRIES

NONMANUFACTURING

MANUFACTURING

INVESTMENT:

BUSINESS FIXED INVESTMENT

RESIDENTIAL STRUCTURES

BUSINESS INVENTORIES
NET CHANGE

ARITHMETIC SCALE

CHART XXI

CHANGES IN U.S. PRIVATE ASSETS ABROAD

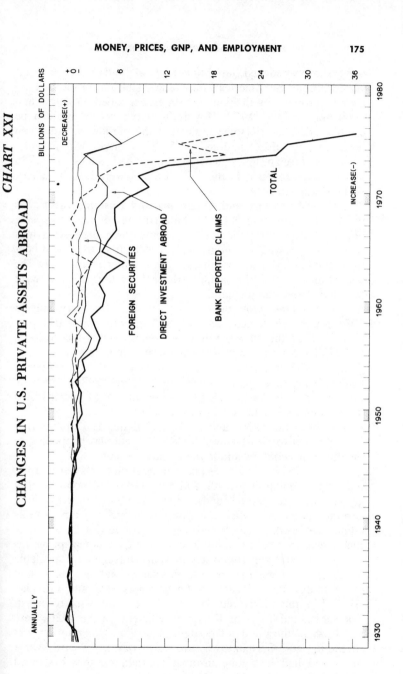

ANNUALLY

BILLIONS OF DOLLARS

DECREASE(+)

INCREASE(−)

FOREIGN SECURITIES

DIRECT INVESTMENT ABROAD

BANK REPORTED CLAIMS

TOTAL

+0
6
12
18
24
30
36

1930   1940   1950   1960   1970   1980

being sharply reduced, large quantities of funds were being invested abroad by American individuals and corporations. Foreign investment in the United States expanded in 1966 and 1969 and again in 1972. Hopefully, a two-way street can be established. There is some indication the outflow of American funds to pay OPEC nations for high oil prices will partially return as foreign investment in the United States. In 1976 OPEC funds invested in the United States were largely in federal government debt.

Capital Shortage and Abundance and Unemployment.   In the Great Depression of 1933 the quantities of savings arising in the private sector pressed the economy down, because savings arising from a weak economy were greater than the investment opportunities even at the sharply lower interest rates. In the depression of 1973 the savings arising from the economy were less than investment demand.

The interest rates on three-month U.S. Treasury bills in 1933 was 0.515 percent, and in 1973 the rate was 7.041 percent. In 1933 the interest rate was moving toward record lows. In 1973 interest rates were moving toward record highs.

In 1933 it became clearly apparent that the portion of income being saved was too high. In 1973 and 1974, it became clearly apparent that the portion of income saved and invested in the domestic private sector was too low.

In both the 1930s and in the 1970s the developing crisis was apparent to all who would examine what was happening to the domestic economy and to the world economy.

In the 1930s birth rates and immigration levels fell sharply, reducing population growth and the traditional sources of a growing need for capital funds. There were few projects with an earnings potential sufficient to permit financing from receipts coming from sale of goods and services produced with the aid of the investment. Neither a big war nor big government programs (such as federal superhighways or space travel) were available to absorb savings. Finally, social security did not exist, and every family had to save to finance accidents and old age. Abroad, in the 1930s, did not look like a good place to invest. The substantial losses on foreign investments of the 1920s were still fresh in the minds of holders of capital. Communism was spreading, and Germany was unable to pay her World War I debts and had just gone through an inflation that destroyed much of the savings of her middle class.

In 1973 the war babies of the birth bulge in 1948 were ready for jobs, homes, and professional education. The United States was still fighting a war that had already resulted in a $60 billion or 22 percent increase in the federal government's debt. The new electronic revolution was affecting every facet of American life. In addition, Europe and many LDCs were realizing economic and social expectations awakened by developments in America.

At the same time as this need for savings expanded, individual need for savings were sharply reduced by expanded social security coverage throughout the world and particularly in the United States and Western Europe. The savings rate remained constant despite an increasing level of disposable income. Consumption as a portion of disposable income increased instead of declining, as it had been assumed in economic analyses of the past forty years.

The result of all these elements in 1973 was a depression and a shortage of savings at one and the same time—something that had been assumed impossible by many observers. The interrelationships that brought this unexpected economic environment into being were a combination of weak federal government fiscal control, i.e., large federal deficits, inflation sensitivity of business and consumers, a tax system encouraging retention of profits, overseas investment, and finally an unindexed income tax that rested heavily on income that was savings prone.

The 1976 and 1977 recovery from the sharp economic decline of 1973–1974 took place on a flood of federal government deficits and a personal savings level as a percent of GNP of 5.34 percent and unemployment estimated to be about 7.5 percent of the labor force. Capital expansion and modernization plus housing were still at modest levels, and price increases were in the 6 percent range with interest rates on three- to five-year issues as high as when unemployment was 4.9 percent.

The estimates of capital needed to provide employment to the 3 to 5 million unemployed who are not needed to provide production flexibility and the 1.5 to 2 million annual additions to the labor force vary considerably. Some of the variation is due to estimates of technological development and the environmental standards to be reached. But even more important are goals as to how modern the capital should be that is used to provide mining, agriculture, transportation, manufacturing, utilities, retailing, and petroleum products. The specifications and data adjustments necessary to come up with a business capital requirement total must be estimates. Some idea is needed of the capital required to make complete use of highest technical development; there data are not available. If, however, cautious estimates are used, a capital shortage arises in the business sector of around 20 percent. This amounts to an increase of business-fixed investment as a ratio of GNP from the 10 percent level in 1976 to 12 percent in 1980.

The capital shortage is substantial, and if current enjoyed productivity efficiency in relation to technical levels available are to be continued along with environment improvement that has been legislated, a 20 percent increase in the savings rate is required to bring about a high level of employment—say at the 4.9 percent of the labor force level. This is more savings as a percent of GNP than the U.S. has experienced since World War II.

In the late 1970s more savings for domestic investment is the road to a high level of employment. In the mid-1930s less savings was the road to a high level of employment.

Chapter 20

Monetary Theory—Prices

The theoretical position under which the Fed was established and given its powers was that if prices were maintained at stable levels, economic development and activity would proceed at the desired level. The development of the Great Depression of the 1930s, which arose after a period of very stable prices (with the exception of security prices), proved this assumption incorrect. Since that time, the job of monetary theory has been to set up the action framework for: (1) stable prices and (2) a high and continuing level of economic activity.

Monetary theory related to the price level is concerned largely with quantitative factors such as the amount of money, the quantity of goods available for exchange, and the like. Monetary theory related to a high continuing level of economic activity is concerned much more with the way in which money receipts and payments flow through the economy.

There are three important classes of monetary theories: (1) the transaction theory, (2) the cash balance theory, and (3) the income-expenditure theory.

Transaction Theory. The transaction type of quantity theory is most frequently summarized in the Fisher equation of exchange:

$$P = \frac{MV}{T}.$$

In this equation, P is the price level, M is the stock or means of payment, V is the velocity of circulation, and T is an index of the physical volume of transactions. This equation is often written $MV = PT$. This equation is a truism as are all equations summarizing the determination of the value of money. The usefulness of the transaction theory and other monetary theories arises largely from the selection of the factors to be considered. This selection has become the basis of the most devastating criticism of the transaction theory. It is pointed out that V is not the appropriate point of emphasis, because it cannot be accurately measured; in addition, its analysis does not yield particularly helpful findings. To overcome a portion of this difficulty, income velocity, i.e., national income divided by the money supply, is used. This eliminates the portion of the problem of measuring V because of the difficulty of separating out spending to purchase and sell securities from spending for goods and services. The same criticism can be levied at T as developed in the transaction theory and is again eliminated by use of national income.

The equation becomes a statement that the quantity of money determines the general price level if it is accepted that the physical quantity of goods (T) is always at capacity level (full employment) and that the velocity (V) remains relatively constant. Also the conventional assumption of classical theory was full employment or capacity production, and the factors affecting V were stated to suggest a great deal of stability; therefore it is justifiable to consider the equation of exchange as an expression of the quantity theory of money.

Cash Balance Theory. The cash balance theory is stated in a formula rather similar to that of the transaction type of quantity theory. In the cash balance analysis the K is the portion of transactions held as cash. The K is the unspent margin and is the reciprocal of the V in the transaction theory. Thus, T multiplied by K and divided into M gives P, or in a formula, $P = \dfrac{M}{KT}$. The cash balance theory considered in this fashion does not aid greatly in making an analysis different from that which can be made with the transaction theory.

The similarity can be clearly shown by inserting numerical values. For example:

$$(P)10 = \left[\frac{(M)10 \cdot 10(V)}{10(T)} \right], \text{ or } (P)10 = \left[\frac{10(M)}{(K)1/10 \cdot 10(T)} \right].$$

The important difference is the change of emphasis. The emphasis of the transactions theory is on speed of expenditure, and that of the cash balance theory is on the quantity of cash holdings.

EMPHASIS OF THEORY. The cash balance theory emphasizes the demand for money as cash rather than the demand for money to complete transactions. The amount of cash that people are willing to hold is determined by a number of motives. The more important of these are: (1) the income motive, (2) the business motive, (3) the precautionary motive, and (4) the speculative motive. These motives are important not only in determining the amount of cash in the sense of bank notes and demand deposits but also in determining the type of asset in which funds will be invested. In the United States today, for example, the liquidity that a person enjoys in holding government savings bonds is practically as great as that which he holds if he happens to have a demand deposit. In the cash balance theory, therefore, federal government savings bonds should be considered money. Also, any determination of what is cash for purposes of economic analysis results partly from what is generally considered cash as well as the characteristics of the item. Actually a fundamental problem of both the transactions and the cash balance theories is the definition of money and/or cash balance (see Index). '

Income-Expenditure Theory. The income-expenditure theory is the final monetary theory possessing a wide acceptance. The theory can be stated in the formula $P = \dfrac{Y}{O}$. In this equation, P is the price level, Y is money outlay (which produces a flow of income), and O is the physical volume of goods and services placed on the market. The theory simply states that when money outlays increase more rapidly than offerings on the market, prices tend to rise. If on the other hand, O increases more rapidly than Y, P may be expected to fall. Recent research has demonstrated that lags between monetary action and results are considerably longer than assumed. This, of course, makes monetary action based on the above theories considerably less helpful than optimists had been assuming.

FACTORS AFFECTING Y AND O. Obviously the size of money outlays is affected by such factors as the quantity of liquid assets, the ability of money to circulate rapidly, and the demand to hold cash balances. However, these factors are not considered of key importance, and many other considerations may enter to restrict or expand Y and also to affect O. Examples of factors influencing Y are the number of marriages, birth rate, degree of competition, type of tax system, and a great list of effects sometimes placed within the group terms "anticipations" and "surprises." O is in turn influenced by a wealth of factors ranging from government power-development programs to labor union policy regarding hours of labor and marketing practices.

ADVANTAGES. The great advantage of the income-expenditure approach to monetary theory is that its use requires continuous examination of the changes in the desires, aspirations, and wants of large portions of the population. The income-expenditure approach leads to economic laws that are stated in terms of how human beings act. This approach to economics substitutes basic economic motives and drives for the previous mechanical adjustments that were required to cause changes based upon a particular set of assumptions.

Link Between Prices and Money: 1970–1976. Cost–push inflation as practiced in the United States has been largely labor pressure to increase wages above improvement in productivity. The higher prices arising from this practice are not expected to result in reduced sales and employment because the Fed will add to bank reserves the amount required to float the new higher prices. The money supply is determined by the wage rates negotiated.

The oil embargo of late 1973 was and continues to be, under price and quantity controls, an example of cost–push inflation much broader in its impact than any labor contract. The establishment of high international oil prices through control over marketings raised the price of energy relative to all other products. All these other products had their costs increased depending on the energy and particularly the oil used in their manufacture and transportation. The new production–consumption balance developed includes somewhat less-energy-intensive goods and services and somewhat more low-energy-intensive goods. Under these new conditions satisfaction will come less from energy exerted mechanically and more through human, animal, and vegetation energy. Also the availability of many customary goods and services decreased, and costs have gone up.

A decrease in living standards arises either as prices increase at a more rapid rate than wage rate expansion, or unemployment of a larger portion of the labor force arises when wages are set high enough to absorb the added energy cost. The realized adjustment likely takes place to some degree in both areas.

The higher prices and increased unemployment were not the result of monetary decisions. The expansion of monetary resources merely acted to bring about part of the adjustment to a lower real GNP through the more acceptable money illusion route rather than through reduced money wages.

Under the cost–push inflation initiated by the international control of oil the people of the world, as represented by energy use and particularly by oil consumption, became poorer —i.e., consumer prices rose relative to income. If it were to act to maintain price stability through monetary actions the Fed would have had to contract the money supply to compensate for the speeded-up velocity. If the Fed entered into this type of monetary action as labor was pushing actively for higher wages to avoid a real decrease in living standards, a very serious economic crisis could have resulted. The business firms would find it difficult to maintain needed liquidity during the adjustment under a restrictive credit policy. The labor leadership would be unable to report money compensation increases to their membership, resulting in disorganization of labor groups. Finally, despite the Fed's restrictive monetary policy, prices would rise because reduced production due to strikes would place demand pressures on reduced supply.

In a nutshell we have here how monetary and supply forces work to affect price levels. The general increases in prices in 1974 were caused by restrictive oil marketing action by governments. The support of these price increases and additional price increase support actions were the result of the Fed acting in a fashion that seemed to be the best adjustment approach to a changed supply situation. The activating force of the inflation was a shift in supply.

The adjustment to the new situation through a price increase was supported by the Fed by providing additional reserves. Monetary action was a secondary element that may have increased or may have decreased prices from the level that would have developed through domestic institutional disorganization and international dislocation under another adjustment procedure.

Prices are linked to money, because it is in money terms that prices are stated. Prices of particular products have an established price linkage with all other goods and services. When this linkage is destroyed through supply shifts or sudden shifts in demand, a period of adjustment to reestablish linkages is needed. This period of adjustment can be accomplished in a number of ways and without Fed action. However, Fed action pressing the adjustment through the good old money illusion appears to be helpful under current institutional arrangements but apparently will be less helpful in the future because of increased inflation sensitivity.

Increasing the Moneyness of Debt. The existing manner in which the federal government assures repayment to holders of debt (i.e., deposits, bonds, mortgages, and other miscellaneous debt) affects the moneyness of debt instruments. The insurance of deposits of banks, savings and loan associations, and credit unions by the federal government, even though the limit is set at $40,000 per deposit, must substantially reduce the level of reserves held, the quality of loans and investments, interest rates earned and paid, and therefore the costs of attracting and holding deposits.

The federal government's activity in guaranteeing mortgages under the FHA, the VA, and other agencies, works toward reducing the cost of attracting funds to meet the financing needs of the construction industry. It therefore expands the quantity of credit that will be available to finance new housing. This happens because the moneyness of these guaranteed debt instruments has been increased.

The credits extended to those selling and investing abroad and to those operating small businesses have also had their moneyness increased by federal government action. Here the international action has been carried out through a federal insurance program (Overseas Private Investment Corporation) and the Export-Import Bank. The Small Business Administration has provided guarantees of loans by commercial banks to small businesses. All of these guarantees basically protect the moneyness of deposits in financial institutions that are in excess of the deposit insurance maximums.

This brief excursion into federal financial activity, beyond that of ordinary money and high-powered money creation and contraction, has been taken to point out that institutional arrangements are a very important group of real-world determiners of perceived liquidity, the interest rate level, and the structure of interest rates.

The insurance and guarantee commitments of the federal government are immense. Estimates are made on a variety of bases; because the dollar during the past five years has been very unstable the real potential burden of the commitments has become even more difficult to establish. A total frequently used is $2 trillion.

The question being asked here, however, is not how large is the federal government's potential, and in most cases very real, dollar commitments. Rather it is: has all of this increase in moneyness of obligations by federal government action affected proneness toward inflation and decreased the ability of the economy to adjust to meet new situations? The answer must be yes. These insurance and guarantee commitments obviously act to prevent losses due to a variety of causes, in many cases because investment commitments were made unwisely. Just as obviously these wastes and failures to decrease credit outstanding prevent the loss from being really felt by the individual provider of funds. Instead, everyone pays through inflation as the liquidity of the society is increased without a compensating increase in productivity.

Chapter 21

Monetary Theory—Interest Rates

The theory of the determinants of the rate of interest is best discussed as consisting of two parts. The first part is the Keynesian concept of *liquidity preference*. The second part is the traditional *loanable funds* concept.

When interest rates are considered within the liquidity preference framework it is the money supply working in relation to the willingness to hold liquidity that sets the market rate of interest. When interest rates are considered within the loanable funds framework it is the demand for loanable funds in relation to the supply of loanable funds made available in the capital markets that sets the rate of interest.

The loanable funds approach looks to the *flow* of funds and the demand for the flow during a relatively short period of time. The liquidity preference approach utilizes a *stock* of money and a given liquidity preference or desire to hold this money at an instant of time.

The liquidity preference theory runs in terms of the demand and supply of money. The loanable funds theory runs in terms of supply and demand for debt securities.

Relation to Money Supply. Under conditions of an expanding money supply interest rates are assumed to decline. This decline in interest rates will stimulate investment by reducing the cost of borrowing but will not decrease savings as a portion of income. When income is increased because of the impact of this new investment, savings also will rise. The expanded income therefore lays the basis for more savings and a sustained higher income due to lower interest rates that are maintained after the original push toward lower interest rates that arose from the original expansion of the money supply.

The word *multiplier* has been used as the term that presents the relationship between the expansion of national income and the expansion of investment. Income is usually assumed to increase by 1.7 or 2.0 times the increase in investment. When this relationship is seen to exist, it means that investments have been carefully made so that the productivity of a man working with machines has increased. In LDCs the multiplier relationship often has been assumed, but frequently it has not been there. The investments, instead of increasing real income, caused a decrease because the debt that was incurred bid away from productive uses resources that were later wasted in unproductive projects. The result was an expansion of the money supply and inflation that worked to decrease the soundness in terms of real productivity of many economic decisions not directly associated with the economic growth effort.

Sometimes the analysis of interest rates takes place through use of a diagram such as the one provided below. The *IS* curve, which is normally down-sloping to the right, is the function of the interest rate and the demand for all goods and services. The *IS* slope to the right indicates an expansion of demand generated largely by an increase of investment, i.e., the *IS* curve is very steep if investment has little interest–sensitivity.

The second curve in Diagram I slopes upward and to the right. It is labeled the *LM* curve. It is constructed from a schedule showing the rates of interest and levels of income for which the money market is in equilibrium, i.e., people are neither trying to increase or decrease their money holdings. The analysis summarized in Diagram I permits combining of the traditional loanable funds theory of the interest rate, the *IS* curve, with the liquidity preference theory, the *LM* curve; it also allows us to relate both to interest rates and income levels. The combination permits one to include in a single diagram and in a single analysis model the important roles of the multiplier and the interest rate (the *IS* curve) and the income and transaction demand for these funds (the *LM* curve) as forces working together to determine the equilibrium rate of interest.

Keynesian and Monetarist Models. Diagram I has been popular through the years because it can be modified readily to express changed assumptions or conditions. For example, the monetarists like to demonstrate the special case where demand for money depends on income alone. Under these conditions the *LM* curve is completely vertical, and an increase in the money supply increases *Y* (income) by the money supply times

DIAGRAM I

DETERMINATION OF EQUILIBRIUM INTEREST RATE WITHIN NATIONAL INCOME FRAMEWORK

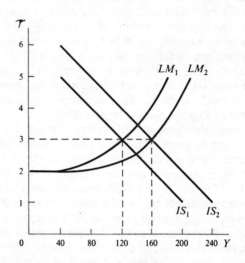

a constant velocity. To show what happens, just draw another vertical *LM* parallel and to the right of the first *LM*. Income expands by money supply times the constant velocity, demonstrated by the slope of the *IS* curve.

Another extreme position is to have a completely horizontal *LM*. This illustrates the famous liquidity trap idea. The *LM* after an increase in money supply is right on top of the old horizontal *LM*. Money is increased without affecting *LM*, and income remains constant.

Another extreme approach is to assume *IS* is vertical and *LM* has the normal upward to the right slope. An increase in the money supply moves *LM* to the right. The new equilibrium interest rate is lower than the previous rate, but income (Y) remains the same. The effect of an increased money supply on income is zero, just as it was when *LM* was horizontal.

When the *IS* and *LM* curves are in the normal position as

shown in Diagram I, an increase in the money supply moves the *LM* curve downward and to the right. The new equilibrium rate of interest is where the new *LM* intersects the original down-sloping *IS* curve. The interest rate has been reduced by the liquidity effect of the new money supply and increased by the income effect, but the downsloping *IS* curve prevents the income effect from nullifying the downward pressure on interest rates caused by the expansion of the money supply.

It is also possible that the demand for funds by investors expands because of the profitability of recent investments. When this happens the *IS* curve is moved upward and to the right. If this happens the new equilibrium rate of interest that results from an original stimulus of the economy by an increase of the money supply is higher than that existing when the original money supply increase was initiated.

Finally, Diagram I can be used to illustrate the effect on interest rates and income of budgetary policy. If the government increases its deficits, i.e., greater demand for savings, the *IS* curve is moved upward and to the right. If, however, *LM* is completely vertical the action does not increase *Y* (income) but is entirely used up in a higher *r* (interest rate). On the other hand, if *LM* is completely horizontal the deficit budgetary program is completely effective, and an increase in the demand for funds to meet liquidity needs does not act to drain off some of the expansionary impact of the deficit-financed spending.

PART V: SELECTED REFERENCES AND SOURCES

Robert D. Auerbach and Jack L. Rutner, "Money and Income: Is There a Simple Relationship," *Federal Reserve Bank of Kansas City, Monthly Review*, May 1975, 13–19.

Stephen H. Axilrod, "Liquidity and Public Policy," *Federal Reserve Bulletin*, October 1961, 1164–1169.

V. Lewis Bassie, "The Real Rate of Interest: A Thesis in Pseudoscience," *Faculty Working Papers #306* (Champaign, Ill.: University of Illinois, 1976).

William Brainard and Michael C. Lovell, "Some Simple Propositions Concerning Cost–Push Inflation," *American Economic Review*, 56, September 1966, 857–866.

E. Bresciani–Turroni, *The Economics of Inflation* (London: Allen and Unwin, 1937).

Business Week, "The New Keynesians Have a New Prescription," May 12, 1975, 42–44, 46.

————, "The Critics Ask: Is Monetarism Dead?" June 7, 1976, 63–64.

Jean Crockett, Irwin Friend, and Henry Shavell, "The Impact of Monetary Stringency on Business Investment," *Survey of Current Business, 67,* August 1967, 10–27.

S. Homer, *A History of Interest Rates* (New Brunswick, N.J.: Rutgers University Press, 1963). (2nd ed., 1977)

J. M. Keynes, *How to Pay for the War* (New York: Harcourt-Brace, 1940).

Tong Hun Lee, "Alternative Interest Rates and the Demand for Money: The Empirical Evidence," *American Economic Review, 57,* December 1967, 1168–1179.

Alan Sweezy, "The Keynesians and Government Policy, 1933–1939," *American Economic Review, 62,* May 1972, 116–124.

Part VI

Deposit Credit Institutions Other Than Commercial Banks

INTRODUCTION

The two largest institutional groupings, the mutual savings bank (MSB) and the savings and loan association (S&L), have many similarities. From their very inception, however, sharp and important differences have existed in the goals, philosophies, portfolio policies, and regulation requirements of MSBs and S&Ls. The third deposit institution is the credit union (CU), and it has developed out of another set of goals and from another organizational background.

The MSB was begun out of a desire to provide working people with a safe place to deposit their savings. The S&L was started so that people would be able to borrow the money needed above their own savings to finance the purchase or construction of a home. The CU arose as a portion of a personnel policy of businesses and government agencies that encouraged employees to save and at the same time provided them with an opportunity to borrow cheaply and readily to meet their household needs for credit.

These three deposit financial groupings, along with the commercial banks, are government regulated and benefit from the availability of government-provided deposit insurance. However, they are privately owned and controlled and are not government institutions.

The growth of the three deposit groupings discussed in this part has been rapid, as has that of the commercial banks and the financial institutions that are a portion of one-bank holding company operations. This growth has resulted in a sharp reduction in the portion of the financing needs of America that are met directly. Instead, surplus units make a deposit, and the institutions receiving the deposit purchase the security or loan contract offered by the deficit unit.

191

This shift to the use of intermediary deposit institutions by relatively small, nonbusiness or farming savers in particular indicates a choice for greater security and reduced earnings from savings. Undoubtedly, the greater security has been provided partially by better government regulatory legislation and inspections; the principal source, however, has been government insurance of deposits.

The flow of funds data of Chapter 17 demonstrate the very dominant place deposit and other types of financial intermediaries occupy in providing the source for funds needed by deficit units.

The exclusion of life insurance, mutual funds, and pension funds plus the many intermediary financial institutions of the federal government and international institutions from this part is justified on the basis of a selection determined by whether savers receive assets that have the basic characteristics of deposits and the moneyness qualities of deposits and whether the ownership and control is in private banks.

The MSBs and S&Ls have been plagued by the instability arising from owning long-term assets, largely mortgages, and owing depositors on short-term deposit commitments. They have not been able to adjust their financial position so that short-term deposits are matched with short-term loan or security maturities. This problem has been exacerbated because interest rates became very volatile during the 1966–1976 period.

Legislation and special credit arrangements have been developed to mitigate the impact on the operations of MSBs and S&Ls of their unhedged credit extension position. The problem still exists, however, and new proposals are being considered by Congressional committees. The difficulty remains partially because institution managers have lagged in establishing new portfolio investment policies. A changed portfolio policy requires reeducation of management to new concepts and the injection of new management that can make judgments about mortgage markets and other financial markets on the basis of scanty information.

Chapter 22

Savings and Loan Associations

The original savings and loan associations were temporary home builders' clubs that operated as mutual or cooperative organizations. The members agreed to pay a certain amount each month, and the funds so obtained were used to finance construction or to purchase houses. Borrowers gave the associations mortgages on their homes and made monthly payments until the mortgages were retired. These clubs later became permanent but still operated on this restricted principle. Some continue to operate in this fashion, but the savings bank procedure is definitely the modern trend.

The 4,600 federally chartered savings and loan associations are cooperatives. This has meant the boards are less stimulated to make profits than are boards representing stockholders. In 1977 the Federal Home Loan Bank Board (FHLBB) cut back on the self-serving actions of savings and loan boards and set down the rule that only one-third of board members could represent management. Savings and loan associations suffered serious losses during the depression of the 1930s through the general economic conditions that caused great reductions in real estate values. In most cases, however, they were able to continue in operation and have experienced a great boom in activity during the post-World War II period. Between 1948 and 1960 they were more successful in attracting additional savings than savings departments of commercial banks or mutual savings banks. Between 1964 and 1968 deposits of commercial banks rose much more rapidly than savings and loan shares. The commercial bank success was largely due to the introduction of the negotiable certificate of deposit (CD) and the modification of Regulation Q by the Federal Reserve Board to permit the payment of higher interest rates on CDs and other time deposits. The S&Ls were hurt by the high interest rates of 1969 and 1974. However, by 1977 they had recovered their ability to compete for deposits.

Legislation of the 1930s. The Home Owners Loan Act of 1933 provided for the Federal Savings and Loan Associations and the Federal Home Loan Bank Board (FHLBB) with regional Federal Home Loan Banks (FHLB). The organization is similar to that of the Fed. Prior to this time all savings and loan associations grew very rapidly despite the prohibition of accepting deposits. The purchase of shares was arranged so that to the depositor, legally a shareholder, the inconvenience was slight. All federal associations must insure their accounts with the Federal Savings and Loan Insurance Corporation (FSLIC), which was established in 1934. State associations also utilize this insurance, which corresponds to the Federal Deposit Insurance Corporation in the banking area.

The modern S&L is a federally chartered, mutual savings bank or a state-chartered capital stock or mutual savings bank. Capital stock S&Ls hold about 23 percent of total S&L assets. All restrictions on deposit differentiation were removed in 1968 and 1971. Deposits are invested in government and industrial bonds as well as in loans on urban residential real estate. The total assets of S&L are about twice as great as those of the MSBs. Geographically, S&Ls are more widely dispersed than MSBs. California accounts for about 17 percent of all assets, with Florida, Illinois, and Ohio following with over 7 percent each.

Deposits are insured up to $40,000 per account. The regular deposit insurance premium paid annually is $1/12$ of 1 percent of all accounts. The percent may not go above $1/8$ of 1 percent, but member institutions also may be called upon for 1 percent of their total savings accounts. Provision also exists in the legislation adopted in 1962, and modified since then, for additional payments into FSLIC reserves when they fall below about 1.5 percent of savings deposits of member S&Ls. The number of insured S&Ls is divided about equally between federal and state-chartered associations. The state-chartered S&Ls of Mississippi have been distinct in being noninsured. They encountered difficulties in 1975, which may result in a growth of FSLIC state-member associations.

If an S&L gets into trouble, the FSLIC can purchase the assets or make a contribution or loan to allow time for a merger

CHART XXII

PRINCIPAL EARNING ASSETS AND LIABILITIES—SAVINGS AND LOAN ASSOCIATIONS

AMOUNT OUTSTANDING; END OF YEAR, 1946–51; END OF QUARTER, 1952–

RATIO SCALE, BILLIONS OF DOLLARS

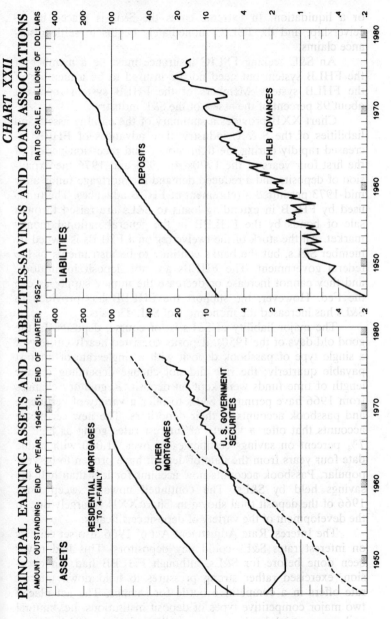

or a liquidation. In extreme cases the S&L is placed in receivership, and the FSLIC immediately begins to settle insurance claims.

An S&L seeking FSLIC insurance must be a member of the FHLB system but need not be insured to be a member of the FHLB system. Members of the FHLB system represent about 98 percent of the assets of the S&L industry.

Chart XXII provides a summary of the earning assets and liabilities of the S & L industry. The advances of FHLB increased rapidly during the tight money and recession period of the first four years of the 1970s. In 1975 and 1976 the expansion of deposits and a reduced demand for mortgage funds after mid-1973 permitted a retirement of FHLB advances. The funds used by FHLB in extending loans to S&Ls are raised through sale of bonds by the FHLBB in the general national money market. All the stock of the twelve regional FHLBs is owned by member S&Ls, but the banks continue to be instruments of the federal government. The FHLBs are not deposit institutions, and they cannot increase or decrease the money supply as can the Fed. However, the support the FHLBB has provided to S&Ls has increased the moneyness of S&L deposits.

The major liability of S&Ls is, of course, deposits. In the good old days of the 1950s, deposits consisted nearly entirely of a single type of passbook deposit with a single rate of interest payable quarterly; the rate did not change depending on the length of time funds were kept on deposit. Regulatory changes from 1966 have permitted S&Ls to offer a variety of certificate and passbook accounts to their depositors. The new certificate accounts that offer a variety of interest rates going as high as 7¾ percent on savings certificates of over $1,000 with a due date four years from the date of deposit have proven to be very popular. Passbook accounts now account for less than half the savings held by S&Ls. The continued upward sweep since 1966 of the deposit total shown in Chart XXII is largely due to the development of the variety of deposit certificates.

The Interest Rate Adjustment Act of 1966 also set ceilings on interest rates S&Ls could pay depositors. This had never been done before for S&Ls, although FHLBB had, on occasion, exercised rather strong pressures to hold down interest rate offers in a competitive battle for savings. The act placed two major competitive types of deposit institutions, i.e., mutual and commercial banks, under similar restrictions, but it excluded credit unions. However, the interest rate MSBs and S&Ls could pay on various types of deposit certificates was set ¼ percent higher than the rate commercial banks could pay. One final point—since 1973 no interest rate ceilings are imposed on CDs of over $100,000; the rate paid is set by all the various competitive forces operating in the money markets of the world. By the end of 1976 interest rates were below the ceiling rates, and the interest rate freedom of CDs of over $100,000 was not being used.

The use of S&L deposits to purchase assets during the past thirty years is also summarized in Chart XXII. The dramatic climb in mortgages other than to finance one- to four-family residences highlights the trends depicted. This is caused partially because Chart XXII is drawn on a ratio scale. The increase in other mortgages during the past fifteen years was about $60 billion, while the total of one- to four-family mortgages grew by $140 billion. The same phenomenon of charting through use of a ratio scale makes the growth of ownership of U.S. government securities appear to be very substantial.

Of course, the growth outside of one- to four-family residential mortgages has been an important aspect of S&L development during the past thirty years. The invasion of the single-family home mortgage market by other lending institutions is another side of this shift. Commercial banks hold substantial quantities of FHA or VA guaranteed mortgages on single-family residences. Also commercial bank-dominated, one-bank holding companies frequently include a mortgage company as one of their operating units (see Index). Nevertheless, S&Ls during the past fifteen years have been able to increase the percentage they hold of total conventional first mortgages on single-family homes. Also in the multifamily mortgage area, the S&Ls are the single largest provider of mortgage funds.

Federal Government Lending. In the 1960s the term *second-layer lenders* began to be used. The term refers basically to federal government agencies created by Congress to assure that funds are available on reasonable terms to finance new housing construction and rehabilitation. They include the Federal National Mortgage Association (FNMA), the Government National Mortgage Association (GNMA), and the Federal Home Loan Bank Board (FHLBB), plus the Federal Home Loan Mortgage Corporation, a component of the FHLB system (see Index). They were stimulated by the money crisis of 1966, the first since the early 1930s, and then again by the money crisis of 1969 and 1973–1974.

Although second-layer lenders have been particularly active in financing mortgage credit during the recurrent money crises of the past ten years, they also have become net providers of funds for mortgage financing during the more normal periods. Undoubtedly a partial explanation of this development was the large housing boom that arose during the late 1960s and early 1970s. Another is the overall shortage of savings to meet domestic public sector and private sector needs. Also, restrictions on interest rates and services that S&Ls could offer reduced the competitive advantage over commercial banks that S&Ls had enjoyed during the 1950s. Finally, the great instability of interest rates during the past ten years reduced the ability of S&Ls to lend long-term and borrow short-term. This has, in turn, stimulated serious thinking about procedural changes; for example, the variable rate mortgage, renewable five-year mortgages, and the sale of bonds with maturities and interest rates corresponding to the mortgages providing the security (see Index).

Chapter 23

Mutual Savings Banks

The first real MSB was established in Scotland in 1810 by the church as a method of helping the poor. They multiplied rapidly in Great Britain. After a number of scandals they were placed under government regulation.

The first MSB was established in the United States in 1816 in Philadelphia as the Philadelphia Savings Fund Society. Each MSB is managed by a self-perpetuating board of trustees that serves without pay. In the past members of the board frequently have been paid indirectly through business developed from their trustee relationship with an MSB.

The MSBs are largely in the northeastern portion of the United States with a very considerable concentration in New York. The geographical distribution of MSB offices and the geographical distribution of deposit growth in 1975 is shown in Table 16. The growth of deposits of $11.173 million in 1975 is about a 10 percent increase; this approximates the inflation rate in the construction industry during the same period. Therefore in 1975 the real resources available from MSBs to finance construction did not expand.

The poor 1975 record was corrected somewhat during the first half of 1976. There can be little doubt but that the basic cause of the weakness in deposit growth in 1975 arose from the immense federal budgetary deficits that necessitated very large placements of new government securities. By September 1975 the yield on U.S. government securities with a three- to five-year maturity were 4 basis points above the 7¾ ceiling rate that MSBs could pay on deposits. The government deficits during this recession period prevented the development of lower interest rates and the stimulating multiplier effect they have on the private sector, through both an increase in the market value of

BALANCE SHEET OF THE MUTUAL SAVINGS BANK INDUSTRY, DECEMBER 31, 1975 AND 1965.   TABLE 15

(Millions of Dollars)

Item	Amounts outstanding Dec. 31, 1975	Amounts outstanding Dec. 31, 1965	Increase 1966-75 Amount	Increase 1966-75 Per cent	Percentage distribution Dec. 31, 1975	Percentage distribution Dec. 31, 1965
ASSETS						
Cash	2,330	1,017	1,320	129.8	1.9	1.8
U.S. Government securities	4,740	5,485	−685	−12.5	3.9	9.4
Federal agency securities	2,767	846	1,923	227.3	2.3	1.5
State and municipal securities	1,545	320	1,241	387.8	1.3	.6
GNMA mortgage-backed securities	3,367	—	3,367	—	2.8	—
Corporate and other bonds	17,536	2,898	14,362	495.6	14.5	5.0
Corporate stock	4,322	1,426	2,953	207.1	3.6	2.5
Mortgage loans	77,221	44,433	32,977	74.2	63.8	76.3
Other loans	4,023	862	3,250	377.0	3.3	1.5
Guaranteed education	557	n.a.	n.a.	n.a.	.5	n.a.
Consumer installment	608	n.a.	n.a.	n.a.	.5	n.a.
Home improvement	444	n.a.	n.a.	n.a.	.4	n.a.
Other	2,414	n.a.	n.a.	n.a.	2.0	n.a.
Other assets	3,205	944	2,268	240.3	2.6	1.6
TOTAL ASSETS	121,056	58,232	62,976	108.1	100.0	100.0
LIABILITIES						
Total deposits	109,873	52,443	57,783	110.2	90.8	90.1
Regular deposits	109,291	52,204	57,415	110.0	90.3	89.7
Ordinary savings	69,653	n.a.	n.a.	n.a.	57.5	n.a.
Time and other	39,639	n.a.	n.a.	n.a.	32.7	n.a.
Other deposits	582	239	367	153.6	.5	.4
Borrowings and mortgage warehousing	555	1,124	1,602	142.5	.5 }	1.9
Other liabilities	2,200 }				1.8 }	
General reserve accounts	8,428	4,665	3,591	77.0	7.0	8.0
Capital notes and debentures	185	2	183	n.a.	.2	*
Other general reserves	8,243	4,663	3,408	73.1	6.8	8.0
TOTAL LIABILITIES	121,056	58,232	62,976	108.1	100.0	100.0

earning assets and an expansion of profitable investment opportunities.

Assets. Table 15 summarizes the balance sheet of all MSBs at the end of 1965 and the end of 1975. During this ten-year period of violent fluctuations in interest rates, but also of very substantial economic growth and a big housing boom in 1972 and 1973, the assets of MSBs about doubled in money terms. This is an increase of about 20 percent when deflated by the wholesale price index and a slight decrease when deflated by the home-ownership Consumer Price Index (CPI).

Although mortgage loans dominate the assets of MSBs, they are also substantial investors in corporate and other bonds, including U.S. government securities. This investment freedom available to MSBs has enabled them to hedge their financial position somewhat through ownership of a considerable quantity of assets with maturities corresponding more closely to those of their deposits. The reduced liquidity of MSBs in 1974 arose from massive disintermediation in the April-October period. This in turn pressured the MSBs to use their available funds in 1975 to purchase short-term corporate and government securities at a considerable sacrifice of earnings, because the yield curve prevailing in 1975 sloped sharply upward as maturities lengthened (see Table 16).

Time Deposit Market. The commercial bank total of time deposits at the end of 1975 was $450,615 million, or over four times the total deposits of MSBs. During the hectic 1972–1975 period for the MSBs the time deposits of commercial banks remained much more stable and grew at a steady rate. The ability of commercial banks to attract year-by-year a higher portion of household savings has been an important element in the development of saving accounts markets. The commercial banks' share of the growth of time deposits grew from 30 percent during the 1956–1966 period to 51 percent in the 1966–1975 period. The reduced demand for business loans in 1975 and 1976 reduced the appetite of commercial banks for savings as CDs or as open-account deposits. This has improved the competitive position of MSBs.

Federal Charter. The MSB is the only one of the four deposit financial institutions that does not have available federal charters. The granting of federal charters would be a continuation of the general practice of dual deposit institution chartering. The first provision of the Financial Institutions Act of 1975,

TABLE 16

DEPOSIT GROWTH OF MUTUAL SAVINGS BANKS BY STATE, 1973, 1974, AND 1975.

State	Net change in total deposits, including interest (millions of dollars)			Percentage change in total deposits		
	1975	1974	1973	1975	1974	1973
New York	5,574	1,082	2,279	10.1	2.0	4.4
City	3,826	274	1,232	9.5	.7	3.2
Upstate	1,748	808	1,047	11.9	5.8	8.1
Massachusetts	1,509	279	640	10.1	1.9	4.5
Boston	333	−104	−27	8.6	−2.6	−.7
Outside Boston	1,176	383	667	10.6	3.6	6.6
Connecticut	1,013	378	539	13.0	5.1	7.8
Pennsylvania	1,127	407	407	17.0	6.5	7.0
New Jersey	715	222	315	15.0	4.9	7.4
Washington	336	197	146	15.7	10.1	8.1
New Hampshire	167	54	110	11.3	3.7	8.2
Maine	192	90	106	13.8	6.9	8.9
Rhode Island	156	90	144	15.0	9.5	10.1
Maryland	92	27	60	9.2	2.4	5.8
Vermont	64	30	30	14.5	7.3	8.0
All other states	228	98	80	12.1	5.5	4.7
TOTAL	11,173	2,954	4,856	11.3	3.1	5.3

which was the result of five years of effort including intensive study by the Hunt Commission, was to authorize federal charters to MSBs. The legislation proposed permitted MSBs choosing to convert to federal form to retain those assets and departments allowed under state law at the time of conversion.

One of the departments some MSBs are going to wish to retain under federal charter is the life insurance department. MSBs in New York, Massachusetts, and Connecticut sell life insurance directly to the public. Another department of importance provides for negotiable orders of withdrawal, i.e., NOW amounts. When national uniform legislation for federal chartering of MSBs is adopted, the preservation of state grants of NOW accounts and other provision for third-party payment powers, i.e., checking accounts or payment order accounts, will be insisted upon. Currently, NOW accounts legislation has been adopted in the New England states and New York and New Jersey, with Oregon granting its single MSB the power to establish checking accounts.

Account Transferability, Safety, and Interest Rates. This whole matter of payment order accounts became very important to MSBs when the social security administration began the direct deposit of checks in October 1975. The availability of checking accounts at the same institution that receives social security checks is very important to many actual and potential users of MSB services.

Although membership of an MSB in the Federal Reserve has not been prohibited the cost has outweighed benefits, and MSBs have not joined. There is a possibility that a new type of membership will be established that permits long-term advances during periods of disintermediation at a nominal annual membership charge and suitable interest charges on advances made.

The MSB can join the Federal Deposit Insurance Corporation (FDIC) and the Federal Home Loan Bank System. Most MSB's outside of Massachusetts, which has its own deposit insurance plan, are members of FDIC. FDIC, of course, was established by Congress largely to insure the deposits of commercial banks. It was not until 1966 that the FDIC and the Fed applied interest rate ceilings to thrift institutions as well as to commercial banks.

The thrift institution ceiling was first set $\frac{1}{2}$ percent higher than for commercial bank savings accounts. On November 1, 1973, the differentiation was reduced to $\frac{1}{4}$ percent. In June 1975 the commercial banks requested that the FDIC and the Fed eliminate the $\frac{1}{4}$ percent differentiation as it applied to Individual Retirement Accounts (IRA). Because IRA deposits are ideal (due to the length of the commitment) for hedged mortgage lending, the appeal was turned down. Chart XXIII provides a summary of growth of MSB earning assets and deposits.

Access to automated clearinghouses (ACH) is one other area of great concern to MSBs as they move toward providing one-stop financial services for savers. ACH regional facilities are available down the east coast and at Portland, Oregon. Action has been initiated to gain full access to the Fed's national transfer of funds facilities. This development again is necessary because of the social security direct-deposit program and the development of NOW accounts and other third-party payment powers.

The Financial Institutions Act of 1975 failed to include many of the provisions of the Hunt Commission report. The development of a financial institution system that would better

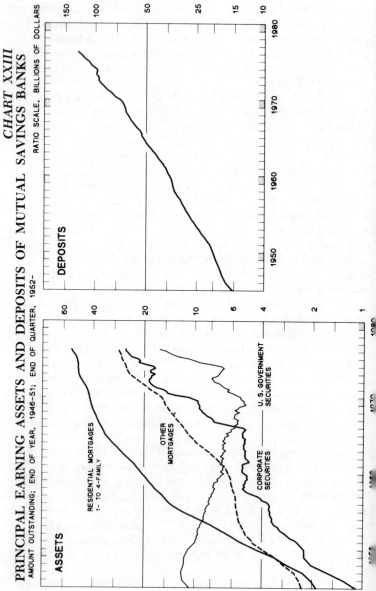

CHART XXIII

PRINCIPAL EARNING ASSETS AND DEPOSITS OF MUTUAL SAVINGS BANKS

AMOUNT OUTSTANDING; END OF YEAR, 1946–51; END OF QUARTER, 1952–

RATIO SCALE, BILLIONS OF DOLLARS

DEPOSITS

ASSETS

RESIDENTIAL MORTGAGES
1- TO 4-FAMILY

OTHER MORTGAGES

U. S. GOVERNMENT SECURITIES

CORPORATE SECURITIES

meet the needs of consumer groups is, however, being pushed actively with considerable success by MSBs and also S&Ls and CUs. The MSBs are well on their way to becoming a much more competitive group of consumer-oriented deposit institutions and larger providers of investment funds. Prospects are very good that added MSB services will stabilize the growth rate in the future. The desirability of continuing to be organized as mutuals now that the scope of activities has broadened will be a subject of conversation, at the very least, during the next few years.

Chapter 24

Credit Unions

The resources of the credit union (CU) are about one-third that of MSBs, but they have been growing faster during the past five years than any of the other deposit institutional groupings. Between 1971 and 1975, as shown in Chart XXIV, savings on deposit in CUs grew from $18.3 billion to $33.6 billion. A large portion of the increase, of course, was eaten up by the 53 percent slide in the value of the dollar.[1]

Also in 1976 there were about 23,000 CUs, half with federal charters, half with state. They had about 31 million members, an increase in membership of about one-third in the five years past. In 1975, a slow year for consumer borrowing, the CUs accounted for about all the growth that did take place in the United States. An important aspect of the recent strong growth record of CUs has been the expansion of family income of working people, more generous state regulatory legislation, and the provision of federal insurance of deposits up to $40,000.

Background. The CU movement dates back to 1849 in Germany as an effort to avert starvation among workers. Unlike MSB and S&L groupings, which also trace their origins to European development, the CU has continued as an international movement that now extends around the world. The first CU founded in North America was in Quebec in 1900. The first CU in the United States was established in Boston in 1909. In 1934 federal legislation providing for chartering of CUs was adopted. In the same year, the Credit Union National Association (CUNA) was formed, and in 1970 the World Council of Credit Unions was founded. CUNA has become a very active

---

[1] As measured by wholesale price index.

CHART XXIV

SAVINGS AND LOANS OUTSTANDING IN
CREDIT UNIONS   1971–1975

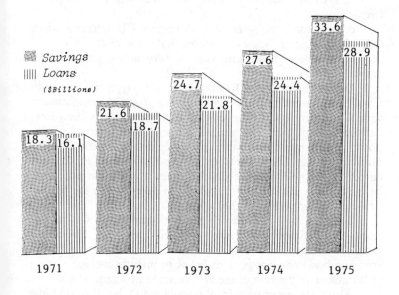

▓ *Savings*
▥ *Loans*
($Billions)

18.3 16.1

21.6 18.7

24.7 21.8

27.6 24.4

33.6 28.9

1971   1972   1973   1974   1975

organization providing training for CU employees and many services to CU management.

CUNA.   A listing and brief description of some CUNA's activities gives an idea of the importance of this organization in tying the CUs of the United States into a national, dynamic, deposit organization grouping.

1. CUNA data provide uniform CU accounting and a nation-wide funds transfer system for CUs of all sizes.

2. ICU Services Corporation provides investment advice and in cooperation with the Congress of Central Credit Unions is able to provide a system of total liquidity management. This has given CUs the capability of competing for tax-sheltered pension fund accounts.

3. Two insurance affiliates sell insurance to CU members and to CUs directly.

4. CUNA directly:

a. Coordinates CU activity among the armed services of the United States.

b. Establishes and provides personnel for leadership and development of management seminars.

c. Provides the U.S. input into the World Council of Credit Unions.

d. Organizes lobby activity to protect CU interests when federal legislation is being considered that could affect CUs.

e. Stimulates leadership for the very active youth movement of CUs.

Deposit Sources and Regulations. CUs typically are made up of people working for a company or a group of organizations with a common bond. The cost of management has been low, and because of their cooperative ownership by holders of deposits (sometimes called shares) CUs do not make profits in the ordinary sense. They therefore are not subject to the federal corporate income tax. The depositors in a particular CU must be included in the *common bond* group described in the federal or state charter under which it operates.

Since the days of the work group association by CU depositors, the definition of *common bond* has been liberalized greatly by federal and state legislation. This broadening of the common bond concept goes so far as to include everyone living in Wisconsin in the case of the Wisconsin State Credit Union.

Also CUs are exempt from Regulation Q, but they do have government-imposed deposit interest rate limitations. However, the interest rate ceilings are more liberal than those current under Regulation Q, which controls commercial bank, MSB, and S&L interest rate ceilings. Federally chartered CUs pay 7 percent, while some state CUs offered 8.75 percent in 1976 on savings that can be withdrawn at any time without a penalty. Also, by being a CU depositor you become eligible for loans that are generally extended more liberally than those available from a commercial bank or an MSB or an S&L.

Loan Restrictions. The federal and many state CU regulations forbid CUs to make personal loans for more than $2,500 for five years and secured loans for more than $10,000 for ten years. Currently CUs are pushing to have this federal legislation liberalized. The states have been moving to do this for their chartered CUs.

CUs, in addition, are busy having legislation changed to broaden their lending and investing powers. For example, many state-chartered CUs can extend home mortgages. Currently over 4,000 CUs hold over $2 billion of real estate loans. The portion of CU deposits invested in U.S. government and agency securities and short-term market credit instruments has been increasing. To do this wisely, investment advisory services have been developed by CUNA.

A very large share of CU lending continues to be used to finance purchase of durable consumer goods and automobiles. Currently CUs provide about 20 percent of automobile financing. The commercial bank share is about twice as large.

The expansion of the scope of CU lending is being vigorously opposed by commercial banks at both the state and federal levels. Regarding lending and the development of the Electronic Fund Transfer System (EFTS) and such check substitutes as share drafts, plastic cards, and other third-party instruments, banks take the position that if CUs want to offer all bank services they should be taxed like banks and be required to keep reserves like banks.

However, all commercial banks don't see the expansion of CU services as undesirable. The banks provide clearing services for share drafts and collect a service charge plus requiring a compensating balance. This is a good, profitable business. However, CUs are not stopping at this stage of their EFTS development. The use of point-of-sale credit cards has been introduced. These permit tie-in through computer terminals for immediate transfer of funds as purchases are made.

The CUs also will soon have a central credit agency to perform services for them something like the FHLBs do for the S&Ls. It will be called U.S. Central Corporate Credit Union System (CCCUS). Each CU will contribute 1 percent of assets. When the CCCUS is in place it will increase the credit worthiness of the CUs of the nation. This will help CUs ride out an emergency such as the closing of a plant or a serious economic slow-down in some regions of the United States.

The CU's basic strength lies in its close association with working people and the sources of their wage income. There can be little doubt but that the strengthening of this relationship goes along with current interest in tying employer and employee economic interests more closely together, as has been demonstrated by pension fund developments (see Index).

Chapter 25

Structural Reform

of Thrift Institutions

The Canadians have trust companies that are like our MSBs and mortgage loan companies that are similar to our S&Ls. But there are very important differences that could provide guidelines for one type of reform in the United States.

Perhaps the most important area for concern and possible reform is the new interest-rate volatility that has existed since 1966. A procedure is needed that will permit thrift institutions to operate successfully in the money market under the existing unstable conditions. In Canada this is accomplished through attraction of five-year deposits without interest rate ceilings and the granting of renewable five-year mortgages. This means that Canadian home mortgage loans are in effect lagged variable-rate loans.

The American thrift institutions have not been pushing for this kind of development, and neither has the construction industry or the consumers of housing. The explanation of this general agreement is that all three groups see themselves suffering if the approach is introduced, although some movement in this direction exists.

The undesirable aspects of the Canadian approach are as follows:

1. Thrift institutions would experience reduced earnings when interest rates are stable or declining.

2. The cost of mortgage money will be higher, and this will reduce construction activity. (In Canada mortgage money costs about 2 percentage points more than in the United States.)

3. Depositors will be forced to tie up their money for five years to earn substantial interest rates.

Obviously with the groups most intimately involved with the finance of housing directly losing something, if the Canadian method is adopted as a reform, some offsetting gains must be experienced. These basically consist of greater stability in thrift institution deposits and therefore stability in the availability of funds and stability in the construction industry. The stability obviously does not extend to interest rate levels or to housing demand fluctuations due to such demographic determinants as birth rate fluctuations and world-wide interest rate instability.

The general population has a stake in thrift institutions reform that seldom surfaces. Introduction of the Canadian system as a reform of our thrift institutions would eliminate a considerable portion of the subsidy of these institutions now taking place through use of the federal government's monetary (debt guaranteeing) power (see Insurance and Housing in Index). The use of this power to help stabilize housing is done at a cost to all others needing and using credit. The size of this cost and the manner in which it is distributed can be estimated in only a very gross way. These cost characteristics of the subsidy of housing credit prevent benefits from their removal from having an important impact on the federal government's decisions.

Variable-Rate Mortgage. Considerable push by specialists has been demonstrated in testimony before Congressional committees, professional journals, and academic meetings for a reform that is somewhat related to the Canadian method. It is called variable-rate mortgages (VRM).

VRM provides for a shift in the interest rate on all outstanding mortgages along with the change at the average rate of interest on all new fixed-rate mortgages. The rate would change for all outstanding mortgages, and the remaining time the mortgage had to run would not affect the interest rate paid. Under this procedure the original mortgage could bear a higher or lower interest rate than the one the borrower would be paying. Whether you, as an individual borrower, suffered from the introduction of VRM would depend on whether your original mortgage was taken out when interest rates were high or low.

The basic goal of VRM reform is to permit savings institutions to pay the interest rate required to hold the deposits that provided the funds for holding outstanding mortgages. VRM during periods of high interest rates would be increasing the income of depositors and increasing the costs of those with mortgaged properties. Some of these depositors under current conditions of interest rate ceilings withdraw their deposits; others are lethargic and permit their funds to remain on deposit, even though higher earnings on the savings are available in the market. Under current interest rate ceilings and original interest rate mortgages, the loser is typically the small, unsophisticated depositor who has few alternative investments. The gainer is the holder of the low-interest-rate mortgage who does not have to pay higher interest rates as the market rate increases.

It has been estimated that for each ten dollars saved in lower interest on mortgages under the present system by families below the median family income, thirty dollars in interest on savings is lost. This is the result because mortgage loan borrowers have higher incomes on average than thrift institution savers. But it is clear that the dynamics of both the political and economic environment in this matter is not with the depositors in thrift institutions, but with the borrower.

In both Vermont and Massachusetts efforts to increase mortgage interest rates when money was tight were cancelled by direct political intervention. Efforts of S&Ls in California to use permissive legislation has not been fruitful. The borrowers and the contractors like the current system. This is even true of the federal government as its attitude is reflected in FHA and VA mortgages (see Index). Federal legislation forbids FHA and VA mortgages from being VRM mortgages.

VRM is used widely in Europe. Currently VRM is successfully used in the United Kingdom, Sweden, the Netherlands, and Finland. Also, the Hunt Commission (see Index) and the Fed recommend that federal government and state government legislation impeding development of VRM be repealed. And that is where this structural reform rests.

Chapter 26

Taxation of Financial Institutions

Special treatment of how taxation operates when applied to financial institutions is justified because special treatment has been the order of the day since the early days of the Republic.[1] In the National Bank Act of 1864, "section 5219" circumscribed the authority of states to tax national banks, and this protection, through court decisions and additional state and national tax legislation, has been extended to other financial institutions chartered by the federal government and state governments. The 1864 "section 5219" was amended only three times in the next 100 years—in 1868, 1923, and 1926. Starting with court decisions of the late 1960s that definitely prevented the application of state and local sales or use taxes or a documentary tax to national banks, Congress was forced to act to modify "5219."

The law passed by Congress in 1969 was general in nature and did not specify just exactly how a national bank may be taxed. Instead the legislation only required that national banks be treated like state banks in the jurisdiction where the national bank has its principal office. From January 1 until August 16, 1973, states were free of all special federal statutory restrictions on their authority to tax a bank doing business within their borders.

The next step in the evolving bank tax drama was federal legislation on August 16, 1973, requiring a moratorium through 1975 on state and local government application of normal "doing business" taxes applied to other corporations. In the meantime a study was carried out. The moratorium was contin-

[1] U.S. Supreme Court case of *McCulloch* v. *Maryland* (1819) declared chartered banks instrumentalities of the national government and therefore free of state and local taxation.

ued through 1977. This restriction on state and local government action extended to all "federally-insured out-of-state depositories." The study that was completed recommended that an out-of-state depository be out of bounds to state and local "doing business" taxes if it does not have an office and employees sited within the state or local jurisdiction. Therefore the existence of a substantial physical presence in a state or local area was necessary to subject to local taxes the business carried out by the financial institution.

The taxation of businesses including financial institutions by different states and local governments shows great diversity. The federal government has been active in enforcing the constitutional restriction on taxation that restricts interstate commerce or that burdens imports. Using the same income, for example, as a tax base in several states has been considered burdensome by the federal courts. The nub of the problem becomes which state should give up some or all of the base taxed. The practice among states in dealing with nonfederally insured depositories, i.e., regular businesses, is to use a formula that establishes, through an average of the portion of wages, property, and sales taking place in a state, the portion of total profits a state may include in the base they tax. To regulate the manner in which this or similar allocation formulas are administered and enforced, the Departments of Revenues of the various states have established the Multistate Tax Commission headquartered in Boulder, Colorado.

The taxation powers of the states and the application of these powers to interstate businesses remains an area of uncertainty. New legislation restricting state taxation of individuals and business proposed in 1965 after an extensive study of the Willis Subcommittee of the House Judiciary Committee never became law. The people of the country and their elected representatives to states and local government offices have remained jealous of their taxation powers. Also, it must not be forgotten that residual taxing powers were given to the state by the writers of the Constitution, and the taxing powers of the national government were specified.

The development of state and local taxation of depository institutions was sharply restricted by "section 5219." By restricting taxation of national banks "section 5219" also restricted taxation on all state-chartered depository institutions. No state was going to place higher taxes on its institutions than it could place on federal-chartered competing institutions. Now there is a new ball game, and states and local governments are busy modifying their tax legislation to treat depository businesses basically as any other business. However, the last inning has not been played, and the large banks are trying to preserve their immunity from taxation by states other than their home states. In this regard, they remain fearful that like insurance, depository activity may lose its interstate commerce protection (see Index).

As was pointed out, great diversity exists among the states in the definitions used in establishing the tax base to which their income, sales, and property taxes apply. For example, in thirty of the fifty states using income taxes to tax businesses, an excise-type net income tax has been legislated especially to apply to depository businesses (financial institutions). This has been done in order to include in the tax base the income from ownership of federal government securities within the income tax base. When treated as income, the interest on federal government securities is exempt from state income taxes, just as the interest of state and local securities is exempt from the federal income tax—therefore the use of the excise-type tax using income as its measure but not as its base.

Federal Government Taxation.   In the early 1960s commercial banks actively protested to Congress that their taxes were much higher than those of other depository institutions. Since 1962 new federal legislation and IRS rulings have substantially reduced taxes paid the federal government as percent of net income of commercial banks and increased the percent of net income paid by other thrift institutions. Consequently the shoe now is on the other foot, and it is the other financial institutions that are complaining about unfair tax treatment by the federal government.

Prior to 1952, S&Ls and MSBs were not subject to the federal corporate income tax, which is far and away the biggest tax collected by the federal government from depository businesses. For the next ten years thrift institutions were able to avoid paying federal corporate income taxes by making large contributions to bad debt reserves that were deductible in calculating taxable income. Finally, in 1962, new federal tax legislation tightened the rules applying to thrift institution transfers of taxable income to reserve accounts. Tax payments increased from $0.5 million to $3.4 million.

Again in 1969, tax structure changes sharply increased thrift institution tax liabilities. As a result, the federal corporate income taxes paid by thrift institutions increased to $567 million in 1975. The effective tax rate (taxes as percent of net income) for S&Ls rose from 14.4 percent in 1968 to 24.8 percent in 1974. During the same period the effective tax rate on net income of commercial banks declined from 25 percent to 14 percent.

Table 17 provides a very informative summary of how tax shelters are used to reduce sharply the effective tax rate of depositories below the legislated corporate tax rate of 48 percent on net income. Tax shelters available to financial institutions approximate those of other businesses except in the provision for bad debts. Nonfinancial businesses are basically limited to actual historical losses from credit extensions in their bad debt reserve account, whereas depository institutions can use 2.4 percent of eligible loans as the bad debt reserve credit. They also have available to them an experience approach based on losses over the past six years.

The biggest tax shelter used by commercial banks is the tax exemption afforded under the corporate income tax to interest earned from ownership of state and local securities. The tax exemption status is available to all holders of these securities, and therefore the interest rate is driven down to compensate for this tax advantage. To the extent the market makes these interest rate adjustments, the commercial banks benefit by less than the amount indicated when this tax-free income is reported as benefiting from a tax shelter.

Chart XXV provides a summary of the absolute and comparative tax burdens of three major categories of thrift institutions. These data do not take account of tax paid by member commercial banks through loss of earnings of the funds they keep deposited in the Fed to meet reserve requirements (see Index).

Another interesting aspect of the federal taxes collected from depository institutions is the relative burden between small and large institutions. Smaller CBs (commercial banks) and MSBs do not enjoy as great benefits from tax shelters as do the larger CBs and MSBs. Currently in the case of CBs this is due largely to the greater use of accelerated depreciation by those offering equipment leasing programs, taking investment and foreign tax credits, and benefiting from merger and holding-company accounting rules. The Tax Reform Act of 1969 removed a major tax advantage used largely by large CBs. The act made all income and losses from sale of securities and mortgages ordinary income and losses. This largely eliminated the big CB tax game of alternating years of security gains and losses. The game increased after tax profits, because losses were deductible from regular income and gains treated as capital gains.

Taxing of Banking Abroad. It is only the CBs that carry out significant operations in foreign countries. Therefore this discussion is limited to taxation of foreign CB operations.

When activity is initiated abroad, a branch relationship usually is adopted because losses are likely to be realized at the start and these are directly deductible from total profits of the CB. Later, when the operation becomes profitable and a relatively substantial operation exists, the operation usually would be incorporated in the foreign country. This results in the elimination of foreign earnings as taxable U.S. income unless the profits are taken home.

This general rule of tax exemption of foreign operations of U.S. banks has been modified since 1962 by what has become known as subpart "F" income. If the income of a controlled foreign corporation (CFC) (in this case, say a corporation established in a foreign country by an American banking corporation) with a considerable share of the corporation's stock owned by the American banking firm, the income, even if not brought home, may become taxable by the U.S. Treasury as subpart "F" income. The income that would become taxable even though not brought home includes foreign personal holding-company income, foreign base company and sales and service income, income from insuring U.S. risks, and earnings invested in U.S. property.

The definition of tainted or taxable income is not as broad as appears at first glance. For example, all income arising from ordinary banking activity is excluded. Income from related persons also is excluded in holding-company income if both parties are engaged in banking.

The ability of CBs to benefit from lower taxes on foreign operations is related closely to treatment given earnings through use of tax havens around the world. In addition, the ability to move income legally assigned to these tax havens for investment in other parts of the world without paying a normal level of income taxes is important. These world-wide operations of CBs

TABLE 17

SELECTED TAX ADVANTAGES FOR MAJOR FINANCIAL INSTITUTIONS, 1973

Deductions From Income	In Thousands of Dollars	Estimated‡ Increase in Tax Burden Without Tax Provision (Per Cent)	Credits or Additional Taxes	In Thousands of Dollars	Estimated‡ Increase in Tax Burden Without Tax Provision (Per Cent)
Interest on state and local securities			**Investment tax credit**		
Savings and loan associations	16,892	0.3	Savings and loan associations	4,992	0.2
Mutual savings banks	52,982	3.3	Mutual savings banks	2,083	0.3
Commercial banks	3,862,232	20.8	Commercial banks	99,616	1.1
Bad debt losses on loans*			**Foreign tax credit**		
Savings and loan associations	699,456	12.6	Savings and loan associations	0	0.0
Mutual savings banks	155,451	9.7	Mutual savings banks	78	0.0
Commercial banks	856,908	4.6	Commercial banks	343,809	3.9
Gross depreciation†			**Minimum tax on preference items**		
Savings and loan associations	166,918	3.0	Savings and loan associations	44,479	-1.7
Mutual savings banks	61,429	3.8	Mutual savings banks	19,267	-2.5
Commercial banks	1,681,793	9.0	Commercial banks	9,087	-0.1

*Bad debts for savings and loan associations and mutual savings banks were estimated from changes in reserve accounts and thus may reflect changes in reserves for reasons other than transfers to loan loss reserves.

†Depreciation deductions cannot be separated between normal depreciation for ordinary bank assets and accelerated depreciation nor can depreciation on leased assets be determined.

‡The calculation of the percentage increase in taxes assumes a marginal tax rate of 48 per cent applicable to all institutions. Insofar as some banks would have been subject to lower tax rates, the tax benefits shown would be overestimates.

Per Cent

Insured Commercial Banks

Insured Savings and Loan Associations

Insured Mutual Savings Banks

1952 '54 '56 '58 '60 '62 '64 '66 '68 '70 '72 '74

and their multinational corporation (MNC) customers has become the subject of international and domestic studies and some action. For example, the Organization for Economic Co-operation and Development (OECD) is in the process of revising its rules relative to domestic taxation of income controlled by foreign interests. The United Nations (UN) also has become active in considering MNC taxation. The taxation of income and wealth that moves from nation to nation has become an area of great concern, and attempts aimed at control can be expected. The same concern is developing relative to the operations of the Eurodollars market (see Index).

PART VI: SELECTED REFERENCES AND SOURCES

Robert P. Black and Doris E. Harless, *Nonbank Financial Institutions* (Richmond: Federal Reserve Bank of Richmond, 1975).

William J. Byrne, "Fiscal Incentives for Household Saving," *IMF Staff Papers*, *23*, July 1976, 455–489.

Walter E. Erikson, "Another Look at Directors Responsibilities in Savings and Loan Associations," PMM & Co., *Management Controls*, October–November 1976, 163–166.

Federal Home Loan Bank Board, *Study of the Savings and Loan Industry* (Washington, D.C., 1970), four volumes.

Federal Reserve Board, "Nonbank Thrift Institutions in 1974," *Federal Reserve Bulletin*, February 1975, 55–59.

L. Grefler, *The Future of Thrift Institutions* (Danville, Ill.: Joint Savings Banks Exchange Groups, 1969).

Robert W. Johnson, *Methods of Stating Consumer Finance Charges* (New York: Columbia University Graduate School of Business, 1961).

H. E. Kroos and M. R. Blyn, *A History of Financial Institutions* (New York: Random House, 1971).

Alexander A. Robichek, Alan B. Coleman, and George H Hempel, *Management of Financial Institutions*, 2nd ed (Hinsdale, Ill.: Dryden Press, 1976).

Tony Thomas and Anne Segall, "A Survey of American Financial Institutions," *The Economist*, January 22, 1977.

U.S. News and World Report, "Home Mortgages with Variable Rates—How They're Working," September 6, 1976, 70-72.

U.S. Treasury, "Role of ESOP's in Broadening the Base of Stock Ownership," *Treasury Papers*, January 1976, 12.

Wall Street Journal, "New York Checking Accounts to Cost Less As Service by Thrift Institutions Is Voted," May 20, 1976.

Weldon Welfing, *Mutual Savings Banks: The Evolution of a Financial Intermediary* (Cleveland: Western Reserve, 1968).

Part VII

Credit Intermediation Developments

INTRODUCTION

Consideration in this part is given chiefly to evolving procedures for getting the saver and the borrower together. Although on-going deposit credit institutions are a portion of the descriptive and analytical discussions, the emphasis is on change, and ways in which the intermediation credit role is carried out under a variety of circumstances.

Chapter 27

One–Bank Holding Companies
(OBHC)

One approach to the provision of financial services that has become very important and possesses additional potentials is that of the bank holding company. The one-bank holding company was considered briefly in the sections concerned with commercial banking. Now that the entire area of financial intermediation within the private sector has been opened up, the time has come for a careful consideration of the very important bank holding company development and the characteristics of the death and growth of financial institutions.

The assets controlled by OBHCs are very substantial. At the end of 1975 the total assets of the ten largest OBHCs totaled $322.5 billion. This approximates the total assets of all the S&Ls of the United States. The total assets of the 100 largest OBHCs is about double that of the ten largest OBHCs or twice the assets of all S&Ls. The figure in 1975 was $626.3 billion.

The real estate investment trusts (REITs) turned out to be the aspect of OBHC operations that has attracted the greatest attention. This happened both because of the size of the operations and the repayment difficulties encountered in 1973 that continue to be troublesome.

The REITs (see Index) were established by the largest OBHCs. The commercial bank of the OBHC is usually the dominant member, but it does not own the REIT that may be a portion of the OBHC operation. The OBHC merely advises the REIT, and presumably so does the dominant bank of the OBHC, which typically also lends heavily to the REIT.

When this apparatus was being put in place in 1969 or so, much was made of the fact that the OBHC or its dominant bank was under no legal obligation to bail out the REIT if it en-

TABLE 18

DATE OF ENTRY BY ONE-BANK HOLDING COMPANIES INTO NONBANK ACTIVITIES
BY TWO-DIGIT SIC CLASSIFICATION

Primarily in SIC No.	Description of activity	Before 1930	1930-39	1940-49	1950-59	1960-64	1965-70
01	Agricultural production		2	1	1	10	15
07	Agricultural services and hunting				2	7	12
08	Forestry	1					1
10	Metal mining						
12	Bituminous coal and lignite mining	3					4
13	Crude petroleum and natural gas				1	2	3
14	Mining and quarrying nonmetallic minerals, ex. fuel				2	1	19
15	Building construction—general contractors	1			1	4	5
16	Construction other than building					3	14
17	Construction—special trade contractors		1		1	1	7
19	Ordnance and accessories						11
20	Food and kindred products	1			4	4	21
22	Textile mill products					2	16
24	Lumber and wood products, ex. furniture	1				1	7
25	Furniture and fixtures						6
26	Paper and allied products					2	11
27	Printing and publishing				4	6	13
28	Chemicals and allied products	1	1	2	3	4	8
29	Petroleum refining and related industries				3		1
30	Rubber and misc. plastic products		2			1	3
31	Leather and leather products						3
32	Stone, clay, glass, and concrete products				3	2	10
33	Primary metals				6	1	16
34	Fabricated metal products		1	1	1	4	20
35	Machinery, ex. electrical				2	2	24
36	Electrical machinery				3	1	23
37	Transportation equipment				2	2	6
38	Instruments						2
39	Misc. manufacturing industries						3
40	Railroad transportation	1					
41	Local suburban and interurban passenger transportation						3
42	Motor freight transportation and warehousing			1	2	4	11
44	Water transportation		1		6	1	33

SIC	Activity						
45	Transportation by air				1	2	5
46	Pipeline transportation					1	2
47	Transportation services			2	3	1	27
48	Communication					8	27
49	Electric gas and sanitary services	3			5	7	12
50	Wholesale trade	1	1	3	13	14	51
52	Building materials, hardware, farm equipment dealers	1	1	1		3	6
53	Retail trade—general merchandise					4	8
54	Food stores				1	10	2
55	Auto dealers and gasoline service stations					4	9
56	Apparel and accessory stores				1		
57	Furniture, home furnishings, and equipment stores					1	4
58	Eating and drinking places					2	4
59	Misc. retail stores					2	16
60	Banking	10		5	3	5	99
61	Credit agencies other than banks		9	1	60	115	359
62	Security and commodity brokers, dealers, exchanges				4	8	61
63	Insurance carriers	1	2	5	24	32	147
64	Insurance agents, brokers, and service	1			12	27	140
65	Real estate	7		3	57	105	478
66	Combinations of real estate, insurance, loans, law offices		4	22			1
67	Holding and other investment companies	5	3	7	33	46	481
70	Hotels, rooming houses, and other lodging				2		7
72	Personal services	2			2	1	1
73	Misc. business services		3	4	10	22	168
75	Auto repair, auto services, and garages		1			2	19
76	Misc. repair services				1		1
78	Motion pictures				3		2
79	Amusement and recreation services	1					6
80	Medical and other health services					2	7
82	Educational services						3
86	Nonprofit membership organizations				3		3
89	Misc. services		1		1	2	77
99	Nonclassifiable establishments					2	1
	Total	43	34	58	290	503	2,571

1 Tabulation is based on the "principal" SIC activities reported for nonbank subsidiaries. It includes each nonbank subsidiary of a holding company regardless of how many subsidiaries are reported in the same principal two-digit group. Inactive subsidiaries are excluded. There are 18 nonbank subsidiaries for which either the principal SIC activities or the date of acquisition or formation was not provided. These data should be interpreted with caution because the number of entries into the various activities for each time period reflect only those nonbank subsidiaries that were still owned by one-bank holding companies as of December 31, 1970. If, for example, a one-bank holding company acquired or formed a nonbank subsidiary between 1930 and 1939 and disposed of that subsidiary prior to December 31, 1970, it would not be reflected here. Consequently, the number of formations and acquisitions reported is understated in earlier time periods.

NOTE.—Periods showing date of entry indicate when OBHC's formed or acquired nonbank subsidiaries.

TABLE 18 (Continued)

SIC No.	Description of activity	Number[1]	SIC No.	Description of activity	Number[1]
011	Field crops	11	301	Tires and inner tubes	2
012	Fruits, tree nuts, and vegetables	7	302	Rubber footwear	1
013	Livestock	59	303	Reclaimed rubber	1
014	General farms	28	306	Fabricated rubber products n.e.c.	4
019	Misc. agriculture	1	307	Misc. plastics products	8
071	Agricultural services, ex. animal husbandry and horticulture	6	311	Leather tanning and finishing	1
			312	Industrial leather belting	1
072	Animal husbandry	11	314	Footwear, ex. rubber	2
081	Timber tracts	4	321	Flat glass	1
086	Gathering forest products	1	323	Glass products	1
			325	Structural clay products	1
101	Iron ores	1	326	Pottery and related products	6
102	Copper ores	1	327	Concrete, gypsum, and plaster products	5
103	Lead and zinc	1	329	Abrasives, asbestos, and misc. nonmetallic mineral products	6
105	Bauxite	1	331	Blast furnaces, steel works, and rolling and finishing mills	6
108	Metal mining services	1			
109	Misc. metal ores	2	333	Primary smelting and refining of nonferrous metals	1
121	Bituminous coal and lignite mining	10	334	Secondary smelting of nonferrous metals	2
131	Crude petroleum and natural gas	1	335	Rolling, drawing, and extruding of nonferrous metals	3
132	Natural gas liquids	1			
138	Oil and gas field services	9	336	Nonferrous foundries	2
141	Dimension stone	2	339	Misc. primary metal products	1
142	Crushed stone	1	341	Metal cans	2
144	Sand and gravel	3	342	Cutlery, hand tools, and general hardware	3
145	Clay, ceramic, and refractory minerals	3	343	Heating apparatus, ex. electrical, and plumbing fixtures	3
148	Nonmetallic minerals, ex. fuels	2			
149	Misc. nonmetallic minerals, ex. fuels	1	344	Fabricated structural metal products	16
151	General building contractor	19	345	Screw machine products	4
161	Highway and steel construction	1	346	Metal stampings	3
162	Heavy construction, ex. highway and street	8	347	Coating and engraving	2
171	Plumbing, heating (ex. electrical), and air conditioning	3	349	Misc. fabricated metal products	5
			351	Engines and turbines	2
172	Painting, paper hanging, and decorating	3	352	Farm machinery and equipment	4
173	Electrical work	4	353	Construction and mining equipment	6
175	Carpeting and flooring	1	354	Metalworking machinery	9
176	Roofing and sheet metal work	1	355	Special industrial machinery	4
177	Concrete work	7	356	General industrial machinery	4
179	Misc. special trade contractors	2	357	Office computing and accounting machines	3
192	Ammunition, ex. small arms	1	358	Service industry machines	6
195	Small arms	1	359	Misc. machinery, ex. electrical	3
196	Small arms ammunition		361	Electrical transmission and distribution equipment	3
199	Ordnance and accessories n.e.c.		362	Electrical industrial apparatus	3

No.	Code	Industry
2	202	Dairy products
6	203	Canned and preserved fruits, vegetables, and seafood
3	204	Grain mill products
2	205	Bakery products
2	206	Sugar
2	207	Confectionary and related products
5	208	Beverages
4	209	Misc. food preparation
3	222	Broad woven fabric mills, manmade fibers, and silk
1	223	Broad woven fabric mills, wool
1	224	Narrow fabrics
4	225	Knitting mills
1	226	Dyeing and finishing textiles
4	227	Floor covering mills
5	229	Misc. textile goods
4	242	Sawmills and planing mills
6	243	Millwork, veneer, plywood
1	244	Wooden containers
4	249	Misc. wood products
5	251	Household furniture
2	252	Office furniture
1	253	Public building furniture
1	254	Partitions, shelving
3	262	Paper mills, ex. building paper mills
1	263	Converted paper and paperboard products
5	264	Paperboard mills
5	265	Paperboard containers and boxes
1	266	Building paper and board mills
4	271	Newspapers: Publishing and printing
2	272	Periodicals: Publishing and printing
8	273	Books
9	274	Miscellaneous publishing
1	275	Commercial printing
2	276	Manifold business forms
3	277	Greeting card publishing
1	278	Blankbooks and loose leaf binders
1	279	Service for printing
7	281	Industrial inorganic and organic chemicals
4	282	Plastic materials and synthetic rubber and resin
3	283	Drugs
7	284	Soap, detergents, perfumes, and cosmetics
4	285	Paints, varnishes, and lacquers
1	286	Gum and wood chemicals
4	287	Agricultural chemicals
3	289	Misc. chemical products
4	291	Petroleum refining
3	295	Paving and roofing materials
1	299	Misc. products of petroleum and coal

No.	Code	Industry
2		[...] appliances
4	364	Electric lighting and wiring equipment
6	365	Radio and TV receiving sets
9	366	Communication equipment
12	367	Electronic components and accessories
5	369	Misc. electrical machinery
7	371	Motor vehicles and equipment
1	372	Aircraft and parts
1	374	Railroad equipment
3	379	Misc. transportation equipment
1	381	Engineering, laboratory, and scientific equipment
5	382	Instruments for measuring and weighing physical characteristics
3	383	Optical instruments
2	384	Surgical and medical supplies
3	386	Photographic equipment
1	387	Watches and clocks
3	393	Musical instruments
2	394	Toys and athletic goods
1	395	Pens and pencils
2	399	Misc. manufacturing industries
3	401	Railroads
1	411	Local and suburban passenger transportation
8	421	Trucking
1	422	Public warehousing
18	423	Terminal facilities for motor freight transportation
1	441	Deep sea foreign transportation
2	442	Deep sea domestic transportation
1	444	Transportation on rivers and canals
1	445	Local water transportation
3	446	Services for water transportation
4	451	Air transportation, certified carriers
5	452	Air transportation, noncertified carriers
1	458	Fixed facilities for air transportation
4	461	Pipelines, ex. natural gas
3	471	Freight forwarding
3	472	Arrangement of transportation
36	473	Stockyards
3	474	Rental of railroad cars
1	478	Misc. services for transportation
1	481	Telephone communication
11	483	Radio and TV broadcasts
7	489	Communication services n.e.c.
2	491	Electric companies and systems
2	492	Gas companies and systems
7	494	Water supply
7	495	Sanitary services
3	497	Irrigation systems

TABLE 18 (Continued)

SIC No.	Description of activity	Number[1]	SIC No.	Description of activity	Number[1]
501	Wholesale motor vehicles and auto equipment	9	628	Services allied with the exchange of securities or commodities	32
502	Wholesale drugs, chemicals, and allied products	5	631	Life insurance	73
503	Piece goods, notions, apparel	4	632	Accident and health insurance	38
504	Groceries and related products	11	633	Fire, marine, and casualty insurance	40
505	Farm products, raw materials	7	635	Surety insurance	32
506	Electrical goods	10	636	Title insurance	12
507	Hardware, and plumbing and heating supplies	2	639	Insurance carriers n.e.c.	7
508	Machinery, equipment, and supplies	11	641	Insurance agents, brokers, and service	604
509	Misc. wholesalers	34	651	Real estate operators (ex. developers) and lessors	439
521	Lumber and building materials dealers	16	653	Agents, brokers, and managers	127
523	Paint, glass, and wallpaper stores	1	654	Title abstract companies	10
524	Electrical supply stores	2	655	Subdividers and developers	91
525	Hardware and farm equipment	11	656	Operative builders	28
531	Department stores	8	661	Combinations of real estate, insurance, loans, law offices	7
532	Mail order houses	6	672	Investment companies	35
533	Variety stores	1	673	Trusts	22
535	Direct selling establishments	1	679	Misc. investing institutions	57
539	Misc. general merchandise stores	7	701	Hotels and motels	20
541	Grocery stores	10	703	Trailer parks and camps	5
542	Meat and fish markets	1	704	Membership hotels	2
545	Dairy products stores	3	721	Laundries and cleaning plants	4
551	Motor vehicle dealers	9	726	Funeral services and crematories	3
553	Tire, battery, and accessory dealers	2	729	Misc. personal services	1
554	Gasoline service stations	7	731	Advertising	18
559	Misc. aircraft, marine, and auto dealers	6	732	Consumer credit reporting agencies	9
561	Men's and boy's clothing stores	1	733	Duplicating, mailing, and stenographic services	2
562	Women's ready-to-wear stores	2	734	Services to dwellings and other buildings	11
563	Women's specialty stores	1	739	Business services n.e.c.	214
564	Child's and infant wear	1	751	Auto rentals w/o drivers	28
565	Family clothing stores	2	752	Auto parking	3
571	Furniture and home furnishings, ex. appliance stores	6	762	Electrical repair shops	2
572	Household appliance stores	1	769	Misc. repair shops	3
573	Radio, TV, and music stores	2	781	Motion picture production and distribution	4
581	Eating and drinking places	14	783	Motion picture theaters	1
591	Drug and proprietary stores	6	793	Bowling alleys and pool establishments	2
595	Sporting goods and bike stores	1	794	Sports promoters and commercial operators	10
596	Farm and garden supply stores	7			
598	Fuel and ice dealers	4			
599	Retail stores n.e.c.	7			

Code	Industry	Number	Code	Industry	Number
602	Commercial and stock savings banks	36	806	Hospitals	2
603	Mutual savings banks	1	809	Health and allied services n.e.c.	5
604	Trust companies not engaged in deposit banking		811	Legal services	1
605	Establishments performing functions closely related to banking	78	821	Elementary and secondary schools	1
611	Rediscount and financing institutions for credit agencies other than banks	5	822	Colleges and universities	3
612	Savings and loan associations	27	824	Correspondence and vocational schools	3
613	Agricultural credit institutions	18	829	Schools n.e.c.	1
614	Personal credit institutions	114	862	Professional membership organizations	1
615	Business credit institutions	173	863	Labor unions	6
616	Loan correspondents and brokers	61	867	Charitable organizations	2
621	Security brokers, dealers, and flotation companies	42	869	Nonprofit membership organizations n.e.c.	4
622	Commodity contracts brokers and dealers	6	891	Engineering and architectural services	136
			893	Accounting, auditing, and bookkeeping services	4
			899	Services n.e.c.	
			990	Nonclassifiable establishments	9

1 Number of one-bank holding companies that are engaged in the activity either directly or through a subsidiary. Subsidiaries classified as inactive are not included in this tabulation.

countered difficulties. However, the largest banks of the country have not been willing to permit REITs in which they are involved through an OBHC they dominate to file under Chapter XI of the Bankruptcy Act.

The banks apparently became deeply involved in providing funds to REITs when they began to play the liability management game instead of the traditional intermediary role. Funds were loaned to associated REITs without carefully considering if this was a safe use of depositors' funds. It has become abundantly clear that REITs were financing construction in the areas of office building and recreation condominium second-homes, and that the banks providing the funds were not supervising the REITs because they didn't own them.

Because of the potential for monopoly and unwise expansion of finance-related activities, the Banking Act of 1933 provided the Federal Reserve Board with some control over the voting of member bank stock owned by corporations. The legislation required, among other restrictions, the withdrawal of bank holding companies from the securities business (see Tables 18 and 19).

Right after World War II bank holding company activity expanded all over the lot. These holding companies usually included more than one bank within the group. The ability of these holding companies to take over finance-related business of other organizations caused Congress to act again in this field. In 1956 a new Bank Holding Company Act was adopted.

The legislation of 1956 required multiple-bank holding companies to divest themselves of ownership or control of any kind of business other than banking. It also largely cut out any more buying by the holding company of stock of banks located outside the state where the holding company's principal office was located. In 1966 this legislation was amended to require prior approval by the Federal Reserve Board of any acquisitions within or outside the state of the company's principal office.

This restrictive and regulatory federal action did not apply to one-bank holding companies, and their number nearly doubled between 1968 and 1970. As a result, operators of businesses that competed actively with the expansion developments of one-bank holding companies pressed Congress for new restrictive legislation. Congress acted and adopted the One-Bank Holding Company amendments of 1970.

These 1970 amendments placed OBHCs under federal control. At the same time, however, the amendments in effect broadened the types of activities in which OBHCs could become engaged and permitted them to acquire nonbank firms across state lines. The Federal Reserve Board retained the power to declare the business areas appropriate for OBHC operation. The OBHC law as amended in 1970 provided in Section 4(c) (8) that the Fed would decide what activities were "closely related to banking" and therefore eligible for OBHC control and operation.

Some recent examples of OBHC requests and actions are summarized in several of the following paragraphs. They give you an idea of the complications and forces involved in this whole business of OBHC expansion and at the same time control of the expansion by the Fed.

Since 1956, Sec. 4(a) (2) of the BHC Act permitted the offer of management consulting services to any bank of which the BHC owned 25 percent of the voting shares. In 1974 the Fed amended Regulation Y to permit OBHCs to provide management consulting services for nonaffiliated banks. The expansion of the right to offer management consulting services was combined with restrictions to minimize the potential of unfair competitive practices.

For another example, in 1974 the board added leasing of real property as an activity "closely related to banking." At the same time, the existing right to engage in the leasing of personal property, i.e., machines, trucks, and so on, was modified to correspond with the newly developed real property leasing procedures that require the lease to be the functional equivalent of the extension of credit.

At about the same time the Fed decided that mortgage guarantee insurance and operation of S&Ls may not be appropriate activities for OBHCs, despite the fact that both activities obviously were related closely to banking. The basis of the decision was that the public interest would not be served by permitting OBHCs to engage in this activity.

The kinds of permitted businesses of OBHCs are many as is demonstrated by the listing on the following pages. Recently the Fed has become concerned with the efficiency with which basic banking activity is carried out. A Fed attitude of favoring sticking with your banking "knitting" has reduced the acceptance of OBHC activity requests. The Fed also has become very concerned with two basic issues: potential competition and capital adequacy.

Capital adequacy and the desire to increase leverage by investors in financial institutions are perennial problems that never will be solved (see Index).

The impact of change on competition is also an ongoing area where honest difference of opinion can be expected. The degree of monopoly can be both expanded and decreased by the expansion of facilities of one of the providers of the service. A branch of a big city bank in a smaller town can increase the competitiveness with which financial services are offered. This change also can be seen as an increase in the stranglehold of big city banks on the life-giving processes of the local economy.

Competition in providing financial services has increased as finance companies, S&Ls, and retail store credit facilities have grown. The growth of the institutions demonstrate that traditional banking has left a void in the financial services market. The next question is: Should the banks be prohibited from offering these services, or should they be permitted to compete by setting up similar arrangements under an OBHC?

These registration statements of the one-bank holding companies in existence at the end of 1970 provide the only comprehensive body of data available on bank holding companies. These data demonstrate that:

The majority of both holding companies and their affiliate banks are small, and large holding companies tend to be involved in nonbank activities to a greater extent than small companies.

Banking is relatively less important in the operation of large companies than of small companies.

One-bank holding companies, as a group, engage in a wide range of nonbank activities, but most of them taken singly engage in only a few such activities.

The most important nonbank financial activities among holding companies are establishments performing functions closely related to banking, personal and business credit institutions, and loan correspondents and brokers.

The most important nonfinancial activities are insurance agents and brokers, real estate operators and agents, and business services.

And finally, large holding companies account for a rela-

TABLE 19
OBHC AREAS OF ACTIVITY

ctivities APPROVED by the Board

1. Dealer in bankers' acceptances
2. Mortgage company
3. Finance company
4. Credit card company
5. Factoring company
   Operating an industrial bank
7. Servicing loans
8. Trust company
9. Adviser to real estate investment trusts and other investment companies
9. General economic information and advice
1. Portfolio investment advice
2. Full pay-out leasing of personal property
3. Full pay-out leasing of real property
4. Community welfare investments
5. Bookkeeping and data processing services
6. Insurance agent or broker in connection with credit extensions
7. Underwriting credit life and credit accident and health insurance
8. Courier service
. Management consulting to nonaffiliated banks
20. Sale of travelers checks
21. Bullion broker

Activities DENIED by the Board

1. Equity funding (combined sale of mutual funds and insurance)
2. Underwriting general life insurance
3. Real estate brokerage
4. Land development
5. Real estate syndication
6. General management consulting
7. Property management

Activities UNDER CONSIDERATION by the Board

1. Armored car services
2. Mortgage guarantee insurance
3. Savings and loan associations
4. Travel agencies
5. Underwriting and dealing in U.S. Government and certain municipal securities

tively large share of the nonbank activities in which one-bank holding companies are engaged.

Will competition be increased by bank activity in these financial service areas? Or will it be another example of banks increasing the control they hold on the entire area of the provision of financial services?

The Hunt Commission (see Index) proposed changes that would substantially reduce the government-enforced restrictions on how financial institutions carry out their responsibilities. The Hunt Commission recommended removal of all interest rate restrictions and all limitations on branch banking as well as the ability of deposit institutions to provide checking account services. These recommendations were justified basically on the basis of providing more competition in the allocation of credit and the gathering together of savings.

All of these protestations of inefficiency because of government restrictions seem to be statements that demonstrate great enterprise independence and a willingness to do or die in the fields of free competition. But this impression is modified when one recalls that these financial institutions want government insurance of their deposits and insurance and government subsidy on many of their loans. One is tempted to contemplate what would have happened when the OBHCs were experiencing huge REIT losses in 1974 if such props as government insurance, Fed discounting, and government subsidies had not been available.

Chapter 28

Finance Companies

Finance company operations consist largely of extending credit based on sales receivables consisting of installment paper from retail sales of automobiles, mobile homes, motor scooters, boats, planes, and home improvements not secured by real estate. In addition, finance companies make secured and unsecured loans to individuals and families. The third loan category includes making funds available to businesses through short- and intermediate-length loans secured by accounts receivable and equipment of businesses and farmers. The definition used by the Fed in its study of finance companies is: a company (excluding commercial banks, credit unions, mortgage banking firms, mutual savings banks, and S&Ls) in which the largest portion of its assets are in one or more of the asset types listed above.

There are about 3,400 finance companies. Of this total 88 have loans outstanding exceeding $100 million. These largest finance companies account for 81 percent of the total assets of the finance industry, which were $98 billion in mid-1977.

Finance companies are not deposit institutions and therefore must raise their funds through equity capital investments, sale of debt instruments, and loans from institutions and individuals. In 1975 capital and surplus at $14 billion were 15 percent of total assets. The smaller firms, by and large, were less highly leveraged than the large firms. The equity of small firms runs around one-third of total liabilities and capital, whereas for large firms it is about 50 percent of that.

The direct placement of commercial paper by the largest finance companies was the source of $24 billion of funds. The other large source of borrowed funds was long-term senior debt

TABLE 20

ASSETS AND LIABILITIES OUTSTANDING AT FINANCE COMPANIES BY SIZE OF RECEIVABLES, JUNE 30, 1975

IN MILLIONS OF DOLLARS

Balance sheet item	Total	Size of company (in thousands of dollars of short- and intermediate-term loans outstanding)								
		100,000 and over	25,000–99,999	5,000–24,999	2,500–4,999	1,000–2,499	500–999	250–499	100–249	Under 100
Assets										
Consumer receivables	42,760	37,378	2,712	1,253	419	416	268	181	93	40
Retail passenger car paper	9,938	9,351	290	91	53	70	49	19	9	5
Mobile homes	3,461	3,247	170	30	……	8	2	1	1	……
Revolving consumer instalment credit	5,752	5,304	395	36	……	14	2	……	……	……
Personal cash loans	16,715	13,122	1,661	895	312	279	188	147	78	33
Loans secured by second mortgages	1,946	1,064	449	264	62	58	25	18	5	1
Other	14,769	12,058	1,213	631	250	221	164	129	72	31
All other consumer instalment loans	6,895	6,354	196	200	52	45	28	13	5	2
Business receivables	39,286	35,930	2,148	904	147	99	25	20	9	4
Wholesale paper	10,945	10,297	532	60	24	19	8	4	1	1
Automobiles	7,713	7,632	58	13	……	2	……	1	……	……
Other consumer goods	1,273	1,031	193	26	10	6	3	2	……	……
All other	1,960	1,634	280	21	11	10	3	2	……	……
Retail paper	11,067	10,558	340	122	17	19	4	3	3	1
Commercial vehicles	5,012	4,966	5	22	6	7	……	1	1	……
Business, industrial, and farm equipment	6,055	5,592	335	100	11	11	5	2	2	1
Lease paper	8,065	7,575	293	151	31	11	7	1	2	……
Auto paper	2,343	2,297	23	18	……	7	7	……	……	……
Business, industrial, and farm equipment	3,950	3,562	243	106	30	3	5	1	1	……
All other	1,772	1,716	26	28	……	4	2	……	……	……
Other business credit	9,208	7,500	983	572	75	55	9	11	1	3
Loans on commercial accounts receivable	3,388	2,701	309	303	34	34	4	3	2	……
Factored accounts receivable	1,400	1,012	326	30	15	12	3	1	1	……
Advances to factored clients	203	138	47	……	17	……	……	……	……	……
All other receivables	4,218	3,649	301	239	9	9	2	6	1	2

Other receivables	3,948	3,748	127	37	9	15	4	4	3	1
Total receivables—gross	85,994	77,056	4,986	2,195	575	530	298	205	105	45
Less: reserves for unearned income	7,684	6,831	448	230	60	53	31	21	8	2
Less: reserves for losses	1,623	1,411	100	58	18	17	8	7	3	1
Total receivables—net	76,687	68,814	4,438	1,906	496	460	259	177	94	42
Cash and non-interest-bearing deposits	2,667	2,224	267	98	25	23	12	9	5	5
Time deposits	2,202	111	37	11	6	18	10	4	5	2
Other loans and investments	6,745	6,220	296	81	26	78	14	13	9	7
U.S. government securities	63	36	21	2		1	1			
Other marketable securities	683	611	36	4	4	2	4	2		1
All other loans and investments	5,998	5,573	239	75	22	58	9	11	6	6
All other assets	2,416	1,929	272	97	20	41	22	15	12	8
Total assets—net	88,716	79,299	5,310	2,193	573	620	317	219	122	64
Liabilities and capital										
Loans and notes payable to banks	8,617	5,829	1,485	783	207	175	73	35	22	7
Short-term	7,900	5,518	1,351	654	161	123	51	24	14	4
Long-term	718	312	134	130	46	52	22	11	7	3
Commercial paper	25,905	25,167	632	85	19	1				
Directly placed	23,686	23,360	247	59	19	1				
Dealer placed	2,218	1,807	385	26						
Other short-term debt	2,815	1,842	446	351	57	51	30	22	9	7
Deposit liabilities and thrift certificates	1,480	834	413	119	45	44	16	6	2	
Other current liabilities	3,113	2,497	463	67	19	25	24	11	4	2
Other long-term senior debt	23,404	22,614	530	119	30	59	21	19	8	1
Long-term subordinated debt	3,609	4,875	410	173	56	53	22	17	9	3
All other liabilities	3,823	3,600	60	71	30	29	13	9	2	
Capital, surplus, and undivided profits	13,951	12,039	872	423	111	182	119	100	67	39
Total liabilities, capital, and surplus	88,716	79,299	5,310	2,193	573	620	317	219	122	64
Memoranda:										
Short-term debt	36,620	32,527	2,428	1,090	238	176	81	47	23	11
Long-term debt	29,730	27,801	1,074	422	131	165	64	47	18	8
Total debt	66,350	60,328	3,503	1,512	369	340	146	94	41	19
Number of companies	3,376	88	102	204	162	338	415	563	641	863

that totaled $24 billion. Borrowings from commercial banks totaled $8.6 billion.

Another breakdown that is useful in developing a picture of the finance company business is to relate type of loans made to size of the institution. Finance companies with over $25 million in receivables held 94 percent of all consumer loans and 97 percent of all business loans outstanding. In contrast, firms with less than $5 million in loans accounted for 88 percent of all finance companies, and most of their receivables are personal cash loans.

Between late 1974 and 1976 finance companies issued substantial quantities of long-term debt to rebuild liquidity and to fund short-term borrowing that they entered into during the high-interest period of 1973 and early 1974. This period of tight money combined with special government favors to credit unions and S&Ls caused finance companies to enjoy a declining share of the consumer credit market. The overall erosion was from 33 percent of the total in 1970 to 28 percent in 1975. In May 1976 the installment credit outstanding of finance companies was $37 billion. For commercial banks it was about twice as much. The finance companies' total was about 30 percent greater than credit unions' and about twice as much as for retail outlets and others.

Within this declining share of the total consumer loan market, finance companies continued to specialize in consumer personal loans that accounted for 39 percent of their total consumer activity. The decline of finance companies in the retail financing of automobiles has been most noticeable and is attributed to a weak automobile market in 1975 and stiff competition from credit unions and commercial banks. To supplement their consumer-lending activity, finance companies have become fairly active in providing the funds needed in the marketing of mobile homes.

Lending to businesses has picked up some finance company slack resulting from some weakness in consumer lending. Business lending increased from 40 percent to 46 percent of total finance company loans between 1970 and 1975. The strong segment of this activity has been in the finance of automobile leasing. Leasing of automobile fleets by businesses has been encouraged by weaknesses in many balance sheets arising from too much debt and too little equity. In addition, leasing offers special tax advantages over buying and borrowing. The advantage arises because under leasing the total cost month-by-month is deductible as expense and therefore capital as well as out-of-pocket money costs are expenses.

Finance companies, as mentioned above, have become big users of commercial paper as a method to tap the money market. This source of financing is really available, however, to only the very largest finance companies, and 67 percent of them accounted for 97 percent of the finance company paper outstanding in 1975.

Finance companies with a large continuing need for funds (making up about 91 percent of the total) sell directly to lenders, and the interest rate paid is generally less than the commercial bank prime rate. The remaining 7 percent, with only a seasonal need for funds and with a less well-known name, sell through dealers at an additional cost of about ⅛ of a percentage point. The attractiveness of the commercial paper rate has reduced the involvement of commercial banks in the financing of business and consumer credit needs through loans to finance companies.

Table 20 provides a summary of finance company activities by size of company. The Fed conducts a study of the finance company industry every five years. Table 20 is the result of the 1975 study.

Chapter 29

Investment Companies

Mutual funds, i.e., investment companies, account for 26.5 percent of common stocks owned by the principal nonbank financial institutions. The funds provide a procedure for the small investor to enjoy security diversification and portfolio management at a reasonable fee. The managers of the funds are interested in maximizing earnings and capital gains of the investors and not in acquiring management control, as are holding companies. It is currently a troubled industry, but from 1945 to 1973 it was very healthy and experienced a fantastic 12 percent annual growth rate.

The typical private investor in a mutual fund has committed about $5,000 of his savings. These individual accounts plus other investors add up to over $50 billion of assets. The earnings are typically reinvested in more stock. The advantages of the mutual fund procedure in managing investments in common stocks also have made mutual funds attractive to schools, hospitals, labor unions, pension funds, and the like.

In addition, the term *investment companies* includes what are called *closed-end companies*. These companies issue a given quantity of shares, and investors must purchase their stock from other investors holding stocks issued by the company. These shares trade just like the shares of any company. The company manages the funds originally received when the offering of its stock was made. The assets of these closed-end companies are largely invested in common stocks. Total investment is about $7 billion.

Finally, there have been since 1967 the *dual-purpose, closed-end companies*. They issue securities of two types. One issue is called *income shares*, and the other issue *capital shares*. The income shares receive all income from company investments and have a minimum dividend that is cumulative. The capital shares receive all capital gains but do not receive dividends. The company has redemption dates of ten or fifteen years after establishment. The capital value appreciation at redemption date goes entirely to the owners of capital shares. These funds were popular in 1973 to 1974, but the earnings and capital gains record since then have not been sufficiently attractive to support new issues.

Operations. The open-end mutual investment company acquires funds to invest through the sale of its shares. The purchasers of these shares can sell them back to the company at a price equal to the value of the portion of total assets represented by the shares presented. Since 1971 these funds have been making larger payments to meet redemption requests than they have been receiving from new purchasers or from an increase in the value of assets held. In other words, the assets available to these funds have been declining.

The decline in the popularity of open-end funds lies basically in the decline in the market value of common stocks in 1973 and 1974 and the failure of the market to regain the level existing in 1968. Also, investors found interest rates available on bonds to be much higher than were dividends as a percent of stock prices. These conditions in turn affected the general attitude toward mutual funds. The investing public also was exposed to studies that appeared to demonstrate that the investment management skills of the mutual fund professionals were not great enough to keep up with the popular market averages.

Funds specializing in particular investment goals have become more popular in the mid-1970s than the basic "balanced funds" developed during the 1960s. Some of these funds specialize in securities of Japan or of Europe; others limit their purchases to a particular industry. The relatively high interest rates of the 1970s encouraged the development of money market funds. These funds invest in commercial paper, bankers acceptances, and U.S. Treasury bills. The managers of these funds, by spreading investments and taking some risks, have been providing more safety and higher returns than could be enjoyed by an individual investor.

In 1976 a new group of funds specializing in municipal bonds became possible as a result of a provision of the 1976 tax-reform law. The new provision permits investment companies owning municipal bonds to pass the interest payments to shareholders without any loss of tax exemptions. This had not been possible previously.

Taxation and Regulation. The federal government's Investment Company Act of 1940 laid the basis for thirty years of investment company growth. Prior to this legislation the Securities Exchange Act of 1934 had regulated investment companies along with other sellers of securities. The Investment Company's Amendments Act of 1970 set new standards for establishing charges for management and sales. Some of the 1970 sale regulations appear to have hurt the industry's competitive posture.

The taxation of investment companies by the federal government operates on the basis that investors made the security purchases directly. Therefore the companies themselves do not pay income taxes. To enjoy this tax immunity, 90 percent of net investment income and net short-term capital gains must be paid out to investors. Realized long-term capital gains need not be distributed, but in this case the maximum capital gains tax applicable to long-term gains is due. The amount paid is, of course, deductible by individuals from their tax liabilities.

Conclusion. The mutual fund, a Dutch invention, has been an important element in the secondary security market in the United States and of some but less importance in Europe. The willingness of funds to trade has caused security market impact to be considerably greater than indicated by their asset totals. Undoubtedly, the growth of tax-sheltered private sector pension arrangements (see Index) has at this point reduced the portion of the savings pot total that investment companies can expect to attract. More than likely, mutual funds are going to move over toward pension-type activities to gain the available tax shelter advantage for their investors.

Chapter 30

Real Estate Investment Trusts

The National Association of Real Estate Investment Trusts (REITs) reports that construction and development (C&D) loans dominate the investment portfolio of their members. These short-term mortgages are used to finance clearing the land and preparing it for construction and for financing the building of the structures on the land. The worth of the mortgages and payments of the high rate of return promised depend on the willingness of future owners and renters to take over the properties. In 1973–1974 many REITs found these user investors hard to find.

The REITs are very similar to the closed-end investment company. The big difference is that they are restricted to real estate investments. The equity holders are largely small investors as is true of mutual funds. In addition, pension fund managers and other trusts have been attracted by the opportunity REITs seemed to offer to invest in real estate and participate in the big real estate boom of the early 1970s.

As noted, many of these REITs were closely associated with many of America's largest and most prestigious commercial banks, and the names of these banks were used by the REITs to attract equity investment. In addition, the prestigious banks lending to REITs that were a part of their holding company found that they could not push them through bankruptcy to collect their loans and also that asset values backing C&D mortgages were grossly inadequate. The result in 1975 and 1976 was huge commercial bank losses from these sources that more than likely matched the investor equity losses arising from the sharp drop in the market value of REIT common stock.

The income of REITs was considered federal taxable income from the mid-1930s until it was changed in amendments to the Internal Revenue Code in 1960. This was the same year that the Real Estate Investment Trust Act was passed. To enjoy tax exemption, the REIT, like the mutual funds, must distribute to equity holders 90 percent of the profits exclusive of capital gains. To qualify as a REIT, the company also must at the end of each quarter have 75 percent of its assets in cash, government securities, or real estate mortgages and at least 75 percent of its gross income must come from earnings related to real estate investments. They are taxable on income earned from temporary management of property acquired through mortgage foreclosure.

The REITs are not really corporations and are headed by a board of trustees. However, these trustees are elected by the shareholders and are responsible to them just like a corporation's board of directors. A REIT could operate entirely on its own as do many mutual funds, but this is not the usual practice. A typical REIT contracts with an investor–adviser consisting of a mortgage bank within the same holding company arrangement to which the REIT belongs. The payment procedure for these services varies, and undoubtedly new incentive-related contracts will develop as REITs get back on their feet again.

The regulation of REITs in the past has been looser than that of other financial intermediaries. However, they must meet regular SEC disclosure requirements when securities are initially offered and make regular reports to the SEC when the securities are listed on a stock exchange. Also, state "blue sky" laws apply to REIT securities as to other securities sold in a particular state.

The REITs controlled about $20 billion of assets in 1973, before the roof fell in. In 1976, the value of their assets is being questioned seriously as foreclosures result in half-empty, half-completed office buildings, condominiums, and shopping centers as the assets rather than the numbers on a mortgage contract. Also, the commercial banks with large loans outstanding to REITs have been forced to reduce contracted payment requirements in order to avoid becoming property managers. It will take a few years to determine exactly what the value of REIT assets are. In some instances it appears that the value of equity investments has been absorbed largely in meeting interest and losses on loans to real estate developers.

In addition to stockholders and commercial banks, the REITs drew funds from commercial paper sales. When REITs were operating under favorable conditions commercial paper provided about 20 percent of the funds used. (Some losses later were suffered by the owners of this paper.) Here, of course, is a very clear example of speculation on the relation between short-term interest rates and long-term rates. When really tight money pushed short-term interest rates up to 12 percent in July 1974, the long-term borrowers from REITs could no longer pay the even higher rates required, so that the commercial paper-sourced financing from REITs could be continued.

Conclusion. The strength of the REITs in 1968 when they began to become popular was supposed to be in their flexibility as to source of funds and their specialization in real estate. These strengths were envisaged as making it possible, through purchase of shares of stock freely traded on stock exchanges, for a new group of investors to participate in financing new construction and to enjoy an income flow from rental receipts. In addition, ownership of real estate would provide inflation protection to investors in REITs just as it had to direct owners of homes and farms.

As it turned out, the strengths became weaknesses. The availability of short-term credit pushed REITs into speculative C&D mortgages rather than into the development of a long-term real estate income base. The REIT may have a permanent place within our intermediary financial institution structure, but some observers have doubts.

Chapter 31

Replacement of Financial Institution Credit

A considerable trend away from using commercial bank credit and toward the use of funds of nonfinancial firms has developed during the past ten years, i.e., since the first tight-money experience of 1966. This nonfinancial institution substitution and therefore financing by nonregulated institutions has a number of advantages that forecast continued growth.

Three main areas of development and change are in consumer installment and commercial credit, commercial paper, and bankers' acceptances. The expansion in all three areas has been at a fantastic rate. Avoiding financial intermediation is big business.

Installment Credit. The data on the provision of installment credit by major automobile manufacturers, nation-wide retail stores, and distributors of gasoline is incomplete. The data available, however give some idea of the importance. Three non-bank installment lenders have receivables outstanding equal to 11 percent of the quantity held by all commercial banks. One of these giant installment lenders has more receivables than the combined total for all commercial banks in New York and Chicago.

The provision of installment credit directly by the seller to the buyer is obviously convenient for all concerned. Also, the manufacturer and/or marketing group frequently has internally generated funds needing placement for short periods. Investment in its own agency to provide credit to the buyers of its products avoids the middleman, i.e., the intermediation credit institution. Therefore it avoids the costs of these services that result in a reduced earnings rate on funds available for lending. Also these nation-wide and in some cases world-wide business undertakings can raise funds at a lower cost than regulated financial institutions. Of course, the cost of government insurance of deposits is not a portion of the operation, but the assurance of insurance is not needed.

The cost-of-funds side favors the development of nonbank-financed installment and commercial credit. Other major advantages arise from the nation-wide and unregulated manner in which these finance operations can be managed. For example, national recognition and advertising of services is possible. Funds also can be moved readily from one area to another as demand for funds dictates.

The finance activities of a nonfinancial business firm need not be and are not limited to sales of products produced by these firms. For example, in 1972, only 2 percent of the credit acquired by one large credit corporation controlled by a nonfinancial business consisted of products produced by the business providing the funds.

Also, when a given finance company (see Index) wishes to sell out, the offer made by a nonfinance corporation will look better than one made by an OBHC. This is true because the seller doesn't have to worry about regulatory rejection as he does when negotiating with an OBHC.

One more point, a nonfinance corporation does not have to worry about capital adequacy as set down by a regulatory agency as does an OBHC. Capital of a nonfinance corporation is determined by security market judgments—and that is all.

Commercial Paper. The financing of sales activities often is provided through the sale of commercial paper to treasurers of other companies. These companies purchase commercial paper directly rather than accumulating deposits in commercial banks that might be used by the banks to purchase commercial paper. The step of intermediation is avoided. The economic source of funds, i.e., the corporate treasurer with excess funds, lends directly to the corporate treasurer or finance company with a need for funds. The lending treasurer earns more on his excess funds, and the borrowing treasurer gets the funds he needs at a lower rate than if they both had used a commercial bank as an intermediary.

The commercial paper market is the source of funds for some of the largest finance companies (see Index) as well as for corporations generally. The market grew rapidly in 1966 when interest rates rose to new highs and commercial banks could pay no more than 5½ percent on large CDs (over $100,000).

It was not until January 21, 1970, that these interest rate ceilings were removed.

Between the end of 1966 and the end of 1969 the total quantity of commercial paper outstanding increased from $13.6 billion to $32.6 billion. The quantity remained relatively constant for the next three years, and then along with the money crisis of 1973 came a 12 percent prime interest rate that was set by commercial banks on July 5, 1974. The quantity of commercial paper outstanding leaped from $34.7 billion at the end of 1972 to $71.1 billion by the end of 1973 and down to $49.1 billion by the end of 1974. This level has been maintained since then. In July 1977 the level of outstanding commercial paper was $60.3 billion.

Nearly three-fourths of the borrowing through issuance of commercial paper is done by finance companies. The other one-fourth of commercial paper is issued by nonfinance organizations. The buyers include all individuals, institutions, and groups that have funds to be put out on a short-term basis and that are willing to take a slight risk to earn more than U.S. Treasury bills pay or than can be earned on a CD with a short maturity.

The American commercial paper market extends beyond the national borders and is used to adjust liquidity balances throughout the world. On the other hand, there are short-term credit markets in the United States that are very local and informal. Here credit is extended on the basis of an intimate knowledge of needs and potentials. These credit transactions, although performing the function of commercial paper, do not become a portion of the total reported.

Bankers' Acceptances. The bankers' acceptance is another method of avoiding financial intermediation. When a banker's acceptance is used, credit is granted by the bank only to the extent that the bank guarantees payment. The actual funds to carry the credit are gotten through sale of the acceptance to an investor who may be the bank writing the original acceptance; most likely, however, it is an acceptance dealer who in turn sells it to an investor, who becomes the party who provides the funds to finance the credit extended.

The bankers' acceptance is closely associated with the financing of international commerce. Currently about 44 percent of the total dollar value of bankers' acceptances are based on imports into and exports out of the United States. The growth in the quantity of bankers' acceptances also has been very substantial since 1966. In this instance, however, the growth was relatively steady at about 20 percent a year until 1974, when the total more than doubled that of 1973 and reached the level of $18.5 billion where it has remained, with only minor growth, into 1977. The very substantial growth was financed very nearly entirely with noncommercial bank funds. Also, some 70 percent of the sharp jump in 1974 was based on financing activities other than imports and exports of the United States.

The dramatic 1974 increase arose from what are called "third-country bills." At the end of 1975 third-country bills accounted for about 55 percent of all bankers' acceptances outstanding. Most of the surge has been due to increased use of the U.S. acceptance market by the Japanese. It is estimated that less than 15 percent of Japanese exports and 3 percent of its imports are settled in the Japanese yen.

The bankers' acceptance is an ideal instrument to finance foreign trade shipments and needed off-shore storage. However, it is estimated that only about 15 percent of U.S. international merchandise trade was financed through use of bankers' acceptances.

Bankers' acceptances are rated on the basis of the reputation of the accepting bank. Therefore the activity is limited mostly to the very largest commercial banks. The attractiveness of the acceptance as far as a bank is concerned arises from the earning of a fee, usually $1\frac{1}{2}$ percent of the face value of the acceptance, for merely lending its name and credit rating by accepting a draft. The percentage is earned, of course, without tying up any of its funds. It is easy money for the bank. The only cost is that of carrying out the regular staff work needed to check credit ratings and the like of the parties involved plus the risk of nonpayment.

Chapter 32

Employee Stock Ownership Plan (ESOP)

This ESOP program is the result of the work of two men. One was Louis Kelso, a lawyer who wrote the book *Capitalist Manifesto*, which advocated that worker pension payments be paid directly by business firms rather than by government with funds collected from businesses. The second man was Senator Russell Long, the Chairman of the Senate Finance Committee who successfully fought for ESOP in 1974 and 1976.

The basic aim of the ESOP philosophy is to make capitalists out of employees. A secondary aim is to make employees realize that the reason retirement payments they receive have a value is because businesses are producing and that pensions are not the result of the bounty of government except to the extent that government, through the use of its police power, collects the taxes. Most unions fear employee stock ownership plans of any kind including ESOP. They are seen as devices to make workers relate less to their unions.

The benefits of ESOP are threefold. It is a procedure for management to work out arrangements for a new benefit for its workers in the form of ownership in their company. Secondly, it gives the company an inexpensive way to raise additional equity capital. Finally, it gives special tax advantages to the company entering into the arrangement. It works like this . . .

The company typically creates an employee stock ownership trust. The trust in turn borrows a substantial sum from the company's bank to purchase a good-sized block of the company's stock. The loan agreement provides for the company to make annual payments to retire the loan. As the loan is liquidated the shares providing the security for the loan are distributed to the employees according to the agreed-upon arrangement, but the stock is held in trust. The worker cannot sell or get possession of the stock until he quits, retires, or is fired. The company can deduct from its taxable income both the interest and the amount of loan repayments if it is under an ESOP plan; otherwise only interest is deductible.

The worker owns stock, the company has raised additional equity capital, and both benefit from improved worker morale. In addition, the bank has enjoyed a profitable loan. Everyone is better off except the U.S. Treasury, and in the long run it may benefit from an improvement in the efficiency of the company's operations.

In addition to the tax saving related to new capital, having an ESOP permits a company 1 extra percentage point of investment tax credit. This extra 1 percentage point of tax rate reduction can be enjoyed only if the saving is contributed to a company ESOP. This extra tax credit has not been used widely because the company using it must give its employees full voting rights on the ESOP shares held in their names.

There are a number of pitfalls in the introduction and operation of ESOPs. These largely are related to problems that could arise if the company didn't do well and its stock lost value. Nevertheless, ESOP's attractions have caused growth to be rather rapid among small and medium-sized companies. It is a procedure to turn ownership of a company over to the employees; and if it caught on in a big way, for example, by making dividends paid to ESOP deductible in calculating company taxable income as are interest payments, it could bring about a major worker finance–ownership revolution.

Chapter 33

Life Insurance Companies

The first life insurance company in the United States was called "The Corporation for Relief of Poor and Distressed Presbyterian Ministers and of the Poor and Distressed Widows and Children of Presbyterian Ministers." Many of the purposes of this first life insurance company established 220 years ago have been taken over at least partially by the U.S. social security system. Nevertheless, the private sector—through life insurance companies with about $300 billion of assets (compared with commercial bank total assets of about $1 trillion) and a 6 percent compounded asset growth rate—provides a significant portion of retirement and death benefits enjoyed by widows, their children, and the insured. Approximately two-thirds of life insurance company payments are for purposes other than to meet directly death benefit requirements. The face value of life insurance in force is over $2 trillion.

Organization and Purpose. The funds flowing into life insurance companies are based largely on long-term contractual arrangements. These whole life contracts, and to a lesser extent the rapidly expanding term life insurance contracts of the outstanding life insurance policies, provide for the accumulation of savings. This accumulation of a cash surrender value from whole life insurance policies, under conditions of loan-on-demand at a set interest rate, has been an additional advantage largely available only on whole life insurance contracts. During the Great Depression and again when unexpectedly high market interest rates appeared in 1966, 1969, and 1974, these cash loan values were utilized because the interest rate set in the contract was substantially below the market rate. The effect of this was to reduce temporarily the assets of life insurance companies and to increase emphasis on liquidity in the investment of life insurance company assets.

Term life insurance has been favored by personal finance advisers on the basis that the purchase of the protection provided by life insurance should be entirely separated from the savings decision. Whole life insurance, with its considerable savings element arising from flat rates that cause overpayment when the policy holder is young, has combined with a declining death rate to give life insurance companies a substantial long-term investment fund.

The difference in the value to the life insurance company of whole life insurance providing the same death payments as term insurance is demonstrated by the difference in the commission paid. The commission on the sale of a $100,000 term life policy is only about thirty dollars. The commission on the sale of a $100,000 whole life policy is about ten times greater.

The cash or loan value accumulated on a whole life policy does not increase payment in event of death. And if a loan had been negotiated the loan plus accrued interest is deducted from the death benefit. Really the cash or loan value of a whole life policy is the amount the policyholder is contributing toward his own death claim.

The life insurance industry is divided between the mutual (cooperative) companies and the stock companies. The competition of the mutuals in charges assessed for life insurance protection has been countered by the stock company emphasis on annuities and benefits from the accumulation of cash balances. Both the mutual and stock life insurance companies have benefited from favorable tax treatment at the federal level and suffered some from uncertain tax treatment at the state level.

Taxation. The federal income tax effective rate, i.e., as percent of life insurance company earnings, was around 7 percent or 8 percent in 1960. Gradually the treatment of life insurance company income by the federal government has been tightened, and today the effective corporate income tax rate applicable to life insurance company earnings is around 22 percent. This makes taxation of life insurance by the federal government in line with the effective rate paid by deposit financial institutions. To get around the vexing problem of taxable income of cooperatives (mutuals), a limitation on the deduction of policy owner dividends exists on both stock and mutual life insurance companies.

Another aspect of life insurance taxation by the federal government remains favorable. Reference here is being made to the exemption of accumulated earnings of cash balances to the insured as they accumulate. Of course, the insured is liable for taxation on the portion of later annuity payments coming from these earnings. The advantage lies in the fact that interest earnings on accumulations are not taxable as they arise.

Yet another tax break to life insurance buyers rests in the treatment of insurance as a portion of an inheritance. In their inheritance taxes the states typically give a special exemption of $50,000 to $100,000 to the portion of inheritance consisting of insurance. The estate tax benefit from having an estate of the deceased include insurance has decreased as a result of the 1976 federal tax legislation. The legislation changes the approach to exemptions of estates and more than doubles the effective maximum. Under the new procedures a tax credit, rather than an exemption of a portion of the base, is provided. This decreases the value of the insurance exemption to large estates. Also, the doubling of the effective maximum exemption to everyone makes the exemption of the insurance portion of the estate less helpful. All medium-sized estates are largely exempt from the estate tax under the 1976 federal tax legislation.

The insurance business still operates under the McCarren Act of 1945, which for all practical purposes exempts life insurances from the interstate commerce clause of the federal Constitution. As a result, states are not prohibited from giving favored treatment to companies incorporated in their state.

This opportunity has caused all but a few states (the states excluded include the home offices of a number of large insurance companies) to include in their statutes regulating and taxing the insurance industry a provision called the "retaliatory" clause. The provision of the clause requires the insurance commissioner to levy equivalently higher fees and taxes upon a foreign or alien insurer when the domicile state of that insurer charges its nondomestics more than the home state charges its nondomestics. This is aimed at keeping all states honest and causes an administrative nightmare in the process.

/   The basic insurance tax used by states is a premium tax, i.e., a percentage, say 2 percent or 3 percent of premiums received by a company. Many states exempt all or a portion of premiums on domestic risks that are paid to companies having a head office or that are incorporated within the state. The effect of this discriminatory tax treatment is to limit access to insurance companies by residents of some states. The state of Texas has been particularly active in encouraging domestic insurance companies. Texas, for example, requires that the ratio of investments of an insurance company doing business in Texas to total investments be at least equal to that of premiums collected in Texas to total premiums. In 1975 California repealed a law that exempted insurance company real estate consisting of the home office, a move away from favoring domestic insurance organizations.

Investments.   At the end of World War II, about 50 percent of life insurance company assets consisted of U.S. Treasury securities. Today only about 1.7 percent of life insurance company assets consist of these securities. Life insurance companies have become big investors in mortgages and corporate bonds with policy loans absorbing about 8 percent of investment funds.

There are a number of basic and sound money management reasons for life insurance company investment in mortgages. First and foremost, it provides the companies with a safe, long-term, high-yield use of funds in an investment with steady amortization of principal year by year. Second, mortgages in apartments and industrial facilities can be written to permit participation in equity and profits arising from the underlying investment. Mortgages and real estate have been accounting for about one-third of investment funds.

Corporate bonds absorb nearly one-half of life insurance investment funds. Most of these bonds are purchased on the basis of direct placement and do not pass through investment bankers and competitive bidding procedures. Life insurance companies have become a very important source of business debt capital. Also, the ready availability of life insurance funds to purchase debt issues has combined with the federal income tax treatment of interest payments as an expense to stimulate debt rather than equity financing of American businesses.

The higher federal taxes on life insurance earnings in recent years have made state and local securities with their tax exempt interest more attractive. They now have reached a level that approximates that of federal securities, or 1.7 percent of assets.

The final large absorber of life insurance company funds is stocks; nearly 78 percent are common stocks. Currently about 10 percent of life insurance company assets are accounted for by holdings of stock. This investment area is expected to ex-

TABLE 22

LIFE INSURANCE COMPANIES

(IN MILLIONS OF DOLLARS)

End of period	Total assets	Government securities				Business securities			Mort-gages	Real estate	Policy loans	Other assets
		Total	United States	State and local	Foreign¹	Total	Bonds	Stocks				
1971	222,102	11,000	4,455	3,363	3,182	99,805	79,198	20,607	75,496	6,904	17,065	11,832
1972	239,730	11,372	4,562	3,367	3,443	112,985	86,140	26,845	76,948	7,295	18,003	13,127
1973	252,436	11,403	4,328	3,412	3,663	117,715	91,796	25,919	81,369	7,693	20,199	14,057
1974ʳ	263,349	11,965	4,437	3,667	3,861	118,572	96,652	21,920	86,234	8,331	22,862	15,385
1975	289,084	14,582	5,894	4,440	4,248	135,014	106,755	28,259	89,358	9,634	24,389	16,107
1975—Apr	273,523	12,374	4,608	3,719	4,047	126,256	99,725	26,531	87,638	8,782	23,459	15,014
May	275,816	12,464	4,678	3,739	4,047	127,847	100,478	27,369	87,882	8,843	23,570	15,210
June	278,343	12,560	4,738	3,762	4,060	129,838	101,238	28,600	88,035	8,989	23,675	15,246
July	279,354	12,814	4,843	3,902	4,069	130,298	102,675	27,623	88,162	9,058	23,794	15,228
Aug	280,482	13,022	4,895	4,039	4,088	130,659	103,496	27,163	88,327	9,112	23,919	15,443
Sept	281,847	13,150	4,914	4,122	4,114	131,524	104,529	26,995	88,445	9,210	24,048	15,470
Oct	284,829	13,793	5,505	4,148	4,140	133,237	105,473	27,764	88,655	9,356	24,171	15,617
Nov	286,975	14,129	5,762	4,210	4,157	134,495	106,385	28,110	88,850	9,464	24,271	15,766
Dec	289,084	14,582	5,894	4,440	4,248	135,014	106,755	28,259	89,358	9,634	24,389	16,107
1976—Jan	293,870	15,380	6,446	4,652	4,282	138,965	108,130	30,835	89,395	9,661	24,498	15,971
Feb	296,479	16,142	6,458	4,790	4,894	140,332	109,321	31,011	89,543	9,726	24,633	16,103
Mar	299,552	15,723	4,967	5,220	5,536	143,105	111,385	31,720	89,781	9,812	24,755	16,376
Apr.ᵖ	299,983	15,917	5,198	5,100	5,619	143,197	111,757	31,440	89,489	9,852	24,873	16,655

¹ Issues of foreign governments and their subdivisions and bonds of the International Bank for Reconstruction and Development.

Note.—Institute of Life Insurance estimates for all life insurance companies in the United States.

Figures are annual statement asset values, with bonds carried on an amortized basis and stocks at year-end market value. Adjustments for interest due and accrued and for differences between market and book values are not made on each item separately but are included, in total in "Other assets."

pand as management of retirement funds and equity tie-ins with mortgage financing expand in importance. Also, a number of states have reduced their restriction on the investment of insurance reserves in common stocks. Nevertheless, because life insurance companies find the fluctuating market value of common stocks difficult to manage, life insurance companies are not likely to become large investors in common stocks.

Regulation. The types of investments, quantity of reserves, prices charged, and commissions paid by life insurance companies are subject only to state legislation. The license to do business as a life insurance company is issued by a state. Also the right to do business in any state is determined by that state. A life insurance company can do a nation-wide business and is not restricted to one state, an interstate business freedom not enjoyed by deposit institutions. On the other side of this advantage is the multitude of regulations that have to be met in each of the fifty states and the fierce competition met in each state by homegrown companies that have been granted tax and other advantages.

Table 22 provides a summary of life insurance company investment trends since 1971. The expansion of the quantity of assets since 1971 has not been much more than enough to keep up with the decline in the value of the dollar as measured by the consumer price index. The CPI increased by about 49 percent between 1971 and 1976, and the increase in the assets of life insurance companies was about 34 percent during the same period. Inflation hurts the industry.

The loss in the value of the monetary unit does not affect the liquidity of life insurance companies, because all benefits promised are in dollar units. Some activity in what are called *variable annuities* took place in the 1960s; benefits are related to value of stocks purchased, and some pension fund management is on this basis. However, the industry remains basically on the current monetary unit basis as of course is true of all deposit credit institutions.

Chapter 34

Property Liability Insurance
Companies

(CASUALTY INSURANCE COMPANIES)
(NONLIFE INSURANCE)
(PROPERTY–CASUALTY INSURANCE)

The first property liability insurance in the United States developed in Philadelphia with Benjamin Franklin one of the leaders. The company was called the Philadelphia Contributionships for the Insurance of Houses from Loss by Fire. The year was 1794. A few years later the Insurance Company of America (INA) made fire insurance available on properties anywhere in the country.

Fire insurance continues to be a very important portion of property liability insurance, but the danger from fire has fallen rapidly as modern heating facilities have expanded. Today automobile liability premium payments are more than five times as great as fire insurance premiums.

The property liability insurance, excluding accident and health insurance, has become an industry with annual gross receipts of $45 billion. The industry becomes a provider of savings and a source of investment funds as a result of unearned premium reserve accounting. The quantity of reserves required is set by the state legislation of the different states in which the companies do business.

Until insured losses are realized the casualty insurance companies have funds to invest in primary securities. The loss liabilities have proven to be difficult to forecast, and as a result casualty insurance companies are much more interested in short-term, highly marketable securities than are the life insurance companies. About 19 percent of funds are invested in short-term securities. Also, because the investment return is an important portion of the earnings of these companies, they have been interested in the higher earnings and capital gains available from holding corporate common stock.

The capital gains possibility from common stock owner-ships has been important because casualty insurance stock companies have been subject to the full impact of the 48 per-cent federal income tax and the additional 4 percent to 8 per-cent state corporate income tax rates. This relatively heavy potential tax liability also has caused casualty insurance com-panies to be active purchasers of state and local government securities, because interest payments arising from ownership of these securities are exempt from federal corporate income taxes. Corporate stocks make up about 40 percent of investments, and state and local government securities another 30 percent.

An investor in the stock of a nonlife insurance company is to a considerable extent making an investment in a mutual fund. The investor is purchasing professional management of funds invested in common stocks and municipals. The common stocks purchased are primarily those of utilities, banks, insurance companies, and other similarly conservative companies. Port-folios hold some mortgages and preferred stocks, but not much. To an extent the investment portfolio is just the reverse of that of life insurance companies. Common stock investments for stock nonlife insurance companies are particularly attractive, because they can deduct from taxable income 85 percent of dividend income from domestic corporations.

Large mutual companies are taxed just like stock com-panies, but small mutuals benefit from more favorable tax treat-ment. The smallest are taxed only on income they may earn on activities other than that arising from their own business. Re-ciprocals are taxed like mutuals. Domestic Lloyds (investors purchase a share of a risk) are taxed as partnerships.

The companies are nearly entirely regulated by states. However, certain activities concerning stocks and stockholders are subject to federal regulations. The states typically require reserves equal to 60 percent of liabilities compared to around 10 percent for S&Ls. This requirement has held down growth.

The total assets of nonlife insurance companies is less than $100 billion, making them about the size of finance companies and larger than credit unions or REITs. The average size of the 913 nonlife stock companies (1973) was $68.1 million in assets compared with $7.5 million each for the 312 largest mutual, nonlife insurance companies.

Chapter 35

Investment Clubs

Neighbors, employees, and social groups sometimes organize their own investment funds. They are called *investment clubs*, and they operate under a loose national organization called the National Association of Investment Clubs (NAIC). In 1975 the assets of NAIC member clubs was above $155 million, and if the total of the nation's estimated 32,000 clubs is included (on the assumption each of the non-NAIC clubs has assets equal to NAIC member clubs) the total gets close to three-quarters of a billion dollars. This is down from about $1.6 billion in 1969, when the dollar was worth about 40 percent more than in 1976.

The problem of investment clubs as of mutual funds is dropouts. Members become discouraged and wish to withdraw their funds when the market drops. Other members stay, waiting to recoup their losses; and as soon as they are about even in money terms (not purchasing power), they also sell out.

The clubs tend to consist of about twenty members, and each member invests a given amount every two weeks or so. The amount required is not apt to be more than $100 a month. The clubs meet every month or more often, and under NAIC regulations members are supposed to research selected shares individually. Some clubs, however, merely analyze the recommendations presented by the broker used by the club in making its purchases. As commercial banks become more active in arranging for sale and purchase of common stocks, the investment clubs can be expected to use these facilities, as they are oriented toward doing their own research.

The members of investment clubs aim to educate themselves. In addition, they hope to reduce costs of sale and purchase of common stock through larger transactions. Finally, by investing regularly, when the market is high and when it is low, they expect to benefit from averaging the price paid for their shares. The advice of NAIC to its member clubs is to invest regularly, irrespective of market outlook, and reinvest all earnings and purchase stocks of companies growing more rapidly than the general economy.

The NAIC has more advice and actually prepares what it considers to be a model portfolio for an investment club. For example, clubs are advised to invest in small and large companies but to concentrate in the stock of medium-sized corporations. Finally, the NAIC attempts to cheer up its member clubs by pointing out that the largest banks in the management of their trust departments didn't do any better than they did.

Member clubs benefit from NAIC-made statistical summaries of purchases and sales of common stock of all club members. These summaries permit clubs to compare the results they are experiencing with other club results around the country. To a degree, this gives the clubs a useful indication of investor psychology in the different regions of the country. The problem arises in the interpretation of these experiences.

Conclusion.   The investor club has proven to be able to exist when the market is weak as well as when it is strong. More than likely, an enterprising broker can develop new customers from club members who are dipping their toe into equity investing for the first time.

The new pension legislation (see Index), its tax sheltering provisions, and the requirement that established financial institutions be used will weaken the attractiveness of investment clubs. This pressure toward less use of investment clubs will be countered by extra convenience and lower trading charges available to those not wanting or needing investment advice.

Chapter 36

Pension Systems

Company noninsured pension plans now must meet the funding requirements of the Employee Retirement Income Security Act of 1974 (ERISA). The act requires that each qualified, defined pension program include a standard funding account. This account must be set up to show how the funds provided are going to meet the future costs of the benefits. The funds are to be provided by the employer, and no provision is made for voluntary employee contributions.

ERISA Requirements. If the employer does not make the payments into the account required to meet the minimum funding established in the standard funding account he becomes liable for payment of an excise tax. The tax is assessed on the amount of the fund deficiency. The rate of the tax is 5 percent and is imposed for each plan year of fund deficiency.

Employer-sponsored pension plans that meet certain safeguard requirements and specifically treat high- and low-ranked employees alike enjoy substantial tax benefits. The payment made into the established account is deductible from the taxable income of the firm but does not become a portion of the taxable income of the employee. In addition, reinvested earnings of the funds deposited in the account are not taxable. Of course, when the employee starts to receive benefits these payments are taxable.

Uninsured pension plans have become very popular as a portion of fringe benefits in labor contracts. This popularity has decreased as a result of the stiff funding, reporting and disclosure, and asset management requirements of the 1974 ERISA legislation. In addition, the cost of providing a level of benefits with a purchasing power equal to that originally contemplated has increased sharply as a result of the weak stock market of

1973–1977 and the restriction on acceptable investments. ERISA establishes a Pension Benefit Guarantee Corporation to insure payment of entitlements. Payments for this insurance is required for most plans.

The legislation does not require an employer to provide a pension plan, but it does make it possible to establish individual pension programs. The added costs and administrative difficulties of uninsured company pension programs and the availability of individual alternatives apparently have been reducing the use being made of company programs. In 1975 the number of pension plans dropped exceeded those started. And during the first quarter of 1976 only one-third as many corporate plans were approved as in the same period a year before. In addition, plan approvals were only about one-half as great as terminations.

IRA. The Individual Retirement Account (IRA) was also a portion of the 1974 pension legislation. It provides for the deduction of up to $1,500 from individual taxable income, or 15 percent of earned income, whichever is less. This amount must be put aside in an approved institution or fund. Banks, insurance companies, and thrift institutions have been the recipients of most of the funds.

The IRA provision of ERISA, in addition to providing a way for a firm to provide a tax-sheltered pension program for its employees with a minimum of administrative difficulties, eliminates much of the pension rollover problem. The IRA provides for payout from an abandoned company program or when a new job is taken without becoming liable for the income taxes deferred. The invested funds, those that the employee receives, can avoid tax liability if they are deposited in an IRA program within sixty days. Also, once placed in an IRA deposit, the interest earned is not taxable. Moreover, should the employee later join a company with its own pension program the funds in the IRA account, in certain circumstances, can be reinvested in the new employer's plan. A counterelement in the IRA plan is that the amount transferred cannot exceed the allowable limits without becoming liable to a nondeductible 6 percent annual excise tax on the excess as long as the excess remains in the account. Also, the amount the employee had contributed to the company pension plan may not be transferred to an IRA deposit.

There are some other shortcomings, but when all has been

TABLE 23

Assets of Private Noninsured Pension Funds, Book Value (1976)
(Millions of dollars).

Cash and deposits	$ 2,220
U.S. Government securities	12,343
Corporate and other bonds	38,301
Preferred stock	1,194
Common stock	86,823
Mortgages	2,382
Other assets	6,960
Total assets	150,223*

* Includes assets of profit-sharing funds.

TABLE 24

MARKET VALUE OF STOCKHOLDINGS OF INSTITUTIONAL INVESTORS AND OTHERS
(BILLIONS OF DOLLARS, END OF YEAR)

	1967	1968	1969	1970	1971	1972	1973	1974
1. Private Noninsured Pension Funds	51.1	61.5	61.4	67.1	88.7	115.2	90.5	63.3
2. Open-End Investment Companies	42.8	50.9	45.0	43.9	52.6	58.0	43.3	30.3
3. Other Investment Companies	7.5	8.3	6.3	6.2	6.9	7.4	6.6	4.4
4. Life Insurance Companies	10.9	13.2	13.7	15.4	20.6	26.8	26.3	22.2
5. Property-Liability Insurance Companies [1]	13.0	14.6	13.3	13.2	16.6	21.8	19.7	12.6
6. Common Trust Funds	3.9	4.8	4.6	4.6	5.8	7.4	6.6	5.3
7. Personal Trust Funds	75.9	83.6	79.6	78.6	94.1	110.2	94.7	70.9
8. Mutual Savings Banks	2.5	2.8	2.7	3.1	4.1	5.4	4.4	3.3
9. State and Local Retirement Funds	3.9	5.8	7.3	10.1	15.4	22.2	20.6	16.8
10. Foundations	20.2	22.0	20.0	22.0	25.0	28.5	24.5	18.4
11. Educational Endowments	7.7	8.5	7.6	7.8	9.0	10.7	8.8	6.2
12. Subtotal	239.3	276.1	261.6	272.0	338.7	413.7	346.0	253.6
13. Less: Institutional Holdings of Investment Company Shares	2.8	3.4	4.0	4.9	6.0	6.7	6.7	5.7
14. Total Institutional Investors	236.5	272.7	257.5	267.1	332.7	406.9	339.3	247.9
15. Foreign Investors [2]	24.0	28.8	26.9	28.7	32.7	40.8	36.6	26.3
16. Other Domestic Investors [3]	563.4	674.4	574.9	557.0	630.5	689.2	528.5	363.9
17. Total Stock Outstanding [1]	823.9	975.9	859.3	852.8	995.9	1136.9	904.4	638.0

[1] Excludes holdings of insurance company stock.
[2] Includes estimate of stock held as direct investment.
[3] Computed as residual (line 16 = 17−14−15). Includes both individuals and institutional groups not listed above.
[4] Includes both common and preferred stock. Excludes investment company shares but includes foreign issues outstanding in the U.S.

said there remain undeniable attractions of the IRA in a roll-over situation and for general use by employers and employees in establishing a tax-shelter pension program. However, complete portability of private and government pension programs has eluded the bill writers. A Joint Pension Task Force is supposed to be working on this badly needed reform.

Assets. The assets of private noninsured pension funds at the end of March 1976 are summarized in Table 23. The investment in common stocks at $86,823 million makes pension funds the second largest institutional holder of common stocks. Only personal trust funds are larger investors, and common stock holdings of open-end investment companies are not much greater than one-third as large.

Table 24 provides a summary of the stock ownership of institutional investors. The market value of these holdings fell sharply during 1973 and 1974 due to sharp stock market declines and to reduced popularity of common stocks as an investment.

Private pension funds and other trust, estate, and public funds are of tremendous importance in meeting business need of equity capital. Private pension funds alone are providing about $10 billion of new capital annually. They have become a major demand component in the capital markets of the United States.

The aggregate data of Table 24 are limited to stock ownership of the organizations of various types that are investing individual savings. Each of them also invests in government and corporate bonds and mortgages as Table 23 shows is the case with private noninsured pension funds. The group figures hide the great variation in investment policy followed by the various funds.

Insured Pension Funds. Insured pension funds have assets equal to about one-third that of noninsured pension funds. The insured pension fund is not a separate financial organization in the same sense as a noninsured fund. The savings deposited are used as received to purchase retirement benefits in the form of individual or group annuities. This premium income now can be invested separately from other insurance funds. This has given them considerably more leeway in investing pension funds. The investment of these premiums makes up a considerable share of life insurance company funds that are used to purchase common stock. About 80 percent of these separate account assets are so invested.

TABLE 25

CASH AND SECURITY HOLDINGS OF STATE AND LOCAL EMPLOYEES' RETIREMENT SYSTEMS BY TYPE OF ASSET

END OF FISCAL YEARS 1960 AND 1974

Type of asset	Amount (billions)		Percent of total	
	1960	1974	1960	1974
Cash and deposits	$ .2	$ 1.5	1	2
Federal securities	6.0	5.3	32	6
State and local securities	4.3	1.4	23	2
Corporate bonds	6.1	47.4	33	54
Corporate stocks	.4	19.6	2	22
Mortgages	1.2	6.6	6	8
Other	.3	5.7	2	6
Total	18.5	87.5	100	100

TABLE 26

RECEIPTS OF STATE AND LOCAL EMPLOYEES' RETIREMENT SYSTEMS BY SOURCE

SELECTED FISCAL YEARS, 1960–1974

Year	Total	Employee contributions	Government contributions	Earnings on investments
	Receipts (millions)			
1960	$ 3,393	$1,140	$1,652	$ 601
1965	5,260	1,626	2,418	1,216
1970	9,848	2,788	4,600	2,460
1971	11,310	3,159	5,241	2,910
1972	12,620	3,400	5,750	3,471
1973	14,878	4,166	6,649	4,064
1974	16,527	4,207	7,821	4,500
	Percentage distribution by source			
1960	100.0	33.6	48.7	17.7
1965	100.0	30.9	46.0	23.1
1970	100.0	28.3	46.7	25.0
1971	100.0	27.9	46.3	25.7
1972	100.0	26.9	45.6	27.5
1973	100.0	28.0	44.7	27.3
1974	100.0	25.5	47.3	27.2

STATE AND LOCAL EMPLOYEES
RETIREMENT SYSTEMS (SLERS)

The SLERS have assets equal to about one-half those of the uninsured pension funds. Since the late 1960s they have become more active in the stock market but remain much less committed than the uninsured pension funds. It is in corporate bonds where the SLERS have found their favorite investment. Table 25 shows that in 1974 they held $47.4 billion in corporate bonds, which represented about 54 percent of total assets. The SLERS have become providers of a substantial quantity of debt capital for investment in the private sector, with some indication that they will become larger providers of equity capital in the future.

The funds flowing into SLERS come from employee contributions, employer payments, and earnings from previous investments. During the past several years the employee share has tended to decline, and the share coming from earnings has increased by about the same percentage. The employer payments share has remained fairly stationary (see Table 26).

Reform Actions. The SLERS were not included in the provisions of ERISA as was mentioned above. Recent problems of cities in meeting pension commitments point to a need for guidelines. Congress responded to this clearly felt need and set up four committees to complete studies by 1977 in the following areas:

1. The adequacy of existing levels of participation, vesting, and financing arrangements.

2. Existing fiduciary arrangements.

3. The necessity for federal legislation and standards with respect to public plans.

A serious overcommitment pension problem has been plaguing the pension systems of many, if not all, government units including the federal government. The serious New York City crisis in the spring of 1975 highlighted the state and local government problem. A respected study released in the fall of 1975 by the American Enterprise Institute concluded that state and local government pension systems are falling short of what they will need to meet their obligations by a very conservative $3.5 billion a year.

In studying the funding adequacy problem each committee

has been asked to consider establishing funding minimums as well as the taxing powers of the various governments maintaining the pension programs. One approach to the determination of adequacy of the funding of SLERS is to apply the standards ERISA has set for uninsured pension systems in the private sector. When this is done, the SLERS do not come out badly.

Of the thirty-two states with firm information, twenty-eight have provided for funding of past service liabilities within a forty-year period. For most private plans the forty-year amortization period meets the requirements of ERISA. So in this important area the major systems of many states meet private pension-required standards. This is less true of large-city pension systems. For example, Atlanta, Indianapolis, and Seattle have pay-as-you-go retirement systems, i.e., no funding provided.

In the area of vesting, state and local practices are less well known, but it appears that they generally meet ERISA requirements for private systems. A study of police systems, however, concluded that vesting was seldom available in police retirement plans.

In the manner of investing funds received the SLERS are generally more conservative than the ERISA standards. Therefore if ERISA rules also were applied to SLERS, the result would be a general loosening of investment restrictions. However, ERISA rules would cut out some unconscionable pension fund raids to support deficit governments and also the use of pension funds to support the market for securities issued by weak state and local government units.

Keogh Plan. The Keogh plan program to assist self-employed owner or partner individuals to develop a retirement income is not an acronym. It is the name of the New York congressman largely responsible for the 1974 legislation setting up the program.

Under the plan the lesser of $7,500 annually or 15 percent of earned income plus the interest earned on the funds accumulated are sheltered from the federal income tax. Benefits from the straight life annuity commence at age 65 or after 5 years, whichever is later. These payments are taxable.

Keogh plan receipts have become a growing portion of the investment funds of investment companies and of deposit financial institutions. Very competitive conditions in terms of investment plan, interest rates, and services have developed between institutions with qualified programs. It is a new growth area that may be promising more than can be delivered.

Conclusion. The provision of pension systems outside the federal government's social security system is going through a period of considerable change. The net result is likely to be a stimulation of savings of those in the middle-income brackets. These additional savings may help to meet the heavy capital needs of American industry and the housing sector, but the result may instead me largely reduced deposits in savings institutions. Also, a broad coverage by pension systems outside the social security programs will reduce the need for expansion of the benefits available from these programs to aid in the financing of retirement years of average income receivers.

PART VII: SELECTED REFERENCES AND SOURCES

Business Week, "More Employees Raise the ESOP Banner," March 1976, 58–60.

————, "The Overloading of the Nation's Insurance System," September 6, 1976, 46–50.

Loring C. Farwell (ed.), *Financial Institutions* (Homewood, Ill.: Irwin, 1966).

Federal Reserve Board, "Survey of Finance Companies," *Federal Reserve Bulletin*, March 1976, 197–207.

————, "One Bank Holding Companies," *Federal Reserve Bulletin*, December 1972, A99–A101.

Edward P. Foldessy, "Holding-Firm Concept Turns Sour for Banks as Profits Fall Short," *Wall Street Journal*, April 20, 1976, 1, 24.

J. G. Gurley and E. S. Shaw, "Financial Aspects of Economic Development," *American Economic Review*, June 1955, 515–538.

Insurance Information Institute, *Insurance Facts*, 1976 (New York: 1976).

George Katona, "Consumer Investment and Business Investment," *Michigan Business Review*, July 1961, 18–19.

Gigi Mahon, "Competition for Retail Brokerage Business Sharpens," *Barrons*, July 12, 1976, 5, 20.

Thomas B. Marvell, *The Federal Home Loan Bank Board* (New York: Praeger, 1969).

Margaret D. Pacey, "Investment Clubs Are Still Ready to Go," *Barrons*, April 7, 1975, 3, 22.

F. H. Schott, "Disintermediation Through Policy Loans of Life Insurance Companies," *Journal of Finance*, June 1971, 719–729.

Tax Foundation, *Employee Pension Systems in State and Local Government*, Research Publication No. 33 (New York, 1976).

U.S. Department of Labor, *Often-Asked Questions About the Employee Retirement Income Security Act of 1974* (Washington, D.C.: 1976).

———, *Fiduciary Standards Employee Retirement Income Security Act* (Washington, D.C.: 1975).

———, *Reporting and Disclosure Employee Retirement Income Security Act of 1974* (Washington, D.C.: 1975).

U.S. Treasury, "Consumer Would Benefit from Financial Institutions Bill," *Treasury Papers*, August 1976, 14–15.

D. Wrightsman, "Pension Funds and Economic Concentration," *Quarterly Review of Economics and Business*, Winter 1967, 29–36.

Part VIII

Federal Government Lending

INTRODUCTION

The federal government in recent years has used credit subsidies and guarantees to meet many demands coming out of rising citizen entitlements. These actions have included financial service-providing agencies plus regulation and control of financial institutions and their credit instruments. This part is concerned largely with the portion of federal government financial actions that combine fund provision and regulation in their operations. These agencies and activities have been divided into four groupings: housing, agriculture, international, and business.

A few years ago the Joint Economic Committee of Congress made a staff study of federal government credit provision programs. They identified forty-two major federal programs, i.e., rated major if credit extended exceeded $10 million. The programs were designed to finance housing, agriculture, commerce, economic development, natural resources, education, and medical care. The loans outstanding totaled over $80 billion, and the loan guarantees were another $200 billion; the budgeted cost was about $10 billion.[1]

Between fiscal years 1965 and 1975, the cumulative net borrowing of the federal government for off-budget programs (which is a broader concept than the one used in the estimates of the previous paragraph) totaled $173 billion. This is $30 billion greater than the cumulative unified regular budget deficits during the same period. The federal government has been sopping up and allocating for legislatively determined social purposes an enormous portion of the savings pool available. In the mid-1970s crowding out became the "in" words to explain

[1] Totals are rough estimates.

high interest rates and large federal government deficits. Along with government largess comes government regulation. Or as was once said, "You can't get the federal government off your back until you get your hand out of its pocket."

On the other side of this continuing debate as to whether a nation's savings are used most wisely if determined by market or political decisions is the feeling that the financial marketplace gives too many advantages to the strong. This tendency of the financial marketplace is bad for democracy and reduces the efficiency of the economy. Where the federal government has the power to correct the weakness it should use it. The federal government is doing what needs to be done for the good of the market system when it brings about considerable social allocation of savings and regulates the credit rationing activities of financial institutions and other controllers of investment funds.

Credit Gap Concept. The primary reason offered through the years for federal government provision of credit has been to fill credit gaps. True credit gaps exist only when prospective private benefits that would arise from the equal treatment of all credit needs exceed cost caused by barriers of one sort or another faced by some credit users. A true credit gap is quite a different animal from a situation where subsidy is· justified because social benefits will exceed private costs.

If federal lending were limited to true credit gaps, the appropriate policy of the federal government would be aimed at eliminating the credit gap so the federal credit program also could be eliminated. This, as the following discussions demonstrate, has not been the experience in the United States during the past forty years.

Federal government provision of credit has grown because social and political policy pointed to needs that could be met more cheaply with subsidized credit than with immediate budgetary commitments. The result has been some replacement of some unsubsidized borrowing with government-guaranteed loans. This has in turn increased the cost of credit in the unsubsidized private sector and developed pressure for an expansion of the money supply and resulting additional inflation.

As each of the government credit programs are considered in this part and in the two parts dealing with government international credit activity that follow, keep in mind the basic analytical concept of opportunity costs. In other words ask yourself the question: "If the credit had been allocated strictly by the market and therefore where return expectations—after allowing for risk—were the greatest, would the overall economic and social welfare have been greater than under a group of government credit gap filling and credit subsidy programs?" To arrive at an answer is complex, and room for difference of opinion exists.

One of the truly fundamental financial developments of the past century is the expansion of the activities of the federal government in the extension of credit and the insurance and guarantee of lending by private institutions. From a very small start in the area of long-term agricultural credit in 1916, federal government credit activities and federal government department balances have grown to include over twenty specialized government agencies with securities outstanding of $100 billion (1975). In addition, FHA insurance and VA guarantees have underwritten another $150 billion of residential loans (1975).

Types of Lending. In nearly all cases federal government loan and credit agencies have not entered into direct competition with private lenders. Basically the federal government has commenced lending activities in the absence or inability of private sources to provide needed funds and in order to bolster private enterprise. The federal government does not engage in lending as a straight business transaction. Nearly without exception it has lent money only to further the accomplishment of a public purpose—social or economic. This general purpose has been reached by the following broad categories of objectives.

1. Government financial assistance has been used to build up mutual credit institutions for the purpose of broadening the availability of credit and increasing the stability of credit systems. These activities include the Federal Reserve banks, the Federal Home Loan banks, the Federal National Mortgage Association, and the Federal Intermediate Credit banks of the Farm Credit Administration.

2. Government financing has been used to build up mutual credit insurance institutions as experiments in the underwriting of institutional stability. As a result we have the Federal Deposit Insurance Corporation, the Federal Savings and Loan Insurance Corporation, the Credit Union Insurance Corporation, the Federal Housing Administration, the Veterans Administration, and the Rural Housing Insurance Fund; the latter three are underwriters of home-mortgage insurance.

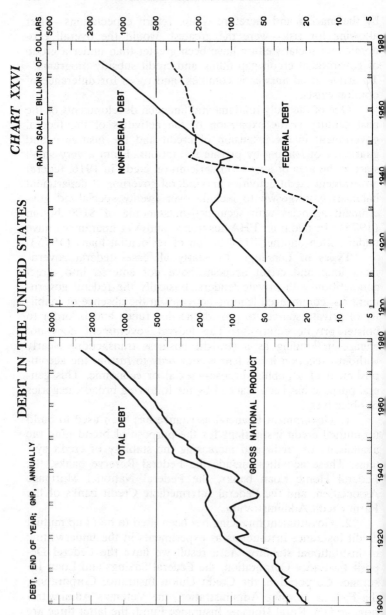

CHART XXVI

DEBT IN THE UNITED STATES

RATIO SCALE, BILLIONS OF DOLLARS

NONFEDERAL DEBT

FEDERAL DEBT

DEBT, END OF YEAR; GNP, ANNUALLY

TOTAL DEBT

GROSS NATIONAL PRODUCT

3. Government financing has been used to build up the nation's industrial potential in response to the requirements of war and national security. The Reconstruction Finance Corporation, the facilities of the Federal Reserve System, the Export–Import Bank, the Foreign Operations Administration, and other agencies were employed in these activities.

4. Government funds have been loaned directly to private individuals and business concerns in financial distress, for purposes not associated with war or national security. The Export–Import Bank, Banks for Cooperatives, and the Reconstruction Finance Corporation are active in this field at the present time, and the Farm Credit Administration conducts a curtailed program, having been engaged more extensively in emergency programs in previous years.

5. Government lending has been employed in programs undertaken primarily to subsidize the activities of individuals or business enterprises. The programs of the Farmers' Home Administration, the Public Housing Administration, the Rural Electrification Administration, the Commodity Credit Corporation, Banks for Cooperatives, and the Small Business Administration are examples.

Chart XXVI shows a parallel growth of debt and GNP. The federal debt grew very rapidly between 1925 and 1941; since then nonfederal debt has been the area of rapid growth. Much of the nonfederal debt is directly and indirectly guaranteed by the federal government. The federal insurance of deposits (see Index) underlies all of the special programs in the chapters in this part.

In addition to the federal government's direct and guaranteed debt obligations there exist immense insurance liabilities. These go from deposit insurance to riot insurance. It was estimated in mid-1975 that these totaled $1.5 trillion and were climbing every day. Finally there exist about $30 billion of contingent international claims. The total works out to about $2.5 trillion.

Chapter 37

Housing Credit

The United States is a big user of savings to finance housing. Total mortgages on housing are about $700 billion (see Chart XXVII). This is over three times the total of all installment debt and about twice the total of interest-bearing public debt. About $130 billion of the housing debt is guaranteed by the federal government, and another $90 billion of mortgage debt is owed by agencies of the federal government.

Much of the federal government housing activity consists of extending and guaranteeing loans. The program was initiated in 1932 and resulted in the establishment of a number of agencies. The Home Owners Loan Corporation (HOLC) is now inactive, but its role was reassumed by the federal government in the Emergency Home Purchase Act of 1974. The HOLC was formed to refinance home mortgages. The development of low-rent housing and slum clearance is still active and is organized within the Public Housing Administration (PHA). The aid is extended as loans and also as annual subsidies by the Housing Act of 1937. The Federal Housing Administration (FHA) was established to increase housing loans through guarantee of payment and lower interest rate and collateral requirements. It is very active and has guaranteed a large number of home mortgages. The Public Housing Administration (PHA) was also established during the 1930s. Legislation of 1949 restored this program to major significance, and the Housing and Urban Development Act of 1968 went off in new directions to increase the supply of low-cost housing.

World War II Program. During World War II, programs to provide emergency housing needs functioned under the Lanham Act and have been liquidated. These programs did not make extensive use of loans to achieve their aims but rather entered directly into construction activity.

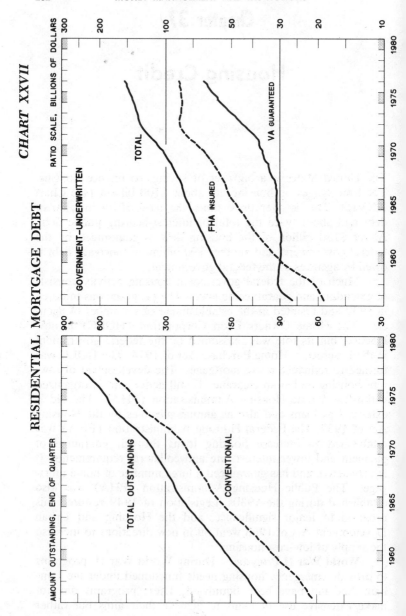

CHART XXVII

RESIDENTIAL MORTGAGE DEBT

During the 1950s federal government guarantee of loans to provide housing expanded greatly. The "G. I. Bill of Rights" provides for the guarantee of home loans by the Veterans Administration. VA guaranteed loans are obtainable with a minimum of red tape, with extremely low down payments, small monthly payments, and low rates of interest. The program was extended to cover Korean veterans, and in 1966 the program was expanded to cover all veterans of the service after January 31, 1955. Between 1945 and 1962 more than one-fifth of all private, single-family construction involved loans guaranteed by the VA.

Chart XXVII summarizes the role of VA and FHA mortgages in financing the growth of housing and construction since 1955. The VA guaranteed mortgage total remained constant from 1955 to 1967, while FHA totals increased steadily and rather rapidly from 1956 to 1970 and then flattened out.

Housing and Urban Development (HUD). The loan guarantee program and housing assistance programs of HUD are worthy of additional consideration. Existing legislation provides for different insurance programs. The former FHA insurance program and some of the added insurance provisions are as follows:

1. Title I. Insurance of loans to alter, repair, improve, and, within certain limitations, construct both residential and nonresidential properties.

2. Section 203. Insurance of mortgages up to 80, 90, or 95 percent of appraised value on new and existing one-to-four-family homes. A Section 203(n) initiated in 1975 makes benefits available to those purchasing stock of a cooperative housing project.

3. Section 207. Insurance of mortgages up to 80, 90, or 95 percent of value on multifamily residential rental projects.

4. Section 608. Insurance of mortgages on multifamily residential rental projects on special terms designed to stimulate production of rental housing under present economic conditions.

5. Section 609. Insurance of loans for the manufacture of housing by industrial processes and short-term notes incident to the sale of prefabricated homes.

6. Section 610. Insurance of mortgages executed in connection with the sale by the federal government of certain federally owned housing.

7. Section 611. Insurance of construction loans on groups of twenty-five or more single-family dwellings constructed by modernized, large-scale, site-construction methods.

8. Title VII. Yield insurance for investors in large-scale rental housing projects.

9. Section 235, which was reactivated in 1975, provides for an interest-rate subsidy to qualified home buyers.

10. A new program aimed at assisting the Indian Housing Authorities was introduced in 1975.

11. Section 8 provides housing assistance payments for lower income families occupying new or substantially rehabilitated or standard rental housing.

12. Section 202. Authorizes long-term direct loans for rental or cooperative housing for the elderly and handicapped.

13. Section 236. HUD assists tenants who cannot afford to pay "basic rents" with 25 percent of their adjusted incomes.

The finance of these programs is assisted by the Federal National Mortgage Association (FNMA, or Fannie Mae), a federal-related agency that buys and sells government-backed home mortgages in the secondary market; it does not make direct mortgage loans. It was established in 1938, and pursuant to Congressional action in 1954, FNMA was rechartered by Congress into a mixed-ownership corporation. In 1968 Congress divided FNMA into two separate corporate entities. One was FNMA, which became completely privately owned with stock listed on the New York Stock Exchange. The other was the new Government National Mortgage Association (or "Ginnie Mae" —GNMA).

FNMA engages in the sale of participation certificates at public offerings. Mortgages are pooled and participation is sold at going market interest rates. The receipts from the mortgages permit FNMA to make the interest payments and to retire the certificates of participation. This procedure has eliminated the need to use federal funds to finance FNMA operations.

By 1977, in terms of assets Fannie Mae was the sixth largest American corporation. Some feared that Fannie Mae was becoming so large that it could crowd other private corporations out of the debt market. As a result, HUD began to use its power over FNMA to force it to sell some of its huge mortgage portfolio and use the funds to finance low- and moderate-income mortgages.

The nickname for the Federal Home Loan Mortgage Corporation is Freddie Mae. An acronym "flimic" would just not work.

Freddie Mae is an offspring of the Federal Home Loan Bank Board (FHLBB) established to also help develop a secondary mortgage market. It does this through the same procedures as Ginnie Mae established by the government's National Mortgage Association.

The pass-throughs (bundle of mortgages bought from S&Ls, banks, and other sources and sold to investors participating in the pool who receive the interest on the mortgages) of Freddie Mae come no smaller than $100,000.

Bonds or certificates backed by guaranteed mortgages are sold by private organizations as well as through the FHLBB and its Freddie Mae. To increase safety, and therefore marketability, privately offered bonds and certificates backed by guaranteed mortgages often also benefit from a private mortgage insurance policy. These bonds and certificates bear an interest rate about one percentage point above federal government securities with a comparable maturity. They are offered in denominations as low as $10,000. Freddie Mae mortgage holdings totalled $3.4 billion in August 1977.

GNMA on the other hand assumed responsibility for those mortgage purchasing functions that could not economically be carried out in the private sector. During fiscal year 1976 it lost money, about $550 million. The wholly federal government-owned GNMA operates within HUD to administer three types of activities:

1. The guarantee of securities based on government-backed mortgages.

2. Assistance to certain types of housing and to the mortgage and housing market during periods of tight credit through purchase of mortgages.

3. Management of a portfolio of mortgages owned by various agencies of the federal government.

In its activity to find buyers for mortgages bearing interest rates below the market rate and held by recognized mortgage lenders such as banks and S&Ls, GNMA operates under the *tandem plan*. Under this procedure GNMA uses U.S. Treasury borrowed funds to purchase mortgages at face value and subsequently sells them at market price. The loss suffered is absorbed by GNMA. Since 1974, GNMA can carry out these activities using conventional mortgages as well as FHA and VA insured mortgages. GNMA, through its tandem plan, provides a federal subsidy to those borrowing to construct or hold housing. It is an important aspect of why structural reform in the U.S. housing mortgage market has made little progress.

The funds provided at below-market-rate interest levels through GNMA under the Emergency Home Purchase Act of 1974 have been substantial. Mortgages were financed at a 7½ percent rate of interest when the market rate was 9 and 10 percent. Some $18.5 billion were released under the program through the first portion of 1976. This was sufficient to support the financing of over 620,000 housing units or about one-half of all new housing during the housing slump period.

GNMA is constantly working to develop new procedures of marketing to private investors the mortgages it acquires. The disposition of mortgages is, of course, the very heart of the tandem procedure as well as of the desire of HUD to develop a national market for mortgages.

In January 1975 a new procedure enabled GNMA to combine sales of mortgages with the issue of mortgage-backed securities. Loan sources of mortgages purchased are invited to pool mortgages for the purpose of backing securities. Then the pooled mortgages are sold at auctions on the basis of highest-bidder-take-all. The security dealers then market the mortgage-backed securities to investors.

Another one is the whole loan auction. Investors make offers to purchase FHA project mortgages held in GNMA's Special Assistance Functions portfolio. Sometimes only an option to purchase at a given price is sold.

Finally, conventional mortgages can be repurchased by the original mortgagee. The GNMA weekly establishes a price reflecting money market conditions. The difference between this current value of the mortgage and the original face value is the amount the repurchaser would receive from GNMA when the deal is made.

Summary. All of these procedures are methods to keep an adequate portion of savings as seen by Congress flowing into the housing mortgage market. The devices are complex and multiple in nature. Also, many of them require considerable administrative attention. Whether any of these actions are proper in a society dedicated to market allocation of savings has been answered politically, because growth has been continuous since the beginnings in 1932 and 1937.

TABLE 27

HUD/FHA MORTGAGE AND LOAN INSURANCE
WRITTEN DURING CALENDAR YEAR 1975

(DOLLAR AMOUNTS IN THOUSANDS)

Program	Number	Amount	Units
Grand Total	508,419	$7,941,327	N/A
Home Mortgages	255,061	6,166,115	266,994
Unsubsidized	249,769	6,058,061	260,980
Subsidized	5,292	108,054	6,014
Multifamily Housing Mortgages	325	776,139	38,044
Unsubsidized	157	346,534	17,981
Subsidized	168	429,604	20,063
Other Mortgages[1]	74	200,114	N/A
Title I Loans	252,959	798,959	N/A
Property Improvement	245,112	720,819	N/A
Mobile Homes	7,847	78,140	N/A

[1]Includes mortgages and loans insured on Section 207 mobile home spaces, Section 213(j) supplemental loans, Section 223(d) two year operating loss loans, Section 232 nursing home beds, Section 241 supplemental loans and nursing home beds, and Section 242 hospital beds.

N/A – Not Applicable

Table 27 provides a summary of HUD financing activities during a year in which the construction of houses was a depressed industry. The total of new housing units constructed in 1975 was about 1.1 million. Over one-half of this total benefited from federal mortgage insurance, loans, and subsidies.

GNMA securities since 1973, the year of the money crunch, have become a favorite investment of pension funds, bank trust departments, and insurance companies. This activity is induced by the competitive interest rates offered and the marketability of the securities. The result is a secondary market for housing debt of greater depth and breadth. It also means the mortgage debt market has an advantage over the corporate bond market that lacks a GNMA and its government guarantee and subsidy.

Chapter 38

Agriculture Credit

Agricultural lending by the federal government is conducted through a number of major agencies with ancillary institutions and groups, some permanent and some quite temporary. Some of these agencies are largely privately owned and managed, whereas others are nearly entirely government owned. They are engaged in a great variety of agricultural-related lending activities.

Since 1952 the productivity of agriculture has increased more rapidly than that of the rest of the economy. This productivity expansion required increasing levels of investment and ready availability of short- and long-term credit. The federal government, through specialized credit institutions, actively assisted the commercial banks to meet the need.

Short-term credit is extended by the Federal Intermediate Credit Banks (FICB), the Banks for Cooperatives (BC), the Production Credit Corporations (PCC), and the Production Credit Associations (PCA). These comprise a total of 37 federal government corporations and about 500 associations. The FICBs and PCCs are entirely owned by the federal government. This is also largely true of the Banks for Cooperatives, but it is no longer true of PCAs. At present about 86 percent of the stock of PCAs is owned by farmer members.

LONG-TERM LENDING. Long-term loans have been made by the Federal Land Banks (FLB) and the Federal Farm Mortgage Corporation. These two agencies hold about one-third of all farm mortgages. The Federal Land Banks were established in 1916 to extend loans on farm mortgages that had been previously accepted by the cooperative mortgage-credit associations provided for under the original Federal Farm Loan Act. These loans have been extended only if the value of the security was considerably (usually 50 percent) greater than the amount of the loan.

DEPRESSION LENDING. The sharp drop of agricultural prices in the 1930s necessitated financing upon a more liberal basis. The Federal Farm Mortgage Corporation established in 1934 was designed to meet this need. It obtained its funds for lending from the federal government and from the sale to the public of bonds guaranteed by the federal government. The lending authority of the corporation expired in 1947.

Production and Mortgage Credit. The three federal agricultural lending agencies that raise funds from the sale of bonds to investors are the Banks for Cooperatives, Federal Intermediate Credit Banks, and Federal Land Banks. Between 1970 and 1975 loans to cooperatives by BCs increased from $2 billion to $4 billion, loans and discounts of FICBs increased from $5 billion to $10 billion, and mortgage loans of FLBs increased from $7.2 billion to $16.6 billion.

The $27.8 billion of agriculture-related credit provided by these three federally sponsored credit agencies does not place a drain on the U.S. Treasury. The funds used are raised directly from sale of securities. The pertinent question to ask is: When have conditions that existed when the government entered a financing area changed enough to justify abandonment of the activity?

A fairly good case can be made that agriculture credit conditions have stabilized and the agriculture industry has been strengthened so that federal government support is no longer needed. In fact, the very substantial increase during the past five years of the mortgages held by the FLBs can be pointed to as a harmful influence. The availability of mortgage funds on favorable terms from the FLBs has been an element in the bidding up of agricultural land prices. To the extent that this is true the FLBs have added to costs without increasing efficiency or the level of production in agriculture. FLB lending has been another element in the creation of inflation, and it has indirectly encouraged corporation farming by reducing the ability of family farmers to cover the heavy land investment required to have a commercial farm.

The Farmers Home Administration. The Farmers Home Administration (FmHA) has always been less of a business-type government agency than the other agriculture credit groups. The FmHA traces its beginnings back to 1935 and the Resettlement Administration (RA). The RA had the job of making short-term loans to low-income farmers, which is continued by FmHA in its farm operating loan program. The RA was also responsible for a program to resettle and rehabilitate a large group of farmers racked by drought and depression.

The basic thread running through the various forms of RA down to the current FmHA is that assistance is given only to farmers and then only to those unable to qualify for financial assistance from some other source. This limited area of responsibility was pristine when the RA went through its first evolutionary stage in 1938, became the Farm Security Administration (FSA), and was placed under the Department of Agriculture.

The loans (forty-year loans) to marginal farmers aimed at farm ownership combined with technical and supervisory assistance proved to be a very successful program and provided the background for the Bankhead–Jones Farm Tenant Act of 1937. The first addition made to this limited rural teaching and financing program was the takeover of the farm water facilities in 1942. From this small expansionary step has come a whole galaxy of programs.

The stem explanation of why the original RA became what it is today is: (1) it had an organization extending from Washington, D.C., into nearly every county and therefore it provided a convenient administrative tree on which additional farm-related assistance actions could be hung; and (2) the Department of Agriculture was interested in continuing control over programs that in one way or another affected rural America.

It was in 1946 that FSA was replaced by FmHA. At the same time a new, insured farm ownership loan program was introduced. Prior to this funds for loans came from the U.S. Treasury. With the development of insurance for these farm loans, funds from the private sector became available. The idea of supervision and training of farmers of the original RA programs was continued. The insurance was and is provided through the Agricultural Credit Insurance Fund (ACIF). ACIF is based on federal government capital provided by the U.S. Treasury. Annual appropriations to ACIF are limited largely to amounts needed to cover losses. Prior to 1974 ACIF through FmHA also acquired funds through the sale of obligations directly to individuals and finance institutions. Since 1974 the

Federal Financing Bank (see Index) deals with the investing public.

The water facilities program expanded from helping in financing sanitary pumps for farms to water systems to villages and cities with populations up to 5,500 and waste disposal systems for communities up to the same population maximum. In 1975 grants and loans for these purposes totaled $869 million.

In addition to the expansion of the traditional farm loan program and the water provision program, FmHA since the early 1960s has been assigned responsibility for development of a rural housing program and a rural and small town business and industrial program.

For example, loans under the rural housing program at an interest rate as low as 1 percent were made available to developers of low-priced rental housing. The community in which the development was located could have a population of up to 20,000. Another important aspect of the FmHA housing program is the offer of a second lien on housing mortgaged both for the FmHA and other lender loans. This, of course, becomes a program that is extended considerably beyond the basic rural loan to farmers unable to borrow in the market. The program is an active one, and loans and grants, which do not include insured mortgages, were $2.3 billion in 1975.

The Rural Housing Insurance Fund established in 1965 provides insurance on the rural housing loans developed under the FmHA programs. In addition, there are grants to develop adequate farm labor housing and grants to qualified organizations to help low-income families complete home construction projects.

The new FmHA business loan program was established under the Rural Development Act of 1972. This legislation also substantially lifted ceilings on farm operating loans and expanded community facilities financing programs. This legislation strengthened the hand of the Department of Agriculture in programs concerned with rural development and greatly expanded FmHA responsibilities.

The business and industrial financing may be extended to cities with populations as large as 50,000. The 1972 legislation established the Rural Development Insurance Fund to provide insurance coverage of loans for business and industrial development and also for the community facilities expansion. The FmHA insurance covers up to 90 percent of the loan and in the case of these business loans the requirement of unavailability of funds from other sources is dropped. The lender is charged a one-time 1 percent fee for the FmHA guarantee. For fiscal year 1977, $350 million was allocated to this business financing program.

In December 1976, FmHA's business financing program was stimulated by two basic actions. One change allows the primary lender to sell off the guaranteed portion of the loan, thereby establishing a secondary market. The other stipulates that FmHA must immediately make good on the guaranteed portion of the loan in case of default.

The political philosophy that has stimulated FmHA growth is that the nation would be well served if people were encouraged to live on the farm or in small communities. Crime and unemployment in the cities have strengthened the support for FmHA. The result is a program that had a direct call on the U.S. Treasury in 1975 of $5.5 billion and is growing; in addition, it has a potential for severe loss levels arising from introduction of new insurance and guarantee programs. Also the organizational structure belonging to FmHA that extends into nearly every county makes it a convenient vehiclé for fund and aid distribution when disaster strikes in rural or semirural areas.

Conclusion. FmHA has become a giant development bank, a continuing provider of succor to the needy, and an economic support for a back-to-the-country movement. The growth and return of small-town America is seen by some as scatteration (the wasteful use of land), the encouragement of the inefficient, a failure to conserve fuel, and therefore not deserving of encouragement. But there is another side.

Chapter 39

Small Business Administration

One of the unsolved problems of our economy relates to the financing of small businesses. The conventional source of their financing is the commercial bank. However, the CB is not well suited to the extension of long-term loans to businesses. And when small businesses are in the greatest need of assistance, for example in 1974, the CB is short of loanable funds and is experiencing defaults on its loans to small businesses. Under these conditions studies have demonstrated what one would expect, i.e., loans to small businesses are cut back more than are loans to safer and usually larger businesses.

Our Constitution was written to meet the political and economic needs of small businesses and relatively small agricultural operations. Our tax laws also have been written with these members of the U.S. economy in mind. The relatively favorable aspects of this economic environment, however, don't appear to be sufficient to guarantee realization of the American dream of being your own boss after accumulating a little capital working here and there.

Business Lending. Business lending of the federal government is as old as the government, but it experienced a great expansion during the period of large-scale railroad construction of the 1870s and 1880s. The next period of rapid growth was during the depression of the 1930s. In 1932 the Reconstruction Finance Corporation was established by the federal government through the purchase of $500 million of stock. The corporation was to assist financial institutions, railroads, farmers, business firms, and governmental units who found the deflation of the depression too difficult to bear. Despite the distressed conditions existing when extended, these loans have been largely repaid.

The RFC loans extended at this time to the railroads and financial institutions were particularly important. This lending activity reduced the harm arising from the depression and in nearly all instances developed into good financial investments.

The activities of the RFC expanded greatly during the World War II period. It was utilized by the federal government as a convenient institution available when policy dictated stimulation of economic activity in a particular area. The RFC went out of existence on June 30, 1954, and its assets and activities were transferred to the National Mortgage Association, the Small Business Administration, and the Export–Import Bank.

WARTIME ACTIVITY.   During World War I the loans to businessmen increased to meet the needs of war production; these were largely private loans. Again during World War II loans provided an important share of the capital required for enlarged and reconverted production capacity. This time, however, the program was much larger; this in turn necessitated a huge expansion of lending activities.

Business firms engaged in producing goods or services vital to the war effort were provided the following credit sources through federal government action:

1. A loan from a bank, secured by an assignment of claims under a government contract, or otherwise.

2. A Regulation V loan from a bank or other financing institution guaranteed pursuant to the provisions of the executive order and the regulation issued thereunder.

3. A loan from the RFC.

4. A loan from a Federal Reserve bank under the provisions of Section 13 (b) of the Federal Reserve Act.

5. A loan from the Smaller War Plants Corporation.

6. A direct loan from the War Department, Navy Department, or Maritime Commission.

7. A combination of two or more of the foregoing.

8. Advances from the War Department, Navy Department, or Maritime Commission if the business enterprise held a prime contract.

V LOANS.   The most important device developed by the federal government during World War II to extend credit to business was the V loans. These were loans for less than five years to businesses producing goods for the Army, Navy, or Maritime Commission, and they were guaranteed by one of these three agencies. The loans were extended by the Federal

Reserve System or a commercial bank; most were extended by commercial banks. A V loan to a producer of goods helpful to the War Department was often obtained in the following manner:

The contractor applied for the loan at his local bank. The local bank presented the application to the district Federal Reserve bank, who drew up the terms with the local loaning bank. The army liaison officer stationed at the Federal Reserve bank then checked with the prime contractor (in the case of a subcontractor's application) or the technical branches of the army to determine that the production was necessary and that the contractor had the ability to produce the product at the price stated. If the results were satisfactory, a loan was granted.

A complete case report on all loans was sent to the Financial Contracting Officer in Washington through the Federal Reserve System. The army liaison officer also sent a report. The producers paid a maximum rate of interest of 5 percent on the loan, plus the fees charged by the three services (Army, Navy, and Maritime Commission) for their guarantees. These guarantee fees varied from 10 percent to 50 percent of the loan rate. The guarantee fee expanded with the rise of the percentage of the total loan guaranteed. V loans extended totaled $10.3 billion at the end of World War II. The V loan program was not reinitiated during the Korean and Vietnam wars.

Small Business Lending. The federal government agency most active in extending credit to business has been the Reconstruction Finance Corporation (RFC), which became inactive in 1953 and went out of existence in 1954. While functioning, the RFC frequently was attacked for being too liberal and for not being liberal enough, for taking too great risks and for not taking enough risks, for lending to those who were able to obtain credits from private institutions and for lending to those who did not have a credit standing, for lending to too many Republicans and for lending to too many Democrats. Despite these constant complaints the RFC's record, considered now after the heat of the conflicts, seems to have been good.

The RFC was replaced in 1953 by the Small Business Administration (SBA). In 1958 the Small Business Investment Act was passed, and the SBA was made a permanent agency to fill the small business "credit gap" in the American financial system.

The SBA is authorized to assist small businesses through

loan assistance and business management help. The SBA usually participates with a private lending agency in making a loan. The SBA loan permits the private lender to extend a larger loan with a longer maturity. The program has proven to be helpful.

The Small Business Investment Companies. SBICs authorized by the Small Business Investment Act of 1958 receive financial support from the SBA after they are licensed. The SBICs are private investment companies interested in providing equity capital and long-term loan funds to small business concerns. The ratio of private capital to government capital has turned out to be approximately 7 to 3. Investors in SBICs also receive tax favors.

The SBIC industry has provided over $2.4 billion through some 45,000 disbursements to new and small businesses. The assets of the industry are a little over $1 billion. Currently there are about 270 operating SBICs. Some of them are owned by small, local investor groups; some are large companies with stock traded on the exchanges. Many SBICs are affiliated with banks and nonfinancial corporations.

The SBA has two revolving loan funds. One is called the Business Loan and Investment Fund (BLIF), and the other is the Disaster Loan Fund (DLF). Since 1969 in addition to disaster funding, the DLF also has provided loans to small firms to assist them in meeting new health and safety standards.

In 1975 the BLIF program resulted in 22,348 loans totaling $1.4 billion, and SBA direct funds made up only $144 million of this total. Most of the funds came from the banks and other lenders encouraged to act because of SBA assistance or guarantee.

The physical disaster loan portion of DLF activities resulted in 9,114 loans totaling $127 million in 1974. The loan amounts required in this program fluctuate widely from year to year, depending on the seriousness of the disaster occurring during the period. There were 74 disaster declarations that triggered DLF activity in 1975 in 38 states and Puerto Rico and the Virgin Islands.

The nonphysical disaster loan portion of the DLF approved about $42 million of loans in 1975. These varied from loans to firms to assist them in complying with the Clean Air Act of 1970 to helping firms to relocate that were depending upon major military installations that were being phased out.

In addition to funds utilized by SBA in the BLIF and DLF

programs there are two revolving funds. One fund is called the Lease Guarantees Revolving Fund and the other the Surety Bond Guarantees Revolving Fund. The lease program assists small businesses to compete with large firms in renting locations in desirable real estate developments. The bond program enables small contractors to obtain bid performance and payment guarantee bonds through the established surety bond industry channels.

Recently the loan program of the Economic Opportunity Act was assigned to SBA. This legislation provides for the making of loans to socially or economically disadvantaged persons. The loan assistance has been made largely to the minority business population. In 1975, some 5,290 loans were made.

Through its minority enterprise program the SBA also works to assist minority men and women through the regular SBA loan and capital formation programs. In 1975 minority enterprise accounted for 2,462 of regular SBA loans that totaled $137 million. Also legislative provision exists for Limited Minority Small Business Investment Companies (MESBICs). In 1975 MESBIC financing totaled $11 million extended to 307 firms.

Considerable political activity related to a substantial expansion of government aid to small and large businesses arose during the recession of 1973–1974. However, the actual loan activity of SBA declined during the recession period, and none of the proposed new programs seemed to possess much potential and they were not enacted. Nevertheless, the federal government did provide massive aid to several financial institutions scattered from New York to San Diego that was reminiscent of the RFC aid of the 1930s. In fact, considerable support existed in 1974 for a revival of RFC.

Conclusion. It has been said that to be against aiding small business is un-American. Nevertheless, at this juncture, the right tool to do the job has not been developed. The SBA, however, has demonstrated a staying power in its twenty years of life and therefore must be judged to be providing part of the answer.

Chapter 40

Export–Import Bank (Eximbank)

The Export–Import Bank was established in 1934 to stimulate the foreign trade of the United States. It operates under the provisions of the Export–Import Bank Act of 1945, and it is an independent, wholly owned agency of the federal government. Eximbank was continued and powers expanded by the Export Expansion Act of 1971. The size of the activities of the bank has expanded gradually since 1934, with a substantial jump in loan guarantees and insurance in 1971.

Usually, the bank's credit has been extended only when there is a reasonable assurance of repayment and generally only if the credits granted are to be used to purchase American goods and services. Finally, the bank does not compete with private capital seeking foreign use but supplements and encourages it. In doing this the Eximbank has been offering subsidies to exports through cheap and liberal credit. The Eximbank does not operate directly in deficit; however, it did receive as a gift $1 billion of capital, and it has retained nearly $1.5 billion in earnings that it accumulated without paying corporate income taxes and that it relends without paying interest or dividends to the providers of the capital, the U.S. taxpayers.

The Eximbank originally was established as an arm of United States foreign policy. Its first efforts were aimed toward developing trade with Russia. However, the Trade Act of 1974 outlawed Eximbank dealings with Russia. This 1974 action demonstrates the continued political nature of U.S. foreign trade policy.

Originally its lending was limited to facilitating trade through greater availability of financing. This continues to be the main thrust of Eximbank, but its powers since have been broadened to include development and reconstruction loans. Its activities somewhat duplicate those of the International Bank for Reconstruction and Development (the World Bank, see Index). Its unique usefulness lies in the fact that it can operate directly as an agent of the United States, which the World Bank does not. A further U.S. development in development lending took place in 1957, when Congress granted funds for a Development Loan Fund to be administered by the International Cooperation Administration (ICA) and to be used to finance economic development investment projects in underdeveloped areas of the world.

United States policy, as developed in the World Bank and the Eximbank as well as other international financial activities, is coordinated through the National Advisory Council on International Monetary and Financial Problems. Members of this council represent all federal government agencies interested in international financial operations, i.e., Department of State, U.S. Treasury, Federal Reserve, Eximbank, and the Department of Commerce.

Since 1968 the Eximbank has been engaged in three major programs and several minor programs. All programs are related to making loans in foreign areas that are unacceptable to private lenders. All materials used in the project that are available in the United States must be purchased there, and the loans are repayable in dollars. Participations are sold in these loans to encourage private capital to become involved.

Direct Lending and Participation Financing Plus Commercial Bank Guaranteed Programs. Since 1971 the Eximbank has been able to borrow in the money market with the benefit of federal government guarantee. However, the receipts and disbursements of Eximbank are not included in the totals of the unified budget of the United States. Also, Eximbank operations and lending are exempt from any limitations that might be placed on the federal budget.

Recently, as the ability of private financial institutions to profit in the long run from borrowing short and lending long has been called into question, the very similar approach to financing followed by Eximbank also has been scrutinized. In 1975, the U.S. Comptroller General pointed out that Eximbank currently is paying more interest on borrowings than it is receiving as interest payments on its long-term commitments. In fact, between 1972 and 1975 Eximbank's income declined as loan commitments expanded. Late in 1976 Eximbank moved into the public bond market to correct this weakness. It offered fifteen-year term bonds with a 30-basis-point advantage over outstanding Treasury bonds of comparable maturity. This gave Eximbank low-cost funds to lend.

On large international projects in which American firms have an interest, the financing when Eximbank is involved normally works out like this: The foreign borrower makes a cash payment of 10 to 15 percent of the U.S. contract price. The remainder is financed equally by loans from Eximbank and private capital sources. In addition, Eximbank is prepared to enter into a loan guarantee agreement with the private lenders and will agree further to permit them to be repaid from the early maturities of the overall repayment period.

Eximbank guarantees on loans made by U.S. financial institutions include the guarantee of repayment of export paper arising from exports of Americans who have granted credit to foreign buyers of their product. Also, loans by U.S. financial institutions directly to buyers in other countries can be guaranteed.

The Eximbank's *long-term loans* have been primarily to finance purchase from American producers of nuclear power plants, oil extraction and refinement equipment, and jet aircraft. In addition, Eximbank typically provides direct credits for the export of raw cotton, soybeans, and tobacco. In 1977 Eximbank financing of nuclear power plants was questioned.

The Eximbank *preliminary commitment program* provides buyers, sellers, and financial institutions with an advance indication of a willingness to grant credits and assistance under certain terms. These commitments permit active development of export prospects. More than half of the actual credits or guarantees granted by Eximbank arise through preliminary commitments.

Local costs related to the use of products exported from the United States are financed by Eximbank in developing countries when the export sale is dependent on this assistance. Local cost financing in developed countries is only provided when foreign competition is doing this. The amount of assistance in both cases is limited to 15 percent of the total cost of the U.S. exports. Non-U.S. source funds are used, and the lender must be a financial institution acceptable to Eximbank.

Eximbank supports U.S. export sales through *financing feasibility studies*. In addition, activity in general support of

U.S. engineering, planning, consulting, and technical assistance has become a growing area of Eximbank activity. Eximbank's Royalty Guarantee Program also has been useful to a number of U.S. firms.

The *lease financing guarantee* was initiated in 1972, and it has stimulated foreign marketing of American-manufactured equipment. The American products used abroad under rental arrangements under Eximbank have included data processing equipment, construction equipments, aircraft, and so on.

The very active *cooperative financing* facility of Eximbank is used largely by businesses in LDCs anxious to borrow funds to purchase capital equipment from American producers. Under the program, cooperating banks located in the area in which the potential purchaser and borrower is located assume the credit risk of their customers. The cooperating bank receives from Eximbank one-half of the funds required at an attractive interest rate. Many of the loans are used to finance purchase of construction equipment.

Working alongside the cooperative financing facility is an Eximbank *relending program*. This facility provides 100 percent of the loan. The loans are limited to finance of purchases of U.S. products that should develop further U.S. sales. Sales in countries where the U.S. share of the business is particularly low also are stimulated through the relending program. Typically, the same banks making use of the cooperative facility negotiate relending arrangements.

The discount loan facility guarantees funds to banks financing exports at an interest cost below that paid by the borrower. The interest spread, except for very large, short-term loans, is 1 percent. The short-term program makes funds available for less than one year, and the medium-term discount program is for credit extensions of between one and five years. The two programs cover the entire range of export credit normally extended by banks and exporters.

A basic aspect of Eximbank operations has been its provision of *payment guarantees to exporters*. Most of this activity now is carried out through the Foreign Credit Insurance Association (FCIA). Since 1971 FCIA has been a cooperative arrangement among fifty leading property and marine insurance companies of the United States and the Eximbank. Political risk coverage under the policies is underwritten solely by Eximbank.

FCIA's master policies provide under a single insurance contract for all of an exporter's short-term and medium-term sales. Again it was the small and medium-sized exporter who found the programs most helpful. The premiums charged vary according to political and economic risk.

Conclusion. The Eximbank exists because the Congress has decided that U.S. exports should receive government credit support comparable to that enjoyed by exporters of other countries. The desirability of using government resources to stimulate the quantity of exports frequently is questioned by classical economists. The basic point they made is that if we export less, adjustment to the relative value of the U.S. dollar soon will bring about the needed adjustment to prices required to bring our international trade into balance. Also, U.S. firms borrowing to purchase American equipment such as aircraft find themselves competing with foreign firms that purchased the same aircraft on more favorable credit terms because of the guarantees of Eximbank. This is expected to be less likely in the future as Eximbank follows a policy stated to de-escalate export credit competition with other countries.

Chapter 41

Federal Financing Bank

In 1974, Congress passed legislation establishing the Federal Financing Bank (FFB). This was the culmination of many years of effort by the Treasury.

The FFB gradually has been replacing the proliferation of federal agency issues with the homogeneous FFB obligations. Instead of each agency making a trip to the money market when it needs additional borrowed funds, the FFB combines the needs into a single offering. A number of very substantial government agencies cannot obtain their funds through FFB, because they have become privately owned. These government-sponsored but not government-owned agencies include FHLBs, FNMA, the three farm credit agencies, plus the Federal Home Loan Mortgage Corporation.

The Student Loan Marketing Association (SLMA) is also a government-sponsored agency. This means it cannot use the FFB to directly meet its financing needs. About the same effect is enjoyed by SLMA, however, when it issues its securities and the FFB steps in and purchases them when they are placed on the market.

The offerings of some government agencies enjoy special privileges that will encourage them to continue to borrow through their own securities. For example, the HUD-guaranteed urban renewal notes are exempt from federal income taxes. Another example is the offerings of Eximbank. Its securities can be purchased by Domestic International Sales Corporations (DISCs) and are counted as investment in foreign sales efforts making the DISC eligible for a 50 percent saving on its corporate income tax liability.

How the FFB Works. The FFB has a board made up of assistant secretaries of the Treasury and the Treasury's General

Counsel. The Secretary of the Treasury presides. In addition, the FFB has an advisory council made of the secretaries of the Treasury, Agriculture, Commerce, HEW, HUD, Transportation, the President of Eximbank, and the Postmaster General. The provider of funds, the Treasury, and the advisory council consisting of the big borrowers make up the board.

The original FFB grant of borrowing power was set at $15 billion. In addition, the Secretary of the Treasury may be required by the FFB to purchase $5 billion of its obligations, and the secretary has discretionary authority to purchase more. These provisions have the effect of making FFB obligations the same as public debt and backed by the full faith and credit of the federal government.

The funds raised by FFB are exempt from the public debt limit that exists on Treasury direct borrowing, and its loans are outside the budget. Although the interest on HUD-guaranteed housing notes is subject to state and local taxation, the funds raised through FFB for HUD's use enjoy tax exemption. Also, the TVA (Tennessee Valley Authority) and U.S. Postal Service obligations are subject to the national bank 10 percent limitation. This is not true of FFB borrowing for their use.

The FFB has not worked out as intended, because it was not able to raise money as cheaply as the Treasury. Only one eight-year note was sold to the public, and it had to pay a higher tab than the Treasury. Instead, FFB has borrowed from the Treasury. This means that FFB borrowing is included in the debt under the ceiling. However, it does not mean that FFB borrowings are included in the budget.

The federal government's deficit for fiscal year 1976 was $65.6 billion. If the FFB lending were included it would have been $10 billion or so higher.

Currently FFB has been turning to the purchase of outstanding loans guaranteed by the federal government. There exists about $275 billion of these loans. When these loans are switched, let's say, from a commercial bank to FFB, it really means the federal government is no longer guaranteeing the loans but is funding them. As FFB increases its purchases of guaranteed loans, the Treasury has to ask Congress for higher debt ceilings. The Office of Management and Budget doesn't like the drift of FFB activities and favors its getting out of the business of buying federal guaranteed loans.

Those feeling this way see the FFB loan purchase program

as a way to crowd out nonguaranteed borrowers. As they see it, the borrowing of FFB may be so great that it is boosting the interest costs of ordinary borrowers who want to tap the capital market. The loans outstanding of FFB as of July 31, 1976, are summarized in Table 28.

The net purchase of government obligations by the FFB was $12.7 billion in fiscal year 1975, and in 1976 the total was $9.4 billion. It appears as though the fiscal year 1977 (October 1, 1976, to September 30, 1977) total will be about $12 bil-

Conclusion. The FFB is an attractive alternative to the practice of each agency entering the money market to meet its borrowing needs. However, with the exception of one issue of eight-month bills that has matured, the FFB has financed itself by borrowing directly from the U.S. Treasury. When operating in this fashion, the FFB is not much more than a convenient method of assembling new agency borrowing to be met out of funds borrowed by the Treasury. The goal of a single agency entering the money market to meet borrowing needs of federal agencies has not been met.

TABLE 28

FEDERAL FINANCING BANK:
LOANS OUTSTANDING AS OF JULY 31, 1976

	Millions
Chicago, Rock Island & Pacific Railroad	$ 0.8
Department of Defense (Foreign Military Sales)	1,011.5
Export–Import Bank	4,984.6
Farmers Home Administration	9,200.0
General Services Administration	70.4
Department of Health, Education & Welfare (Medical Facilities Loan Program)	123.5
Department of Housing & Urban Development (New Communities Administration)	27.5
National Railroad Passenger Corporation (Amtrak)	555.1
Overseas Private Investment Corporation	5.4
Rural Electrification Administration	997.3
Rural Electrification Administration—CBO	166.4
Secretary of the Treasury (New York City)	855.6
Small Business Administration	163.1
Small Business Investment Companies	77.1
Student Loan Marketing Association	405.0

Tennessee Valley Authority	2,495.0
United States Postal Service	2,748.0
United States Railway Association	89.9
Washington Metropolitan Area Transit	177.0
Total	$24,153.2

Source: Federal Financing Bank, *Annual Report*, 1976.

PART VIII: SELECTED REFERENCES AND SOURCES

Banking and Currency Committee of Congress, *A Study of Federal Credit Programs* (Washington, D.C., 1964).

Gary L. Benjamin, "The Farmers Home Administration," *Federal Reserve Bank of Chicago, Business Conditions*, December 1975, 3–8.

Business Week, "A Box Score on the Controversial SBA," June 30, 1975, 100–101.

Stanley Diller, *Credit Allocation* (New York: Citibank, 1976).

Export–Import Bank of the United States, *Eximbank: How It Works* (Washington, D.C., 1975).

Federal Home Loan Bank Board, *Annual Reports*, Washington, D.C.

First Boston, *Handbook of Securities of the United States Government and Federal Agencies* (27th Edition, 1976).

Forbes, "Everybody Loves Ginnie Mae!" November 1, 1976, 69–70.

Stewart Johnson, Warren A. Law, James W. McKie, O. Gale Johnson, James Gellies, Robert C. Turner, Ross M. Robertson, and J. Fred Westson, *Federal Credit Programs* (Englewood Cliffs, N.J.: Prentice-Hall, Inc., 1963).

Anne Marie Laporte, "The New Federal Financing Bank," *Federal Reserve Bank of Chicago, Business Conditions*, May 1974, 9–15.

Addison W. Parris, *The Small Business Administration* (New York: Praeger, 1968).

Murray L. Weidenbaum, "A Reevaluation of Federal Credit Programs," *Tax Review, 31*, November 1970, 47–50.

Part IX

International Banking and Lending

INTRODUCTION

Total foreign assets of private U.S. businesses and American citizens totaled $246 billion at the end of 1975. This is countered by claims on the United States by foreign businesses and individuals of $123 billion. The total private claims of Americans on foreigners is just exactly twice the private foreign claims on the United States. Foreign government claims total another $87 billion. Most of these claims arise from central bank ownership of U.S. government securities. Foreign government claims on the United States were $29 billion greater than U. S. government claims on foreigners.

The two pie charts given in Chart XXVIII depict the international investment position of America by type of asset and by area. The total of private and public U.S. foreign investments was $304.1 billion, and the private and public investments of foreigners in the United States was $210.5 billion. U.S. claims on foreigners were $93.6 billion larger than foreign claims on Americans. This net U.S. position in 1975 was $16.2 billion greater than in 1974.

The U.S. direct investment (ownership of property and production facilities) abroad, at $133.2 billion, is about five times greater than foreign direct investment in the United States. This comparison provides a good idea of the relatively greater importance of American business enterprise in the economies of foreign countries.

The $58 billion of foreign investment of the U.S. government consists largely of gold and SDR (Special Drawing Rights) holdings. The total, in addition, includes investment in the World Bank, the International Monetary Fund (IMF), and other international and U.S. agency investments largely in LDCs. A final component consists of foreign currency holdings.

CHART XXVIII

INTERNATIONAL INVESTMENT POSITION OF THE UNITED STATES AT THE END OF 1975

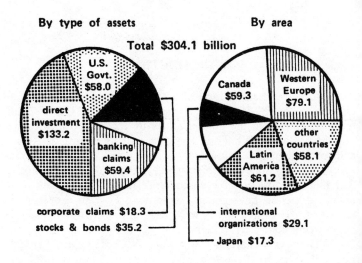

By type of assets　　　　　　　**By area**

Total $304.1 billion

U.S. Govt. $58.0

direct investment $133.2

banking claims $59.4

corporate claims $18.3

stocks & bonds $35.2

Canada $59.3

Western Europe $79.1

other countries $58.1

Latin America $61.2

international organizations $29.1

Japan $17.3

The U.S. international commitment is substantial and growing. The large earnings surpluses arising in the international accounts of OPEC countries with relatively small populations can be expected to be the source of funds for additional foreign claims on the United States in the forms of ownership of securities and direct investment in real estate. The foreign direct investment in America is likely to continue to be less actively employed than are U.S. direct investments.

Chapter 42

International Finance Concepts

Definition of International Finance Terms.   The discussion of international financial activity involves use of terms that are largely new or whose exact meaning is vague to the nonspecialist.

International finance is concerned with means of payment and transfer of capital assets between countries. The term *foreign exchange* is used to refer to the money of foreign countries. A dealer in foreign exchange purchases money of foreign countries and has it available to sell to any person desiring foreign money to purchase a good or service, to repay a debt, or to finance a trip. Foreign exchange is usually not in the form of currency and is not desired in that form. It is wanted and used in the form of drafts, checks, letters of credit, acceptances, and similar credit instruments. Foreign exchange is frequently referred to as a *bill of exchange*. Either term can be used to indicate the supply of foreign money.

BALANCE OF PAYMENTS.   The balance of international payments is considered unfavorable when the demand for foreign exchange is greater than the total demand for the national currency by foreign nations. This frequently is determined by the *international balance of trade*. The international balance of trade is unfavorable when the value of goods purchased by a country from all foreign nations is greater than the value of goods that foreign nations purchase from it. The international balance of payments is, in addition, affected by (1) service items and (2) short- and long-term international capital movements, that is, changes in the type and quantity of investments held by the nationals of different nations.

Chart XXIX provides a summary of U.S. international

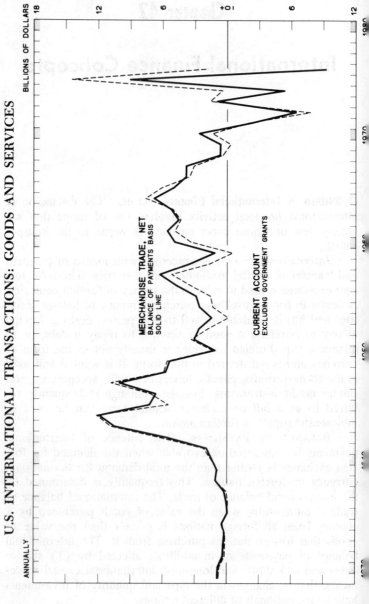

CHART XXIX

U.S. INTERNATIONAL TRANSACTIONS: GOODS AND SERVICES

BILLIONS OF DOLLARS

MERCHANDISE TRADE, NET
BALANCE OF PAYMENTS BASIS
SOLID LINE

CURRENT ACCOUNT
EXCLUDING GOVERNMENT GRANTS

ANNUALLY

transactions in goods and services since 1930. The overall balance of U.S. international trade has been in surplus nearly continuously since 1930. However, since the mid-1960s, the relative U.S. position has been less favorable than earlier and in 1977 the United States ran a deficit of $25 billion.

DEVALUATION.   The term *devaluation* is used to refer to a national monetary policy aimed at reducing the currency's value in terms of foreign currencies. This policy tends to increase the nation's exports by causing a relative decrease in the price of goods and services exported. It was a very popular type of monetary policy during the depressed period of the 1930s and was successful in expanding exports, raising prices, and reducing imports when initiated by economically unimportant nations that exported a large portion of their total product. When later in the 1930s the policy was initiated by the great commercial nations, it quickly degraded into competitive devaluation which was, and still is, considered to be economically harmful to all nations.

Devaluation was utilized again in the post-World War II period to increase exports. This time rising domestic prices are not wanted, but decreased imports, especially from the United States, are a very important goal of the program. In the postwar period devaluation of over 10 percent was possible by members of the International Monetary Fund only with the fund's approval. This control by international agreement broke down in August 1971 (see Index).

PURCHASING POWER PARITY.   This term is used when equilibrium in the exchange rates of different national currencies is discussed and analyzed on the basis of the domestic price levels. Equilibrium exists if the exchange rate is such that approximately the same quantity of goods can be obtained if the currency is spent within the country of issue or if it is used to purchase the currency of some other country and that currency is spent within the country of its issue for goods and services.

Purchasing power parity and the balance of payments are among the most important considerations utilized in evaluating the soundness of a nation's money.

EXCHANGE CONTROLS.   The purpose of direct *exchange controls* is to hold the price of foreign currencies in the domestic market at a different level than would arise in a free market. It is the resulting rationing that constitutes the direct control of foreign exchange. This procedure will achieve a balance of a nation's foreign transactions and reduce the cost of imports, but it will also decrease the total quantity of foreign trade.

Foreign Exchange Operations. The use of many foreign exchange rates for a particular currency has arisen from national efforts to maximize returns from exports and minimize costs of imports. In addition rates vary depending on date of delivery and degree of risk. The commercial banks generally handle the actual transactions for they are the institutions possessing claims on foreign (currency) exchange. Banks have claims on foreign exchange in the form of deposits in foreign banks against which bankers' bills may be drawn, or the claims are in the form of deposits in their foreign branches. Banks acquire their deposits because exporters and others sell their claims to foreign funds to banks in the form of commercial bills.

EXCHANGE RATES. The price paid for foreign exchange is called the *exchange rate*. There are many types of rates. A few of them are listed and briefly described below:

Spot Rate. The price at which claims to foreign exchange can be immediately obtained.

Forward Rate. The price of foreign exchange for future delivery. It follows the spot rate very closely. It is used to eliminate speculation in exchange rate changes. At the same time that foreign exchange is sold for future delivery, similar exchange is purchased for delivery when the exchange sold must be delivered.

Cable Rate. The rate used by bankers in selling their claims to foreign exchange. The funds are made available immediately.

Sight Rate. This rate is slightly lower than the cable rate because funds are not available until the paper is presented.

Official Rate. The rate established by a government for the sale of its currency.

ARBITRAGE. Dealers in foreign exchange may sometimes make profits from discrepancies in the exchange rates. It is a sure-thing speculation. They make large commitments for a few minutes in the currencies of different countries or in the prices of securities and commodities. They buy where the quotation is low and sell where it is high. This, of course, decreases the supply of exchange, securities, or commodities where the price is low and increases the supply where the price is high. The effect is to equalize the prices of the two areas.

The Problem of International Exchange. An individual

nation through the use of its police power can declare its money legal tender, ration goods and services, and establish price controls. These powers are quite effective in maintaining the value of a monetary unit and guaranteeing (unless the state's police powers are very inadequate) that the money will be utilized in exchange activity; that is, the money will be accepted by a domestic seller in exchange for goods or services.

CONTROL OVER INTERNATIONAL VALUE. A particular nation cannot extend to its monetary units the power of legal tender in foreign countries. The value of a nation's money in terms of goods and services of foreign nations is largely determined by the quantity of its own goods and services desired or purchased by nationals or governments of foreign nations. And this in turn is determined by the types of goods and services produced within the nation and the relative prices of these goods and services to the foreign government or foreign nationals requiring them.

If a nation has relatively large exports and small imports, the value of its monetary unit tends to increase; if international trade balances are in the opposite direction, the value tends to decrease. This relationship sets in motion forces tending toward stability in the value of the monetary unit of any particular country. If a government is going to try to prevent the relative change in the value of its monetary unit caused by the movement of goods, services, and investment, it must restrict the free exchange of goods and services by its nationals. The devices to achieve the needed restriction are numerous, but none are completely effective in preventing a decrease or an increase in the value of a nation's monetary unit if the *balance of payments* continually tends in one direction.

RELATION TO DOMESTIC ECONOMIC CONDITIONS. Modern nations are very much interested in preventing unemployment and a reduction in the scale of living of their laboring population. If these policies cause the imports of the nation to increase more rapidly than its exports, the government and its nationals will experience a shortage of money from foreign nations (foreign exchange) to be used to purchase the goods they wish to buy from foreign areas. At the same time foreigners will find that their supply of the currency of the country in question is greater than needed to pay for the purchases they desire to make.

The result is that if the scale of living of the country in

question is dependent upon the purchases of goods and services from foreign countries and the sale of goods and services in foreign areas, the scale of living will decrease. This decrease arises both from the higher price that must be paid for foreign goods and from the unemployment that will develop if the prices of goods exported are not permitted to decrease. This has actually been the situation in many countries of Western Europe during the postwar period. A drastic reduction in wages and the scale of living in these areas was largely prevented by extension of loans by the United States. These aid programs have had the same effect as if those countries had sold large quantities of goods and services to residents of the United States and today the scale of living of Western Europe approximates that of the United States.

AUTOMATIC GOLD STANDARD. Prior to the Great Depression of the 1930s (the automatic gold standard was actually destroyed by central-bank policies of the 1920s), the nations of the world operated to a greater or lesser degree on what is called the *automatic gold standard*. This standard was to provide the adjustments required for a free, and assumed desirable, flow of trade among the nations of the world. Briefly, the scheme operated in this fashion. Each country set its monetary unit as equal to a certain weight of gold. Anybody could exchange a monetary unit for this amount of gold. The relative weights of gold into which monetary units could be transferred determined their relative values. Prices in the different nations were to be adjusted by the flow of gold from nation to nation.

If prices in country A were relatively high, its international purchases would increase and its international sales decrease. This would cause the money of A to accumulate in the hands of foreigners in quantities in excess of needs. They would demand gold for this money, and gold would flow from country A into country B. The flow of gold through its effect on the size of the base upon which credit could be issued would decrease prices in country A and increase prices in country B. The effect was that domestic price levels were at the mercy of changes in the international flow of gold. This was partly justified if gold flowed as the result of price differentials of the type indicated. However, gold also flowed as the result of investors' switching their security holdings and mere speculation in the currencies of different countries.

In addition, the political leaders of many nations became

unwilling to permit domestic prices to fluctuate to meet the requirements of an automatic gold standard. The result was the establishment of central-bank policies to prevent gold movements from affecting the general price level and the establishment of different weights of gold for the standard unit. Both practices destroyed the basis for an automatic gold standard, and both arise from a political unwillingness or inability to permit the fluctuations in the domestic level of prices that the automatic gold standard required.

THE INTERNATIONAL MONETARY FUND'S USE OF GOLD. In 1944 the nations of the world provided for the establishment of the International Monetary Fund (see Index). The original fund agreement established means for the orderly change of the gold content of a nation's standard monetary unit, which means a procedure for the change of the relative value of the currencies of the different nations. Although the different standard monetary units are stated in relation to gold, the actual meaningful relationships were stated in terms of dollars. The original fund arrangement assumed that exchange rates will fluctuate and domestic price levels will remain rather constant or at the level considered desirable by domestic and impartial monetary authorities. The automatic gold standard concept assumed that exchange rates would remain relatively constant and that domestic price levels would be left to fluctuate. Since 1972 the IMF exchange rate powers have consisted only in quoting the SDR values of national monetary units.

Chapter 43

U.S. Government International Lending

The United States did not engage in important international lending activities until after World War I. At that time the nation extended large government-to-government loans to aid in reconstructing Europe. These loans became the World War I debts that were a source of considerable international financial difficulty. Repayment of the loans became tied to the payment of reparations by Germany. The Dawes Commission in 1924 and the Young Commission in 1929 attempted to provide workable plans for the payment of German reparations and indirectly for the repayment of the United States war loans to European nations. The plan established by the Young Commission failed to solve permanently the German reparation problem but did establish the Bank for International Settlements (BIS), which continued to function as an international institution throughout World War II. The bank still exists in Switzerland and functions largely as a monetary information exchange center.

The depression of the 1930s caused the suspension of German reparation payments and a moratorium on war debt payments. Both the reparations and the war debts now are almost forgotten, and the expectation of payment is nearly completely gone.

Shortage of Private Lending. Private American international lending activity was substantial in the period of the 1920s. These loans enabled foreign nations to purchase a greater quantity of goods and services from the United States than would have been possible otherwise. The decline of the post-World War I boom caused difficulties in the repayment of the interest and principal of these loans. The losses of American investors were so substantial (although they were perhaps less extensive than the losses in the domestic stock market) that until the revival of internationalism in the 1960s, Americans avoided foreign investments.

Lend–Lease. During World War II the federal government directly extended even larger credits than during World War I. This time the credits were extended as a lend–lease rather than as loans to be repaid. Lend–lease was treated as a device of mutual aid; the United States provided materials, and our allies provided troops and other support.

U.S. Economic Aid. At the conclusion of World War II (1946) the federal government extended to Great Britain a line of credit totaling $3.75 billion at an effective interest rate of approximately 1.65 percent. The agreement provides that interest payments be waived if the British possess an inadequate quantity of dollar exchange, but it does not provide for cancellation of principal payments. The loan must be repaid within fifty years. In addition, under the Marshall Plan, the United States through the federal Treasury provided large quantities of dollar exchange as gifts to be used by Western European countries in their reconstruction activities. The manner of the use of these funds has been controlled partially by the United States. In the 1950s additional dollar credits were made available to Greece, Turkey, and China.

Through the *Agency for International Development* (AID), established in 1961, the United States has continued a program of economic assistance to friendly developing nations. The assistance is granted largely as loans repayable in dollars. A large portion of the loans extended are required to meet debt servicing charges on former loans.

From 1961 to 1976 the programs of AID have remained pretty much the same. However, the energy with which they are pushed and the growth of the funds provided by Congress to pursue the goals of AID have been declining in recent years.

The principle aim of the legislation establishing AID was to move the federal government toward trade and loans and away from grants and gifts in its efforts to improve the economic well-being of LDCs. The legislation prohibits application of the program to countries where American property has been expropriated or where government action has been taken to repudiate previous contracts and agreements, and more recently where democratic procedures are openly violated.

One useful provision of the AID legislation makes it possible for a private borrower to repay a loan in the local currency of the host country. The repayment in dollars to the United States is made by the host country under a long-term and usually much lower interest rate arrangement. The funds loaned, whether to government or private operators, must be spent largely for goods and services provided by American sellers.

The staff of AID have said over and over that their interest is primarily in assisting long-term development projects. This aim is advanced largely through investment insurance and payment guarantees of developmental goods and services purchased through approved host country programs that now exist in about 100 different nations. Eligible U.S. investors can receive protection for a period of twenty years by payment of stipulated rates for various types of protection.

The risk insurance is available to protect against (1) inconvertibility of currency, (2) expropriation or confiscation of property, and (3) war, revolution, or insurrection and resulting destruction.

Through AID the United States has about $8 billion of specific risk insurance outstanding. In addition, an extended risk program allows coverage, up to 75 percent of an investment, against losses of all types, except fraud or misconduct. This later program is expensive to the insurer and is not greatly used.

Under the so-called Cooley Amendment to Title I of the Agricultural Trade Development and Assistance Act (Public Law 480) certain of the local currency earnings from sale of agricultural products may be allocated to AID. The funds can be loaned by AID to host country or American companies operating where the earnings arose. However, loans may not be made to companies planning to export to America. The interest rates charged correspond to charges being made in the host country.

For the past several years agricultural surpluses have been low. Therefore, Cooley funds have not been large recently, but expansion is expected in 1978.

Finally, under AID, the United States has actively assisted in the financing of housing; most of this activity has been in Latin America.

In Latin America, AID is authorized to issue guarantees to eligible American investors assuring against loss of loan investments made in the following:

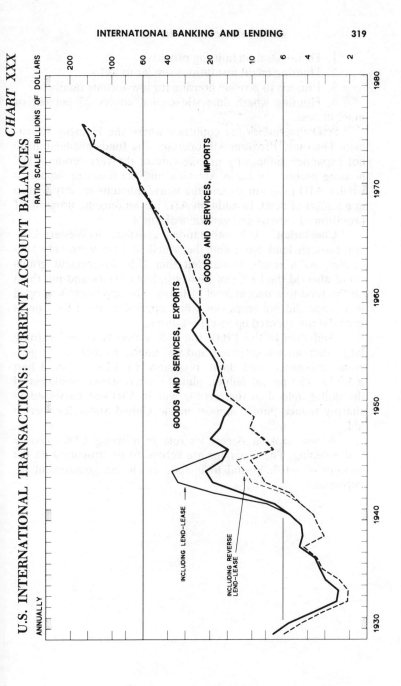

CHART XXX

U.S. INTERNATIONAL TRANSACTIONS: CURRENT ACCOUNT BALANCES

ANNUALLY

RATIO SCALE, BILLIONS OF DOLLARS

GOODS AND SERVICES, IMPORTS

GOODS AND SERVICES, EXPORTS

INCLUDING LEND-LEASE

INCLUDING REVERSE LEND-LEASE

1930 1940 1950 1960 1970 1980

200 100 60 40 20 10 6 4 2

1. Demonstration housing projects.
2. Housing credit institutions similar to S&Ls.
3. Projects to provide housing for low-income families.
4. Housing where domestic capital covers 25 percent or more of cost.

AID determines the countries where the Housing Investment Guaranty Program will operate. The funds available have not expanded sufficiently to take care of the very serious LDC housing problem in Latin America, and the funds to support a similar AID program around the world amounts to only a drop in a bucket of need. In addition AID has an ongoing program of provision of experts and general assistance.

Conclusion.   U.S. international assistance to Western Europe through lend–lease and the Marshall Plan were very successful. As a result, it was felt that U.S. government grants could also rid the LDCs of their grinding poverty and put them on the road to a decent level of living. The approach developed in Europe did not work out when applied in the LDCs or at least did not succeed up to expectations.

And then in the 1960s the U.S. economy ceased earning large international surpluses and was unable to continue its generous assistance and loan programs to LDCs (see Chart XXXI). The partial failure, plus the international weakness of the dollar, added to the terrible war in Vietnam combined to sharply reduce public support in the United States for foreign aid.

A new look at America's role in relieving LDC poverty is developing. The programs are certain to be structured on the concept of self-help and to include much less government involvement.

Chapter 44

U.S. International Commercial Banking

During the past ten years the commercial banks of the United States have expanded and have changed the character of their international activities. The forces bringing about the changes arose from shifts in both domestic and foreign economic and legislative conditions.

Monetary Crisis. In 1964–1965 the U.S. balance of international payments began the deterioration that finally resulted in the closing of the U.S. gold window in August 1971. To prop up the dollar, a federal program to control the outflow of capital was initiated by the federal government. The programs included the Foreign Direct Investment Program (FDIP), the Interest Equalization Tax (IET), and the Voluntary Foreign Credit Restraint (VFCR) program.

Each of these programs set in motion pressures that pushed for the establishment of a network of foreign banking branches by the major American domestic commercial banks. These capital controls sharply decreased the ability of U.S. commercial banks to meet the needs of their MNC (multinational corporation) customers. The result was that banks located in such cities as Chicago, Pittsburgh, and Detroit actively and aggressively entered into foreign banking operations for the first time.

Another element in the decision of American commercial banks to go international was the provisions of Regulation Q and the rate of interest existing in the money markets. Regulation Q interest rate payment ceilings that were applied to commercial banks reduced the ability of commercial banks to attract domestic deposits. To supplement their traditional sources of funds, commercial banks turned to their foreign branches that were not under U.S. interest rate ceilings and could therefore compete actively for funds. The deposits that were attracted overseas were transferred back to America as needed for use by the domestic offices of the bank.

Another element in the original attractiveness of overseas branches in 1965 was the absence of reserve requirements on these deposits. This, of course, caused funds arising abroad to possess a greater profit potential. Also, the branches could pay interest on dollar deposits with maturities of less than thirty days. This is prohibited in America. Finally, in 1966 a New York bank introduced the Eurodollar certificate of deposit.

The result of all these elements of the economic and regulatory environment was a growth in the number of overseas branches of Federal Reserve member commercial banks from 180 to 732 between 1965 and 1975. And the member commercial banks with foreign branches grew from 11 in 1965 to 125 in 1975.

The regulation climate in the United States changed significantly by mid-1970. The Fed removed the reserve-free status on any increase in deposits of member banks in their overseas branches. Any deposit additions were required to meet a 10 percent reserve requirement.

The Fed also worked the other side of the street and took actions modifying Regulation Q to encourage domestic deposit expansion. The interest rate ceilings on large CDs (over $100,000) were suspended in two steps. The first step was taken in June 1970 and the second step in May 1973. As a result, the tight money conditions of 1973–1974 did not result in huge American bank-sourced deposits in foreign branches as had happened in 1969. Nevertheless by mid-1977 the total assets of foreign branches of U.S. banks were nearly double the 1973 level and stood at $236 billion.

Independent Operations.   With the home office demand for funds from overseas branches diminished, the management of overseas branches of U.S. banks entered a new and more active phase. For example, it was during this period that what is called the *floating rate Eurocredits* were initiated. Under this procedure relatively long-term credits, in fact for as long as seventeen years, are extended at an interest rate tied to the six-month London interbank deposit rate. These lengthened credits were very useful to LDCs without oil reserves as they attempted to keep their heads above water when petroleum prices rose rapidly. Also, lower interest rates could be offered, because the rate negotiated need not provide protection to the lender in case of higher rates in the future.

During this same period some attention was paid to what is called *cash flow financing* rather than the standard practice of *asset-protection lending*. This permitted lending without being so concerned about the collateral the borrower could provide. The lending risk became acceptable if the flow of cash appeared to be adequate to cover interest and regular payments to retire the debt.

Another aspect of the greater spread of overseas branches grew out of the expertise developed by the staffs of these branches. MNCs (multinational corporations) began to use branch managers as their financial advisers in the particular area where they both were located. This activity generated commissions and stimulated expansion of the services provided by foreign branches.

Weaknesses and New Directions. Out of these new relationships there developed an expansion of cooperative activities with foreign banks. U.S. banks became active participants in jointly owned consortia of banks or became shareowners and partners of foreign banks. In this manner, U.S. banking funds have become a portion of loans extended to communist countries and LDCs. This activity could, and has, become a source of difficulty as the loans come due.

Another aspect of the overseas expansion of U.S. banks was rather closely related to the VFCR legislation that was repealed in January, 1974, and the earlier repeal of FDIP and IET legislation. The Fed permitted the smaller U.S. banks to establish *shell branches* overseas. These shell branches are approved by a letter from the Fed that gives its OK to the activity providing there is no contact with the local public at the branch.

Shell branches constituted the activity of 76 of the 175 commercial banks with overseas branches in 1974. They are used largely to make interbank money market placements and for purchases of small shares of syndicated loans. In addition, very large U.S. banks sometimes use the shell branch technique to fund credits originating within the large overseas network of the banks.

All shell branches also possess two continuing, attractive, profit-making features: 1) they can benefit from the loopholes in U.S. taxation of foreign-sourced income, 2) the Fed does not require reserve assessments against the deposits booked.

Since 1974 a reversal in the direction of the flow of banking funds has arisen. The freedom of the U.S. money market has been attractive. Also, foreign borrowers of U.S. funds have become aware that they can borrow at lower costs when they directly use their credit lines with the home office rather than with one of its overseas branches. The experience of 1975 seems to demonstrate that without VFCR and when credit conditions in the United States are relatively favorable, the head offices of U.S. banks will supply the funds required by lending activities of their overseas branches. Therefore, the role of foreign branches as holders of funds is likely to be dependent on the comparative ease and tightness existing in the American money market.

In addition, the availability of long-maturity funds in the American money market has made the United States very attractive to foreign borrowers needing funds for extended periods. On the other side of the marketplace American investors have found foreign bonds attractive because of higher interest rates relative to risk apparently existing.

Regulation of Overseas Operations. In America banks are not permitted to establish full banking organizations outside the state of the bank's home office. In France, on the other hand, banks are not restricted to one province but may locate at the major cities around the country.

This situation could cause equal treatment of foreign and domestic banking in the United States to result in unequal treatment of overseas operations of American banks. France, for instance, could follow the well-established and widely accepted mode of international operations of allowing U.S. banks no greater freedom than French banks enjoyed in America.

The operation of foreign banking activities on a more favorable basis than domestic banking activities cannot be an acceptable solution. Also, American banks deserve treatment equal to domestic and other foreign banks in their foreign operations. Some hard bargaining is yet to be done to work out operating procedures.

International Commercial Bank Operations. The Steering Committee on International Banking Regulation established in February 1973 has been the policy-making agency in the development of guidelines for regulation of American banks operating branches or other facilities overseas and foreign banks functioning in the United States. The committee of seven is made up of four members of the Fed's Board of Governors and three Fed bank presidents.

However, the power of the Fed in the area of American international banking is not complete. It must share the regulatory responsibility with the Comptroller of the Currency with respect to all national banks and with state banking authorities with regard to nonmember and member state banks. However, the Fed has full control over foreign activities of Edge Act Corporation (see Chapter 45) foreign subsidiaries and of domestic bank holding companies that control state banks.

Since 1962 the Fed has had the power to allow foreign branches of American banks to carry on activities abroad that they were not permitted to carry out in the United States. The activities permitted have been those typically being implemented by competitors in the market in which the foreign branch of a U.S. banking firm was operating. This usually has meant power to create acceptances against trade taking place wholly within a foreign country and to guarantee payments of customs duties. The Fed has been much more conservative in the manner in which bank branches are permitted to operate than in the permissible activities of bank-owned organizations that assume any form other than the branch form.

In determining acceptable activities for overseas operations of American-controlled financial institutions other than branches, the Fed concentrates on the competitive environment in which the operation takes place. This has resulted in the inclusion of investment and venture capital financing in the overseas operations of U.S. financial institutions. These activities cannot be a part of domestic operations. The Fed, on the other hand, has not permitted all types of activities that are a normal part of the operations of foreign competitors. For example, general insurance underwriting has been ruled out by the Fed, even though competitors engage in the activity.

The Fed generally has followed a cautious policy in its granting of new powers to American banks in their foreign financial activities. It usually has held back when foreign operations seemed to be increasing general risks or when it was endangering banking services to basic U.S. industry or when the possibility of the growth of considerable additional monopoly power was a possible result.

Foreign-owned banks and bank branches have become an increasing element of the U.S. banking industry. The general rule adopted by the Steering Committee on International Banking Regulation is to treat foreign banking offices and operations the same as domestic activities. The principle of nondiscrimination encounters some difficulties because other nations are generally less restrictive of banking activities than are the federal and state governments of America. Therefore, if U.S. overseas banking is treated like foreign domestic banking, it enjoys more freedom of action than foreign bankers do in their U.S. operations.

Legislation in the House Banking Subcommittee on International Trade, Investment, and Monetary Policy provides mandatory Fed memberships of state-chartered subsidiaries and Fed reserve requirements for branches and agencies of foreign banks operating in the United States. The legislation would permit multistate branching of foreign banks to continue if the license to operate was granted by a state before December 3, 1974. In addition, the foreign branch would have to acquire a federal license.

Conclusion. The banks have found themselves deeply involved in the efforts of nations to meet the international requirements of their citizens under the new conditions that were initiated in the late 1960s. More than likely, a basic new long-term approach to international management of money and banking is in its formative stages. We are going to see more foreign-headquartered banks operating in America. On the other hand, overseas operations of American banks, particularly in Western Europe, may decline somewhat as basic banking business activities are carried out in the home office more frequently. A 1977 study by the Conference Board showed that of 1,546 American firms with sales of $20 million or more, 46 percent owned manufacturing facilities in two or more countries. These firms provide a minimum customer base to foreign units of American CBs.

Chapter 45

Edge Act and Agreement Corporations

In 1916 federal legislation provided for bank investment in the stock of corporations principally engaged in international and foreign banking. The corporations formed under this legislation are called *Agreement Corporations*. The term *agreement* is used because each corporation established is based on an agreement with the Fed regarding limitation of operations. These corporations have state charters and are available to banks only if the bank has capital and surplus of at least $1 million and if not more than 10 percent of capital and surplus is invested in the Agreement Corporation.

In 1919 further amendment to Section 25 of the Federal Reserve Act provided for federal chartering of international banking corporations. The legislation was sponsored by Senator Walter Edge of New Jersey, and so was born the Edge Act Corporations. Edge Act Corporations can avoid state regulatory laws and state incorporation requirements, but the corporation must have $2 million of capital; no minimum exists for Agreement Corporations. Because the maximum investment rule of 10 percent still applies, a parent bank must have $20 million or more of capital and surplus.

Most Edge Act and Agreement Corporations function as active extensions of the parent bank's international department. The preferred location for carrying out these activities is New York—the international banking capital of the United States.

A study of the assets of these corporations operating in New York singled out Cash & Due from banks as the dominant asset category. This indicates the bank-owned finance corporations are used extensively to liquidate parent bank foreign exchange obligations. However, they had not been used extensively to generate acceptances that arise in the implementation of international commercial financing. Apparently the parent bank's international department does not allocate this business to its affiliate corporation.

The Edge Act and Agreement Corporations provided the original approach for American banks to become involved in the development investment companies established by LDCs. Frequently these activities are carried out through offshore affiliates that are owned jointly by a number of American and foreign bank-related institutions. The investments benefit from special favors that countries grant to new investors. It also has been a way to cooperate with the World Bank's International Finance Corporation.

Finance companies owned by bank corporate affiliates have proven to be useful approaches to becoming actively engaged in the money markets of foreign nations. For example, the financing of installment purchases and leasing operations have proven to be profitable. Also, a considerable portion of the funds needed in the financing activities often has been acquired through the domestic sale of short-term commercial paper.

The Fed always has placed some restrictions on the acquisition of equity in foreign operations by Edge Act or Agreement Corporations. In legislation currently applicable, the Fed gives its general consent to equity purchase up to $500,000 if it does not represent more than 25 percent of the voting shares and if the foreign corporation does not do business in the United States, and if the investment is likely to further the development of U.S. foreign commerce. Joint ventures of this type have been quite popular. They represent an example of how the Fed has permitted more liberal bank investment activity abroad to meet foreign bank competition than is allowed domestically.

Another aspect of Edge and Agreement corporate activities lies in the extension of credit to purchase into foreign banking houses. It is an alternative to direct foreign branching and a useful procedure to strengthen correspondent bank relationships.

Foreign-chartered banks generally can operate more freely than U.S. banks. The Edge and Agreement Corporation legislation partially corrects this situation abroad as well as at home because the legislation makes out-of-state domestic "banking" locations possible as long as the business carried out is international and deposits are not accepted.

Chapter 46

International Money

When American banks provide financing for the overseas operations of American business they must use their dollar resources to purchase foreign currencies of one type or another. The all-prevailing difference between foreign and domestic activities is that money other than the U.S. dollar must be acquired. The Bretton Woods agreement of 1944, which established an international money arrangement built on a U.S. dollar that could always be traded for 1/35 of an ounce of gold, broke down in August 1971 when the United States stopped selling gold at $35 an ounce to foreign possessors of dollar exchange. In fact the United States as a government stopped selling gold. The U.S. gold window was closed.

The first amendment of the 1944 Articles of Agreement, which set up procedures for establishing international values of monies of member nations, was adopted in 1969 at Rio de Janeiro. The amendment gave the *International Monetary Fund* (IMF) the authority to issue special drawing rights (SDRs, see Index).

The original authority to use and issue SDRs is limited to supplementing existing reserve assets available to provide liquidity to the nondomestic transactions of the world. The SDRs created by the fund since its establishment total SDR 9.3 billion. (As of September 1976 1.15 U.S. dollars equaled 1 SDR.) All SDRs issued are allocated to member countries in need of additional monetary reserves. The last allocation of SDRs by the fund was made in 1972.

The total of official holdings of gold and foreign exchange exceeds SDR 180 billion. The SDRs are therefore a small portion of the world's liquidity. However, they gradually have become widely used as a unit of account for international central-bank contracts, and many adjustments between treasuries of nations are made with them. Since July 1, 1974, the value of the SDR is based on an index of sixteen currencies.

SDR Index. This basket of currencies is used to set the value of the SDR by giving currencies of the sixteen nations a weight dependent on world exports of goods and services during the five-year period 1968–1972. The result is that the U.S. dollar's weight is relatively small when considered in relation to the relative GNP of America.

To arrive at an exchange rate for a currency in terms of the SDR, it is necessary to calculate the equivalent of all the components of the SDR in terms of that currency on the basis of market exchange rates. The first amendment establishing the SDR defined it in terms of gold that corresponded to the par value of the dollar established at Bretton Woods in 1944, or 0.88867 gram of fine gold. This meant that 1 SDR equaled 1 dollar, or $35 purchased 35 SDRs; and the gold content of 35 SDRs was equal to 1 ounce of gold. When the dollar window was closed in August 1971 and when floating exchange rates were initiated in 1972, the SDR's tie to a definite weight of gold was abandoned. This was when the basket valuation method was introduced. The second amendment to the IMF's articles of agreement adopted in 1976 provides for the elimination of any use of gold in setting quantity or value of SDRs.

The value of the SDR was set as the equivalent of the sum of 40 U.S. cents, 38 German pfennings, 45 new pence (United Kingdom), 40 centimes (France), and so on down through the sixteen currencies. The calculation of the value of the SDR based on this basket concept is calculated each day for a number of currencies in addition to the sixteen currencies included in the basket. These rates are reported daily by a number of wire services and daily newspapers. The Fed in 1977 held SDRs valued at $1.2 billion and gold certificates representing gold with a value of $11.5 billion, with the gold price set at $42.22 an ounce.

Use of SDRs. The finance officers of MNCs and international agencies are following the lead of national monetary agencies. For example, SDRs are used in setting transfers between different airlines under the rules of the International Air Transport Association. Some international bond issues also are denominated in SDRs.

The second amendment of the fund's articles does not replace the gold clause with another definition of the SDR in real terms. Neither does it provide for the basket of currencies that seems appropriate under current floating exchange rates. The SDR has come to occupy such a central role in fund operations that the establishment of any new method of setting its value will only be taken after long deliberations.

Currently 117 of the 128 fund member nations participate through the SDR Department in the transfer of SDR balances. Any participant nation with a balance of payments shortage difficulty can purchase foreign exchange needed with its SDR balance. The purchase can be made without question from any other participant nation with a strong international position. The fund decides who these nations are. A participant under an agreed procedure can also buy back with SDRs quantities of its own currency held by other nations or from the fund.

A participant nation with a stock of SDRs in excess of original allocation receives interest on this amount. (During the September 1976 quarter the rate was 3.75 percent.) A nation with less SDRs than its original allocation pays the same interest rate on the amount by which its SDR stock has decreased below the original allocation. The rate currently is set at 60 percent of a weighted average of short-term market interest rates in the United States, Germany, the United Kingdom, France, and Japan. The goal is to make SDRs usable by participant nations and the fund for all transactions among them.

PART IX: SELECTED REFERENCES AND SOURCES

James E. Boyce and Francois J. Lombard, *Columbia's Treatment of Foreign Banks* (Washington, D.C.: American Enterprise Institute for Public Policy Research, 1976).

David K. Eiteman and Arthur I. Stonehill, *Multinational Business Finance* (New York: Addison-Wesley, 1972).

Federal Reserve Bank of Boston, *Monetary Policy in Twelve Industrial Countries*, Karel Holbik, (ed.) (Boston: 1973).

Federal Reserve Bank of Chicago, "International Lending," *International Letter*, No. 282, July 9, 1976.

International Monetary Fund, IMF Survey, "Manila Meetings," (October 18, 1976), *International Financial Statistics*, monthly (Washington, D.C.).

Francis A. Lees, *International Banking and Finance* (New York: Wiley, 1974).

Walter F. O'Connor and Harold L. Sirkin, "Operating a Bank Abroad," *PMM & Co., Management Controls*, March 1973, 61–70.

U.S. Treasury, "More Control Sought Over Operations of Foreign Banks," *Treasury Papers*, February 1976, 18–19.

Part X

International Government
Financial Institutions

INTRODUCTION

The multinational finance institutions of the world have become involved in an increasing portion of the financial activities of governments and businesses. The abandonment of $35-an-ounce gold in August 1971, the successful organization of the major oil producing nations into OPEC in 1973, and the provision of an expanding role for Special Drawing Rights (SDRs) at the 1976 Manila Conference of the International Monetary Fund (IMF) are the major turning points in the evolution of the international credit system as it functions today.

The abandonment of thirty-five-dollar gold by the United States opened the doors to international monetary confusion. The control over oil prices by OPEC created unbearable foreign exchange requirements for LDCs to attempt to meet. The SDR is the fledgling international answer to the wildly fluctuating changes in the relative value of money that appears to be a part of a world money system based on floating exchange rates.

In 1976 all the nations of Western Europe and North America experienced serious balance-of-trade deficits, with the exception of West Germany, Switzerland, and Sweden. In addition, East European countries were expanding barter arrangements with western oil-exporting nations in order to continue importation of capital to build up particular domestic enterprises.

The need for capital and basic imports by the non-oil-exporting nations is outrunning the foreign exchange they can muster after settling with OPEC. The foreign exchange surpluses of OPEC tend to be invested in the handful of nations able to cover their imports of oil and other products with international sales and earnings from other sources including investments out of OPEC funds. These pressures push nations away from international trade based on comparative world prices quoted in some generally accepted monetary unit and toward barter arrangements with relative value based on individual national need and production capability.

The job of bringing order and economic efficiency to the international trade and investment arena is immense. The existing institutions and arrangements grew up largely under conditions of the 1950s. To make them efficient in meeting current needs would be very difficult even if a decision road map existed. Unfortunately, a modification consensus is still in the development stage, but progress can be reported; and institutional shifting to meet the changed international needs is taking place.

Chapter 47

The International Monetary Fund (IMF)

The articles of agreement of the International Monetary Fund were agreed upon formally at the United Nations Monetary and Financial Conference held in Bretton Woods, New Hampshire, July 1–22, 1944. The fund came into existence on December 27, 1945, when twenty-nine governments representing 80 percent of the quota signed the articles of agreement in Washington. An inaugural organizational meeting of the Board of Governors (one appointed by each member nation) of the fund was convened at Savannah, Georgia, on March 8, 1946, at which time the bylaws were approved, the site of the headquarters of the organization at Washington, D.C., was agreed upon, and the Board of Executive Directors was chosen. The Board of Executive Directors met for the first time on May 6, 1946.

On December 18, 1946, the fund announced its agreement to the official par value of the currency of thirty-two of its members, and on March 1, 1947, it was open for business "in the form of exchange transaction." In the fall of 1949, the values of nearly all currencies were reduced, with the U.S. dollar the outstanding exception. This general devaluation was expected to alleviate the chronic dollar shortage.

Purpose.   The International Monetary Fund is an association of nations that have bound themselves together to further the purposes of stability in international currency values and of an expansion of world trade by accepting the fund's articles of agreement. These nations agree, in effect, to outlaw the competitive exchange practices that characterized the international economic disorder of the 1930s and also to stimulate international trade. They had hoped to accomplish this goal by:

1. Working toward the eventual removal of restrictions on foreign exchange transactions.

2. Setting up a schedule of exchange rates—that is, currency prices in terms of gold and U.S. dollars—so that traders who wish to buy in foreign countries can obtain the currency they require at known and stable rates.

3. Insuring that any major changes in foreign exchange practices will be submitted to international consultation before being put into effect.

To help achieve this objective, the fund's articles of agreement also authorize it to engage in foreign exchange and gold transaction with members; thus the fund provides a secondary line of monetary reserve. In August 1971, the United States found it impossible to continue keeping the dollar convertible into gold at thirty-five dollars an ounce, and the IMF dream of exchange rate stability with the dollar as the key currency convertible freely into an unchanging quantity of gold was shattered.

Membership.   At the beginning of 1977, 128 nations were members of the fund. New members may be admitted by the Board of Governors on the terms and conditions set by the fund. It should be noted that fund membership is a prerequisite to membership in the International Bank for Reconstruction and Development.

Administration.   The top authority of the fund is exercised by the Board of Governors, one governor representing each member country. Normally the board meets once a year, but it occasionally takes between-meeting votes on certain matters by mail or other means. The Board of Governors has delegated many of its powers to the Board of Executive Directors. However, the conditions governing the admission of new members, any revision of quotas, the election of the executive directors, changes in bylaws, and certain other important decisions remain the sole responsibility of the Board of Governors.

The Board of Executive Directors is made up of five directors appointed by the countries having the five largest quotas and seven others who are elected by all the other members. The Latin American members are by the articles of agreement entitled to two places on the Executive Board. There is also a managing director.

Operation Procedures.   The fund works very closely with the World Bank. The information available through the World Bank is utilized by the fund in making its decisions. The executive directors of the fund are in some cases also executive directors of the World Bank, and the same is true of several governors.

The three principal methods by which the fund works to achieve its objectives are:

1. By affording to its Board of Directors a sort of continuous monetary conference for full consultation when certain financial matters are conducted.

2. By furnishing, upon request, expert technicians to advise and assist members in working out their financial and monetary problems.

3. By making its foreign exchange resources available under proper safeguards to its members to meet short-term, current-payment difficulties.

With all these activities, the fund approaches the problems of its members from a realistic, international point of view, applying the principles of the fund agreement to meet the changing circumstances of the world today.

1949 Devaluations. The greatest problem faced by the fund up to 1950 was the general devaluation of the currencies of many countries in 1949. This general devaluation was spearheaded by the deteriorating position of the British pound. The factors considered by the fund in granting devaluation permissions under the Bretton Woods agreements are best understood by examination of the British crisis.

The immediate cause of the British crisis was heavy losses of British monetary reserve (gold and dollar exchange balances). These heavy losses arose from reduced British sales in the American market that were related to price declines in the United States and the slight recession of the summer of 1949. These reduced British sales had forced introduction of rigid restrictions on British foreign spending. These restrictions in turn further reduced confidence in the British pound, which caused buyers to delay purchase of British goods and avoid converting balances into pounds. The impact of the crisis was the unsettlement of world financial markets, which adversely affected postwar reconstruction. The solution adopted was reduction of the par value of the British pound from 3.58134 to 2.48828 grams of fine gold, or from $4.03 to $2.80. Although the British pound has been under heavy pressure frequently, the new rate established in 1949 was not changed until November 18, 1967, when it was devalued, under conditions quite similar to those of 1949, to $2.40.

The scope of the fund's activities expanded considerably in February 1961. This was the date when nearly all currencies used in international trade became convertible under the conditions set forth in Article VIII of the fund's Articles of Agreement. This meant that these countries were required to avoid restrictions on currency payments, multiple exchange rates, and discriminatory currency practices.

In January 1970, the governors of the IMF officially accepted Special Drawing Rights (SDRs). At the same time, provision was made for their introduction into the international monetary reserve base. In August 1971, all of the arrangements developed by the fund under the 1944 Bretton Woods agreements began to become unstuck. Within two years the international understandings on exchange rate stability that had been developed slowly for nearly thirty years by the fund were in shambles.

The Second Coming. From August 1971 to October 1976, the IMF struggled to work out a new international monetary role for itself. During this period new relative values for the monetary units of member nations were agreed upon in an effort to establish a new system of fixed exchange rates. When this failed and the United States negotiated another 10 percent devaluation of the dollar in 1973, the world was launched on an experiment in free-floating currency values. The relative value of currencies have fluctuated widely, and accusations of dirty float were leveled against nations that took advantage of the opportunities offered now that the Bretton Woods understandings of 1944 were dead. Added difficulties arising from OPEC oil price increases after the 1973 embargo and the need to eliminate gold as a monetary metal kept international exchange rates in a turmoil through 1976. However, at Rambouillet, France, in November 1975, the six largest noncommunist industrial nations agreed to the need to work for greater monetary stability. At Kingston, Jamaica, on January 8, 1976, definite procedures were decided upon. The Kingston meeting also directed the IMF to sell 25 million ounces of its gold. Most of the profits, i.e., the amount the sales price is over the official $42.22 price, will be used to assist desperately poor nations such as Chad and Bangladesh. The gold sales will be completed in four years, and the profit is expected to total $1.5 billion.

Finally, at the October 1976 Manila meeting of the IMF

Board of Governors, an overall effort to modify the organization of IMF was ratified. The purpose was to provide IMF leadership toward monetary stability under the new conditions initiated by America in August 1971. The proposed new Article IV and related schedules, which include the crux of the IMF purpose, was agreed upon at an IMF interim committee meeting during the Kingston sessions. The new Article IV, "Obligations Regarding Exchange Arrangements," includes the following points:

Section 1 of the new Article IV reaffirms the IMF role in carrying out policies that foster orderly economic growth with reasonable price stability, while avoiding an international monetary system that produces erratic disruptions and in addition prevents exchange rate manipulations that prevent effective balance of payments adjustment.

Section 2 requires all member countries to make arrangement for managing their currencies to meet the goals of Section 1. In doing this, each member nation maintains a value for its currency in terms of SDR or other denominator other than gold. The special role of gold and the U.S. dollar in the 1944 Bretton Woods arrangement is eliminated. Provision is also made, if an 85 percent majority of IMF voting power is gained, for the fund to establish a new general exchange arrangement. The general arrangement, however, would not prevent individual national arrangements consistent with Section 1.

Section 3 grants power to the fund to oversee the actions of member nations. However, the supervision will respect the domestic, social, and political policies of member nations as long as they are consistent with Section 1.

Section 4 goes a step further toward fund leadership in stabilizing exchange rates. It gives the IMF power, if an 85 percent majority exists, to introduce a widespread system of exchange arrangements based on stable but adjustable par values. The system would require both surplus and deficit nations to take prompt, symmetrical action to adjust their exchange rates.

Finally, Section 5 defines the area covered by the currency of a member nation.

World Afloat. Schedule K of the new fund provision is concerned with currency par values of member nations. In its first paragraph, it is made clear that the common denominator of a currency or group of currencies with a par value cannot be gold or a currency. The old Bretton Woods dollar and gold denominator arrangement is out.

A nation not intending to establish a par value for its currency must consult with the IMF to make certain that arrangements are consistent with the purposes of the fund.

Each country establishing a par value agrees to prevent its currency from varying more than $4\frac{1}{2}$ percent from the currencies of other countries that have agreed to set a par value for their currency under the fund arrangements. And the par value established may not be changed except in case of an emergency or a fundamental disequilibrium. Efforts to maintain an unrealistic par value will be discouraged by the IMF. Also, any country deciding to give up the par value for its currency may at a later date without prejudice propose another par value.

Conclusion. The action of the IMF in 1976 was a very careful approach toward the fundamental problem of managing independent national currencies so that the nations of the world can enjoy productive economic relations with one another. The philosophy adopted by the fund is basically that foreign exchange markets are a very useful guide to the identification of developing problems but a very poor master of an international currency policy. Management of inflation through floating exchange rates and high interest rates has not proven to be particularly satisfying. The alternative approach is cuts in government overspending in LDCs as well as in many of the major industrial countries, including the United States. The IMF, in its new Article IV and Schedule K, will be applying continuing pressure on the irresponsible elements affecting the world's supply of currencies. In 1978 the IMF is running short of resources and borrowing nations are finding loan terms most onerous.

Chapter 48

The International Bank for Reconstruction and Development (World Bank)

The International Bank for Reconstruction and Development (World Bank) is an international, cooperative institution created through the efforts of the member countries, designed to help finance sound projects for reconstruction and development —reconstruction in war-torn countries and development of world economic resources, particularly in underdeveloped regions. It may be described as a bridge from war to peace, and from government to private financing in the underdeveloped countries.

The Articles of Agreement of the World Bank were drawn up by the United Nations Monetary and Financial Conference at Bretton Woods, New Hampshire, in July 1944. On December 27, 1945, the Articles of Agreement were signed by twenty-eight governments. After an inaugural meeting of the Board of Governors held at Savannah, Georgia, in March 1946 at which the first Executive Directors were elected, the bank officially began operations in Washington, D.C., on December 25, 1946. In 1975 there were over 127 member countries. Russia and her satellites are among the nonmember nations.

Administration. All powers of the World Bank are vested in the Board of Governors, which consists of one member appointed by each member country. The board elects one of its members as chairman. The Board of Executive Directors is responsible for the general operations of the World Bank. There are twelve members, five of whom represent the five nations having the largest number of shares. The remaining seven members are selected by the board, excluding the governors representing the five nations having the largest number of shares.

The Board of Governors may not delegate to the executive directors eight vital powers listed in the Articles of Agreement. These restrictions are similar to those existing in the IMF agreement.

Purpose. The World Bank is a joint effort on a world-wide scale to guide international investment in economically sound channels. It seeks to facilitate international flow of capital to increase production, both in war-devastated countries and in relatively undeveloped areas of the world. It aims to aid its member countries to attain and maintain a balanced national economy where exports of goods and services eventually can pay for an adequate volume of imports and thus contribute to healthy expansion of international trade. These purposes and general policies of the bank are defined in its Articles of Agreement.

The World Bank's first emphasis had been on reconstruction, because in that field there was not only urgency but also great opportunity for rapid improvement in the level of productivity, and with it, improvement in the level of world trade among all members of the World Bank.

In 1976 some $27.8 billion of capital subscriptions of member nations were unpaid. This unpaid capital is subject to call if needed. The unpaid subscription of the United States amounts to $7 billion.

In general, the World Bank aims to stimulate and to help to create conditions that will foster the flow of both domestic and international private investment into productive enterprises in low-income nations. For example, the World Bank may invest varying amounts, depending on need and without government guarantee. Table 29 provides a summary of the scope of World Bank operations during the 1966–1976 period.

METHOD OF LENDING. The World Bank lends funds in three definite ways:

1. It may lend funds directly, either from its capital fund or from funds it borrows in the investment market.

2. It may guarantee loans extended or participate in such loans.

3. It may make, guarantee, or participate in loans to member countries directly or to any of their political subdivisions or to business enterprises in the territories of members. When a member government in whose territory the loan is located is not itself a borrower, this member government, its central bank, or comparable agency acceptable to the bank

must guarantee the loan. The World Bank is primarily a co-operative rather than a profit-making institution. Its objective in fixing interest and commission charges is to secure only enough margin on its operations to meet its own expenses, including the cost of borrowing, and to provide reasonable reserves.

For the fiscal year 1975, net income amounted to $275 million, of which $165 million was placed in the supplemental reserve and $110 million was transferred by way of grants to the International Development Association (IDA). The interest rate charged is currently $8\frac{1}{2}$ percent.

The World Bank does not propose to wait for people to come and ask it for loans. However, thus far the principal work has been to consider loan applications presented by its members. In considering the applications, the World Bank has examined them in relation to the economies of the respective countries as a whole and has made constructive recommmendations designed to adapt the proposed projects to the needs of the respective economies. Apart from its consideration of loan applications, the World Bank constantly studies the financial and economic developments throughout the world and vigorously pursues its objective of encouraging international real investment.

Loanable Capital Funds. Although calls will be made on all members in proportion to the amount of stock they own, the obligation of each member to meet such calls is independent of the obligations of other members. Each member, including the United States, is liable to the full amount of its unpaid subscription if it is required to meet the bank's obligations, irrespective of whether other members meet their calls for this purpose. The Bretton Woods Agreement Act authorized the United States Secretary of the Treasury to pay this subscription of the United States to the bank from time to time when payments are required.

The 18 percent of the World Bank's capital stock that is paid in the currency of the respective countries can be lent only with the approval in each case of the member whose currency is involved.

Expanding Loanable Funds. Measured against world needs, the funds available for lending from the World Bank's capital stock, which was increased by $8.4 billion in 1976, are inadequate. For that reason, the Articles of Agreement of the World Bank specially empower it to borrow money with the

TABLE 29

SUMMARY OF OPERATIONS OF WORLD BANK 1966–1975

AMOUNTS IN US$ MILLIONS

	Fiscal Year									
	1966	1967	1968	1969	1970	1971	1972	1973	1974	1975
World Bank										
Operations Approved	37	46	44	82	69	78	72	73	105	122
Loan Amounts[1]	839	777	847	1,399	1,580	1,921	1,966	2,051	3,218	4,320
Countries	29	35	31	44	39	42	40	42	49	51
Disbursements[2]	668	790	772	762	754	915	1,182	1,180	1,533	1,995
Total Income	292	331	356	410	504	578	646	758	929	1,157
Net Income	144	170	169	171	213	212	183	186	216	275
Total Reserves	954	1,023	1,160	1,254	1,329	1,444	1,597	1,750	1,772	1,902
Borrowings: Total	288	729	735	1,224	735	1,368	1,744	1,723	1,853	3,510
Borrowings: Net	64	503	222	698	299	819	1,136	955	990	2,483
Subscribed Capital	22,426	22,850	22,942	23,036	23,159	23,871	26,607	30,397	30,431	30,821
Member Countries	103	106	107	110	113	116	117	122	124	125
Professional Staff	667	734	767	961	1,170	1,348	1,516	1,654	1,752	1,883
IDA										
Operations Approved[3]	12	17	16	29	50	51	68	75	69	68
Credit Amounts	284	353	107	385	606	584	1,000	1,357	1,095	1,576
Countries	8	13	14	28	33	34	38	43	41	39
Disbursements	267	342	319	256	143	235	261	493	711	1,026
Usable Resources, cumulative	1,682	1,767	1,807	2,176	3,182	3,343	4,204	7,019	7,433	11,608
Member Countries	96	97	98	102	105	107	108	112	113	114

[1] Excludes loans to IFC of $100 million in FY1967, $100 million in FY1970, $60 million in FY1972, $40 million in FY1973, $110 million in FY1974, and $50 million in FY1975.
[2] Excludes disbursements on loans to IFC.
[3] Joint Bank/IDA operations are counted only once, as Bank operations.

approval of the government from whose market the money is borrowed. The first sale of bonds by the World Bank was made in the United States in July 1947. As conditions permit, and as the World Bank has needed funds, it has periodically sold its securities in the major money markets of the world. In 1955, bonds to cover financing needs were sold entirely outside the

United States. In 1975 bonds and notes were sold and placed in twelve different nations.

In the United States, subject to various qualifications as to amounts and certain other conditions in some states, the World Bank's bonds at this time are legal for investment by commercial banks in thirty-nine states and the District of Columbia, by savings banks in twenty-one states and the District of Columbia, by insurance companies in twenty-seven states, and by trust funds in twenty-eight states and the District of Columbia. The United States Comptroller of the Currency has ruled that national banks can invest in the World Bank's bonds up to 10 percent of their capital and surplus funds. The interest is fully taxable in America.

The bonds of the World Bank are a general obligation and are not secured by any pledge of specific assets. As a general obligation, the bonds have behind them the entire resources of the World Bank. It is estimated that the World Bank's total outstanding obligations will increase from $13.7 billion (1976) to $42 billion by 1985. About $7 billion are U.S. dollar obligations. Some $6.5 billion are denominated in Kuwaiti dinars, Lebanese pounds, Libyan dinars, Netherlands gilders, Swiss francs, Japanese yen, and so on.

Funds the World Bank obtains through sale of bonds and grants from the governments of the richer nations are used to make loans. These loans are made only for production purposes and only after due consideration of the prospects of repayment. Further, the World Bank is required to make appropriate arrangements to insure that the proceeds of the loan are used for the purposes for which the loan was made. Currently 39 percent of the loans of the World Bank are made to the poorest nations, those with annual per capita income below $200.

Basis for Loan Grants. In its consideration of a loan, the World Bank must satisfy itself on the following points:

1. The borrower is not able to obtain the loan elsewhere on reasonable terms.

2. The terms proposed for the loan—interest, other charges, and schedule of repayment—are fair to the borrower and appropriate to the project.

3. There is a reasonable prospect that the borrower and a grant guarantor also, if there is one, will be able to meet the obligations contracted under the loan.

4. If the member of the World Bank is not the borrower,

the loan must be guaranteed by the member in whose territory the project is located or by its central bank or comparable agency to be acceptable to the International Bank.

From its establishment to 1976 the World Bank approved loan commitments to ninety-four countries. The amount totals $30 billion.

The World Bank's International Centre for Settlement of Investment Disputes (ICSID) is available to contracting states and investors. By 1975, seventy-one nations had ratified the convention and had become members of ICSID.

In 1959 the World Bank fostered the development of IDA. The purpose was to establish an agency to make development loans to countries unable to receive additional aid from either private investors or the World Bank. The high-income member nations make funds available to IDA, and in addition earnings of the World Bank are on occasion transferred to IDA. Although IDA has loaned approximately $6.6 billion, the amount falls far short of the demand for loans of the type extended by IDA.

Currently IDA and the World Bank proper are concentrating their lending on agricultural projects in low-income nations. These projects are currently absorbing 25 percent of funds loaned.

The World Bank has been growing rapidly, but so have the needs for funds by the poorer nations. Its ability to help the citizens of poor nations is limited largely to throwing money at the problems. This apparently hasn't worked much better in the LDCs than in our domestic poverty pockets. Nevertheless, someone must try; and the World Bank has become the center of where the effort is being made. Ironically, Vietnam has become an eligible reconstruction borrower.

Conclusion. The World Bank continues to grow, as its securities are considered sound investments. Of course, the job the World Bank has set itself is much larger than anyone envisages could be carried out by the World Bank alone. However, its current leadership is very useful. Its programs are less tainted, perhaps, than other LDC aid programs. However, it cannot avoid completely the shortcoming of aid programs financed by middle-class taxpayers of rich nations that enrich the rich of poor countries.

Chapter 49

International Finance Corporation (IFC)

IFC was established in 1956 by the World Bank's member countries as an affiliate. The job set for IFC is to provide a stimulus for private investment in areas where private capital is not available under reasonable terms. These are largely the less developed countries.

The original capital was $78 million subscribed by thirty-one member governments. Twenty of the governments were LDCs.

Early growth was slow, partially because the original charter prohibited equity investment. The IFC during its first four years could make loans but could not operate as an investment banker. So in 1961, the charter was amended to permit equity investment, and IFC began the second stage of its corporate life.

The loans made by IFC do not benefit from government guarantee. However, the IFC, by entering into underwriting of new security issues or standby commitments, was able to broaden share ownerships by citizens of LDCs. IFC began to promote projects and to mobilize risk capital for investment in these undertakings. In 1962 the IFC joined in its first underwriting of a major share issue. The issue of capital shares was made by Mexico's largest steel company.

The third stage of the growth and development of IFC was introduced by another amendment of the articles under which the World Bank functions. These amendments, which were adopted in 1967, permitted IFC to borrow from the World Bank up to a limit of four times its own unimpaired subscribed capital and surplus. These amendments, which made about $150 million available to the IFC for its own loans, came at a time when the funds of IFC available for additional investment had fallen to $1 million.

The third stage of IFC operations has been highlighted by the attraction of outside capital to finance sponsored projects. This outside capital comes from private investors in the country where the investment will be made and from private investors around the world. The IFC has proven to be a very workable catalyst in bringing together private foreign and domestic capital and investment projects that have been carefully evaluated and have benefited from the expertise of the IFC technical and financial staff. Surprisingly, the domestic capital attracted from LDCs to benefit from an IFC-sponsored investment has been on the average greater than outside capital. Nevertheless, more local financial support is needed to meet strictly capital needs; and in addition, local capital is important in assuring a desirable investment–productivity climate.

The need for local capital support if IFC is to reach its private investment goals has caused IFC to work actively in cooperation with the World Bank toward improvement of capital market arrangements. To progress further, a joint Capital Markets Department (CMD) was established in 1970. The stated aim of CMD is to help create and support local institutions to channel domestic savings into productive private enterprise.

Since 1971, the Eurocurrency market has proven to be a source of relatively substantial funds for use by the LDCs. The growth of credit extensions to developing countries has been most remarkable. Accurate totals of additional credit, excluding traditional financing and transportation of products, is not available. An OECD (Organization for Economic Co-operation and Development) estimate places the total through 1972 in the neighborhood of $8 billion.

The IFC, in commenting on this rather unexpected Eurocurrency development in the early 1970's (i.e., prior to the oil embargo and the sharp increase in the costs of oil to LDCs without petroleum resources), pointed to possible future problems. The Eurocurrency debt management procedures were not developed adequately. This made for simplicity, but at the same time it encouraged loose practices that could result in future problems. One practice identified as a sure source of future trouble was the use of the floating interest rate and therefore uncertainty as to cost of credit. Nevertheless, in 1976 floating interest rate loans were used by the Bank of America as private lender consortium leader in Asia, South America, and Central

America loans. The public lender was the World Bank and the Inter-American Development Bank and Asian Development Bank.

The Eurocurrency interest rate in the 1970s has been one of the most volatile in the world. The institutions operating in the Eurocurrency market also are typically short in equity financing, leaving the lenders very vulnerable to shifts in monetary conditions. Finally, the maturities of Eurocurrency loans are relatively short, necessitating refinancing before fixed investments have had a chance to prove themselves. On the other hand, it is the floating interest rate provision that private lenders require if they are to lend long-term to LDCs.

Unfortunately, many of the problems foreseen by the IFC in large LDC borrowings from the Eurocurrency market have been realized in 1977. In addition, the continued high price of oil since the 1973 embargo and the decline in the price of many traditional LDC exports have combined to make the economic position of many developing nations very uncertain. The IMF and the World Bank plus a number of the oil-rich LDCs and multinational corporations are deeply involved in efforts to alleviate the economic stringency that has arisen. The IMF, for example, is committed to rather substantial regular sales of gold to finance additional assistance to developing countries.

In 1977, Korea introduced a new concept. It is called *syndicate-to-syndicate financing*. A group of Korean commercial banks borrow from a group of lending banks at a floating interest rate $1\frac{7}{8}$ percentage points above the London interbank offered rate. The lending syndicate is headed by Asia Pacific Capital, which is 70 percent owned by Citibank Bank of New York and 30 percent owned by Fuji Bank of Tokyo. The Korean borrowing syndicate is headed by the Korean government-controlled Korean Exchange Bank. Each bank of the Korean borrowing syndicate is responsible for the entire loan.

Under these new conditions introduced in the early 1970s and still working toward a new equilibrium, the role of the IFC shifts somewhat from the original purpose. This change in international finance circumstances has created the fourth stage of IFC activities.

In its fourth stage, the IFC becomes an active, rather specialized partner of both the borrower and the lender using the Eurocurrency market. First the IFC can provide a thorough appraisal of the project to be financed. This can be very helpful in establishing the credit worthiness of the borrower. The participants in the Eurocurrency market have been relying too heavily on broad syndication (many lenders) risk distribution.

Second, the IFC can provide a portion of the financing to make the total credit package more attractive. For example, planning plus some long-term support financing can be supplied to go with the major Eurocurrency lending.

Third, the IFC in its long-term financing can provide fixed interest rates to reduce credit cost fluctuations. Along with these contributions, the IFC continues to provide both borrowers and lenders with access to private and government leaders of both developed and developing nations. These organizational conditions can facilitate the traditional IFC role of bringing domestic and foreign investors together in joint ventures. Also, of course, the World Bank and IFC staffs possess the technical know-how required to mobilize capital, personnel, and materials on a world-wide scale.

Conclusion.   The encouragement of the private sector and the growth of productive investment continues to be a top-priority goal of free-world economic development. The IFC undoubtedly has been helpful and can point to many accomplishments. The great question is whether or not the approach followed has been too slow and too deliberate.

In addition, the antagonism toward the rich and capital-abundant, developed countries by the developing countries has increased in most of the international institutions. The problems traditional in relations between the powerful and the weak have been intensified by the sharply higher oil prices since 1973.

The future and success of IFC seems to rest on its ability to combine the labor and natural resources of developing nations and the capital and markets of developed nations into a productive package. The key does not yet exist, but realism appears to be expanding, and that is good.

Chapter 50

Eurodollar Market

The development of high Eurodollar interest rates can arise from a tight U.S. monetary policy. High interest rates in the Eurodollar market can attract funds from all over the world and maybe the moon, too. This causes a shortage of funds to carry out normal business activities in the economies of the world.

In many respects the Eurodollar market has been a fairly good substitute for a European integrated money market that has never developed. It can be said with considerable confidence that the added efficiency provided in international financing and investment by the market outweighs losses created by speculative excesses stimulated by creation of deposits by private financial institutions free of the restrictions imposed on them in their home countries.

A temporary but very important aspect of the functioning of the Eurodollar market took place between mid-1965 and mid-1970. In mid-1965 Regulation Q prevented U.S. banks from paying an interest rate that was high enough to attract funds as the United States initiated a very tight monetary policy. To find a market where market rates could be earned, U.S. funds had to be placed in the Eurodollar market. This market, which was dominated pretty much by the same banks that at home were restricted by Regulation Q, could offer considerably higher rates because regulation did not exist; and liquidity shortage that was world-wide had grown out of the tight U.S. monetary policy. The Eurodollar market also was at the center of the network of national money markets, making it a very convenient liquidity source for the large multinational corporations.

The maximum interest rate restrictions, the high market interest rates, and the tight money resulted in an outflow of funds from the United States, which in turn caused the enactment of new restrictive American legislation on foreign money operations. In mid-1970 all this changed as the Regulation Q interest rate ceiling on large CDs was removed. This development also substantially reduced the impact of legislation regulating the outflow of funds from the United States.

Under these new conditions of mid-1970, the Eurodollar market lost most of the demand for funds from America. The U.S. banks no longer had to borrow from the market to acquire funds needed to meet the needs of their domestic customers. Under the new conditions, U.S. corporations used the Euromoney market as a portion of a strategy to delay payment of U.S. corporate income taxes on foreign earnings.

During the period of 1965–1970, when the Eurodollar market became a major supplier of funds needed by U.S. business, it attracted some funds from the United States that were looking for the higher interest rates offered. The World Bank estimates that about 11 percent of the funds came from the United States, and that about 52 percent of the new lending was channeled to the United States. Major European countries provided 50 percent of the new funds, and the remaining 39 percent came from the rest of the world.

Since the reversal of American monetary policy in 1970, the closing of the U.S. gold window in August 1971, and the dismantling of the U.S. international regulatory system in 1973, the Eurodollar market has become a tax-avoidance technique that occasionally proves to be helpful, as far as MNCs from America are concerned. The major new element in the market since 1973 is on the supply side. A portion of the huge earnings from oil sales of the OPEC countries have found their way to the Eurodollar market. Much of the demand for the funds has been supplied by nations that are short of oil and therefore in many cases are running large balance-of-payments deficits. In addition, the market has provided liquidity to the growing Eurobond market.

Although some data are available to support the position that the funds in the Eurodollar market are limited to the quantities of dollars transferred from accounts in American bank domestic deposits, the sources of the large quantities of dollar-denominated deposits remain somewhat of a mystery. One answer is that the denominated dollar deposits are not all primary deposits but consist also of derivative deposits, i.e., deposits arising from lending activity and and not accompanied by an equal primary deposit increase by the lending institution. As long as loans are made to banks within the system of European banks or to a corporation doing business in Europe, and not to an American bank or a company operating outside the Euro-dollar market network, derivative dollar-denominated deposits should not cause serious difficulties. The process, however, engenders a sequence of additional Eurodollar loans and an expanded liquidity. By recently introducing a 10 percent reserve requirement on deposits held by foreign branches of U.S. banks, the United States has reduced the deposit expansion potential of the unregulated Eurodollar market.

PART X: SELECTED REFERENCES AND SOURCES

Bankers Trust Company, *The Euro-Dollar Market* (New York: Bankers Trust, 1964).

Eugene A. Birnbaum, "Doubts About Floating Rates," *Wall Street Journal* (May 16, 1976).

Chamber of Commerce of the United States, *Competitive Export Financing for the Seventies*, Washington, D.C., 1970.

Charles A. Coombs, *The Arena of International Finance* (New York: John Wiley, 1976).

Fred Hirsch, *The Pound Sterling: A Polemic* (London: Victor Gollancz, 1965).

Irving B. Kravis and Robert E. Lipsey, "A Report on the Study of International Price Competitiveness," *American Economic Review*, 57, May 1967, 482–491.

International Monetary Fund, *Exchange Restrictions* (Annual Report), Washington, D.C., 1970–1975.

Hal B. Lary, *Problems of the United States as World Trader and Banker* (New York: National Bureau of Economic Research, 1963).

Fritz Machlup, *Euro-Dollar Creation: A Mystery Story* (Princeton, N.J.: Princeton University, International Finance Section, 1970).

World Bank Group, *International Finance Corporation* (Annual Reports), Washington, D.C., 1970–1975.

———, *World Bank Annual Report* (Annual Reports), Washington, D.C., 1970–1975.

Part XI

Finance Systems of Other Countries

INTRODUCTION

The manner in which financial affairs are carried out in other countries often provides an insight into the basic functions of the financial system of a nation. In addition, the way in which bothersome problems are treated in another financial system can point out possible reform directions. Finally, offshore business undertakings and travelers must have dealings with foreign banking systems. These activities are made easier if some familiarity with differing approaches exists.

The communist nations encounter banking and finance problems that bear many similarities to those of democratic, capitalist nations. In these nations, money—as power to be allocated by private individuals through the extension of bank loans to other private individuals or groups desiring to build a house or expand an inventory—is very limited. On the other hand, money as a common denominator, or *numéraire*, remains very important. Money valuation of goods and services continues in communist countries to be a very productive device. Aggregation, projection, evaluation, and the like are very difficult without stable prices that can be compared over time and between different products.

The American society is unique in the decentralization that exists in its banking system and in its education system. No one has theorized that the decentralization of these two basic activities are interrelated. Nevertheless, the banking systems of all the Western developed nations, the LDCs, and the communist nations are more centralized than is the banking system of the United States, and so are their education systems.

Currently, legislation is under consideration to increase the centralization of the American finance system. Here and there, year by year, new legislation and new technologies chip away at the basic concept under which the American finance system has functioned. The consideration given to foreign finance systems in this part is relatively brief. However, on the basis of what is brought to light, one cannot conclude a centralized finance system is obviously the best approach.

The British banking tradition as well as its political tradition is to operate without centrally written and enforced regulations. The British political constitution is unwritten, and its banking community has operated rather more on the basis of convention and understandings than have the banking systems of other Western nations. This British approach to banking and monetary management generally is being nibbled away by scandals and frauds that reach even up to the Bank of England itself. The basic element of private flexibility in monetary management that was nurtured by the British example is being diminished. As this takes place, the management of national money systems becomes more bureaucratic. Other private areas, maybe that of wage negotiations, will have to step in to provide the flexibility needed for capitalism to retain its resilience.

Chapter 51

British Financial Institutions

The Royal Mint and the Bank of England are the two historical mainstays of the British money and banking system. The Bank of England is controlled by the majority party as is the executive division. Therefore, official differences of opinion regarding appropriate monetary policy cannot develop as in America. Also, all regulation of both banking and nonbanking institutions resides in the Bank of England. It is a very centralized system.

The Royal Mint can trace its coinage as the London Mint back to A.D. 610. It functions now as any other government department, except that it serves a considerable international clientele. This overseas business in coins and paper money is extensive and perhaps accounts for more than one-half of the total, world-wide international sale of coins, decorations, and medals.

Domestic Commercial Bank System.   Eleven commercial banks with 14,000 branches account for more than 80 percent of the commercial banking of the United Kingdom. The banks with head offices in London have branches throughout the country. The banks with headquarters in other cities are more regional in nature.

The volume of checks cleared through London and provincial clearinghouses is very large. Despite a stamp tax collected on each check, the British write checks to cover relatively small payments.

The government does not enforce statutory reserve requirements on commercial bank deposits. Convention having approximately the force of law sets an 8 percent reserve requirement for the eleven large banks. Half of this reserve must be kept in cash reserves payable on demand and the remainder as deposits at interest and subject to notice. In addition, the Bank of England may call upon the banks to place special deposits with it that are not considered a portion of the conventional reserve.

Overseas Banks and the International Money Market. Despite the chronic weakness of the monetary unit, the British pound, London continues to be the world's greatest international monetary center. The New York money market is considerably larger in terms of assets of participants but smaller when measured on the basis of transactions including a largely international input.

The London area houses some thirty British and Commonwealth banks that are largely engaged in nondomestic activities. They provide a comprehensive banking service in various regions of the world, i.e., West Indies, Middle East, Africa, and so on.

Also representative offices, bank branches, and full-service operations are carried out in London as a necessary portion of the operations of any bank in the world that intends to meet the overseas banking needs of its customers. This international activity has resulted in London becoming the headquarters of the operations of the Eurocurrency and Eurodollar markets (see Index).

The Eurocurrency activities are of immense importance, totaling between $205 billion and $260 billion in 1975. These activities have been taken over by the 150 or so authorized foreign exchange banks and departments in London. The expertise of these authorized institutions is not matched any place else in the world. In addition, these foreign exchange banks and departments deal in the interbank British pound market that was initiated in the mid-1960s. The purpose here is to utilize more completely the credits developed by domestic and overseas British banks.

London Gold Market. The London gold market is indivisibly related to London's foreign exchange market dominance. The basic market consists of five firms dealing in gold bullion; two are merchant banks, two are owned by a merchant bank, and the fifth is tied to commercial buyers of gold. The representatives of these five firms meet each day to establish an official price of gold in the various major currencies in the world and particularly in terms of the U.S. dollar. When the market is volatile, considerable buying and selling of gold throughout the day will take place at prices that vary from the official morning fixing. In the 1960s when a gold pool operated, the Bank of England actively participated in the market to carry out the wishes of the IMF and the participating national central banks. Between 1973 and 1977 the London gold market operated as the world's leading completely free gold market. In 1977 the New York gold market reached the London level of activity.

The existence of the London gold market has strengthened the city's position as an international money center as the price of gold has become free floating. In addition, the use of gold by communist countries in their dealings with the West causes London to be a convenient place to complete the financial side of sales and purchases. Finally, the large earnings of OPEC countries frequently have been held in gold as well as in short-term British and U.S. Treasury bills. Again, the convenience of the London gold market as well as Euro- and dollar currency markets was recognized and led to further growth of London as the international money center of the world.

London Discount Market. Another basic element of the London money market consists of the twelve discount houses that together form the London Discount Market Association (LDMA). This association plus the commercial banks and the Bank of England make up the market. As is true of the other principal elements of the London money market, a large central structure to house the participants does not exist. Contacts necessary to set prices and buy and sell are carried out nearly completely by telephone.

The LDMA purchases all bills offered weekly by the U.K. Treasury. These bills later are marketed to the commercial banks.

The LDMA also provides an active market for commercial bills originating all over the world in the financing of trade. London's unique position as an international finance market is built upon the finance of trade and a ready market for commercial bills.

Finally, LDMA has become the center for making a market for short-term British government bonds. To carry out the task, they were offered jobber's facilities at the Bank of England for government bonds maturing in not more than five years. These securities are acceptable security for borrowing from the Bank of England. This, of course, made central-bank credit available to hold government debt.

The assets of LDMA prior to the current crisis of the British pound have been divided about equally between treasury bills, commercial bills, and short-term British government bonds.

The Accepting Houses. This market is made up of the seventeen merchant banks that are members of the Accepting Houses Committee. To be a member, the bank's acceptances must enjoy the lowest interest rate being paid, and its paper must be eligible for discount at the Bank of England.

One of the chief functions of an accepting house, i.e., merchant bank, is to guarantee payment of bills of exchange drawn on it by third parties that are dealing with customers of the bank. This is always done on the condition that the customers, who are dealing in the underlying goods, will pay the acceptance firm the amount required to meet the bills when the bills become due. The acceptance house charges to cover the risk involved that payment may not be made and for the advantage it offers its customers in lending its name to the bills of exchange drawn on them.

In addition to this basic function of acceptance of bills of exchange, merchant banks perform ordinary banking activities as acceptance houses. For example, they borrow and lend Eurodollars and other currencies. They also act as investment bankers and issue and place shares and debentures for British and other companies raising capital in the London market.

NONBANK DOMESTIC FINANCING

Building Societies. The British use the term *building societies* in referring to institutions dedicated to the financing of housing. These institutions were originally temporary groups brought together to finance gradually a house for each member through payment of a fixed monthly sum during the life of the society, i.e., until each member had his house. As each house was built it was allocated to a member either by ballot or by payment of a premium.

These temporary building societies were introduced early in the nineteenth century. After mid-century, new and more permanent building societies were introduced. The regulations for their operation were formalized under the Building Societies Act of 1874, which also provided for incorporation. Currently, regulation of the societies is as provided under 1962 legislation. Advice as to interest rates to be paid and charged is offered but need not be followed. Mortgage interest rates typically vary with market rates and deposit rates are not set as in the United States.

The borrowers and investors are two distinct groups under the permanent building societies. The investors consist of share purchasers and depositors. The shares of a society are not traded on the market but may be withdrawn at par in cash, on giving notice. Deposits can be withdrawn with one month notice, a formal requirement. Deposits are treated as creditors and are paid off before shareholders in case of financial difficulties. The interest paid on shares is usually ¼ percent more than paid on deposits. Income tax on earnings on both deposits and shares is paid by the society and not by the individual investors. Special tax rate levels are negotiated with the income tax people.

The societies lend on mortgages secured on owner-occupied houses. The mortgages may be for thirty years, but they frequently are repaid in advance. The societies also make short-term investments in a group of securities. These investments act as reserves to meet withdrawal requests by depositors and shareholders.

These building societies have grown very rapidly since 1920. It is estimated that about two-thirds of privately built houses in Britain are erected with building society finance.

Finance Corporations. Specialized financial institutions to provide medium and long-term capital to businesses that find the traditional sources inadequate have developed since World War II. The development was based on the careful recommendations of the Macmillan Committee (Cmnd. 3897) published in 1931.

In 1945, after some earlier experience during the 1930s, the Finance Corporation for Industry (FCI) was established to provide credit facilities to medium to large businesses unable to find the funds needed from private credit sources. At the same time, the Industrial and Commercial Finance Corporation (ICFC) was set up to meet the legitimate credit needs of smaller businesses. In both cases the capital was provided largely from private sources, i.e., insurance companies in the case of FCI and commercial banks in the case of ICFC, with the Bank of England making a substantial contribution.

The FCI has loaned funds to the steel, aircraft, and chemical industries, all large users of capital. The largest loan was made to the Cunard Steam-Ship Company. The ICFC normally makes five- to twenty-year loans to purchase equipment. About 20 percent of ICFC investments are made to the engineering and electrical industries and about 12 percent to the distribution industry. The remainder is spread quite evenly throughout industry.

Other Finance Developments.   The United Kingdom has a complete array of financial institutions to meet local, national, and international needs. The insurance industry is highly developed and is active in meeting insurance needs around the world. The Society of Lloyd's with its many activities is one of the world's greatest financial institutions. Also many major insurance companies of the United States and other nations maintain offices in London and place reinsurance business in the London market.

Another important area has developed out of the funded pension schemes of England. Associated with this investment and savings activity is the old Registered Provident Societies of England. These societies now cover the countryside, and their regulation takes place under the Industrial and Provident Societies Act of 1965. The societies are basically cooperatives organized to carry out wholesaling and retailing activities. Some societies, however, carry on a banking business and are engaged in the main branches of insurance. All in all, they have proven to be a most flexible organization and have adjusted well to the changing financial and purchasing needs of the ordinary British citizen.

Conclusion.   The British have proven to be very adept at working out procedures to meet both international and domestic finance-related needs. The close connection between the various financial institutions and the Bank of England works to provide a very responsive money market mechanism. It has proven itself through the years, and London remains the banking capital of the world.

Chapter 52

Banking in India

Until July 19, 1969, India had an extensive, privately owned banking system based on the British model. On that date, fourteen large commercial banks were nationalized. Prior to this development, nationalization of two of India's largest banks that previously had been partially publicly owned had taken place in 1949 and 1955.

After 1969, the nationalized banks of India accounted for 85 percent of total bank deposits. The commercial banks of the private sector that remain consist of sixty-one small Indian banks and fifteen foreign banks.

The purpose of nationalization as stated by the then-ruling political party was "to give the people convincing proof the government would follow a socialist program of economic development." The nationalization of banking was followed up by a takeover of the insurance business by the government in May 1971. In addition, a number of basic industries, somewhat along the British line, have been nationalized.

The actual nationalization of banking through issuance of bonds and cash payments to the stockholders came about as the climax of a series of steps started in 1967. The Banking Law Amendment Act of 1968 was aimed at channeling savings and bank credit toward development goals and away from harmful speculative uses. The act provided for a National Credit Council to coordinate and assess the lending policies of the banks of the nation. At the same time, the government placed its representatives on bank boards. The aim here was to reduce the decision-making powers of the large businesses of India.

Each of these steps acted to demonstrate the seriousness of the problem and the inadequacy of steps short of complete control. In the words of Indira Gandhi, "It is widely recognized that the operations of the banking system should be informed by a larger social purpose and be subject to close public regulation . . . [and] that the desired regulation and rate of progress [of banking business] consistent with the urgency of our problems could be secured only through nationalization."

The "social purpose" is of course to use bank credit and the savings of the people. A portion of the savings of the people in India traditionally has been funneled through the banking system, but a much larger share has sought out gold, land, and foreign deposits as the depository of savings. The government's approach to achievement has been two-pronged.

First, the government has, through branches and offices, made banking available to the villages where banking services did not exist and to urban sections where there was a shortage of banking facilities. Second, bank credit availability was expanded at a reasonable interest rate to all segments of the economy and regions of the country.

The program has been pursued actively. More new banking facilities have been established during the past seven years than had been organized during the prior quarter of a century. It is judged that the result has been bank facility availability to all groupings down to a population of 10,000. In addition, mobile banking facilities have been introduced to serve working groups and schools. The aim is to spread the banking approach to saving and borrowing.

Lending has been expanded at the grass-roots level. The priority sectors have been agriculture, small businesses, and retailers. As a result of this emphasis, the portion of bank credit going to these borrowers has approximately doubled. To stimulate further the government role in expanding the economic progress of the nation, the concept of Lead Bank Scheme (LBS) was introduced in 1970.

The LBS provides for a Lead Bank in each designated administrative district of India. The bank acts as an innovator in the area. The activities emphasized are determined by the credit needs as seen by the managers of the Lead Bank. Competition between banking units of other banks is not diminished, and the Lead Bank does not aim at monopolizing the credit business of the district.

The LBS is aimed at turning around banking from an examination of the individual project alone to examination of how the project being proposed fits in with overall economic and social needs of the area. To make this new approach more bankable, a substantial loan insurance program was introduced in 1971. The government, aided by the commercial banks, provided the capital for a Credit Guarantee Corporation of India.

Since the bank reform program of India was initiated, the government has assumed wide administrative controls, and most of the traditional democratic institutions of India have been throttled. The success of the program in expanding growth rests on the success of the government in gaining control over the resources required to expand investment. One aspect of this is to offer sufficiently high interest rates and great enough safety to attract savings. The other side of the coin is to assure the investments are productive and not wasteful. The 1977 Indian government looks upon government banking with less favor than past governments.

Chapter 53

West German Financial Institutions

A unique and significant feature of German banking is its system of municipal-owned and managed savings institutions. These institutions were established to protect small savers and businesses from fraud and to encourage the general spirit of saving.

These municipal financial institutions carry out about one-fourth of the total German lending to the nonbank public. The system includes a central bank or lending office in each state. It is called the Girozentralen, and the institutions are particularly active in making long-term loans to large corporations. These institutions plus savings banks have one-third more assets than the commercial banking system, and they participate along with commercial banks in every field of German banking endeavor.

Prior to 1967 all sectors of the German finance industry operated under very restrictive legislation. Interest rates on both loans and deposits were set by the government, and advertising was sharply restricted. Today banks are completely free in setting deposit and lending rates. Competition between institutions is only limited by the rather strict German laws against monopoly promotion tactics.

The central bank of Germany, called the Bundesbank, provides basic interest rate guidance through its setting of the discount rate. The three-month savings deposit rate is the base private sector rate around which lending and deposit rates cluster. Demand deposits in Germany can earn interest, but the payment is very low, perhaps down to $\frac{1}{8}$ of 1 percent.

The interest rate on short-term loans fluctuates with money market conditions. However, the interest rates of consumer and housing loans are set for the duration when the loan is granted.

The funds for most of these loans are obtained through sale of mortgage-secured, long-term bonds. In this manner the problem of losing funds to support outstanding mortgage lending when market interest rates increase is avoided.

Commercial loan interest rates are flat rates and about 3.5 percent above the Bundesbank discount rate. The rate differential to non-prime-rate customers is about 1 percent more. The German banks do not use compensating balances as a portion of the loan agreement, but accounts with a high turnover are subject to additional charges.

To establish a new bank the proposer does not have to demonstrate that a need for additional banking service exists, as is necessary in the United States. Demonstration of a need was required in Germany up to 1962, when it was declared unconstitutional by the German Supreme Administrative Court.

Nation-wide branch banking is available to commercial banks. The physical location of savings banks and Girozentralen institutions are limited, however, to the state granting the charter.

Although every commercial bank has the potential of covering all of West Germany, only four banks with a total of 3,000 branches have a nation-wide network of branches, i.e., Deutsche Bank, Dresdner Bank, Commerzbank, and Bank für Gemeinwirtschaft, which is controlled by the labor unions. Savings bank services are supplied abundantly, with branches available in more than 34,000 different locations. Only 47 German banking offices are operated by foreign banks, and most of these are American. Also, German banks operate very few foreign branches or offices. This relatively low level of foreign bank participation is not due to restrictive legislation, which is really very liberal. Apparently, the banking market abroad as seen by German bankers has not been as attractive as the domestic market.

The German government does not provide a savings deposit insurance system such as the FDIC or FSLIC in the United States. However, since 1969, the banking community has established a fund to reimburse depositor losses up to 20,000 DM (Deutschemarks) equivalent to $8,000. The Bundesbank has the power to set reserve requirements as well as to engage in open market operations, and in this way it can press for sound credit conditions. The failure in 1974 of Bankhaus I.D. Herstatt, a medium-sized German bank, caused considerable international uneasiness and some rather large losses by American bank clients.

The German commercial banks are able to become much more involved with equities than is possible for U.S. banks. They can, for example, own stock in other companies of all sorts. In addition, the banks can carry on a stockbrokerage business.

The stock-selling side of the business of German bankers has expanded just recently to meet the potential of the market. The stimulus for action came from an American company called Investors Overseas Services Ltd. (IOS), which later encountered serious management problems. Nevertheless, IOS and its mutual fund activities set the spark that resulted in a very substantial expansion of bank and citizen interest in ownership plus sale and purchase of corporate stock. One result of the increase of public holdings of corporate shares has been a questioning of the German system of electing members of corporate boards of directors.

In the past, banks have selected a large portion of the directors of German corporations. The power of management to control boards of directors in Germany is much less than in America. Also, the exercise of direct power in the management of corporations of all types is possessed by the banks of Germany to a much greater degree than in the United States.

The only government restriction on the investments held by banks in Germany is that their investment in real estate and participations may not be higher than the bank's capital plus reserves. As a result, German banks are deeply involved in the promotion of new companies, in the purchase of large blocks of shares, and in generally operating as corporate conglomerates.

Conclusion. The political forces in Germany have permitted the commercial and savings banking systems to accumulate a great deal of economic power. The strength demonstrated by the German economy since World War II plus basic anti-monopoly legislation has made the procedure acceptable. In addition, the success of the huge Girozentralen and cooperative savings institutions has given the citizen, as both a political and economic participant, a stake in the system. Finally, the increasing relative value of the DM in the international money markets and the relatively low level of inflation strengthen the entire system.

Chapter 54

Financial Intermediaries in France

In mid-1965, the French government introduced a somewhat different approach to the regulation of its financial institutions. The change was made as France acted to reduce the role of the Treasury in financing economic growth and turned to the savings institutions of the private sector.

A basic legislative change to bring about this shift in the source of investment funds provided for the abandonment of the compartmentalization of the financial system. Commercial banks were allowed to hold savings and other term accounts and to pay interest competitive with that offered by savings banks. A second provision of this legislation forbade interest payments on demand deposits of commercial banks. This resulted in a very large expansion of commercial bank term and savings deposits. Most of this increase came from a decrease in demand deposits, but in addition the commercial banks actively sought and acquired deposits from households throughout the country. The competition between savings banks and commercial banks for time deposits became very intense.

The savings banks of France are members of a semipublic system and are related to the Caisse des Dépôts et Consignations, a national public bank. This bank in turn uses the savings coming in through its affiliation with savings banks to finance local governments, social facilities, and housing. It provides about 15 percent of the total value of new housing. This special relationship of the savings banks to the national government and investment programs possessing a high political importance has resulted in a special tax privilege. The interest paid on ordinary savings deposits within these savings institutions is exempt from the French income tax.

These deposits earning tax-exempt interest are very popular and account for 75 percent or so of total savings bank deposits. The size of these deposits that can be held by one holder is limited, and each time the maximum level has been increased new deposits flow in, even though the interest rate offered is considerably below the rate of inflation. Under these conditions this activity demonstrates that a substantial portion of the deposits come from those in the high progressive income tax brackets. The assets of a very large portion of wealthy Frenchmen include a savings bank deposit equal to the maximum interest, tax-exempt level.

A few years ago, France initiated what is called the *housing savings account*. The procedure ties a savings account to eligibility for an interest-subsidized housing loan. The account also makes the borrower eligible for a more expensive supplementary loan. The program has been successful in attracting savings and in stimulating housing.

The national public mortgage bank of France is the Crédit Foncier. It has established a very useful secondary national mortgage market. The market trades in notes issued by commercial banks that have extended mortgage loans. These notes corresponding with mortgage maturities are purchased and sold by participants in the market including the Crédit Foncier. No special additional guarantee is granted to these instruments. The market appears to have been strengthened by the French practice of not issuing variable-rate mortgages.

The banking system of France is largely government owned. These nationalized institutions appear to operate about the same as they would if they were privately owned. In France, the specialized banking institution is being replaced by the department-store bank, along the lines of American and German development. Specialized, short-term deposit banks offer long-term credits. On the other hand, investment banks have begun to offer short-term deposit service.

Chapter 55

Banking in Communist Countries

The take-over of banking activities is an early step of communist governments. The capital allocation and the gathering together of resources for investment in a communist nation rests largely with budgetary decisions and not with the banking system. Banks and financial institutions in general in a communist country are concerned largely with carrying out the transaction function of money (*numéraire*), with fulfilling some role in encouraging citizen savings, and with dealing with noncommunist suppliers of needed imports and noncommunist purchasers of exports. All planning in communist nations is accomplished through the allocation of material balances and not money balances, i.e., the money illusion is removed.

People's Republic of China. Shortly after the Communist Revolution (1949), the People's Bank of China was established as the only bank authorized to issue currency. By 1960 the Director General was able to announce that "in the main, the socialist transformation of the private banking organization, ending the capitalist monetary system and laying the groundwork for the socialist transformation of capitalist industry and commerce, was completed."

The role of banking in the transformation of China is concentrated in implementing plans, setting group responsibility, and allocating rewards to individuals. As a result, money as a unit of exchange and measure of value is used to calculate wages and measure profits of group undertakings. A monetary unit with a constant value is therefore very important. The patterns of distribution and production are for the most part set by government budgetary decisions and not by relative prices offered in the market. Prices, wages, and production are set by government fiat and are affected very little by developments in the market.

The monopoly power of the People's Bank is very great, but there are several basic banking functions implemented by other semiautonomous agencies. The most important of these is the Bank of China. This bank, with branches in the Far West and London, conducts the foreign exchange business of the Republic. Its operations are strictly controlled, but in the cities where branches are located a rather normal international commercial banking business occurs.

The rural banking business was spun off by the People's Bank shortly after it assumed its monopoly position. The new Agricultural Bank of China was created to meet rural credit needs. Its life was short, and after a few years its more than 100,000 branches were absorbed by the People's Bank.

Early in the development of modern China, a People's Construction Bank of China also was established. It has branches in all the principal cities, and its life span continues up to the present. The Construction Bank performs some of the functions expected of an investment bank in a capitalist nation. The bank receives capital funds from the national budget and on behalf of the Ministry of Finance allocates them on the basis of decisions made in the government budget process. The bank is an agency and not an enterprise in its own right as is the People's Bank.

Apparently, about 80 percent of China's fixed capital allocations are provided directly out of budgetary allocations. After being deposited in the Construction Bank these funds are allocated to state enterprises to finance capital expansion and construction.

China has found it difficult to move her economy into the twentieth century. The bureaucratic system introduced early in her development has been replaced largely with procedures based on banking approaches traditional to loan granting and loan management. This has meant more power for the People's Bank and more centralization of planning and administration of projects undertaken.

Repressed inflation exists to some extent and results in the use of rationing procedures. The government has encouraged the deposit of all funds in the People's Bank and the holding in cash of only that amount of currency required to meet daily marketing needs. This program of noncash settlement of accounts has caused the use of cash to account for only 15 percent of payments. This is a very unusual relationship in a nonurban, low-income area.

Efforts to hold funds received by individuals within the system have included insurance and savings bond programs. In addition, state enterprises are expected to provide working capital from internal sources.

All in all, China has been quite successful in avoiding inflationary monetary and banking policies. China also has been quite pragmatic in its use of banking controls over liquidity and loan extensions to carry out investment decisions and to avoid depreciation of the *yuan*.

Russia. Currently Russia, like China, uses only one institution to allocate budgetary appropriations into fixed investments. The Investment Bank (Stroibank) is also a relatively weak institution as is the case of the Construction Bank of China.

The Gosbank does for Russia what the People's Bank does in China. It is another example of a monobank. Gosbank alone meets virtually all the cash, credit, and payment needs of Russia and its 250 million people. It doesn't have any real competition. The Investment Bank is essentially an administrative organization, and the Foreign Trade Bank is actually only a headquarters organization.

The Gosbank is able to meet the growing use of common credit by strengthening a system of credit extension by stores rather than banks. The savings bank system had been taking care of most individual use of banking services; therefore the Gosbank, by absorbing these institutions, took over virtually all accounts and transactions of individuals. The collective farms have become greater users of funds as each collective farm becomes an earner and dispenser of funds. The Gosbank has been hard pressed to develop banking services to fill the void in agriculture banking that had been created by the earlier collective farm procedures that relied largely on payments in kind. The major internal monetary and banking operating problem of the Gosbank appears to be in developing an efficient settlements mechanism between different regions and different industries.

In addition to its very comprehensive, rather traditional central and commercial banking activities the Gosbank performs a myriad of responsibilities related to checking the operations of commercial and production ventures as varied as can be imagined. In the Ukraine alone, some two thousand economists from the staffs of local and regional offices of the Gosbank participate in the work of "public bureaus of economic analysis." These so-called voluntary bureaus have been assigned the task of seeing that managers of commercial and industrial operations perform their duties efficiently. These bureaus are the communist substitute for the profit motive, and the economic specialists are provided by Gosbank.

The Soviet Union is a much larger user of cash than is China, where transfer of accounts dominates the transaction process. It is estimated that in Russia about 90 percent of the money income of the population is represented in currency withdrawals and the return of currency to Gosbank. The failure of Russia to develop a bank account system of making payments and withdrawals makes the management of liquidity a more difficult problem than is true in China.

Opportunities for savings other than first holding onto cash received as wages are very limited in Russia. The savings banks system in Russia is operated on a part-time basis by the regular employees of the postal administration and is completely integrated into the Gosbank. In addition to accepting deposits, these offices sell and redeem government savings bonds and pay out social security benefits, including old-age pensions and aid to large families and dependent children. They also pay lottery prizes, which is how interest is paid on Soviet bonds held by the people. Safekeeping facilities are also available. These savings offices do not lend any of the funds received. All lending is monopolized by the Gosbank.

The average savings account in Russia is around $100. This amount can be spent by check if the depositor desires. Accounts from which withdrawals are permitted without notice earn 2 percent. In addition, lottery savings accounts run by the different states of Russia do exist. Interest is paid in prizes that frequently consist of relatively expensive consumer goods. Savings account balances also have been given special, favored treatment when the ruble has lost value through currency conversions. The traditional communist approach to finance is through government budgetary decisions and not decisions of managers of financial institutions. This continues to be the basic approach to the provision of commercial and industrial credit in Russia. However, since the mid-1960s, a considerable portion of the turnover tax levied on consumer goods is being channeled into Gosbank to provide funds to make loans to finance new and improved technology for producing consumer goods.

The use of interest to allocate funds to various purposes is still nearly banned in Russia. The ideological hurdles set by Marx to thinking of interest as a legitimate cost to be considered in making a decision to build a dam, for instance, are still very high. Interest charges for long-term loans range from $\frac{3}{4}$ of 1 percent to 2 percent. It is an issue that still is largely unresolved.

Higher interest rates are restricted largely to penalty charges made because a loan was not repaid when due. Higher interest also may be charged if the need for funds arose from mismanagement of the enterprise under control of the borrower.

In the future, the Gosbank hopes to rid itself of many of the minute details of supervision of borrowers. The aim is to rely much more on "economic and material stimulants," i.e., as a modified profit-oriented borrower.

East Germany. Right after the occupation of East Germany by the Russians, the Reichsbank and all large commercial banks in the area were liquidated. For replacement, a Deutsche Notenbank and an Investment Bank were established. Later, an agricultural credit institution called the Landwirtschaftsbank was organized; later still, a foreign trade bank called the Deutsche Aussenhandelsbank was established.

The East German banking system continues on a somewhat reduced basis as the traditional cooperative banking system of Germany. The new approach to an old answer consists of a network of about 230 cooperative banks called Banken für Handwerk und Gewerbe. The responsibility still consists largely of providing credit and banking facilities to small producers and traders. Of course, now the activity is supervised by the Notenbank, the East German monobank.

The municipal savings banks of the old Germany also have been preserved under local municipal control, although the network now is under the general control of the Ministry of Finance. There are over 100 of these banks with about 5,000 branches. In addition, a post office, nation-wide savings system has offices in more than 10,000 post offices. East Germany even continues a separate savings bank for the railroad system.

The private sector, although under strict limitation, continues to function in a minor way in East Germany. The Notenbank has some accounts of private firms and farmers. In fact, all firms employing ten persons or more and all farms of fifty acres or more must keep their accounts with the Notenbank. This means the other banking and savings facilities are able to perform only very minor economic undertakings.

The savings system is much more active and inventive in East Germany than is typical of communist banking. The various savings organizations, which even include the Landwirtschaftsbank, offer a variety of private accounts to attract savers. The savings bank and the postal system also provide convenient facilities for the transfer of deposits to make payments or for other purposes.

The agricultural sector utilizes the Landwirtschaftsbank, which offers both short-term and long-term loans. Most of the credit activity is with collective farms, but they also serve as the banker for private farms of more than fifty acres. In addition, it lends to farm credit cooperatives, who in turn meet the credit needs of small farmers and rural consumer groups. The East German government has always seen the breaking up of large private farms to be a basic aspect of its farm program. In the credit area, this has meant the requirement of tougher terms on credit extended to carry out large farming operations than small ones.

In order to assist in the re-establishment of the viability of East Germany's industrial sector, a rather unique communist institutional arrangement called the Industriebanken was initiated. The Notenbank continues to allocate to individuals government budget-provided funds for industrial investment through the Investment Bank, but investment activity is not limited to this budgetary and therefore centrally controlled approach.

The new approach of the Industriebanken has resulted in the creation of about 80 industry associations that are directly responsible for sound operation of about 2,000 enterprises, which account for more than 60 percent of East Germany's industrial output. Each Industriebanken, which is legally a branch of the Notenbank, serves as a special industry bank for up to 3 of the 80 industry associations. Each of these groupings is responsible for drafting its own quarterly plans, although the annual plan of the Notenbank, into which these local plans must fit, is subject to approval or rejection by the Council of Ministers, the top government political group.

As time has passed, more and more of the financing of

each association group has come from internal funds and less from budgetary allocations. Interest charges also are being used to promote completion of projects within the designated time span. The result has been considerable flexibility in industry planning and the allocation of some of the power to manipulate the society's economic levers to the operators of the various activities required to produce and market in the world of mass production and mass buying power.

Yugoslavia. The government has been active in its search for more satisfactory financial institutional arrangements adapted to Yugoslavia's commitment to workers' self-management of economic organizations. The search resulted in a very substantial reorganization of banking and investing institutions in 1965. The new development is aimed at greater decentralization of investment decisions and a greater reliance on nonbudgeting funds to finance investment projects. Both of these broad aims push toward banking and investment procedures more like those of capitalist countries and less like the procedures of communist nations.

By 1965, the National Bank of Yugoslavia had become more of a monobank than was the case even in Russia. Its powers were reduced sharply at the same time as attempts were abandoned to carry out detailed national planning concentrated at the top. Today only two formal banking institutions exist—the National Bank that operates as a limited central bank and business banks that operate very much like American commercial banks. In addition, there is a rather dormant nation-wide postal saving system.

The Federal Executive Council, an arm of the Federal Assembly, sets National Bank policy in all major areas except minimum reserve requirements; however, a maximum reserve ratio of 35 percent is established in the National Bank Law. The federal government's borrowing from the National Bank is sharply limited under federal law, and short-term borrowing to cover budgetary deficits is practically prohibited. This tough policy was initiated after the Yugoslavian dinar had gone through two devaluations in 1971. The business banks can borrow from the National Bank only for a term of ten days, and the amount is limited to 2 percent of the reserves required of the bank. A real effort has been made by the Federal Assembly to prevent an inflationary expansion of the money stock.

The business banks, about seventy of them, plus numerous

branches are a combination of investment and commercial banks. These banks accept savings accounts, and because they are not prevented from operating throughout the nation they have become quite competitive in the interest rates they pay. The deposits and interest on them are tax exempt. The federal government guarantees the deposits but does not guarantee that the business bank will remain solvent.

Any group of economic and sociopolitical organizations may establish a bank by meeting the capital and other requirements established by law. The assembly, in which investors in the bank are represented on the basis of both deposits and initial capital provided, is the highest administrative organ. The assembly must have a minimum of twenty-five members, each having at least one vote and not more than 10 percent of total votes. The bank's statutes must provide for a special voting quota for the employees of the bank. The bank lends funds as it has resources and to those approved by the bank's credit committee, which is bound by guidelines set by the assembly. Capital cannot be withdrawn, but the rights derived from the contributions are transferable.

The earnings of the business banks above interest and other expenses involving yield on funds invested follows the direct participation principle of the Yugoslav economic system. The workers receive bonuses above salary if operations have been profitable. Funds also are expected to be allocated to the reserves of the bank and payments for social security and fringe benefits of employees. If the earnings are not sufficient to cover these costs, the staff is expected to adjust expenditures and take other proper measures to correct the situation. Under these conditions, additional capital payments would be assessed on investors. The federal government and the National Bank are under no obligation to rescue the operation.

The funds loaned by business banks come from individual time deposits, demand deposits from production associations, capital funds, funds from sale of bonds and other securities, government investment resources, and borrowings from abroad from the National Bank. The regulations prohibit the use of short-term funds to grant long-term credits—another indication of a desire to follow a conservative policy.

The decentralization decision of the mid-1960s has meant an abandonment by the central government of a quality or type of credit control. The business banks are in effect free to lend where they think it would do the most good. The exceptions to this approach are in the investment and long-term lending activity of the business banks. The government has pressed for loans to finance certain key infrastructure projects and the operations of the Federal Fund for Accelerated Development of Less Developed Republics and Regions. Also, the Federal Institute for Economic Planning develops suggested credit policy goals.

Nevertheless, the business banks are governed in making their loans largely by economic conditions as they see them. This does not mean narrow regional and institutional thinking dominates credit decisions. The business banks have assembly members and depositors who are interested in national development and international opportunities, also. In addition, the tax program discourages "localist" tendencies. The fixed assets owned by an economic organization are taxed, but the income is not taxed. Therefore, a business bank's credit committee should be attracted to yields available in the capital market rather than in a new local building.

Through the Association of Yugoslav Banks the business banks have worked out an arrangement to distribute funds from surplus banks to needy banks. The National Bank is in the first stages of establishing a federal funds market. The National Bank has developed rather complete and current flow-of-funds accounts and projections. These accounts form the basis of National Bank actions relative to meeting monetary quantitative goals.

The experimental work in Yugoslavia has developed answers to many of the basic problems of banking in a communist country. Problem areas remain, however. For example, insufficient mobility of financial resources and a limited range of marketable securities continue to be troublesome. And the interest rate structure is still too rigid, and insufficient facilities exist to service direct foreign investment.

Although most of the banking controls and procedures of capitalist nations are available and used in Yugoslavia, the federal government through the Social Accounting Service still has the power to directly control the use and allocation of financial resources. The capital market now is dominated by the banks with their decentralized control, but substantial credit resources continue to be centrally allocated by the government sector.

Conclusion.   The communist approach to banking and investment in its pure state sees banks as administrative units of the state. The budget of the national and state governments determines the type and quantity of loans and provides the funds to do the borrowing.

This highly centralized and unitary approach to investment, saving, and financial services remains in its purest form in Russia. The procedure has proven to be clumsy and inflation-prone and therefore somewhat unsatisfactory and subject to modification. A very important area where dissatisfaction has led to modification is in the allocation of credit to agriculture and in the gathering up of savings arising in the agricultural sector.

The brief examination of banking in communist nations demonstrates, if nothing else, that the communist world does not approach the area of banking in an entirely uniform way. There is, nevertheless, a thread of conformity, and this consists of the greater direct role of the national government through budget decisions. Only in Yugoslavia is an effort being made to decentralize both control of the financial institutions and the determination of who will receive loans. The movement toward integration of banks with particular industrial sectors developed in East Germany is another example of communist banking experimentation that has met an economic and administrative need.

The Marx and Lenin position that interest payments and interest rates should not be a part of communist economic planning and development continues to influence banking in the communist countries. The idea dies hard, and in Russia the helpfulness of interest rates as costs in planning for efficient use of resources still is underutilized.

Chapter 56

Brazilian Banking and Indexing*

The existing financial system of Brazil arose from legislation of 1964 and 1966. This legislation established the legal framework for the following seven institutional groupings

1. The National Monetary Council (NMC)
2. The Central Bank of Brazil (CBB)
3. The Bank of Brazil (BB)
4. The National Bank for Economic Development (NBED)
5. The National Housing Bank (NHB)
6. The Federal Savings Bank (FSB)
7. The National Bank for Cooperative Credit (NBCC)

Monetary and Economic Growth: Theory and Policy. Brazil is the land of the economic analytical approach that considers restrictions on the quantity of money unnecessary and believes that economic development is only possible if there is a rapidly expanding money supply. The theory teaches that the resulting substantial inflation should not be feared.

The Brazilian approach to economic problems has been partially formalized under the banner *structuralist*. The structuralist school of economic thought holds that inflation is a natural accompaniment of the economic change required to move a peasant society into the modern era. The bottlenecks that change creates also require inflation for their destruction. To fight the destruction of the restrictions on change by trying to control inflation through fiscal and monetary policies causes such fearful costs in unemployment and lost production that the growth process is destroyed.

* This chapter is based on: José Leite, unpublished doctoral dissertation, University of Oregon, 1976.

The consequence of this economic philosophy during 1957–1964 was the direct manufacture of huge quantities of money by the Bank of Brazil to meet the Treasury's need for funds to meet government commitments. The inflation resulted in money losing its ability to act as a means of exchange or a store of value. To restore to money its basic functions, Law 4357 of July 17, 1964, introduced a broad program of indexing of monetary commitments, i.e., adjustment for loss of purchasing power. The first and basic step under the monetary correction legislation was the issue of Readjustable Treasury Bonds (ORTN). These bonds were indexed for inflation and accumulated interest at 6 percent.

The introduction of indexing on a grand scale in Brazil is called the *gradualist* approach to economic stimulation. The wide use of indexing was expected to be accompanied by reduced government deficits and a carefully planned continuous program of economic expansion.

The procedure provides for two methods of adjustment, *ex post* and *ex ante*. The ex-post approach is applied to contracts in money terms such as house rents, pension funds, wage contracts, mortgage debt outstanding, and bonds. These money commitments are changed in line with a six-month average rate of change in the general price level and pay the contracted interest rate on the indexed amount. When the obligation matures, the full indexed face amount is due.

Time and savings deposits are adjusted on the ex-ante basis. The banks offer depositors a fixed rate of interest plus a calculated inflation adjustment based upon the recent inflation rate. Holders of deposits therefore know the quantity of ruzeiros they will receive on their deposit contracts.

The Brazilian gradualist approach is also an effort to separate the portion of the interest rate caused by inflation from the portion required to cover the sacrifice of savings and productivity of investment. Interest rates are viewed as a cost of production, whereas inflation rates are considered adjustment costs to be borne by the society in carrying out development goals. Therefore interest rates are deemed to be an area where controls are needed, and levels cannot be permitted to adjust freely. Interest rates paid above the index adjustment on deposits are controlled under a system of administered interest rates. The interest rates that are charged borrowers of funds are also set, with rates varying depending on desirability and interest sensitivity of the loan use. The lowest ceilings are set on commercial bank loans, and maintenance of these low rates is encouraged through low rediscount rates available at the Central Bank of Brazil.

The concept of breaking interest rates into two parts, i.e., natural or real and inflationary or monetary is based on much of the analyses relative to interest rates that have been conducted in the free world. Also, the idea of indexing all contracts, including national government securities, has received considerable support as the procedure that may be required under modern conditions of full employment policy.

In Brazil these concepts have been tested partially but through a myriad of institutional adjustments and controls. Nevertheless, all seemed to be going well until 1973 when high oil prices of OPEC drained away the savings of Japan and the Western industrial nations and placed the allocation of these savings into the hands of the leaders of a small group of nations with investment priorities that differed radically from those of the former controllers. In 1976, Brazil's program of gradualism deteriorated, and inflation again went out of control; economic growth came to a standstill. The influence of this development caused indexing to lose much of its support in the United States. It no longer possesses wide support as a workable approach to the control of the ravages of inflation in LDCs or even in developed nations.

Banking and Monetary Institutional Arrangement. Brazil possesses a very centralized and government-directed banking and monetary system. The NMC has direct control over the CBB and all other financial institutions of the national government. In addition, NMC exercises ultimate power over state and private financial institutions. The power is awesome, and its existence explains the belief of Brazilian finance ministers in their ability to control how the monetary and credit system functions.

The NMC Board of Directors, presided over by the finance minister, includes representation from all the economic ministries and credit agencies of the national government plus nominal representation from the private sector. The planning minister is vice-chairman of NMC.

The list of powers of the NMC includes complete authority over banking, credit, and fiscal management activities of the public and private sectors of Brazil. Both the CBB and the BB are utilized by the NMC to carry out its directives. The CBB is a rather conventional central bank with rather more responsibility for the finance and borrowings of state and local governments than is usual.

The BB is a government-owned bank that operates throughout Brazil with nearly 1,000 branches. The BB provides about 50 percent of the credit extended in the private sector.

It ranks thirty-second in size of the commercial banks of the world and first in the quantity of its agricultural loans. In addition, it manages the many special development funds set up by the government. Finally, through its membership, along with CBB in the monetary authorities, it has an important input in the formulation of Brazil's monetary budget.

Brazil has a plethora of relatively small private financial institutions operating as finance companies, S&Ls along the U. S. model, investment banks, credit cooperatives, and commercial banks. All of these institutions operate under a charter granted by the CBB.

Currently, the monetary authorities are pushing conglomeration of these separate financial agencies under the leadership of commercial banks. This effort to reduce the number of independent private financial institutions has met with considerable success.

In the financing of its housing through the NHB, Brazil has turned to pension funds to provide the needed capital. This approach is rather common in LDCs and in most cases has proven to be disastrous to the funds. The pension resources become tied to long-term money obligations that inflation makes nearly valueless in a few years. The index program of Brazil up to 1975 largely prevented this from happening. The number of dollar units owed by the mortgagor to the NHB has increased at the same rate as the money units have declined in value. Also, of course, as was pointed out above, this *ex-post* procedure used in Brazil results in the mortgage interest rate being applied to this expanding monetary base. As a result, interest receipts also keep up with the decline in the value of the monetary unit; pension funds enjoy a growing money flow, and the real value of the contribution base is maintained—something we haven't been able to do in the United States.

Chapter 57

Canadian Banking

Canada, a country of 25 million people, or about the population of California, enjoys the services of five chartered banks that are included in the list of the world's fifty largest banks. These five banks operate more than 6,000 branch offices and provide 90 percent of Canadian banking services.

A very interesting legal quirk in the Canadian Bank Charter legislation provides that renewal of the charter must be made every ten years. The requirement is something like the requirement that TV stations must have their licenses renewed. It puts some pressure on management, but the failure to renew would cause so much commotion that it is not likely ever to happen.

Because Canadian commercial banks are so large relative to the size of the economy, the need for deposit insurance was much less than in the United States. In fact, it was not until 1967 that the Canadian Deposit Insurance Corporation (CDIC) was established by legal action.

The central bank of Canada is called the Bank of Canada. It was established in 1934 and is modeled after the Fed of the United States. However, because the Canadian bank system largely consists of five banks, the Bank of Canada does not have the bank membership problems encountered by the Fed. This fact acts to strengthen its use of regulatory powers. On the other hand, because each bank is so relatively important, any action that would lead to serious problems for one bank would be politically very difficult to impose.

Canada is a very active international borrower and commercial exporter. This has acted to stimulate Canadian commercial banks to operate foreign branches and affiliations, including merchant bank operations in London. The ability of

Canadian banks to operate in the New York money market under less regulation than New York commercial banks also has made them very competitive.

Canada's economic development has been considerably slower than that experienced in the United States. One explanation that certainly is of some importance emphasizes the great difference in the types of commercial banking systems developed in the two countries. In the U.S. banks have been involved constantly in business loans that involve considerable risk. As a result, prior to the Great Depression of the 1930s and the resulting deposit insurance legislation, the United States experienced frequent commercial bank failures. This was not the case in Canada.

Although the decentralized U.S. system (and its frequent bank failures) is often faulted, it was also a system that by financing risks and suffering losses was making it possible to develop new areas and to experiment with new technical developments. On the other hand, the concentrated Canadian system and its conservative lending policy was restricting opportunities for development of the Canadian frontiers in science, agriculture, natural resources, and manufacturing.

PART XI: SELECTED REFERENCES AND SOURCES

British Information Services, *British Financial Institutions* (London, Central Office of Information, 1966).

Business Week, "Now Even Nations Are in Danger of Default," October 12, 1974, 112–116.

Allen B. Frankel, "International Banking: Part I," *Federal Reserve Bank of Chicago, Business Conditions*, September, 1975, 3–9.

————, "International Banking—Structural Aspects of Regulation," *Federal Reserve Bank of Chicago, Business Conditions*, October 1974, 3–11.

George Garvy, *Money, Banking and Credit in Eastern Europe* (New York: Federal Reserve Bank of New York, 1966).

Diether H. Hoffman, "German Banks as Financial Department Stores," *Federal Reserve Bank of St. Louis Review, 53*, November 1971, 8–13.

Karel Holbik (ed.), *Monetary Policy in Twelve Industrial*

Countries (Boston: Federal Reserve Bank of Boston, 1973).

Barry Kramer, "As Peking's Financier, Bank of China Strives to Give a 'Solid' Image," *Wall Street Journal*, December 1, 1976, 1.

Francis A. Lees, *International Banking and Finance* (New York: John Wiley & Sons, 1974).

James R. Piper, Jr., "How U.S. Firms Evaluate Foreign Investment Opportunities," *MSU Business Topics*, Summer 1971, 11–20.

R. S. Sayers, *Modern Banking* (7th ed.) (Oxford: Clarendon Press, 1967).

Pierre Tabatoni, "The Role of Savings Intermediaries in France," *Savings and Residential Financing*, 1968 Conference Proceedings (Chicago: U.S. Savings and Loan League, 1968), 72–84.

J. S. G. Wilson, "Regulation and Control of the United Kingdom Banking and Financial Structure," *Banca Nazionale Del Lavoro*, June 1969, 128–143.

Appendix I

Federal Reserve Operations in Payment Mechanisms: A Summary[1]

Since its origin in 1913, the Federal Reserve System has been an active participant in the Nation's payments mechanisms. At present the System is operationally involved in check processing, distribution of currency and coin, wire transfer of reserve account balances, wire transfer of Federal Government securities, and clearing payments exchanged on magnetic tape. The System also performs an operating function as the fiscal agent of the U.S. Government and of several Government agencies and handles certain financial transactions on behalf of foreign central banks and governments.

Recently, the Board of Governors was asked to provide a summary of the System's operational role in such payments mechanisms. The history, present scope of operations, and legal authority are outlined in this article for each major area of the System's involvement in each payments mechanism. This review does not present an exhaustive treatment of these activities, nor does it examine other Federal Reserve collection activities— notably, the collection of so-called noncash items, such as bonds and coupons of corporations and municipalities.

In addition, this summary describes two of the Board's regulatory actions permitting member banks to transfer funds from savings accounts to third parties. Although these types of transfers are not processed by the Federal Reserve, they are of importance in obtaining a better understanding of current fund transfer systems.

---

[1] From *Federal Reserve Bulletin*, June 1976, pp. 481–489. This article was prepared by the staff of the Board of Governors for presentation to the National Commission on Electronic Fund Transfers.

CHECK COLLECTION

History and Statutory
Basis for Participation

Prior to the enactment of the Federal Reserve Act, checks were exchanged through a system of clearinghouses (or exchanges). Often exchange charges were levied by the bank that finally paid the check,[1] and since the checks were not paid in full, the practice was termed "nonpar banking." The exchange charge was generally $\frac{1}{4}$ of 1 percent of the face value of the checks paid, and many banks engaged in circuitous routing of checks to avoid such exchange charges. Hence, exchange charges resulted in a slow, cumbersome, and costly check collection system and were considered an impediment to commerce and economic growth. The Federal Reserve Act changed these relationships because member banks were required to pay for checks presented to them by Reserve Banks at par and the Reserve Banks were authorized to exercise the functions of a clearinghouse for member banks.

In July 1916 the Board of Governors required all Federal Reserve Banks to function as clearinghouses for member banks. Reserve Banks would receive checks from members that were drawn on a member or nonmember bank agreeing to pay at par for items presented by the Federal Reserve. After that, nonpar clearance was eliminated in many sections of the country and in the major money centers. However, it has continued in certain States in the South; as of June 1, 1976, there were still 64 nonpar banks, operating chiefly in Louisiana, South Carolina, and Texas.

The general provisions of law under which the Federal

---

[1] "Exchange charges" should be distinguished from "collection charges." Collection charges are levied on the payee by the payee's bank for collecting the check. Exchange charges are exacted by the bank on which the check is drawn (the "drawee bank"). Exchange charges developed because funds, except when paid over the counter, were transferred by remitting a draft on the drawee bank's correspondent in the city in which the presenting bank was located. For the service rendered by the drawee bank in remitting funds available for use in the city in which the payee's bank was located, a small exchange charge was made and deducted from the amount of the remittance.

Reserve Banks exercise check collection functions are as follows:[2]

1. The first paragraph of Section 13 of the Federal Reserve Act (12 U.S.C. 342) that provides in part:

Any Federal reserve bank may receive from any of its member banks, and from the United States, deposits of current funds in lawful money, national-bank notes, Federal reserve notes, or checks, and drafts, payable upon presentation, and also, for collection, maturing notes and bills; or, solely for purposes of exchange or of collection, may receive from other Federal reserve banks deposits of current funds in lawful money, national-bank notes, or checks upon other Federal reserve banks, and checks and drafts, payable upon presentation within its district, and maturing notes and bills payable within its district; or, solely for the purposes of exchange or of collection, may receive from any nonmember bank or trust company deposits of current funds in lawful money, national-bank notes, Federal reserve notes, checks and drafts payable upon presentation, or maturing notes and bills; *Provided,* Such nonmember bank or trust company maintains with the Federal reserve bank of its district a balance sufficient to offset the items in transit held for its account by the Federal reserve bank: . . . .

2. The thirteenth paragraph of Section 16 of the Act (12 U.S.C. 360) that provides:

Every Federal reserve bank shall receive on deposit at par from member banks or from Federal reserve banks checks and drafts drawn upon any of its depositors, and when remitted by a Federal reserve bank, checks and drafts drawn by any depositor in any other Federal reserve bank or member bank upon funds to the credit of said depositor in said reserve bank or member bank.

[2] Other important sections of the Act, insofar as payment mechanism services, are Section 4 (12 U.S.C. 341), which permits Reserve Banks to carry on the business of banking, Section 11 (12 U.S.C. 248(i)), which authorizes the Board to establish regulations to enable the Board to accomplish the functions detailed in the Act, and Section 19(f) (12 U.S.C. 464), which permits members to check against and withdraw funds from reserve accounts maintained at Federal Reserve Banks, subject to regulations of the Board of Governors.

3. The fourteenth paragraph of Section 16 (12 U.S.C. 248(o) that provides in part:

> The Board of Governors of the Federal Reserve System shall make and promulgate from time to time regulations governing the transfer of funds and charges therefor among Federal reserve banks and their branches, and may at its discretion exercise the functions of a clearing house for such Federal reserve banks, or may designate a Federal reserve bank to exercise such functions, and may also require each such bank to exercise the functions of a clearing house for its member

In nontechnical language, these provisions have been interpreted to mean that a federal Reserve Bank:

1. *Must* receive deposits at par—that is, must accept deposits for the full face value—and the deposits may be in the form of checks drawn on member or nonmember clearing banks if sent to it by its member banks or other Reserve Banks or by a member bank in another district if permitted by the Reserve Bank of that district;

2. *May* receive from member banks checks payable at par upon presentation anywhere in the country, whether drawn upon member or nonmember banks;

3. *May*, solely for purposes of exchange or collection, receive from other Reserve Banks checks payable at par upon presentation within the receiving Bank's district; and

4. *May*, solely for purposes of exchange or collection, receive from any nonmember bank in its district checks payable at par upon presentation at any bank in the country, provided such nonmember bank maintains a clearing balance with such Reserve Bank.[3]

Pursuant to Sections 11, 13, and 16, the Board has promulgated Regulation J (12 CFR Part 210) designed to afford the public and the banks of the country a direct, expeditious, and economical system for the collection of checks. Regu-

---

[3] The right of the Reserve Bank to present checks to nonmember banks was acknowledged in *American Bank and Trust Co.* v. *Federal Reserve Bank*, 262 U.S. 643. The Federal Reserve does not have the authority, however, to *require* nonpar banks to pay at par. See *Farmers Bank* v. *Federal Reserve Bank*, 262 U.S. 649. Therefore, checks drawn on nonpar banks cannot enter the Federal Reserve clearing system but must be sent directly to the bank on which drawn or presented by a correspondent bank.

lation J details the rights and liabilities of parties using Federal Reserve collection facilities and permits the Reserve Banks to adopt "operating circulars" that detail, in part, the time limits and procedures established by the Reserve Bank for collecting checks as well as other operating matters. Regulations and operating circulars have been issued by the Federal Reserve since 1914. The operating circulars are viewed as contracts between the Federal Reserve and the banks and, as specifically provided in Section 4-103 of the Uniform Commercial Code, the Federal Reserve operating circulars constitute agreements that can vary the effect of the provisions of the Code.

Section 210.4 of Regulation J authorizes any "sender," that is, a member or nonmember clearing bank in the district, to send to the Reserve Bank of the district checks payable at par in any Federal Reserve district. This authorization to senders in effect means that Reserve Banks are required to receive such items in accordance with the provisions of the regulation. Hence, the Reserve Banks do not refuse a sender's items, and the permissive statutory authority described above has been made an obligation on the part of Reserve Banks.

The Federal Reserve Act does not expressly authorize a Reserve Bank to receive checks directly from banks in other districts. Regulation J provides, however, that, as permitted or required by a Reserve Bank, a member bank in one district may send checks directly to the Reserve Bank of any other Federal Reserve district in which the checks are payable. This rule provides an efficient mechanism to handle interdistrict sendings and avoids processing (and the attendant delay) by an intermediate Reserve Bank.

During the late 1950's and early 1960's, the banking industry and the Federal Reserve moved toward automation in handling the mounting volume of paper checks being processed. The initial step permitted the check to be machine processed by adding the MICR (Magnetic Ink Character Recognition) numbers at the bottom of the check. The use of computers and high-speed check handling equipment increased significantly the speed and efficiency with which checks were cleared. During the early 1970's the Federal Reserve implemented the Regional Check Processing Center (RCPC) program aimed at increasing the number of checks cleared on an overnight basis through Federal Reserve facilities. Continued growth in the number of checks led to experimentation with use of encoding payment information on magnetic tape. (Developments in handling magnetic tapes are summarized later.)

Present Scope of Operations

By way of background to the entire check payment system, several relationships and costs should be considered. For example, it can be assumed that the bank receiving a deposit in the form of a check will move expeditiously to obtain possession of the funds from the bank on which the check is drawn. Checks for large amounts are often segregated and subject to expedited handling, and bank messengers may make over-the-counter presentment to the drawee for immediate credit in order that the proceeds of the check may be immediately available. Other items may be sent directly to the bank on which they are drawn, to a clearing house, to a correspondent, or to the nearest Federal Reserve office. A correspondent may, in turn, collect certain items and turn others over to the Federal Reserve. Even though there are a variety of alternative collection arrangements available, after "on us"[4] and local clearing items are removed, most of the checks cleared in the Nation enter directly or indirectly into the Federal Reserve clearing system.

Check collection involves processing and transportation costs. The bank of first deposit must ready the check for subsequent processing and pay the cost of delivering it to the bank on which it is drawn or to a clearing agent—the Federal Reserve, a clearinghouse, or a correspondent. Thereafter the clearing agent, if there is one, has the responsibility for delivery and presentation of items to the bank on which the items are drawn. The transportation costs associated with that delivery may be substantial. Clearinghouses (and check processors permitting "in house" banks to exchange checks) incur nominal delivery costs, but delivery by other clearing agents involves substantial contractual costs for surface and air courier delivery under prevailing operations. Correspondents recoup costs they bear by fees charged or by earnings on collected funds in correspondent balances.

A final but vital aspect of check clearing is the actual

[4] Items that the payee deposits at the drawee bank are termed "on us" items, and often a predominant portion of the total number of checks deposited are of this character, especially in areas in which there are large branching systems or concentrations in demand deposits.

movement of funds. The check serves as documentation for crediting and debiting individual accounts in banks. The matrix of total credits and debits arising from individual items processed at particular times provides the basis for net settlement among all pairs of banks. Generally, settlement takes the form of charges and credits to reserve accounts maintained by member banks at the Federal Reserve, at present amounting to about $35 billion. However, settlements are also made through correspondent balances.

As to the specific Federal Reserve operations, the Federal Reserve presently maintains 48 check-clearing operations. The Federal Reserve clears checks and check-like instruments[5] that have been deposited with member banks[6] and forwarded to the Federal Reserve for collection. The Federal Reserve ultimately presents these items for payment either directly to the financial institution upon which the items are drawn—member or nonmember—or to a processing center designated by that institution.

The Federal Reserve credits the depositing bank with funds in accordance with the Reserve Bank's "availability schedule." This schedule reflects the time that the Federal Reserve normally takes to receive payment from the bank on which the check is drawn. Under current schedules, credit for checks deposited at a Federal Reserve office may be given on the day of deposit, the following day, or the second following day even if the actual time necessary to present the check extends beyond the day credit is made available to the bank depositing the checks. If the item is not collected until after the credit is passed, Federal Reserve float is generated. Currently, Federal Reserve float averages about $2.0 billion. Since the extension of Federal Reserve credit through float has a random effect on the availability of reserves, it hampers the measurement of the money supply. Thus, Federal Reserve System operations are geared to holding float at the lowest possible level.

To accomplish the rapid delivery of checks among Federal Reserve offices (about 40 per cent of the volume is deposited

[5] Among the check-like documents handled by the System are the "NOW account" drafts for thrift and commercial bank institutions, the "share-drafts" for credit unions, and the payable-through draft used by corporations.

[6] In RCPC zones nonmember banks—as agents for members banks—may forward to the Federal Reserve all items *payable in the zone*.

outside the zone in which the item is payable), the System utilizes an air charter service, commercial airlines, and other air courier services. In-zone transportation of checks from Federal Reserve offices to financial institutions on which checks are drawn is accomplished at Federal Reserve expense by contract courier services and the U.S. Postal Service. For all intraterritorial items, however, institutions that deposit items with the Federal Reserve pay for the courier cost of delivering such items to the Federal Reserve.

The Federal Reserve introduces checks received from the Federal Government into this clearing system. With this exception, the Federal Reserve's entire clearing function is determined by the volume of items delivered by member banks and to a limited degree by nonmembers. Thus, in its clearing operations the Federal Reserve's role is one of reacting to flows generated by commercial banks. If the U.S. banking system were concentrated and more like those of the European countries, there would undoubtedly be a less significant clearing role for the Federal Reserve because of the high proportion of "on us" and direct exchange items.

The volume of items cleared through the Federal Reserve's check collection system has grown substantially as shown below (in millions):

Year	Volume	Year	Volume
1920	504	1950	1,955
1930	904	1960	3,419
1940	1,057	1970	7,158
		1975	11,410

AUTOMATED CLEARINGHOUSES

History and Statutory Basis for Participation

The automated clearinghouse (ACH) concept was designed in response to the growing volume and increased cost of processing paper checks. In 1968 a group of commercial bankers in California formed the Special Committee on Paperless Entries (SCOPE) to study the feasibility of exchanging payments on magnetic tape. This system was to augment the check system by providing a more convenient and less costly alternative to the use of checks. As a result of this study, more than 100 banks in California formed an ACH association, and the Federal Reserve Bank of San Francisco was requested and agreed to provide the clearing and settlement facilities for the exchange of such payments on magnetic tape. Subsequently, other Reserve Banks were requested to utilize existing facilities to process the magnetic tapes for other ACH associations. Currently, the Federal Reserve provides the clearing and settlement facilities for such operations in 24 offices. The statutory basis for System involvement is the same as that for checks.

Present Scope of Operations

ACH operations are designed to handle repetitive funds transfers of small dollar amounts, such as salaries and wages and mortgage and insurance premium payments. The Federal Reserve uses its existing computer and courier facilities to clear and deliver such items.

Automated clearinghouse operations and the Federal Reserve's role in such operations essentially parallel check-clearing operations except that the payment information is exchanged on magnetic tape as opposed to paper checks. In an ACH operation, financial institutions create computer tapes of debit and credit items based upon customer instructions and deliver the tapes to their local Federal Reserve clearing and settlement facility, just as those institutions would deliver checks to the Federal Reserve's check-clearing and settlement facility. A Federal Reserve computer—which is also used for other operational purposes—reads, edits, and balances the information on the tape, sorts according to the receiving financial organization, and makes the debit and credit entries in member bank reserve accounts for settlement for both the originating and the receiving financial organization. When the processing has been completed, the computer creates output media consisting of magnetic tapes or descriptive paper listings. The Federal Reserve sends the output media to the receiving financial organization using the same delivery system as that used for delivering checks.

The Federal Reserve is not the sole processor of automated payments. As noted previously, paper checks are cleared through private clearing arrangements apart from the

Federal Reserve facilities, and it should be expected that private facilities will handle certain automated payments.

At the present time, the Federal Reserve will receive items on tapes from any member bank and any member of an ACH association. The Federal Reserve will deliver such items to member banks and members of ACH associations under the following guidelines:

1. Items may be delivered directly to institutions offering demand deposit accounts in the same manner that checks are presented.

2. Items may be delivered directly to institutions not offering demand deposit accounts provided such institution receives a sufficient volume of such items to warrant separate delivery and is located on an existing check-courier route.

3. Items may be delivered to a data processing service bureau provided the service bureau receives a sufficient volume of such items to warrant separate delivery and is located on an existing check-courier route.

4. Items may be picked up at the local Federal Reserve office provided that the volume is sufficient to warrant such action.

5. Items may be delivered to an endpoint that currently receives checks directly from the Federal Reserve office and the institutions may arrange for delivery from that endpoint (that is, the pass-through method).

6. Items may be mailed by the Federal Reserve to any financial organization regardless of its location.

The volume of payments processed in this manner is quite small at present, compared with the volume of checks processed. The 19 operational Federal Reserve offices cleared and settled for approximately 270,000 such automated payments in May 1976.

FEDERAL RESERVE WIRE NETWORK

History and Statutory Basis for Participation

From the first days of the Federal Reserve, there was a need for rapid movement of both financial and administrative messages among Federal Reserve offices. Initially, communication was through Western Union and Postal Telegraph facilities.

In 1918 the Federal Reserve, in recognition of the need for more rapid and secure communication facilities, installed a private Morse code system. This method of transfer continued until 1937 when it was converted into a teletype system. In 1940, in response to a growing volume of traffic, the Board of Governors and the Federal Reserve Bank of Chicago were designated as primary relay stations. The relay station, or "switch," concept was also incorporated when an automatic message system using advanced teletype machines was installed in 1953 with the Richmond Bank designated as the switching center. This system handled 6,000 messages per day initially and linked Reserve Banks and branches, the Board of Governors, the U.S. Treasury, the Commodity Credit Corporation, and the Reconstruction Finance Corporation.

In 1970 the first components of the present automated network were installed, and the system was fully automated in late 1973. Each of the district offices now have installed communications switches to which Reserve Banks, branches, offices, the Treasury, and a number of member banks are interconnected nationwide through a central switch facility in Culpeper, Virginia. This system allows for virtually instantaneous movement of funds among member banks of the System and aids banks in the efficient handling of reserve balances. In view of the need for a quick and efficient method of handling funds transfers of very large amounts in the Nation's money markets, the Board regards wire operations as a necessary and vital tool in conducting its monetary affairs.

During 1975, 17.4 million funds transfers, valued at $31.4 trillion, were handled on the network, as well as 1.5 million Government and Government agency securities transfers and 1.0 million administrative messages. The System's network is designed to handle the very large transfers and to discourage small transfers; a $1.50 charge is imposed for transfers of less than $1,000, and large transfers are handled without charge to members.

The statutory basis for the System's involvement in transferring member banks' reserve balances is basically the same as its involvement in the check-clearing mechanism that has been discussed previously. In addition, paragraph 14 of Section 16 of the Federal Reserve Act authorizes the Board to regulate the transfers of funds among Reserve Banks, and Section 13 authorizes Reserve Banks to receive deposits from their members.

Present Scope of Operations

Three types of messages are handled on the network: (1) transfers of reserve account balances (almost exclusively in large dollar amounts) from one member bank to another, (2) transfers of U.S. Government and Federal agency securities, and (3) administrative and research information. The transfer of reserve balances is used by member banks of the Federal Reserve System to transfer (1) funds as a result of purchasing and selling Federal funds, (2) correspondent bank balances, and (3) funds to other members on behalf of customers. Transfers to other members made by member banks on behalf of their customers include (1) the purchasing and selling of commercial paper, bonds, and other securities, and (2) replenishing corporate demand deposits. For the latter, the Federal Reserve is involved only in crediting and debiting the banks involved in the transfer, and the System does not collect and/or store information related to the corporation that originates or receives the funds transferred.

All money transfers of reserve balances are credit transfers —that is, a member bank instructs the Federal Reserve to transfer funds to another member bank. If the members maintain balances at the same Federal Reserve Bank, each reserve balance is debited and credited accordingly. If the institutions do not maintain balances at the same Federal Reserve Bank, the first Federal Reserve Bank debits the reserve account of the sending bank and credits the account of the Federal Reserve Bank in whose district the receiving bank is located. The latter Federal Reserve Bank debits the account of the sending Federal Reserve Bank and credits the account of the receiving bank. Reserve Banks settle by use of the Interdistrict Settlement Fund. Nonmember banks, other financial institutions, businesses, and consumers may request a member bank to send funds through the Reserve System.

CURRENCY AND COIN

History and Statutory
Basis for Participation

Section 16 of the Federal Reserve Act authorizes the issuance and redemption of Federal Reserve notes. The Federal

Reserve Banks have issued and redeemed such notes since 1914.

On May 29, 1920, the Congress authorized the Secretary of the Treasury to transfer to the Federal Reserve Banks the duties and functions of the Assistant Treasurers in connection with the exchange of paper currency and coin of the United States (41 Stat. 654). Pursuant to this authority, Reserve Banks have been authorized and directed by the Treasury to make an equitable and impartial distribution of available supplies of currency and coin in all cases directly to member banks and to nonmember commercial banks (see 31 CFR 100).

Present Scope of Operations

The volume of currency and coin distribution operations, in millions of pieces, has grown substantially as shown below:

Year	Currency	Coin
1925	1,947	2,329
1935	2,148	2,590
1945	3,016	4,562
1955	4,282	7,008
1965	5,144	5,855
1975	6,551	13,611

There are 37 Federal Reserve offices that process currency and coin. During 1975, 6.5 billion pieces of currency and 13.6 billion pieces of coin were received and counted. In addition 2.6 billion pieces of currency were retired from circulation and destroyed. Fourteen Federal Reserve offices provide coin wrapping services. Almost one-half of the cost of currency and coin operations is for transportation by armored truck of the money requirements of the more than 18,000 banking offices serviced directly by the Federal Reserve.

FISCAL AGENT

History and Statutory Basis for Participation

Section 15 of the Federal Reserve Act states that Federal Reserve Banks, when required by the Secretary of the Treasury, "shall act as fiscal agents of the United States; and the revenues of the Government . . . may be deposited in such banks, and disbursements may be made by checks drawn against such deposits." The Federal Reserve has also been designated as depository and fiscal agent for several international agencies (such as the Inter-American Development Bank) in various other sections of the U.S. Code.

Present Scope of Operations

Federal Reserve Banks act as the Government's principal fiscal agents. Among the activities performed, the Banks maintain banking accounts for the Treasury, handle Government checks, receive applications from the public for the purchase of securities being sold by the U.S. Treasury, allot the securities among bidders, deliver securities, collect payment from the buyers, register and redeem securities, make wire transfers of securities to other cities, make denominational exchanges of securities, pay interest on coupons, and conduct transactions in the market for various Treasury accounts. Most of these activities are under the general supervision of the Treasury, which reimburses the Reserve Banks for most fiscal agency functions.

In addition, the Reserve Banks perform fiscal agency services in connection with the financial activities of various Federal or Federally sponsored credit agencies, and reimbursement is provided by the Treasury (or other Government agencies) for much of the expense incurred.

The fiscal agency functions that relate to the payments mechanism are as follows:

1. DIRECT DEPOSIT OF FEDERAL RECURRING PAYMENTS PROGRAM. Certain Federal recurring payments are received on magnetic tape from Government disbursing centers, processed, and distributed to financial organizations.

The same general procedures and the same computer systems are used to process electronic data representing U.S. Government payments as are used for commercial payments through the Federal Reserve's automated clearing and settlement facilities discussed earlier. Currently, each month approximately 540,000 U.S. Air Force payroll payments are processed and delivered to 9,000 financial institutions. In February 1976 the Federal Reserve Bank of Atlanta distributed the first social security payments under the Treasury's Direct Deposit of Federal Recurring Payments Program. This program is now nationwide with all Federal Reserve offices distributing an estimated 7.5 million payments monthly.

2. TREASURY TAX ACCOUNTS. Payments of Federal taxes (income, Federal Insurance Contributions Act, and so on) made by corporations and some individuals are received from commercial banks, processed, and credited to the account of the Treasury. About 45 million tax payment forms were processed in 1975.

3. GOVERNMENT CHECKS. Government checks are received from banks for charge to the Treasurer's account. This activity, which is essentially a check-collection function, processed more than 800 million Treasury check payments in 1975.

4. INTEREST PAYMENT COUPONS. Coupons representing the payment of interest on U.S. Government securities are processed for the Treasury. Approximately 9 million coupons were processed in 1975.

5. U.S. POSTAL SERVICE MONEY ORDERS. U.S. Postal Service money orders are received from banks for payment. Money orders are charged to the Treasurer's account and shipped to the U.S. Postal Money order processing center in St. Louis. This activity processed more than 170 million items in 1975.

6. U.S.D.A. FOOD COUPONS. Food coupons are received from banks for payment, counted, and destroyed. This activity processed about 2.5 billion items in 1975.

TRANSFERS FROM SAVINGS ACCOUNTS

Bill Payer Services

In July 1975, in recognition of a need for more convenient banking services, the Board amended Regulation Q to authorize member banks of the Federal Reserve System to permit depositors to withdraw funds from savings accounts pursuant to non-transferable orders or authorizations. Prior to this change, the depositor generally[7] had to make requests for withdrawal in

[7] There were exceptions for creditors, administrators of estates, court orders, and so on. See 12 CFR 217.5(c)(i)–(vi).

person, but the bank could permit regular transfers from savings for mortage loans and related payments. The Board was requested to permit banks to offer a full range of bill payment services without regard to the nature of the depositor's indebtedness. In promulgating the changes, the Board relied upon its authority under Section 19 of the Federal Reserve Act (12 U.S.C. 461) to define terms used therein.

The actual transfer from a savings account is not handled by the Federal Reserve since that transfer is an "on us" transfer.

The amendment to Regulation Q authorized member banks to offer bill-paying services but did not specify the form for that service. The following examples may be useful:

1. The depositor will sign a contract with the bank specifying the conditions under which withdrawals will be permitted. Such a contract will be the *authorization* to the bank to honor the depositor's instructions. The bank may be authorized to pay a certain creditor, such as a utility company, every month upon receipt of information by the bank that funds are due and owing. If the creditor maintains a deposit with the same bank, the transfer will be made on the books of the bank; otherwise, the bank would write a check to the creditor.

2. The depositor may write *individual withdrawal orders* to the bank requesting transfers to be made to parties named in the order. These orders may be given at irregular intervals and in irregular amounts. The bank would transfer the funds according to the order. The orders are nontransferable, and only the depositor may send instructions to the bank.

Telephonic Transfers

In April 1975 the Board authorized member banks to permit their customers to transfer funds from a savings account based upon the customer's telephonic instructions. The Board believed that it was no longer true that unrestricted use of the telephone would absolutely destroy the distinction between savings and demand accounts. In its statement, the Board noted that the telephone was an accepted medium for transmitting financial data and that its action would permit more flexibility in communicating the customer's instructions to a bank. In permitting such withdrawals, the Board relied upon its authority under 12 U.S.C. 371b to establish rules governing the payment of deposits.

As with bill payer amendments, the Federal Reserve is not operationally involved in such transfers. However, it appears that growing numbers of banks are now offering such a service to their customers.

Appendix II

The Giro's Scope

One of the paradoxical elements of our present check payments mechanism is that the payment information that the check carries actually proceeds in the *opposite* direction to that of the payment itself.

To the bank upon which a check is drawn, the instructions are concise and explicit, "Pay to Williams & Plenty Co., the sum of $29.88, (signed) Charles A. Struggling." To the check writer, Mr. Struggling, the words *are* the deed. Having written the order (and presumably sent it on its way), he considers the payment made, the chore completed.

However, the check, carrying Struggling's order to *pay* Williams & Plenty Co., goes first—not to Struggling's bank, which will make the ultimate payment—but to Williams & Plenty Co. The company, in turn, deposits the check with its bank, thus "ordering" their bank *to collect* the money.

As Williams & Plenty's bank "forwards" the check through the check collection system, *back* to Struggling's bank, it is in effect requesting each institution—correspondent bank or Reserve Bank—along the route to confirm the actual payment of the amount of the check before sending the check along to the next in line.

It is this "confirmation" of the check-carried information that spirals backward, even as the check moves forward—like the shadow of a moth approaching a candle.

When Mr. Struggling's check finally arrives at his bank and is paid, it "extinguishes" the claim it has represented against Struggling's checking account. When payment is made and the claim is extinguished, the return flow of "confirmations" of the check's accounting information—like the shadow of the moth—stops.

In several European countries, alternative payments mechanisms, called "giro" systems, have been developed to simplify the payments process by making it more direct.

An essential difference between our payments system and the giro approach is that having made out his payment order—his "check"—Charlie Struggling would *not* send it to the Williams & Plenty Co.; he'd send it directly to the local branch of his bank that is a member of a nation-wide "paying institution" . . . in which he maintains (or now opens) an account.

The "paying institution" might be a commercial bank or, in some countries, the post office system. Upon receipt of the order to pay, this institution transmits the information to its branch nearest to Williams & Plenty's home office; and the branch notifies Williams & Plenty that the Struggling payment has been credited to their account.

In some giro systems, the payment order—or a copy of it—is actually sent to the office at which the creditor finally receives payment. In others, only the information is transmitted, perhaps by wire. In either case, however, since both accounts are held by the nation-wide institution, the actual charges and payments to each account can be accomplished by bookkeeping entries at a central "clearing" location.

The giro system—because it enables payments to proceed directly from Charlie Struggling to the Williams & Plenty Co.— eliminates the necessity for the duplication of efforts that our "tentative confirmation of anticipated payments" process requires.

But note that a single institution handles the entire transaction. It may not be necessary that both the payer and the payee (Charlie Struggling and the Williams & Plenty Co.) maintain, or even *have*, "accounts" with the central institution. But the payer must "make the payment" into the system (either in cash, or as a charge to his account, if he has one); and the payee must take the payment out at his end, either in cash, or as a credit to his account. The single institution acts, in effect, as the agent for both parties to the transaction.

Appendix III

Member Bank Income, 1975

Income before securities gains and losses (after taxes) increased $74 million, or 1.4 percent at Federal Reserve member banks during 1975. This increase was far below the $404 million (8.0 percent) gain recorded in 1974. Securities transactions, however, posted a net gain after two successive years of decline. As a result, member bank net income rose $181 million, or 3.4 percent during 1975 (only about one-half as much as in 1974). The ratio of net income to average equity capital and reserves also declined from 10.8 percent in 1974 to 10.3 percent in 1975.

Total operating income at member banks in 1975 declined 4.6 percent after increasing 29.1 percent the previous year. Revenues from loans in 1975 amounted to $35,454 million, down $5,323 million or 13.1 percent from the 1974 level. Contributing significantly to this decline was a sharp drop in the average return on loans from 9.90 percent in 1974 to 8.44 percent in 1975. Investment income at member banks increased $1,322 million, or 18.3 percent in 1975 to $8,558 million, up sharply from the 1974 level. Average investments at member banks rose 11.1 percent, substantially more than the 2.1 percent and 3.0 percent increases recorded in 1974 and 1973, respectively. Slightly higher average returns on securities also contributed to the increase in revenue from this source. Income from U.S. Treasury securities rose 35.1 percent, or $822 million, due both to larger holdings of these securities and to higher return rates in 1975. Holdings of "other securities" also increased substantially as did the rate of return on these investments, thus, resulting in a 10.2 percent increase in revenue from this source. "All other" income, which includes revenues from trust departments, service charges on deposit accounts, and trading account activities, rose $1,530 million, or 26.3 percent.

Total operating expenses at member banks during 1975 decreased $2,408 million, or 5.1 percent as compared to a 33.6 percent increase in 1974. Contributing significantly to this decline was a $5,100 million decline (17.8 percent) in interest paid on time deposits. Salaries, wages, and benefits, however, continued to rise in 1975, although the 8.9 percent increase was significantly less than the 13.1 percent increase of a year earlier. "All other" expenses, which includes net occupancy expense, equipment, provision for loan losses, and other operating expenses rose $1,903 million, or 20.3 percent. Nearly 63 percent of this increase was the result of a $1,193 million or 64.2 percent increase in loan loss provisions.

Reflecting all of the above changes income before securities gains and losses (after taxes) rose $74 million, or 1.4 percent in 1975, significantly less than the 8 percent increase posted in 1974. Security transactions at member banks in 1975 resulted in a very slight gain after two successive years of losses. As a result, net income at member banks increased 3.4 percent in 1975 to $5,545 million.

Income and expenses of member banks usually represent about three-fourths of the total for all insured commercial banks in the country.

Appendix IV

Glossary of Technical Terms

Acceleration principle. The change of investment arising from a given change of consumption expenditures.

Acceptance. A time draft (bill of exchange) on the face of which the drawee has written the word "accepted," the date it is payable, usually the place where it is payable, and his signature. Thus an acceptance is an obligation which the drawee has agreed to pay at maturity. After accepting the draft, the drawee is known as the acceptor. See also Bank acceptance and Trade acceptance.

Acid test. See Quick asset ratio.

Advances. Loans made by Federal Reserve banks to increase the reserves of member banks. Discounts and advances in the Federal Reserve statement include bills discounted, bills bought, and industrial advances.

Aldrich Plan. The plan of the Republican Party to establish a central banking system in 1912. It was based on the findings of the National Monetary Commission provided by the Aldrich-Vreeland Act.

Aldrich-Vreeland Act. An act adopted in 1908. It arose directly out of the panic of 1907. The principal provisions provided for establishment of national currency associations to expand the quantity of money during an emergency; it also authorized Congress to establish the National Monetary Commission.

Amortization. Gradual reduction of a debt by means of equal periodic payments sufficient to meet current interest and extinguish the debt at maturity. When the debt involves real property, often the periodic payments include a sum sufficient to pay taxes and insurance on the property.

Annuity. An allowance or income received in one or more payments annually. Typical from life insurance companies, retirement systems, and others. Annuities are for a stated time or for life.

Antidumping duty. An additional tariff duty assessed on products coming from nations that subsidize exports.

Antifraud acts. Provide for prosecution of violators of blue-sky laws.

Arbitrage. The sale and purchase of foreign exchange to remove the geographical imperfections in the foreign exchange market.

Assignats. French paper money secured by French land and issued between 1790 and 1796 to finance the French Revolution. This money became worthless.

Assignor. The one who transfers rights under a contract to another (the assignee) by an assignment.

Balanced budget. An equality between the bookkeeping budgetary expenditures and receipts.

Bank acceptance. A draft drawn on a bank and accepted by the bank.

Bank Charter Act of 1844. Basic British banking act that gave the Bank of England a monopoly of note issue, set a definite quantity of fiduciary note issue, and provided that all bank notes issued in addition to this amount be backed 100 percent by gold. It was a victory for the currency school and a defeat for the banking school theories.

Bank debits. The volume of checks cleared through clearing associations and debited to individual accounts. The division of bank debits by the average quantity of deposits gives an estimate of deposit velocity.

Bank draft. A check drawn by one bank against funds deposited to its account in another bank.

Bank holiday. President Roosevelt declared a national bank holiday to last from March 6, 1933 through March 10 as a method of halting the money panic.

Bank of England. The central bank of Great Britain. It is now owned and controlled by the British government.

Bankable bill. A note or bill of exchange readily accepted by a bank.

Banking school. Those who believe that the quantity of money should be determined by the needs of business. The needs of business are assumed to be indicated by the quantity of self-liquidating commercial loans.

Barter. The direct exchange of goods and services possessed for goods and services desired. Money is not used as a unit of value or a medium of exchange.

Bearishness. The motive to hold cash that is basic to the speculative motive. Cash is held because prices are expected to fall below present levels.

Bill of exchange. An unconditional written order by one party (the drawer) on a second party (the drawee) ordering him to pay a third party (the payee) a stated sum of money on demand or at some future date.

Bills-only Policy. Open-market operations of Federal Reserve confined to the short end of the government securities market. In effect from 1953 to 1961.

Bimetallism. Two metals, usually gold and silver, serve as the standard metals.

Blue-sky laws. State legislation licensing sellers of securities and permitting only the sale of securities permitted by the state securities commission.

Bond. An interest-bearing debt certificate under seal that promises that the issuer (a government or a corporation) will pay a certain sum of money to its holder on a specified date. In effect, it is a long-term loan by the bondholder (lender) to the issuer (borrower).

Bond reserve plan. Would require commercial banks to hold reserves as government securities as well as deposits in Federal Reserve banks or required reserves of nonmember banks.

Bonus plan, savings and loan account. Saver agrees to deposit a regular amount each month for a period of time. If the agreement is maintained the saver will earn an additional return of as much as 1 percent.

Book value. The value placed on an asset in the accounts of the owner. This may be less or greater than the price that could be obtained at a given moment.

Boot. In finance, the common stock sold as a bonus with other securities. In taxation, the cash or other consideration used to balance an approximately equal exchange.

Broker. A middleman who brings together buyers and sellers of the same security or commodity and executes their orders, charging a commission for his services.

Budget. A plan by a firm or unit of government of its financial activities for the next fiscal period.

Bullion. Uncoined standard metal, usually in the shape of bars. Standard gold bullion is nine-tenths fine and one-tenth alloy.

Bullionist school. The monetary theory of the sixteenth century, which taught that the welfare of a nation depended upon the store of bullion it maintained.

Bullishness. The motive to hold securities or commodities on the expectation that market prices will increase.

Call loan. A loan made on a day-to-day basis, callable on twenty-four hours' notice. Typically, these loans are made to members of the New York Stock Exchange to facilitate the exchange of securities.

Capitalization. The value of an investment determined by dividing the annual net income flowing from the investment by the prevailing rate of interest. It is assumed that the income will flow from the investment indefinitely.

Carrying charge. The addition to the regular price for goods to cover interest and other charges made for installment credit.

Cash-balance approach. Examining the effect of money by determining the reasons why people haven't spent all they have received.

$$\left(P = \frac{M}{KT} \right)$$

P = price
M = money
K = unspent cash margin
T = turnover speed of cash

Cashier's check. A check drawn by a bank on itself and signed by the cashier or other authorized officer. It is also called *officer's check*.

Certificate of deposit. A receipt for funds left with a bank as a special deposit, generally interest bearing. These grew very rapidly in the 1960s and are a portion of the time deposit total. They are called CDs.

Certified check. A depositor's check across the face of which an officer of the bank or another authorized person has stamped the word "certified" and the bank's name and then has signed his own name. By its certification the bank guarantees that sufficient funds have been set aside from the depositor's account to pay the check when payment is demanded.

Chain banking. An arrangement whereby the control of a number of banks is exercised through entire or majority ownership of stock by a group of individuals, who take an active part in formulating the policies of the banks in the group. See also Group banking.

Chancery courts. State courts responsible for guardian or trustee for the infant or the incompetent.

Chattel mortgage. A mortgage with title to some form of personal property given as security.

Clearinghouse. A place where representatives of the banks in the same locality meet each day at an agreed time to exchange checks, drafts, and similar items drawn on each other and to settle the resulting balances. The association operating the clearinghouse also frequently consults to take concerted action on matters of common interest.

Collateral loan. A loan which is secured by the pledge of specific property, the borrower depositing with the lender either the property itself or a document bearing evidence of title to the property.

Commingled Investment Accounts. Similar to trust arrangement at a commercial bank but the customer can increase and decrease amount invested. The arrangement terminates at the death of the investor. Funds invested are not kept separate.

Compensated standard. Amount of metal in standard unit changed to compensate for price changes. If prices were rising the amount of metal in the standard unit would be increased; if prices were falling the amount would be decreased.

Comptroller of the Currency. An appointed official who is responsible for the chartering, supervision, and liquidation of national banks. His office is located in the Treasury Department.

Contract broker. One member of a stock exchange trading for other members. Fee for service was two dollars; hence, *two-dollar broker*.

Convertible securities. Usually a corporate bond or preferred stock that at the option of the investor may be exchanged for some other form of security, generally common stock.

Correspondent bank. A bank that carries a deposit balance for a bank located in another city or engages in an exchange of services with it.

Counterpart funds. Balances in domestic currency of countries receiving U.S. assistance; arise from sale of goods purchased abroad with foreign exchange provided by the United States.

Credit. An advance of cash, merchandise, or other commodity in the present in exchange for a promise to pay a definite sum at a future date, with interest if so agreed.

Credit-Anstalt. Largest bank of Austria, which failed in May 1931 and sparked the international money panic that forced England off the gold standard in September 1931.

Credit exchange bureau. It assembles and distributes facts taken from the ledgers of members. It does not offer ratings; this is left up to the individual credit men of the members.

Crime of '73. The Coinage Act of February 12, 1873, which discontinued free coinage of silver. It was considered unimportant at time of its passage because the bullion value of silver was greater than its monetary value.

Currency. Technically, any form of money that serves as a circulating medium and includes both paper money and metallic money (coins). In banking terminology the term generally refers only to paper money.

Currency exchange. A business establishment whose sole function is to cash checks, money orders, etc., for a fee.

Debt. The other side of the extension of credit. The amount owed by one party to another through having been extended credit.

Default. Failure to meet interest payments and principal payments on the date indicated in the debt contract.

Deficit spending. Financing spending with borrowed funds.

Devaluation. The process of either or both reducing the quantity of gold that the domestic money unit contains and reducing the price of the domestic currency in terms of other currencies.

Disagio. The charge for exchanging a depreciated foreign currency.

Discount. 1. The amount of interest withheld when a note or draft is purchased. 2. A note on which the interest is paid in advance. 3. The process of making a loan by requiring a note larger by the agreed interest charge than the amount paid to the borrower or credited to his account. A discount is distinguished from a loan by the fact that interest on a loan is collected at the time the note is paid.

Disintermediation. Withdrawing funds from institutions to directly purchase securities or make loans.

Double liability. The requirement that stockholders of national banks and many state banks must match the par value of the stock they hold in case the bank in which they are shareholders fails. Since July 1, 1937, national banks have been permitted to terminate the requirement, and it is very uncommon today.

Draft. A signed written order addressed by one person (the drawer) to another person (the drawee) directing the latter to pay a specified sum of money to the order of a third person (the payee).

Drawee. The party who is directed to pay the sum specified in a check, draft, or bill of exchange.

Drawer. The person who makes and signs an order (check, draft, or bill of exchange) for the payment of money. See also Maker.

Dutch auction. The reverse of the ordinary auction with the bidding starting at a higher price and then proceeding downward. Used on occasion by the U.S. Treasury.

ECU. Noncirculating currency used by members of European Payments Union.

Equity. The value of collateral over and above the amount of the obligation it covers.

Equity capital. Capital provided by the owners of a business through the purchase of common and/or preferred stock.

Escrow. An instrument deposited for safekeeping pending the accomplishment of a specified event.

Exchange. 1. An amount charged for the collection of a check or other financial instrument. 2. The volume of funds available for use in another city or country. 3. An organization for trading in securities or commodities. 4. The purchase and sale of goods and services in a market.

Exchange Stabilization Fund. Fund available to the Secretary of the Treasury to purchase foreign currencies.

External drain. The flow of currency from the banks to individuals and businesses.

Face value. The value written on the face of a security. In the case of bonds it is the amount the holder will receive when the bond matures. It is also called the *par value*.

Factor. An agent who markets and aids in the financing of textiles by assuming credit risks.

Federal funds. Excess reserves loaned to banks short of reserves.

Federal Reserve exchange drafts. Drafts drawn on a Federal Reserve bank by any member bank. They are accepted by any Federal Reserve bank or branch.

Federal Reserve note. A noninterest-bearing promissory note of a Federal Reserve bank issued for general circulation as money and redeemable in lawful money on demand.

Fidelity bond. Guarantees the honesty of anyone in a position of trust.

Field warehousing. A warehouse facility at the place where the product in storage is produced, manufactured, or processed. It avoids movement of heavy and bulky commodities.

Float. The portion of a bank's total deposits or of a depositor's account that represents items (checks, coupons, etc.) in the process of collection. They are also called uncollected funds.

Floater policy. An insurance policy covering property for all risks without regard to its location at the time of the loss.

Foreign bill of exchange. A bill drawn in one state or country and payable in another state or country.

Foreign Exchange. 1. The mechanism by which payments are effected between two areas that employ different currency systems. 2. Currency used in making the settlement.

Frazier-Lemke Farm Bankruptcy Act of 1935. A federal measure that provided the requirement of a three-year moratorium on foreclosures of mortgaged farm property.

Free gold. The net amount of gold in the Treasury of the United States that is in excess of the total sum of gold necessary to redeem outstanding gold certificates and other gold indebtedness.

G. Federal Reserve Regulation controlling credit by persons other than banks, brokers or dealers for the purpose of purchasing or carrying registered equity securities.

Gold certificates. Issued by the Treasury under the Gold Re-

serve Act of 1934 to the Federal Reserve System to re-
plenish the reduction of the Treasury Federal Reserve
account arising from its purchase of gold.

Gold points.   Indicate the price of foreign exchange in terms
of the domestic currency at which it would be profitable to
export gold (the gold export point) and profitable to import gold (the gold import point).

Gold Standard Act.   An act passed by the U.S. Congress on
March 10, 1900, which declared the gold dollar to be the
standard unit of value, and directed the Secretary of the
Treasury to keep all other kinds of money on a par with
gold. No longer in effect.

Graham plan.   The commodity reserve standard.

Grain pit.   One of the circular platforms on the floor of an exchange, e.g., the Chicago Board of Trade, where brokers
meet to buy and sell a specific grain.

Gresham's law.   Under bimetallism the monetary metal whose
market price in relation to mint ratio is relatively high is
driven out of circulation and the cheaper metal becomes
the monetary standard.

Group banking.   An arrangement by which a substantial proportion of the stock of each bank in the group is held by a
holding company engaged in the business of banking. The
identity of the local bank remains intact, and its policies
and operations are determined largely by its own board of
directors.

Hundred percent reserves plan.   Requirement that banks keep
100 percent reserves in back of their demand deposits.

Hypothecate.   To give a creditor the right to cause personal
property of his debtor to be sold to satisfy a debt. In a true
hypothecation, the debtor (borrower) usually retains possession of the property until he defaults in meeting his
obligation.

Illiquidity.   The inability to transfer a credit instrument possessing a low degree of "moneyness" into a credit instrument
possessing a high degree of "moneyness."

Inchmaree.   A clause in ocean marine insurance policies covering risks other than perils of the sea.

Income Multiplier.   The multiple increase (decrease) in income resulting from the upward (downward) shift in investment.

Income velocity of money. National income divided by the money supply.

Independent treasury. Fiscal agent of federal government from 1839 to 1913.

Index. A method of combining the prices of a group of goods and services so that relative price levels can be compared.

Indorsee. The holder of a negotiable instrument to whom it has been transferred by indorsement.

Indorsement. The signature plus any other writing on the back of an instrument by which the indorser transfers his rights in the instrument to another.

Indorser. A person who signs his name on the back of a negotiable instrument, such as a check, draft, or promissory note, for the purpose of transferring his title to the instrument or of guaranteeing its payment.

Industrial banks. Banks specializing in lending small amounts to industrial workers.

Inflationary gap. Difference between money value of sales of currently produced goods at current prices and the higher money value that would arise if sold on the free market.

Ingrossing. In law, copying a document into final form from a rough draft.

Interbank deposits. Deposits made by one bank in another. See Correspondent bank.

Interdistrict Settlement Fund. Holds all of the Federal Reserve gold certificates. It settles the differences between the total credits and debits of each Federal Reserve bank and acts as a clearinghouse for Federal Reserve banks.

Intermediation. Deposit of funds in institutions rather than directly purchasing securities or making loans.

Internal drain. The loss of currency by one bank to other banks within the system.

International Finance Corporation. Established in 1956 to supplement the activities of the World Bank. Supplements private capital required to carry out projects in developing nations.

Intestate. A person who dies without making a will.

Investment Companies. See Mutual Funds.

Investment, financial. Purchase of securities. Bank investment also refers to the purchase of securities.

Investment, real. Production of goods and services that are not completely consumed during the period under consideration.

Investment banking. The business of underwriting and distributing corporate and government securities.

Investment bill. A bill of exchange purchased at a discount with the intention of holding to maturity as an investment.

Investment motive. Holding cash as an investment because it appears to be the most desirable type of investment available.

Joint account. An account in the names of two or more persons that requires a combination of signatures for establishment, but only one signature for deposit or withdrawal.

Jus tertii. Latin for the right of a third party.

Kennedy Round. The negotiation in 1967 of multilateral tariff reductions under U.S. legislation of 1962 granting the executive power to negotiate 50 percent reductions of U.S. tariffs for a five-year period. Similar negotiations in 1977–1978 are called the Tokyo Round.

Key Currency. A currency that serves as a unit of account in international transactions, acts as monetary reserves, and is widely accepted in international payments.

Kited check. A check that is given as payment prior to the deposit of funds to cover it. A kite is any fictitious commercial paper.

Labor exchange bank. A scheme appearing in the nineteenth century with the aim of facilitating exchange of commodities in proportion to their labor content.

Latin Monetary Union. Established in 1865, it provided for the adoption of an international bimetallic-standard system by Belgium, France, Italy, and Switzerland. It also provided for issuance of uniform coins that would circulate freely within this international bimetallic area.

Legal reserve. The proportion of a bank's deposits (demand and time) that is required by law to be maintained in the form of cash or readily available balances to meet the demands of depositors. Members of the Federal Reserve

System must keep their legal reserves on deposit with the Federal Reserve banks of their respective districts.

Legal tender. Any kind of money (coin or currency) that the law prescribes as acceptable in payment of debts, unless there is a contract that calls for payment in a particular kind of money.

Letter of credit. An instrument issued by a bank to an individual or corporation by which the bank substitutes its own credit for that of the individual or corporation. Addressed to the seller, it authorizes him to draw drafts on the bank under the terms stated in the letter.

Letter of license. A letter by a creditor permitting a debtor to proceed as stated to avoid bankruptcy.

Leverage. Used in financial circles to indicate the intensified swings of common stocks of firms largely financed with preferred stocks and bonds. The term **trading on equity** is also used to refer to this relationship.

Line of credit. A term applied to the maximum amount of credit that a bank will extend to a particular borrower (usually a business concern) over a stated period, subject to certain conditions that must be met by the borrower, such as maintaining a specified checking account balance.

Liquid holdings. Assets that are considered money or that possess a high degree of cash convertibility.

Liquidity ratios. The principal liquidity ratios are: acid test, cash-to-daily-purchases, current ratio, and quick ratio. These ratios measure the ability of a firm to meet its debts as they come due.

M_1. Currency plus private demand deposits adjusted.

M_2. M_1 plus bank time and savings deposits other than large CDs.

M_3. M_2 plus deposits at mutual savings banks, savings and loan associations, and credit union shares.

Maker. The person who makes and signs a negotiable instrument. See also Drawer.

Midge. The name given to early efforts of the Federal Reserve to raise short-term relative to long-term interest rates.

Mint ratio. Relative values of a given weight of the standard metals established by the mint.

Mint ratio of exchange. See Par of exchange.

Money illusion.   The belief that an economic position has been improved when more money units are received or possessed even though they cannot be transferred into a larger quantity of goods and services.

Money market.   The institutional arrangement consisting of investment banking houses, brokerage firms, organized stock and bond exchanges, and acceptance and commercial paper houses through which the market value of securities and the rates of interest are determined.

Monthly aging report.   Required of borrower using aggregate accounts receivable as collateral. Shows the amounts of account receivables that are delinquent. This total is deducted from the loan base.

Mortgage.   An instrument by which the borrower (mortgagor) gives the lender (mortgagee) a lien on real estate as security for a loan. The borrower continues to use the property, and when the loan is repaid, the lien is removed.

Movable exchange.   Instruments quoted in the currency of the country in which payment is to be made rather than that in which the instrument is drawn.

Mutual Funds.   An organization to pool the investment funds of many individual investors through the sale of fund shares. The funds received are invested in other securities. They are intermediaries through which funds are made available for common stock purchase.

Mutual savings bank.   A bank owned by the depositors and managed for them by a self-perpetuating board of trustees. It has no capital stock and therefore no stockholders.

National Advisory Council on International Monetary and Financial Problems.   Established by Congress in the Bretton Woods Agreement (July 31, 1945) to coordinate the policies of all federal government appointees and agencies engaged in foreign financial, exchange, and monetary transactions.

National Monetary Commission.   Established in 1908 by Congress to survey foreign and domestic banking and currency conditions. Its reports were the basis for the legislation establishing the Federal Reserve System.

National numerical system.   The plan under which every bank in the United States has a distinctive number, which is usually printed below or beside the bank name on all forms in external use including checks. It is used in listing checks on deposit slips, in transit letters, and in many other ways. See also Transit number.

Negotiable instrument. An unconditional written order or promise to pay money, which can be transferred from one person to another free from defenses between the original parties. The law lays down certain standards with which an instrument must conform in order to be negotiable.

Nudum pactum. A promise not legally binding because not supported by a consideration. Literally, "a naked promise."

Numerical rating system. In life insurance, a method of determining the premiums for substandard risks.

Open-market operations. Sale or purchase of securities by the Federal Reserve System. Purchases on the open market increase bank reserves, and sales decrease bank reserves.

Outside lag. Time required for working out impact of monetary policy on decisions of governments, businesses, and consumers.

Overdraft. The amount by which checks paid against an account exceed the balance on deposit in the account.

Over-the-counter market. The market provided by bankers, brokers, dealers, and others for securities not listed on securities exchanges and for the general purchase and sale of bonds.

Par of exchange. The official relative value of two currencies stated in terms of gold, silver, or some third currency.

"Parole credit." A credit transaction in which the agreement to pay was entirely oral.

Payee. The person named in an instrument calling for the payment of money as the one to whom, or to whose order, payment is to be made.

Paying teller. A representative of the bank who is responsible for the proper cashing of checks presented at the window.

Payment bill. A bill of exchange presented for payment instead of acceptance.

Payments approach. Examining the effect of money by determining the manner in which people spend their cash receipts. Also called income-expenditure approach.

$$\left(P = \frac{Y}{O}\right) \quad \begin{matrix} P = \text{price} \\ Y = \text{income} \\ O = \text{output} \end{matrix}$$

"Peg-leg" gold standard. The name applied to the United States monetary standard from 1879 to 1890 because of doubtful convertibility of the silver dollar into gold. The standard had a "peg leg" made of silver.

Penalty rate. Usually refers to a rate charged by a central bank that is higher than that on the instrument offered for rediscount or as collateral for an advance.

Penny stock. A low-priced and often speculative stock selling for less than a dollar a share.

Personal loan. A loan (usually small) made to an individual for his personal needs. See Chapter 13.

Postal savings. Savings system of Post Office Departments of most nations. No longer exists in the United States.

Precautionary motive. Holding sufficient cash to meet possible emergencies arising from an unexpected reduction of receipts and an unexpected increase of expenditures. Also called *margin-of-safety* motive.

Preferential discount rate. A rate of $\frac{1}{2}$ percent set by the Federal Reserve System on advances to member banks secured by short-term federal government obligations. The rate was utilized from October 1942 to May 1946 to encourage commercial banks to purchase government securities.

Present value. The sum of future payments due, discounted back to the present date at an assumed rate of interest.

Prime rate. Rate set on commercial loans to a bank's best customers.

Private bank. An unincorporated bank that is owned and operated by an individual or a partnership. It may or may not be subject to supervision by the banking authorities, depending on the laws of the particular state in which it is located.

Profit break-even point. The intersection of the total income curve (including accruals) and the total cost curve (including accruals).

Promissory note. A written promise made by one person (the maker) to pay a certain sum of money to another person (the payee), or to his order, on demand or at a determinable future date.

Q. Federal Reserve Regulation setting bank interest payments on deposits.

Qualitative credit control. Central-bank credit control activities that determine the conditions under which particular types of credit may be extended.

Quantitative credit controls. Central-bank credit control activities that operate on the total quantity of credit available rather than particular types as do qualitative credit controls.

Quick asset ratio. The ratio of cash accounts receivable and marketable securities to current liabilities. Also called *acid test*.

Raised check. A check on which the amount has been fraudulently increased.

Real Balance Effect. A fall in prices increases the purchasing power of cash balances.

Real-bills doctrine. States that commercial bank loans should be to businessmen, be secured by physical goods in the process of orderly marketing, and be repaid from the proceeds of the sale of the goods.

Receiving teller. A representative of the bank who receives and verifies deposits and issues receipts for them.

Recording statute. Requires notification that borrowing on accounts receivable is to take place before first assignee may collect. See Validation statute.

Redlining. A financial institution practice that marks out large sections of cities as unsuitable for mortgage loans on any terms whatever.

Refunding. The issuance of new debt obligations to replace the old that have matured or that have been called.

Registered check. An ordinary personal check on which the bank teller has imprinted the amount with a check-writing machine. A service charge of 10 cents is usually made.

Revaluation. Process of restoring the former value of the monetary unit.

Revolving credit. Consumer credit usually extended to selected credit risks. Interest is charged monthly on unpaid balances.

Revolving letter of credit. The letter reverts at specified intervals to the original amount. It may be cumulative, in which case the unspent portion of the previous period is added, or noncumulative, in which case it is not. They are usually revocable; used primarily between domestic purchasers and purchasing agencies abroad. See Letter of credit.

Safety fund system. A system that existed in the state of New York from 1829 to 1866 to provide protection of state bank note holders and depositors from a fund built up with assessments based on member bank capital. The plan was judged successful and provided a portion of the basis of the FDIC.

Say's law. Production of goods and services creates the demand for goods and services of an equal value. Production creates its own demand.

Scalp. On the stock exchange, a short transaction made in contemplation of closing out at a profit.

Selective-asset-reserve plan. It would base the quantity of bank reserves required on the character of the bank's assets rather than the quantity of deposits.

Serial bonds. Agreement provides for portions of the bonded debt maturing at different times throughout the life of the debt contract. Eliminates need for accumulation of sinking fund.

Serial plan, savings and loan operation. New accounts are only opened for a group semiannually or quarterly. It requires regular saving by all who join the series, say for one year. See Bonus plan.

Service charge. A charge made by a bank for the cost of handling a depositor's account.

Several account. Several firms underwrite a new issue but each one participates separately rather than jointly as in a syndicate account. Each firm continues to have a definite commitment.

Short-term debt. Debt that matures in any time less than approximately a year after it is acquired.

Short sale. An agreement to deliver at a future date a security or commodity that the seller does not own but that he hopes to purchase later at a lower price.

Sight draft. A draft that is payable on presentation to the drawee—in other words, on "sight" or demand.

Specie. Coins made of precious metal, especially silver and gold. *Specie payments* are payments made in metallic money rather than paper money.

Spot Exchange Market. The market for the immediate delivery of the moneys involved.

Spot price. Price for immediate ownership.

Stabilization fund. Established by nations during the 1930s to make the necessary purchases and sales of exchange to prevent violent fluctuations in the foreign value of their unit of value. The first one was established in Great Britain when she left the gold standard in 1931. The United States fund was called the *exchange stabilization fund.*

Standard metal. Metal selected to be the base of a monetary system; it is purchased in unlimited quantities at a fixed price, and the paper money and subsidiary coins can usually be converted either directly or indirectly into the standard metal.

Standard money. Money made of the standard metal. The bullion value of the coin is as great as the face value.

Standby line of credit. Guarantees funds will be available when needed as opposed to an open line, which can be canceled by the creditor.

Stop-payment order. An order issued by a depositor to his bank instructing it to refuse payment of the check specified in the order.

Straight life insurance. See Whole life insurance.

Structural Unemployment. The skill mix and geographic distribution of the unemployed do not match the skill requirements and geographic location of the job opportunities available.

Subordination agreement. Subordinates the claims against the company of those signing the agreement in favor of the person to whom the agreement is executed.

Sui juris. Used to describe one who is competent to act.

Surety bond. Guarantees a contract, an act, or an undertaking will be fulfilled.

Surplus. The accumulated profits of past periods remaining in the business. In a bank it represents the amount paid in by the stockholders in addition to their capital stock subscriptions when the bank is organized, and the amount (not available for dividends) added to capital from earnings.

Swap Arrangement. A reciprocal and renewable agreement between central banks to exchange their currencies on request.

Symmetallic standard. The standard unit of value is a definite quantity of a fusion or combination of two or more metals in some specified proportion to one another.

Syndicate account.   Underwriting jointly a new security issue. Since 1933 most accounts underwriting corporate issues have been set up on the several account basis.

T.   Federal Reserve Regulation controlling credit of Brokers, Dealers and Members of National Securities Exchanges.

Tare weight.   The weight of a container and the material for packing, or the weight of a vehicle exclusive of contents.

Tax and Loan Account.   U.S. Treasury deposits in over 10,000 qualified commercial banks.

Technocrats.   In the 1930s they advocated the introduction of the *erg* as the unit of account.

Teller.   A bank representative who, in one capacity or another, transacts over-the-counter business with customers.

Testator-trix.   A person who makes a will.

Thomas Inflation Act.   An act that gave the President large discretionary powers that could be used to increase the quantity of money. It was passed by Congress as Title 3 of the Agricultural Adjustment Act of May 12, 1933; the powers granted have been permitted to expire.

Trade acceptance.   A draft drawn by the seller of goods on the buyer. On its face there often appears a statement indicating that the acceptor's obligation arises from the purchase of goods from the drawer of the draft.

Trading limit.   Maximum price change and quantity one trader can buy or sell in one day on the commodity exchanges of the United States.

Transactions motive.   Holding enough cash to take care of necessary expenditures during some future period when cash income is expected to be inadequate.

Transit items.   Cash items that are payable outside the town or city of the bank receiving them for credit to customers' accounts.

Transit number.   A key to the name and location of a bank under the national numerical system. The transit number has two parts; the prefix or first part designates the city or state in which the bank is located, and the second part indicates the name of the bank.

Traveler's checks.   Special checks supplied by banks and other companies at small cost for the use of travelers. Those supplied by the American Express Company are used most frequently.

Treasury warrant. Instrument similar to a check by which all U.S. Treasury disbursements are made.

Tripartite agreement. Established by the United States, Great Britain, and France to stabilize the relative values of their currencies after the French devaluation of 1936. Other countries participated in the plan, which functioned until 1939.

Twist. Holding long-term interest rates down while pulling short-term interest rates up.

U. Federal Reserve Regulation controlling credit by banks for the purpose of purchasing or carrying registered stocks.

Underwriting. In investment circles, an outright purchase of securities offered or an agreement to buy an issue of securities if it is not completely sold by a particular day.

Unearned discount. Interest that has been collected but not yet earned.

Unit Banks. Banks operating only a single banking office.

United States rule. Provides that partial payments of delinquent, interest-bearing debts are to be applied first to the retirement of past-due interest and then to principal.

UNRRA. United Nations Relief and Rehabilitation Administration. Active in relief operations largely with American funds from 1943 to 1947. It was anticipated that problems not solved by UNRRA would be met by the World Bank and the fund. This proved not to be the case and the Marshall Plan was introduced in 1948.

Usury. The collection of interest rates above those permitted by law.

Validation statute. State legislation stating that the first assignee of an account receivable is entitled to collect the proceeds thereof, regardless of notification.

Vault cash. Currency held by commercial banks. Since 1959 counted in meeting reserve requirements.

Walras Law. The concept of general economic equilibrium. The law refutes the notion that money is simply a *numéraire*.

Warehousing mortgages. Original mortgage lenders accumulate mortgages until the quantity is large enough to sell to a life insurance company, Fannie Mae, Freddie Mae, or a mutual savings bank.

Warrant. A right to purchase, usually common stock, that is given to "sweeten" an issue of bonds or preferred stock. (Similar to convertible securities.)

Whole life insurance. Premiums paid over a lifetime and face value of policy paid to beneficiary upon death of insured. Annual premiums are lowest of any of the ordinary insurance policies. After several years there is a loan value and a surrender value. (Also called straight life insurance.)

Wild cat banks. State commercial banks in the 1830s and up to 1866 that issued notes far beyond redemption possibilities. They were usually located in distant and inaccessible places.

Windfall. Unforeseen and unplanned changes in economic well-being.

Window dressing statement. A financial statement that indicates a created temporary situation that makes the economic position of the bank or business corporation seem to be more favorable than the real condition warrants.

Wire transfer. An order to pay or credit money transmitted by telegraph or cable.

Terms not defined in the Glossary are defined in the text and will be found in the Index.

Index